A New Counterterrorism Strategy

A New Counterterrorism Strategy

*Why the World Failed to Stop
Al Qaeda and ISIS/ISIL, and How
to Defeat Terrorists*

AMBASSADOR T. HAMID AL-BAYATI, PHD

Praeger Security International

 PRAEGER™

An Imprint of ABC-CLIO, LLC
Santa Barbara, California • Denver, Colorado

Library of Congress Cataloging-in-Publication Data

Names: Bayātī, Ḥāmid, author.
Title: A new counterterrorism strategy : why the world failed to stop al Qaeda
    and ISIS/ISIL, and how to defeat terrorists / Ambassador T. Hamid
    Al-Bayati, PhD.
Description: Santa Barbara, California : Praeger, [2017] | Includes bibliographical
    references and index.
Identifiers: LCCN 2017023414 (print) | LCCN 2017036134 (ebook) |
    ISBN 9781440847158 (ebook) | ISBN 9781440846878 (alk.paper)
Subjects: LCSH: Terrorism—Prevention. | Terrorism—Government policy. |
    Security, International.
Classification: LCC HV6431 (ebook) | LCC HV6431 .B3763 2017 (print) |
    DDC 363.325/17—dc23
LC record available at https://lccn.loc.gov/2017023414

ISBN: 978-1-4408-4687-8
EISBN: 978-1-4408-4715-8

21 20 19 18 17   1 2 3 4 5

This book is also available as an eBook.

Praeger
An Imprint of ABC-CLIO, LLC

ABC-CLIO, LLC
130 Cremona Drive, P.O. Box 1911
Santa Barbara, California 93116-1911
www.abc-clio.com

This book is printed on acid-free paper ∞

Manufactured in the United States of America

To my hero, to my mentor
To my lovely kind mother
To my oldest oppressed brother
Kidnapped and killed by evil terror
To my sister whose husband was hanged
To my family who stood up and never shivered
To my uncle and my cousin who were detained
and disappeared but had no grave and no coffin
To the great woman in my life, Zeena my wife
To my children and all members of my family
To all Iraqis who face terror and still suffer
To friends who helped, one way or another
To bring to Iraq freedom, dignity and integrity
To the unknown heroes, we will remember forever

Contents

Foreword

It was the International Day of Happiness and once again I was sitting next to Ambassador Al-Bayati on a panel in a United Nations conference room as he greeted streams of high-level delegates and civil society representatives to celebrate this day. Mandated by a United Nations resolution, the day honors the happiness of the people as a measure of the development of a country beyond the money in its coffers.

Ambassador Al-Bayati's PowerPoint presentation showed how he, along with two grandsons of Nelson Mandela and others, had convinced the then-President of the General Assembly and then-UN Secretary-General to pass the resolution. It was a big success for the recognition of happiness in government affairs, and a major step for peace.

That celebration was a stark contrast to the life experiences that Ambassador Al-Bayati has endured. As you will read here, he endured war, torture, assassination attempts, and the murders of his loved ones. He navigated political intrigue and missteps by national powers and years of ongoing terrorism. People in power ignored his wise insights and advice. It's all in the story in these pages about a critical time in the history of his country—Iraq—and lessons learned that have led him to the thesis proposed here—a comprehensive strategy to defeat terrorism. "We need to do it, once and for all," Al-Bayati tells us.

He is right.

Be prepared for a front row seat to the unveiling of a critical time in our history, when Ambassador Al-Bayati had an all-too-close audience to terror in Iraq. Few people can tell this story. Far fewer would have the bravery to have stood up for his opinions in such treacherous times, or to now reveal truths that others may wish he did not speak.

And few could—despite what he has gone through—nonetheless keep the love and laughter that still emanates from this man.

Compellingly, this book offers detailed accounts that will undoubtedly astound you, as they did me. In great detail, characters in the Clinton, Bush, Obama, and now Trump administrations, who determined and now determine our lives, come alive. The ambassador uncovers political intrigue and analysis of what happened—and what now should happen to finally put an end to terror. U.S. policy is not excused from his critique, though he expresses appreciation for U.S. efforts, including to free his country from the evils of Saddam Hussein. And Al-Bayati includes accounts of the emergence of lone wolf terrorists, of foreign fighters, and of the effective tactics of terrorists to raise funds, and to come up with creative ways to exploit the Internet for their evil ends. But each fear-invoking revelation is assuaged by the ambassador's advice about how to turn things around. He shares with us, too, invaluable thoughts on how to turn technology against terrorists, about how to understand the fundamental ideology of terrorists, and how to engage the Muslim community to defeat terrorists.

Readers of all backgrounds and experience will be fascinated with insights into an important period of history that still shapes our current times, and the opportunity to learn from the experiences of a man who was so intricately involved in combatting terrorism in the Middle East, as well efforts to build his country, Iraq, into a modern, democratic, and peaceful nation.

That effort for peace is not over. The lessons in this book have implications for our lives especially today, as we are confused by "fake news" and wonder what may really be happening behind the scenes on the world stage. No matter your current political preferences and thoughts about the present administration, we all seek truth about the deals being struck today.

This book is not just a window on history. The War on Terror, which many of us remember born as a call-to-action by President Bush, is not over. The Al Qaeda of yesterday prevails in the ISIS/ISIL of today, with treacherous beheadings of innocent civilians. We are not safe from bombings in nightclubs, theatres, subways, streets, marathons, and malls, whether here in the United States or in France, Spain, Belgium, Germany, England, or even Turkey. Even Islamic people are not insured from being targeted by terrorists.

For all the references to 9/11 in these pages, my own memories are revived, as a New Yorker and as a psychologist who was immediately posted to "the pit," the harrowing hole where the Twin Towers once stood. Night after night after the tragic attacks when Al Qaeda's hijackers crashed two American planes into the towers killing up to 3,000 people and injuring twice that number, I walked the perimeter, and sat on broken cement blocks with rescue workers trying to cope with the enormity of the event. As psychological first responders, we handed out gloves and coffee, and offered an ear to listen and comfort.

There are many players in this book with which readers will be familiar, but others, who were in top positions then—and became prime ministers and ambassadors—are new to us, and interesting. Your own memories of key figures will be filled out, like Clinton, General Petraeus, and of course, Saddam Hussein.

The first half of this book poses the problem, and the second half gives solutions. As a psychologist I know that once you open a wound, you have to heal it. Al-Bayati does that with his clever counterterrorism plan. Hope is crucial. Reading this comprehensive plan for counterterrorism offers hope.

As a psychologist, I also know the importance of resilience, the ability to survive during, and bounce back after, tragedy. Ambassador Al-Bayati's resilience comes through in these pages. I also know the importance of understanding different cultures—a point the ambassador emphasizes to defeat terrorism. Among so many other approaches, the Sunni and the Shiites need to reconcile their sectarian divide. I know that point up close, from my trips to the Middle East and efforts to raise awareness about the importance of understanding culture for mutual understanding and conflict resolution in another conflict. In *Terror in the Holy Land: Inside the Anguish of the Israeli-Palestinian Conflict*, I presented issues of children, women, belief systems, and practices from both points of view, to effect understanding, and chapters in *Beyond Bullets and Bombs: Grassroots Peacebuilding between Israelis and Palestinians*, profiled peoples form both cultures doing things together—trekking, playing sports, breaking bread, making movies, camping—based on research that when people share experiences together they cannot hate and war against each other. Understanding the mind and motivations and emotional appeals of terrorists is a psychologist's territory, leading me for example, to seminars about the topic by my friend, psychologist Raymond Hamden, and to support a book about *Weapons of Psychological Mass Destruction* by friend and military psychologist Larry C. James (who was deployed in Abu Ghraib). And politician Al-Bayati in these pages leads us to equally revealing "ahas," appealing to reason and intelligent action to counter terrorism.

Through all these horrors and political quicksand, Ambassador Al-Bayati emerges not bitter, but determined—to make peace, and to encourage respect for others. As a moderate voice in the Arab world, he inspires building bridges between the West and Islam. You have only to read his personal statement in this book about his background, and you will undoubtedly respect and honor him as I do, deeply moved by his story— born Muslim, going to a Christian school, growing up in a multicultural setting surrounded by peoples of all faiths, with parents who respected all people and taught him understanding and appreciation for all, in a tight

knit family, respecting women—his cherished wife, and especially ador-
ing his mother, who stood by him through his dangerous rebellion against
the regime at the risk of his family's safety.

Yes, the contrast between this author speaking of happiness at the UN
and his endurance of torture in Iraq under dictatorship and war is pal-
pable. Ultimately the strategy herein is not just an analysis of terror, but it
is a plan and plea for freedom, democracy, human rights, rule of law, and
peace. As Ambassador Al-Bayati reminds us, awareness and action is urgent. We are in drastic times, with Syria plagued with civil war. All Europe and the world face challenges from the dire refugee crisis. And any
one, any day, in any city faces threat from lone wolf and organized terror
attacks. We need to defeat terrorists without missing opportunities, the
ambassador insists.

The time is now for awareness and action, by all sectors of society,
cooperating.

Judy Kuriansky, PhD
May 30, 2017

Acknowledgments

This book is a result of my long search over many years to determine the roots and causes of radicalism, extremism, and terrorism, the most dangerous phenomenon facing the world in the 21st century. Without the help of many people, I would not have been able to finish this work that I hope will help save some lives.

I would like to thank all members of my family for the great support and help. I am grateful to colleagues at Fordham and Fairleigh Dickinson Universities, and especially to my friend, noted psychologist, United Nations NGO representative, and Columbia University Teachers College psychology professor Dr. Judy Kuriansky, who encouraged me to put my plan into this tome and contributed so much to me in conceptualizing, structuring, and editing this book.

I am grateful to colleagues, friends, students, and interns who helped with commenting, editing, and providing valuable feedback. I would specifically like to thank Dr. Fran Biroc, Dr. Yadira Monge, Allison Gillen, Ali Bazzi, Sarah Bosakowski, Katrina Martinz, Mario Hadad, Delia Burns, Frances Fynan, and all the other people who helped me.

I would like to thank everyone at Praeger/ABC-CLIO who participated in the production of this book, especially Debbie Carvalko and Nicole Azze for their superb support and wise judgment and Gordon Hammy Matchado for editing the book.

I also would like to thank all my friends in Wayne Public Library who were a great help over three years, as well as the staff at the library in William Paterson University for their help and assistance.

Most importantly, I would like to thank all the people in Iraq and those who support them, for their courage and good will. It is they who hold the promise for the future stability and democracy in my beloved country.

Introduction

FACING THE DICTATORIAL REGIME IN IRAQ

My main purpose in writing this book is to shed light on the political, military, and intelligence mistakes made in dealing with terrorist groups before and after the 9/11 attacks. U.S. politicians, military commanders, and intelligence agencies had access to information that could have curtailed the actions of the terrorists but were unable or unwilling to act. In this book, I present my 12-step plan for combatting terrorism. My recommendations are based on my many years of experience as a diplomat in firsthand facing the dictatorial regime in Iraq, the movement to democracy, and now the urgency to defeat terrorism in my country Iraq, the Middle East, and worldwide.

I will demonstrate that these mistakes I outlined in this book facilitated the rise of Al Qaeda and its ability to continue executing terrorist attacks since the 1990s. I will also explain how mistakes made in Iraq after the invasion of Kuwait in 1990 and after the war against Saddam's regime in 2003 helped ISIS gain momentum. I will examine why the world failed to stop Al Qaeda and ISIS and propose a new comprehensive counterterrorism strategy to defeat terrorist organizations.

In order to develop a successful counterterrorism strategy for dealing with terrorist groups such as ISIS, it is important to understand the history of the Middle East, the ideology of extremists, and the sectarian strife between Sunnis and Shiites, along with the mentality, traditions, and culture of the Iraqi people. It is also important to understand something about me and my role in this complex time in history.

I have studied history, sociology, philosophy, and politics as well as Islamic movements in Iraq and in the region during my academic studies, acquiring a BA degree from Bagdad University, an MA degree from Cairo University in Egypt, and a PhD from Manchester University in the United Kingdom. I majored in Middle East politics, and my PhD dissertation examined the borders between Iraq and Iran. Later, I became active as a high-level politician in my country and on the international stage at the United Nations.

MY PERSONAL HISTORY

I was born and grew up in Iraq, a country known as the cradle of civilization. Its Sumerian civilization dates back more than 5,000 years, and the country is reputed to be the birthplace of Prophet Abraham, the father of Abrahamic religions (Judaism, Christianity, and Islam). It is also the birthplace of Saddam Hussein, the most brutal dictator in contemporary times, as well as the birthplace of Abo Bakr al-Baghdadi, the leader of ISIS, the most extreme and brutal terrorist group in history. As I write this book, I will leverage my upbringing and my education to examine the root causes and reasons that led to the rise of terrorism, and what can be done to eradicate it now. My approach will look at the issues from a different angle that is acquired through experiences which most Western writers, pundits, and experts do not have.

Although I was born into a Muslim family, my father sent me to a private Christian school when I was four years old. At this early age, I began to attend the church adjacent to the school. I read the Torah, the Bible, and the Quran and learned to appreciate and compare the three books. My father did business with Iraqi Jews, and he used to tell me that doing business with Jews was a good thing because he found them trustworthy. In the neighborhood where I was born, Al-Karrada Al-Sharqiya in southern Baghdad, there were people from all ethnicities, religions, and sectarian background. There were Arabs, Kurds, Turkmen, and Assyrians. The area was also home to Muslims, both Shiites and Sunnis. All these groups, and Christians and Jews, were part of the community. In this area of the world, despite our differences, we lived in peace and harmony for a long time.

The brutal regime of Saddam Hussein and the Ba'ath Arab Socialist Party changed our world. In sharp contrast to my multicultural background of acceptance of all, Saddam played on ethnic differences to get the support of all Arab countries. He did this when he fought the Kurds in Northern Iraq in the 1970s. Saddam presented himself as an Arab leader against non-Arabs. He also played the sectarian card when he fought Iran between 1980 and 1988. Following the invasion and liberation of Kuwait, Saddam crushed the popular uprising of March 1991 when Shiites and

Kurds rose up against him after 30 years of brutal repression. He used religious differences as a crutch when his regime fell into disfavor with the West following the invasion of Kuwait. He presented himself as a Muslim hero standing against crusades orchestrated by Europe and the United States.

In the 1990s, Saddam supported the extreme, brutal, and fundamental Salafi-jihadi ideology in Iraq. He hoped that extremists would defend his regime and stand against U.S. forces and their European allies who tried to topple him in 2003. Saddam's deputy, Izzat Al-Douri, supported the Naqshbandi-Salafi Order, which after 2003, evolved to become an insurgency group called the Army of Men of Naqshbandi Order, referred to as Jaysh Rijal al-Tariqa al-Naqshbandia, or JRTN. The JRTN began fighting American troops and Iraqi security forces in 2003 and continued to support ISIS in attempts to take control of cities and towns in northern and western Iraq.

While in Iraq, I was an active participant against the dictatorial regime of the Ba'ath Party. This was a dangerous position to take. At one point while I attended a funeral of five opposition leaders who were executed, the funeral turned into a demonstration against the regime when security agents started to shoot live bullets at the demonstrators. Protesters were beaten with electric cables and many, including myself, were arrested. This was the beginning of my first-hand experience at the hands of terrorists, and an experience that only strengthened my resolve to defeat them—and my focus on the steps to do that, outlined in this book.

Once captured and arrested, I was tortured at the General Security Directorate and at the Military Intelligence Directorate. They tried unsuccessfully to make me confess that I was part of a secret organization plotting to topple the regime. I denied it, but of course, the truth was that I really was part of a secret organization to topple the regime but I could not admit this. Anyone who rebelled against dictatorship knows this. I was sent to the "Revolutionary Court," where the judge was forced to release me because without my confession, there was no evidence against me. Yet the judge threatened me with execution if I was arrested again. When the security agents did in fact come to rearrest me, I managed to escape. Tragically, many people with whom I was familiar were executed because they confessed or because the regime had managed to get some evidence against them.

When I escaped from Iraq, I traveled through land borders to Kuwait, Saudi Arabia, Jordan, and Syria. Because my brother was studying engineering in Manchester, in the United Kingdom, I was able to get a U.K. visa, so I joined him there. I enrolled in Manchester University and obtained a PhD in Middle East studies. I lived in London between 1991 and 2003, and during that time, I was active in the Iraqi Opposition Movement against the dictatorship of Saddam. As one of my activities, I launched a campaign to spread awareness about the war crimes Saddam was perpetrating on Iraqi people. His crimes included genocide, ethnic cleansing, and crimes against humanity.

FACING TERRORISM IN EXILE 1991–2003

In London, I worked with members of Parliament (MPs), politicians, and journalists to help draw attention to these crimes and violations of human rights perpetrated by Saddam. I requested that United Nations Member States (now there are 193 countries who are members of the UN)—especially the five permanent members of the Security Council (the United States, the United Kingdom, France, Russia, and China)—force Saddam's regime to implement resolution 688 of April 5, 1991,[1] which relates to violation of human rights.

In 1993, I traveled with then-British MP Emma Nicholson, now a baroness at the House of Lords, to New York to meet Jan Eliasson, the first UN Under Secretary-General for humanitarian affairs to discuss Saddam's violations of human rights and the possibility of UN interference to stop these violations.

Emma and I traveled together to the marshes in southern Iraq, along with journalists who made videos and wrote articles about Saddam's crimes. I wrote a chapter about Saddam's destruction of the marshes in a book edited by Fran Hazelton who worked with another British MP Ann Clwyd.[2] I also worked with Ann against Saddam's regime. Getting into Iraq while Saddam was there was a dangerous mission for anyone and certainly for me. When British foreign secretary Douglas Hurd, a conservative politician, heard about our trip, he expressed concern about the potential fate of any British citizen arrested by Saddam. He was even more concerned at the prospect of Saddam abducting a member of the British Parliament. Emma was so moved by the problems of refugees that she established a nongovernmental organization (NGO) to help refugees from Iraq and many other countries. The NGO is still active in the United Kingdom and the United States.[3]

Nineteen years later, while I was Iraq's Ambassador to the UN, I met Eliasson again on July 1, 2012,[4] by which time he had been elevated to the position of Deputy Secretary-General of the UN, the second highest position after the then-Secretary-General Ban Ki-moon. My impression of him as a man of high capability was confirmed by his successful career.

The biggest risk for me as an opponent of the Saddam regime was to publicly and vocally express opposition against Saddam. My name and my face appeared on TV regularly, while most of the Iraqis who agreed with my point of view lived in fear and silence. Those who dared to challenge Saddam covered their faces while doing so. Iraqis working with British and U.S. officials were considered traitors to Saddam; for this "crime," the punishment was execution or assassination. Because I challenged the regime openly, I was a target for Saddam's agents not only in London but also in many of the other countries where I traveled to.

While I worked in London, I came into contact with many U.S. politicians who agreed with my concern about Saddam and supported the Iraqi opposition to Saddam's regime. For example, U.S. Ambassador Frank Ricciardone was appointed by Secretary of State Madeleine Albright as a special U.S. envoy to opposition groups in Iraq in 1999, to lead a team of military and political advisers working alongside diverse Iraqi groups.[5] In November 2002, I also worked with Ambassador Zalmay Khalilzad (Zal), President Bush's special envoy to the "Free Iraqis" movement. I met Zal with other opposition leaders in the United Kingdom, the United States, Turkey, and Kurdistan in northern Iraq. Since he was from Afghanistan, he understood the problems that existed in Iraq and the Middle East and was positioned to help U.S. officials, some of whom had neither visited nor served in Iraq and the Middle East. This was particularly important to me, as you will see in this book, where part of my 12-step plan to defeat terrorism is to take advantage of people who know the region well.

While I was in London, I made many trips to European countries and the United States to explain Saddam's violations of human rights in Iraq, and how the international community could help the Iraqi people. In Washington, D.C., I met with American lawmakers and officials to discuss the situation in Iraq and to propose ways in which the United States could do more to stop Saddam's crimes against humanity, genocide, and ethnic cleansing. These meetings also form the basis of this book.

I did not escape from these activities unscathed, nor did my beloved family. In retaliation for my activities, the regime arrested, tortured, and executed members of my family. In the first round-up, 10 family members were arrested. Some were imprisoned and three were executed, including my brother-in-law and two cousins. In the second round-up, my uncle and his son were arrested and executed. In a third round-up, three family members were executed along with a number of businessmen. In an act of twisted evil, the regime advertised in an official newspaper that the tribe with which I was affiliated had pledged to shed my blood. In an effort to threaten and defeat me, the regime forced my mother, three of my brothers, and a sister to appear on Iraqi TV. Saddam's loyalists interrogated them, demanding to know where I lived, if I was in touch with my family, and why I did not go back to my country.

In addition, Saddam sent people to assassinate Iraqi opposition leaders in London, where I was living at the time. The British police warned me that I was one of the top five people targeted on Saddam's list. Fortunately, during that same time, the British authorities arrested and deported many of Saddam's intelligence agents.

Despite my family's efforts to protect me and keep my location secret, my location in London was known through media interviews and public meetings. One of Saddam's agents came to me in London and threatened me face to face. He said, "If you don't stop your activities against Saddam's regime, your life and the lives of your family members in Iraq will be further in danger." I responded, "Why should I stop my activities if Saddam continues his atrocities?" After the man threatened, he finally softened his approach to ask me that if I continue criticizing the government and the Ba'ath Party, could I at least not criticize Saddam. I was not swayed. My reaction was that Saddam was behind all the crimes committed against the Iraqi people and other nations of the region. Instead of giving in, I was more emboldened and started to focus more on criticizing Saddam, including in my interviews with media.

People ask me how I could have been so bold. My only thought at the time was that someone had to do it, and it had to be me. I was not only speaking out publicly, but also writing about my protest. While I was in London, I published several books in English and Arabic about Saddam's crimes and terrorism. In 2002, I published a book about Al Qaeda, Osama bin Laden, and the 9/11 terrorist attacks in the United States.[6] After I returned to Iraq, I published a second book covering terrorism in 2004 and the rise of Abu Musaab Al-Azarqawi, the leader of Al Qaeda in Iraq (referred to as AQI).[7] AQI became the Islamic State in Iraq (ISI) and evolved to become the Islamic State in Iraq and the Levant (ISIL), also known as Islamic State in Iraq and Sham (greater Syria) (ISIS).

While being so public, fortunately throughout the many years of my protest, I was not alone. For example, I was part of an Iraqi opposition delegation that was invited to Washington, D.C., in August 2002. Many of these individuals went on to assume very high-ranking positions in government—just to show how important these people were. We met with many high-level American politicians at that time, including Vice President Dick Cheney, Secretary of State Colin Powell, Secretary of Defense Donald Rumsfeld, and other officials on the National Security Council. Our delegation included the Patriotic Union of Kurdistan (PUK) represented by Jalal Talabani (who became the president in 2005); the Iraqi National Accord (INA) represented by Dr. Ayad Allawi (who became the first prime minister in 2004); the Kurdistan Democratic Party (KDP) represented by Hoshyar Zebari (who became the first foreign minister after 2003); the Iraqi National Congress (INC) represented by Dr. Ahmad Al-Chalabi (who became a member of the Governing Council in 2003); the Islamic Supreme Council in Iraq (ISCI) represented by Sayed Abdul Aziz Al-Hakim (who became a member of the Governing Council in 2003); and the Monarch Constitutional Movement represented by Sharif Ali Bin Al-Hussein.

These discussions at least presage my point in this 12-step plan regarding the importance of involving the United States, even though they did not lead to the success of defeating terrorism as they could have at the time. Their intentions were in the right direction. Our discussions centered on how the United States could help the suffering Iraqi people, and how they might stop the repression of the Saddam regime. During the meeting, we were told that President Bush had already made the decision to remove Saddam's regime and at that point in time it was a matter of how and when.

During that visit in August 2002, I was nominated to be the spokesperson for the delegation. After the meetings, I read our statement outside the Department of State. The statement said that our delegation opposed military intervention in Iraq and that the best way to remove Saddam from power was to establish an international tribunal to indict Saddam and his top aides for war crimes. The tribunal would be similar to the one set up by the Security Council of the United Nations to address the actions of President Slobodan Milosevic of Yugoslavia. The statement emphasized the point I made many times about the importance of forcing Saddam's regime to implement UN Security Council Resolution 688 with respect to human rights and Resolution 949 to prevent Saddam from using heavy arms and his elite troops, "the Republican Guards," to attack Iraqi people.[8]

Our delegation suggested to the U.S. administration that an Iraqi government be put in place immediately following the fall of Saddam to avoid occupation. Instead, the United States decided to declare occupation in Iraq. This was a big mistake in my opinion, one that I emphasize in this book, since the occupation helped terrorist groups, such as AQI and other insurgency groups, to attract foreign fighters from all over the world to attack the Americans in Iraq.[9]

Our goal was also to bring Saddam and his top aides to justice, with help from British and American high-ranking officials. Fortunately, some officials joined our mission. This supports my point in this book that we cannot defeat terrorism alone. Supporters at the time included British MP Ann Clwyd, U.S. Ambassador Peter W. Galbraith, and other Iraqi, British, and American friends[10] who helped get the process started. Together, we set up INDICT, an organization based in London, to collect evidence of crimes committed by Saddam and his top aides and to establish a tribunal to indict them.

Some politicians proposed views with which I strongly disagreed because they could have led down a dangerous path if it had been followed. For example, Peter W. Galbraith, a Vermont state senator from 2011 to 2015, published a book about Iraq entitled *End of Iraq* in which he argued that Iraq should be "partitioned" into three parts, one part for Shiites, one for Sunnis, and a Kurdish part.[11] I saw major problems with his proposal that could have opened a Pandora's box in the region where separate entities could be exploited by terrorists. Instead, I always maintained, as you will see throughout this book, that Iraqis should work together to solve their problems, to unite as a country, and to build their country for the future. Shiites, Sunnis, and Kurds will be better off if they combine resources to achieve a united Iraq. Galbraith's book is a typical example of diagnosing problems and suggesting solutions from a distance. Such a perspective from a vantage point of an American living in relative security is very different in my view from that of an Iraqi who lived the life first-hand in a terrorist regime, as I have.

RETURNING TO IRAQ 2003

In a move that captured the world's attention, Operation Red Dawn, an American military operation, conducted on December 13, 2003, in the town of ad-Dawr, Iraq, near Tikrit, led to the capture of former Iraqi dictator Saddam Hussein.

A few months before this monumental success, a group of us in the opposition decided to return from exile to our country. When I returned from London to Iraq on May 10, 2003, I accessed a file maintained by Saddam's Intelligence Services, and learned as fact what I already knew—that not only myself but all members of my family were under surveillance. I also found out how they discovered where I was working when I was in exile in London: from informers. Iraqi embassies used Iraqis who needed consulate services to extract information regarding my whereabouts. Reading through the files, I discovered maps covering my movements along with plans for my assassination.

Even though I thought I was safe when I returned to Iraq, in reality those years between 2003 and 2006 were dangerous. I escaped many assassination attempts by the remnants of Saddam's regime and by insurgency groups. One such attempt happened in 2003, when I was invited to speak to a big gathering of Iraqi tribes of Sunnis and Shiites, after I had received many tribal Sheikhs in my house. Fortunately, thanks to the warnings of a friend, the attempt was averted. This friend was the first Iraqi Interior Minister Nouri Al-Badran, who had been a friend for many years when I was living in London (and working with the Iraqi National Accord headed by Ayad Allawi, who became the first prime minister in Iraq after 2003). Nouri contacted me to tell me that American intelligence officers had contacted him from Washington, D.C., to tell him there was a plan to kill me by shelling that meeting with mortars. He insisted that I do not go to the meeting. I listened and did not go.

Other attempts included shootings on my home. Also, many IEDs (improvised explosive devices) were planted on the route from my home to the Ministry of Foreign Affairs in Baghdad, both destinations that were outside the fortified "Green Zone." One event was exceptionally tragic for my family. In 2005, terrorists kidnapped my brother and contacted his wife to tell her that he confessed that he was providing me with information about the Ba'ath Party and the insurgency groups, and that they were going to kill him. They did. He was shot twice in the head and left in the street with a note reading, "This is the fate of traitors and agents."

Of course, this was a message to me personally, and horrific to my family. But it was also a sign of the erratic out-of-control local terrorism. My brother—a businessman who was not involved in politics or any governmental job—was murdered simply because of my status as an outspoken public figure and so a major target. Killing innocent family members and making them appear to turn on family members is a typical action of terrorists. This treacherous tactic is not unlike what the Nazis did during World War II to control and terrorize people.

Very soon after my return to Iraq, several important interactions with U.S. officials further confirmed for me the importance and value of working with the United States in the fight against terror—if steps are taken in the right way, as I outline in this book. One of these events was that Paul Bremer, President Bush's special envoy and head of the Coalition Provisional Authority (CPA), arrived in Iraq on May 12, 2003. He invited recently returned Iraqis including me to a meeting held in Saddam's Republican Palace on May 16, 2003, where he said in his role as the highest authority in the country, he would appoint a Political Council, later called the Governing Council, and a Constitutional Council to draft a constitution.

It is important to note that once back in our country, after Saddam's fall, many of my colleagues in the opposition who had been exiled became political leaders. Members of the group who ascended to high ranks included Dr. Ayad Allawi, who became the first prime minister in 2004; Dr. Ibrahim Al-Jafari who became the second prime minister in 2006; Nouri Al-Maliki who became the third prime minister; Haider Al-Abadi, the present prime minister; Jalal Talabani who became the president in 2006; and Masoud Barazani who became the president of Kurdish region in northern Iraq.

I became Iraq's Deputy Foreign Minister in April 2004 and participated in writing Iraq's National Strategy for Counter-Terrorism with Iraqi officials from the Office of the Prime Minister, Defense and Interior Ministries, the National Security Council, and U.S. military commanders including General David Petraeus, who was then a three-star general. At these meetings, as in so many other meetings, I continued to raise the idea—crucial to my plan outlined in this book—of depending on local people to maintain security, at the same time realizing the Americans' worry—that militias could stage a sectarian war between Sunnis and Shiites. To counter this, I explained that in Sunni areas, local armed Sunni forces would be in control, and in Shiites areas, local armed Shiites forces would be in control.

This approach could also be applied to Kurdish, Turkmen, and Assyrian Christian areas.

SOME U.S. MISTAKES IN IRAQ

While I noted some positive steps by the United States, there are also mistakes. Let me take you through the steps. Paul Bremer issued what is called CPA Order No. 1, which removed the Ba'ath Party's influence from the new Iraqi political system—referred as the "de-Ba'athification" of the system. Following my earlier analogy to Nazi Germany, this move was Iraq's equivalent to Germany's denazification after World War II. The order removed the four highest ranks of the Ba'ath Party from their positions and banned them from future employment in the public sector.[12] I must mention that there were complications in this order. Remember I and the opposition vehemently opposed the Ba'ath Party. But many people had joined the Ba'ath Party solely to get jobs so that they could feed their families, and not because they were loyal to Saddam, his family, or his aides (in fact, many Ba'ath Party members in the northern and southern provinces actually participated in the uprising against the regime in 1991).

Several days later, a major step in the process took place that defines the entire controversy. On May 22, the United States and the United Kingdom decided to announce occupation of Iraq. To confirm the U.S.-U.K. move, UN Security Council Resolution 1483 was adopted, naming the occupying forces as the authority in Iraq.[13] In my view, a big mistake was made, as the advice to set up an Iraqi government immediately after the fall of Saddam's dictatorship regime was ignored.

The decision of the United States and the United Kingdom to occupy the country against the will of the Iraqi people created problems in post-Saddam Iraq. Even Russian and French ambassadors in Iraq at the time supported the Security Council Resolution 1483 that named the occupying forces as the authority in Iraq, with the rationale that occupying forces, according to Geneva Convention, assume responsibilities for maintaining security and for providing services. Given that perspective, the Americans and the British were seen to be meeting their responsibilities.

A day later, the CPA issued Order No. 2—the "Dissolution of Entities"—which disbanded the Iraqi military, security, and intelligence infrastructure of President Saddam Hussein. This order impacted around 500,000 personnel and their families, some of whom were loyal to Saddam's regime, but the majority of whom were not, who had only aligned themselves with Saddam because he instilled fear through tight surveillance on military officers and execution of many, falsely accusing them of disloyalty and of plotting a military coup. But all in all, the occupation by the United States and the United Kingdom remains controversial and is considered by critics to be the biggest mistake made in the immediate aftermath of the fall of Saddam Hussein.[14]

A central point in the criticism, with which I agree, is that Bremer wanted to appoint both the Governing Council and a Constitutional Council I mentioned earlier against the advice that these positions be filled by an election by the Iraqi people. But Bremer rejected the idea of early elections for three reasons: there was no law for establishing political parties in place, there was limited security, and there was no census. I believe that Iraqis should have had election for the members of the Governing Council.

Most the world described the council as a U.S.-appointed Governing Council. There was also opposition to the idea that Bremer would appoint the Constitutional Council. A major voice in this opposition, Grand Ayatollah Sayed Ali Al-Sistani, said that the Constitutional Council should also be elected by the Iraqis, so that the Iraqi constitution would reflect the aspirations of the Iraqi people and would take into account all their ethnic, religious, and sectarian backgrounds that existed in the country. Fortunately, this eventually happened in 2005, when an election for the General Assembly was eventually held, and a constitution was drafted and approved by the Iraqi people in a general referendum.

But the controversy at the time cannot be overstated. It is also crucial to understanding my strategy in this book. I had seriously objected to Bremer's refusal to hold elections by the Iraqi people of the councils. Determined to make my view known, in December 2003, I advised the president of the Governing Council Sayed Abdul Aziz Al-Hakim to write a letter to the UN secretary general, Kofi Annan, to seek the UN's approval to hold elections in Iraq. Ambassador Bremer was angry and asked the president of the Governing Council "Why did you send such a letter without asking me?" This was yet another example of the mistakes made by the United States and the United Kingdom, and things got worse. The insurgency and terrorist groups accused Americans of appointing a puppet Governing Council and the first Iraqi unelected government. They mobilized terrorists to attack the American forces and Iraqi officials. Actually, this situation lasted for years, even after five elections, until 2014; there was still no law for political parties, no census, and no security in Iraq.

My view was clear, and I was not going to be stopped by fear of Bremer, or any others, disagreeing with me or being angry with my position or actions. My colleagues and I wanted national reconciliation among different ethnic, religious, and sectarian groups in Iraq, and to have regional and international reconciliation with governments in the region and the world. So, I advised the president of the Governing Council to visit some countries that were against the war in Iraq to convince them to support reconciliation and reconstruction in Iraq. This action further angered Bremer when he heard news of the trip. He asked the president of the Governing Council, "Why do you want to visit countries which opposed the war against Saddam's regime?"

In spite of these setbacks, my colleagues and I were not derailed. We met with world leaders including President Jacques Chirac of France, Chancellor Gerhard Schroder of Germany, and Vladimir Putin of Russia (who opposed the war of 2003), as well as the U.K. Prime Minister Tony Blair, the Prime Minister of Spain Jose Maria Aznar, and the President of the United Arab Emirates Shaikh Zayed Al-Nahyan, to convince them of our advice.

The next year, in 2004, Iraq's Foreign Minister Hoshyar Zebari asked me to travel to New York to meet with United Nations officials regarding a draft resolution to hand sovereignty back to the Iraqis. Not surprisingly, Ambassador Bremer was upset about this and asked me to postpone my trip. But I refused. On my way to New York, I set up an important meeting to clarify this issue, with Sir John Sawers at the Foreign Office in London, whom I knew when he was in Baghdad representing the British Government in the CPA headed by Bremer. I later worked with Sawers when each of us became an Ambassador to the UN. Later he served as chief of the British Intelligence Service from 2009 to 2013. I set up this meeting because I wanted to ask Sawers why he thought Bremer objected to my trip. He answered that the United States and the United Kingdom were negotiating a draft resolution to the United Nations about Iraq, and Bremer was worried that I would disrupt their plans. In fact, at the time, many high-ranking U.S. officials were talking about handing back *partial or limited* sovereignty to the Iraqis. But, in contrast, I and my compatriots were insisting on *full and complete* sovereignty. This approach is critical when considering the defeat of terrorism.

RISE OF TERRORISM IN IRAQ

You will read in my thesis in this book and my 12-step strategy that I emphasize that the defeat of terrorism must involve the local country, leading actors, and all sectors of the society. That is why I am relating at this point that occupying the country and dismissing the Iraqi army and "de-Ba'athification" created an environment that facilitated the rise of insurgency and terrorist organizations in the post-Saddam era. The "new" Iraq had a huge number of discontented people because they had lost their jobs. Also, eliminating the army—even with good intentions—pushed thousands of well-trained military personnel with long fighting experience to join the insurgency and the terrorist groups. Most of all, the occupation of Arab and Muslim lands—by Western powers, no less—created the best pretext for insurgency and terrorist groups to attract not only discounted local fighters but also brought fighters from all over the world to Iraq to fight against American and British colonial powers.

In this context, let me expand on a new order that was told to our Iraqi opposition leader group in May 2003 (by General David McKiernan and implemented by the CPA) that would ban all arms and mandated that Iraqis hand over their arms to the new police stations. There were strong objections to this proposal—and for good reason! I argued strongly that such a ban on Iraqis to keep arms left the Iraqi people with no resources to protect their properties, business, and homes. Fortunately, the order was altered to allow Iraqi houses, offices, and stores to keep a handgun or an AK-47 machine gun to protect themselves. American officials gave no public explanation for amending what had been a much tougher plan to rid postwar Iraq of heavy weapons, but military officials have said they recognize the difficulties in disarming citizens at a time when Iraqis feel their security is still at risk.[15] Following up on this, General McKiernan requested a one-on-one meeting with me at Saddam's "Al-Fao Palace" near Baghdad International Airport (the notorious palace, surrounded by an artificial lake with a bridge as the only way to reach it, that was partly demolished by air strikes before the fall of Saddam).

During this meeting, General McKiernan observed that the U.S. Army had a major security problem. The palace itself seemed secure because of being surrounded by military tents and satellite dishes positioned to facilitate communications. But the streets were seriously dangerous. In fact, on the previous day, troops distributing candy to children were attacked by an Iraqi man who opened fire and shot two soldiers. It was apparent that American soldiers in Iraq could not distinguish between friends and foes. They did not speak Arabic nor did they understand the culture or traditions of the country. In order to establish a secure environment to protect American troops on the ground, the language barrier and lack of knowledge regarding the country needed to be addressed. This is an important point, because understanding the culture and language is key in my 12-step strategy to defeat terrorism.

Other such incidents ended in tragedy. I told General McKiernan that a store owner who is a friend saw a U.S. patrol on foot coming toward his store. While one soldier sat on the pavement outside, others entered the store. A car stopped across the street and a person got out and crossed the street as if he was going into the store. However, when he reached the soldier sitting on the pavement, he pulled a gun, shot the soldier, and drove his car away. This alarming example demonstrates that Americans could not predict, nor recognize, danger on the streets. I told General McKiernan that if the United States seeks to maintain security in Iraq, it must depend on Iraqis who know the people and can distinguish friend from foe, who are fluent in Arabic so they understand what is being said, and who understand the culture and traditions. My own family illustrates these points. My family lived in the same neighborhood since my grandfather moved from the old city of Baghdad in 1948 and bought a house in a southern suburb. All the members of my family lived in the same neighborhood and knew every house and every person; thus, they could very quickly distinguish friend from foe.

While General McKiernan did not want to establish what he called "armed militias" in Iraq, I emphasized that our group was not recommending militias either, but we recognized the need for local people to help maintain security in the areas where they lived. Tragically in my view, U.S. officials did not agree, and that cost both Iraqi and American lives. Repeatedly, in interactions with high-level U.S. officials, I tried to convince them of the legitimacy of my argument. As an Iraqi native, I was determined to share what I learned from experience in the dictatorship, and to work with the U.S. officials to made conditions better in the complicated country that is my home.

The year after the fall of Saddam was critical in the war against terrorism, in that it was the time when the insurgency took root and began a counterattack. In this time, I continued to insist on my point of view with many top-level officials. These included U.S. general Ricardo Sanchez, who held the top military position in Iraq. For example, in my first meeting with Sanchez in 2003, I informed him that gangs in commercial districts in central Baghdad were intimidating store owners and businesses and collecting monthly payments from them under the pretext of protecting them. Members of my family in these districts who refused to pay had their stores burned at night by people who blackmailed them. I provided the names of the gangs and their leaders. Sadly, and tragically, nothing serious was done about them. This was, in my view, extremely unwise, although I will admit to the value of the American policy change I referred to earlier, whereby Iraqis were allowed to keep AK-47 assault rifles in their homes and businesses.

At times, as you might discern from my recounting of these events, it was very frustrating when U.S. and British officials did not listen to advice that could have averted serious losses. For example, after I became deputy foreign minister of Iraq in April 2004, I was contacted by an Italian friend from Rome who came to Baghdad to seek my help in releasing three kidnapped Italian soldiers. I wrote a letter to the interior minister and asked for information, but received no answer. I had to take matters into my own hands. With help from friends in a news agency, I managed to get information about the place in which they were being held, with eyewitnesses placing them at a local Sunni mosque. Using my contacts in the area, I arranged for the head of my tribe to contact the head of the tribe in the area where the kidnapped soldiers were held, and they were released in June 2004.

In those years, frustration reigned as the situation in Iraq was drastically out of control. Murders and kidnappings were rampant. In July 2003, the five-year-old son of my cousin was kidnapped in my neighborhood in southern Baghdad. My cousin went to the police, but nothing was done for weeks. Then my cousin got a call to warn him to cancel his report to the police and to pay a ransom for the release of his son. Clearly, information had leaked from the police! The caller boldly asked how they could finance jihad (holy war) if people like my cousin refuse to pay. Stopping such kidnappings and funding, you will see later in this book, is part of my 12-step strategy to defeat terrorism.

In all the stories I tell you, you can see that I have learned and experienced as much or even more about terrorism than most of those who are responsible for fighting it, including Americans. I also examined the terrorist situations studiously, including tracing the activities of Al Qaeda in the aftermath of the 9/11 attacks on the World Trade Center, and the rise of insurgency and terrorist organizations evident in the abu Musaab al-Zarqawi al-Tawhid wal-Jihad group, which became AQI. Since then, I have concentrated on issues of fundamentalism, extremism, and terrorism, and the rise of ISIS since its beginnings.

After the fall of Saddam, when I returned to Iraq and became very involved in the government of my country, I learned a great deal about how the American military regarded terrorism in general, and specifically in Iraq. All this experience with the Western approach is at the foundation of my strategy in this book.

I thought at the time that my idea of depending on the local Iraqi people to maintain security was gaining some traction. In one example, the British MP Ann Clwyd, whom I referred to earlier, arranged a one-on-one meeting for me with British Prime Minister Tony Blair. He asked me, "What can we do about security in Iraq?" I said that you have to depend on Iraqis and set up local military units to maintain security. "Do you think the Iraqis can do it?" he asked. I replied, "Mr. Prime Minister, if the Iraqis cannot do it, no army in the world can do it." This interaction is another example of my frustration in meetings with British and American officials who looked at Iraq from a Western perspective and not from an Iraqi perspective. It is why my strategy in this book addresses this failing.

DEFEATING TERRORISM IN IRAQ

Finally, years later, after so much destruction and loss of life in the war against terrorism, in 2009, General Petraeus came up with the idea of "Awakening Councils." Also known as Sons of Iraq, these Awakening Councils were coalitions between tribal Sheikhs in the Al-Anbar province and former Iraqi military officers of Saddam's regime, who united to maintain stability in their communities. The coalitions were initially sponsored by the U.S. military. Finally! My idea was taking hold.

The concept of these Awakening Councils was based on the same principal I had put forward so much earlier, where local people and tribal fighters would protect their communities. This is the same concept I discussed in those earlier years (in 2003 and 2004) that I mentioned earlier, with General McKiernan and General Sanchez. I also advocated for this principle over the years between 2004 and 2005 with other commanders such as General Petraeus during meetings about Iraq National Counter-Terrorism

Strategy at the National Security Council. I continually insisted on those occasions that it was the only way to maintain peace and security from an Iraqi perspective.

Finally, they listened. General Petraeus told his officers, "Tribal engagement and local reconciliation work! Encourage it!" Battalion commanders made it a priority to cultivate tribal sheikhs, imams at mosques, and other influential locals, while the strategic engagement cell contacted insurgent leaders. Thousands of Iraqis came forward to ally with the Americans and eventually became the Sons of Iraq. This was critical move, because it was important to include the Sons of Iraq in the formal structure of the new Iraq.[16] This was an instance of a positive step—and a crucial part of a strategy that must be continued in order to defeat terrorism that I present here.

Through this process, I suffered the loss of lives of many family members, relatives, and friends, but I also managed to save other people's lives. Yet, I am frustrated when I feel that more lives could have been saved, if mistakes had been avoided and lessons had been learned sooner. That is why I hope this book will help save more lives by diagnosing the roots of terrorism and putting forth strategies to uproot this cancer from the human community before it spreads and kills more.

FUTURE OF ISIS AND ITS LEADER IN IRAQ

Terrorist group Islamic State in Iraq and Syria (ISIS), also known as Islamic State in Iraq and the Levant (ISIL), evolved from Al Qaeda in Iraq (AQI), and I will talk about its evolvement later in this book. However in this book I will use ISIS as a short name for the group. ISIS managed to control huge swathes of lands in Syria after the civil war erupted in 2011.

In 2013, ISIS fighters crossed the borders from Syria to Iraq and managed to control several cities and towns in Salah Al-Din and Anbar provinces with the support of former officers of Saddam Hussien's army and members of Saddam's Ba'ath Party. In June 2014, they managed to control Mosul, the second largest city in Iraq and eradicated the borders between Iraq and Syria and called themselves Islamic State (IS) "Caliphate."

By the end of June 2017, the Iraqi Security Forces, the Iraqi Popular Mobilization Forces, and the Kurdish Forces (Peshmerga) were in the final stage to liberate Mosul, the second largest city in Iraq, and defeat ISIS completely.

Iraq's Prime Minister Haider al-Abadi told reporters on Thursday, June 22, 2017, that the full liberation of Mosul was near and it would take only few days. He announced on July 9, 2017, the liberation of the entire city of Mosul.[17]

Leadership in ISIS, as in any terrorist organization, is important for the organization's morale. Thus, confusion over the fate of the head of the Islamic State group, Abu Bakr Al-Baghdadi, was a matter of great concern. In June 2017, Russian media cited a source indicating that the Foreign

Ministry announced it might have killed Al-Baghdadi in an air strike that targeted a meeting of ISIS leaders just outside the group's self-declared capital in Syria. However, U.S. officials said there was no definitive proof of his death.[18]

Just a few days after the questions surfaced about the fate of Al-Baghdadi, Iraqi sources in Mosul said that ISIS distributed a flyer among its members and in the mosques of Talafar city west of Mosul indicating that ISIS would issue a declaration regarding the ISIS leader. The source said there was a clear panic among ISIS fighters after news about his possible killing. However, it is important to point out that the reports were not confirmed. This is relevant given that there was similar news about the demise of the ISIS leader after Iraqi and American air strikes in 2014 and 2015, which proved to be wrong. Also, it was in ISIS's best interests to deny the leader's death, since ISIS was going through a critical time, evidenced by their losing their last important headquarters in Mosul.

If in fact Abu Bakr Al-Baghdadi was dead, the major question became who could be his successor? Experts on Islamist groups saw no clear options, but they believed two ISIS subleaders—Iyad al-Obaidi and Ayad al-Jumaili, former army officers under late Iraqi dictator Saddam Hussein—could be the top contenders, Reuters reported.[19]

Al-Obaiadi, in his fifties, is the war minister of ISIS, while Jumaili, in his forties, was in charge of ISIS security affairs. The two became Al-Baghdadi's top assistants after the killing of at least three of his top leaders, namely, his deputy Abo Ali AL-Anbari, the war minster Abo Omar Al-Shishani, and Abo Mohammed Al-Julani, who was in charge of ISIS media during air strikes in 2016.

PART I

Why the World Failed to Stop Al Qaeda and ISIS/ISIL

The chapters in this part cover the various issues that impact the prevalence and incidence of terrorism. This includes the role of technology, the Internet, and funding sources. They also describe the emergence of the lone wolves who carry out terrorist attacks that have exacerbated the violence caused by organized factions, therefore increasing the importance of new strategies. Importantly, the impact of the U.S. president's strategy is discussed. Understanding all these issues in these chapters sets the stage for my new 12-step counterterrorism strategy presented in Part II.

CHAPTER 1

U.S. Presidents' Counterterrorism Strategy

In this chapter, I will go over U.S. counterterrorism strategy during the presidencies of Donald Trump and his predecessors Barack Obama, Bill Clinton, and George W. Bush Jr., to give some background for comparison, as well as to highlight some mistakes made and lessons to be learned. This provides a context to explore President Trump's impact on the defeat of terrorism. This examination of the American presidents is important to understand my strategy to combat terrorism.

Between 1979 and 1989, the United States and its allies, Pakistan and Saudi Arabia, supported Arab fighters to travel to Afghanistan and fight the Soviet forces along with the Afghani fighters called "mujahideen." They were led by Saudi fighter Osama bin Laden, who established the Al Qaeda terrorist organization.

Following Saddam Hussein's invasion of Kuwait on August 2, 1990, U.S. forces landed in Saudi Arabia to protect the country from Saddam's forces mobilized near the Saudi borders, and to liberate Kuwait. Osama bin Laden objected to the U.S. forces' landing in the holy lands of Muslims in Saudi Arabia and declared war against the United States.

On December 29, 1992, Al Qaeda, under bin Laden's direction, carried out bomb attacks on the hotels in Yemen where U.S. Marines stayed in the port city of Aden on their way to Somalia. Bin Laden ultimately claimed that he and Muhammad Naeem Noor Khan, Al Qaeda senior operative and computer expert, were responsible for the 1992 Yemen attacks.

Almost a year later, in another massive terrorist attack, Al Qaeda helped militias in Somalia attack U.S. forces in Mogadishu on October 3, 1993. Two U.S. Black Hawk helicopters were shot down by rocket-propelled grenades (RPGs), and three other aircraft were damaged.[1] The 15-hour battle that ensued left 18 Americans dead and 73 injured. Hundreds, perhaps thousands, of Somalis were killed. U.S. Army pilot Mike Durant was captured and held by Somali militants for 11 days.

This event was covered widely by the press, and woke up Americans to the deadly drama unfolding. After the Battle of Mogadishu, then-President Clinton said that it was a mistake for the United States to play the role of police officer in Somalia and announced a six-month plan to remove U.S. troops from the country.[2]

Osama bin Laden mistook the withdrawal of U.S. forces from Afghanistan and Somalia as a sign of weakness and a lack of desire to fight. He said, "The youth were surprised at the low morale of the American soldiers and realized more than before that the America [sic] soldiers are paper tigers. After a few blows, the Americans ran away in defeat. After a few blows, they forgot about being the world leader and the leader of the new world order. They left, dragging their corpses and their shameful defeat, and stopped using such titles."[3]

PRESIDENT BILL CLINTON'S COUNTERTERRORISM STRATEGY

The first attack carried out by terrorists connected to Al Qaeda inside the United States occurred on February 26, 1993, namely, the attack on the World Trade Center. Six people were killed and about a thousand people were injured. Notably, this attack was the model later followed by terrorists to carry out the second, and devastating, attack on the World Trade Center on September 11, 2001. In my view, President Clinton's administration underestimated the threat of Al Qaeda, in spite of evidence that terrorists connected to Al Qaeda had bombed the World Trade Center in New York in the 1993 attack.

About a year and a half later, in November 1995, Al Qaeda attacked U.S. forces in Al-Khubar, Saudi Arabia, where nineteen U.S. servicemen were killed and 498 people of many nationalities were wounded. A year later, in October 2000, Al Qaeda attacked the USS *Cole* in Yemen, using a boat laden with explosives, that killed seventeen U.S. sailors, injured many more, and almost sank the destroyer. Yet, the Clinton cabinet was reluctant to respond militarily to what was quite obviously an act of war perpetrated by Al Qaeda. In my view, the lack of a response to the Al Qaeda attack on the USS *Cole* by both Presidents Bill Clinton and George W. Bush Jr. gave the terrorist group a false impression of America as the proverbial "paper tiger"—meaning that Americans are weak, that they have no guts to fight, and that they could be defeated by small-scale attacks. It was a view that the Al Qaeda leadership held, and used to their advantage. Lack of major action was a big mistake.

That false impression emboldened Osama bin Laden and Al Qaeda to plan and execute the major terrorist attacks on September 11, 2001, in which four civilian airplanes were hijacked by terrorists. Two of them targeted—and hit—the World Trade Center towers in New York, a third hit the Pentagon in Washington, D.C., and the fourth plane was supposed to crash into the U.S. Capitol Building of the Congress, but was prematurely crashed in Pennsylvania, as a result of the courageous resistance of passengers and crew members. Around 3,000 people were killed, and twice that number were injured as a result of those 9/11 terrorist attacks. The attacks were the most devastating attacks on the United States since the Pearl Harbor attack carried out by Japan during World War II—an attack that forced the United States to enter the war, and eventually to defeat Germany and its allies. In that example, strong action led to a conclusive ending of the Germans and their allies, in favor of the West. But, in stark contrast, the aftermath of the 9/11 attacks—certainly equivalent if not more so in aggression—did not lead to an end of the terrorist activities. Thus, we are in the situation we are in today, and I am writing this book about counterterrorism.

The foretelling of the escalation of terrorism was clear. More than 3 years before 9/11 in 2001, Osama bin Laden had issued a religious decree (fatwa) when, in February 1998, he said it is the duty of every Muslim to kill Americans wherever they are found. In August 1998, two simultaneous bombings were carried out on the U.S. Embassies in Kenya and Tanzania. More than 200 were left dead.[4] President Clinton took action to declare bin Laden "Public Enemy No. 1." A year later, on June 7, 1999, Osama bin Laden was added to the Federal Bureau of Investigation's (FBI's) "Ten Most Wanted" list, announced by U.S. Attorney General Janet Reno and FBI Director Louis Freeh at a Washington, D.C., news conference. Bin Laden was formally accused of being the mastermind behind the U.S. Embassy bombings in Kenya and Tanzania. It certainly looked like action was being taken.

The CIA spent much of 1998–2001 hunting bin Laden. The goal was to capture bin Laden using recruited Afghan agents or to kill him with a precision-guided missile, according to the 2004 report of the 9/11 Commission and the memoirs of George J. Tenet, director of central intelligence, from July 1997 to July 2004. But, *the intelligence was never good enough to pull the trigger.*[5]

PRESIDENT GEORGE W. BUSH'S COUNTERTERRORISM STRATEGY

While the defeat of terrorism was central in the Bush Jr. administration, and came to be known as the "War on Terror," some factors contributed to the rise of terrorism, as described here.

Clinton's term expired three months after the bombing of the USS *Cole.* In June 2001, five months after President George W. Bush Jr. had been sworn in, Al Qaeda released a videotape claiming responsibility for the USS *Cole* operation. The videotape was broadcast around the world. If the Bush administration needed a reason to destroy Al Qaeda, this was the best one. Instead, "the response was to do absolutely nothing."[6]

By the summer of 2001, the CIA was convinced that Al Qaeda was on the verge of a deadly attack. On August 6, 2001, President Bush received intelligence in the Presidential Daily Briefing (PDB) entitled "Bin Laden determined to strike in US." The report stated that clandestine, foreign government, and media reports indicated that bin Laden since 1997 had wanted to carry out terrorist attacks in the United States. Bin Laden implied in U.S. television interviews in 1997 and 1998 that his followers would follow the example of World Trade Center bomber Ramzi Yousef in 1993 and "bring the fighting to America." After U.S. missile strikes on his base in Afghanistan in 1998, bin Laden told his followers that he wanted to retaliate on Washington, D.C.[7]

On September 4, 2001, at a meeting of the Principal's Committee of Bush's national security advisers, "No one around the table seemed to have a can-do attitude. Everyone seemed to have an excuse." A week later, the 9/11 attacks—the worst terrorist attacks in history—were carried out at bin Laden's direction.[8]

The day after the 9/11 attacks, President Bush declared the strikes by Al Qaeda "more than acts of terror. They were acts of war." Bush's "War on Terror" was "not a figure of speech," he said. Rather, it was a defining framework. The war, Bush announced, would begin with Al Qaeda, but would "not end until every terrorist group of global reach has been found, stopped and defeated."[9]

Despite this, in my view, U.S. counterterrorism strategy was often short-sighted and was a reaction to certain events and developments rather than a long-term and comprehensive global strategy. This is a lesson learned that supports my strategy to finally defeat terrorism outlined in this book.

The reaction of President George W. Bush to the 9/11 terrorist attacks was to launch an "International War on Terror." This rallied the public. Yet, it was a vague definition that kept the identity of terrorists concealed and led officials in the Bush administration to claim that the United States could change many regimes in the Middle East and that they could have armed conflict anywhere.

I know this period and the politics of it firsthand. I was part of the Iraqi opposition delegation invited to Washington, D.C., in August 2002. We met with Vice President Dick Cheney, Secretary of State Colin Powell, Secretary of Defense Donald Rumsfeld, and many other officials in the National Security Council. We told U.S. officials that U.S. official statements about changing regimes in the Middle East frightened governments in the region who will oppose the War on Terror because they were worried about their own country. We also told them that if they are going to remove Saddam's regime, they should explain that it is a special case, since Saddam committed war crimes, genocide, ethnic cleansing, and crimes against humanity.

Other reactions to the 9/11 attacks were to authorized the so-called enhanced interrogation techniques against suspect detainees. Later, President

Obama would call these tactics "torture" that would not be allowed in the United States. But in 2004, the scandal of torture, humiliation, and sexual assaults against detainees in the Abu Ghraib central prison in Iraq fueled insurgency militants and served terrorist groups. The controversy over prisoner treatment related to President Bush's "War on Terror" expanded to the controversial Guantanamo Bay detention center and "Black Sites"— detention centers in many countries outside the United States in which suspects were interrogated and tortured.

Another difficulty in the Bush administration was that the U.S. counterterrorism strategy after the 9/11 terrorist attacks was based on a policy of denying safe havens for terrorist groups. However, this policy failed in Afghanistan and Iraq, with the continued conflicts in the Middle East. This policy of "sanctuary denial" was eventually replaced by a policy of "sanctuary management," which also failed as was seen in Libya and Syria.[10]

PRESIDENT BARACK OBAMA'S COUNTERTERRORISM STRATEGY

The Obama administration thought President Bush overstretched the U.S. Army, and ironically actually motivated rather than deterred jihadists with large ground troops in Afghanistan and Iraq. While the United States did not put pressure on the Iraqi government in 2011 to keep residual forces in Iraq, they were forced in 2014 to send thousands of American troops to face ISIS.

Obama's election campaign included bringing U.S. troops home from Afghanistan and Iraq. He worked hard to keep this promise and to withdraw troops from Iraq by the end of 2011, and from Afghanistan by end of 2016, before his second term ended.

In this way, Obama made dramatic changes to Bush's "War on Terror" on the part of the United States, and key components of the secret structure developed under Bush were swept away. The CIA (Central Intelligence Agency) was prohibited from maintaining its own overseas prisons, and Obama abolished every legal order on interrogations issued by any lawyer in the executive branch after September 11, 2001.[11]

In several key steps in the new national counterterrorism strategy, in June 2011, the United States pushed ahead with more targeted drone strikes and special operations raids, and fewer costly land battles than had happened in Iraq and Afghanistan in the continuing war against Al Qaeda. The new doctrine, two years in the making, came in the wake of the successful special operations raid that killed Al Qaeda chief Osama bin Laden in May 2011.[12]

Part of President Obama's strategy for counterterrorism was a reaction to President Bush's policies that had caused outrage, concerns, and worries among governments, nongovernmental organizations, and human rights activists. The Obama administration's counterterrorism chief, John Brennan, suggested that President Obama's goals "track closely with the goals" of former President Bush, but the new strategy document could not be more emphatic in distinguishing the Obama approach from the Bush doctrine, in saying, "We are not at war with the tactic of terrorism or the religion of Islam. We are at war with a specific organization—Al Qaeda."[13]

While Obama's strategy avoided air strikes in favor of drone strikes and included an increase in the number of drone strikes, the president admitted the lack of certainty with these drone strikes, added to the civilian casualties that resulted. But this approach was justified by saying drones are more precise than air strikes. Obama cautioned that the nature of terrorism makes a clearly defined military victory like those in wars of the past impossible to achieve. Asserting a more long-term view, he said, "We have to pursue a smart strategy that can be sustained."[14]

In the interview I did with television host Jon Stewart on the U.S. television show, *The Daily Show*, which took on political issues albeit on a comedy station and with some comedic intention, on June 19, 2014, I emphasized the importance of U.S. air strikes against ISIS to stop its advance in Iraq and noted that there was no need to send U.S. ground troops. However, President Obama was at that time hesitant to attack ISIS, a position he took until August 7, 2014, when he authorized limited air strikes.

Clearly, one of the most significant events in the War on Terror was the death of Osama bin Laden, by U.S. troops. Obama was entitled to claim this great victory, since the monumental step took place under his administration. Chopping off the head of terrorism at the top is certainly a major step, but others step in to take over leadership, and different methods emerged, with some less-organized means, so terrorism was not cut off at its knees. A victory nonetheless could be claimed.

PRESIDENT DONALD TRUMP CRITICIZED FORMER PRESIDENTS' STRATEGIES

President Donald Trump criticized President Barack Obama for being too hesitant to use force and worrying too much about collateral damage and blowback. Trump's reaction to Obama's "hesitant" policy was to rush to authorize the military attack in Yemen, some would say without proper consultations or appropriate preparation. Indeed, the operation ran into difficulties, as a U.S. Navy SEAL commander was killed, three other U.S. military personnel were injured, and the raid failed to achieve the main objective of capturing the head of Al Qaeda in the Arabian Peninsula, Qasim al-Rimi.

Trump also criticized the strategy of nation-building and regime change implemented by President George W. Bush in Afghanistan and Iraq that was also followed by President Barack Obama in Libya and Syria. Trump said, "We have created the vacuums that allow terrorists to grow and thrive."[15] Trump further blamed President Barack Obama and his Secretary of State Hillary Clinton for the rise of ISIS, saying, "The Obama-Clinton foreign policy has unleashed ISIS, destabilized the Middle East."[16] Trump said, "The failure to establish a new status of forces agreement in Iraq and the election-driven timetable for withdrawal surrendered our gains in that country and led directly to the rise of ISIS." He further insisted that "the failures in Iraq were compounded by Hillary Clinton's disaster in Libya."

This was reported to have "led to a very real and very tragic humanitarian disaster. Her bad judgment and failed policy resulted in the arming of terrorists, months of war and tens of thousands of causalities, the murder of the American ambassador and the deaths of three other brave Americans, continued civil war and the collapse of the Libyan economy, and a failed nation-state contributing to a tragic European migrant crisis."[17]

President Obama has since said he regards Libya as his worst mistake, Trump said.[18] Reflecting on his legacy in a Fox News interview aired on April 10, 2016, Obama said his "worst mistake" was "probably failing to plan for the day after what I think was the right thing to do in intervening in Libya."[19]

PRESIDENT DONALD TRUMP'S COUNTERTERRORISM STRATEGY

At the time of finishing edits for this book, in summer of 2017, President Donald Trump had been elected and was serving as U.S. president for six months; thus, I added this section to this chapter, since I could not ignore the dramatic developments of the new Trump administration regarding terrorism and counterterrorism. In this assessment, I want to be fair, neutral, and rational, since it is a strategy that could save human lives in many countries, including Iraq and the United States. Although President Trump criticized the counterterrorism strategy of both Presidents George W. Bush and Barack Obama and said he will put forth a new counterterrorism strategy, I am worried that there will also be missteps, or issues overlooked, in this new strategy that could be similar to, if not worse than, the mistakes in the previous strategies.

A draft of President Donald Trump's new counterterrorism strategy demands that U.S. allies shoulder more of the burden in combating extremist militants, while acknowledging that the threat of terrorism will never be totally eliminated. The 11-page draft, seen on Friday, May 5, 2017, by Reuters news agency, said that the United States should avoid costly, "open-ended" military commitments.[20] "We need to intensify operations against global jihadist groups while also reducing the costs of American 'blood and treasure' in pursuit of our counterterrorism goals," states the document, which is expected to be released in coming months. "We will seek to avoid costly, large-scale U.S. military interventions to achieve counterterrorism objectives and will increasingly look to partners to share the responsibility for countering terrorist groups," it says. However, it acknowledges that terrorism "cannot be defeated with any sort of finality."[21] Yet, it provides few details on how the United States, that has led global counterterrorism efforts since the 9/11 attacks, can achieve those goals by passing more of the burden to other countries, many of which lack the requisite military and intelligence capabilities.[22]

Actually, in my view, there are negative and positive points in President Trump's counterterrorism strategy that I am going to explain in this chapter. However, I hope that President Trump's administration will study the mistakes committed by previous administrations in dealing with terrorism, avoid repeating the same mistakes, and learn lessons from those mistakes.

MISTAKES IN PRESIDENT TRUMP'S COUNTERTERRORISM STRATEGY

Many commentators have noted mistakes in Trump's current counterterrorism strategy. As one example, critics say that Trump's description of terrorism as "Radical Islamic Terrorism," his anti-Muslim statements, and his ban of seven Muslim nations to travel to the United States, are providing the terrorists with the pretext they need to assert that the United States is waging a war against Islam and Muslims.

Ian Bremer, president of the Eurasia Group, a leading global political risk research and consulting firm, said, "The Trump presidency would make the United States, its citizens and its assets the single most attractive target for terrorist groups. The Clinton, Bush and Obama administrations have all faced this problem. But Trump's intensely anti-Muslim rhetoric will encourage a lot more militants to look beyond softer and more accessible targets in Europe toward the 'big score,' a deadly attack on Trump's America."[23]

Sir Jeremy Greenstock, a former chair of the UN Security Council's counterterrorism committee, said, "If there is to be a global anti-terrorist coalition that is effective, it's got to deal with some of the causes of it, rather than the symptoms . . . I don't see any signs from Trump yet that he has formed a proactive, comprehensive policy that deals with the whole phenomenon of 21st-century terrorism."[24]

In his 2016 book, *The Field of Fight*, Trump's first National Security Adviser Michael Flynn wrote, "We're in a world war, but very few Americans recognize it, and fewer still have any idea how to win it." If the Trump doctrine holds sway, the general, his lieutenants, and their commander-in-chief may indeed get the war they seem to like. Despite what they claim, however, the losers won't be the terrorists, but all of us.[25]

Though designed as measures to make the country safe, other critics assert that Trump's moves are likely to weaken the counterterrorism defenses the United States has erected over the past 16 years. The administration has alienated allies, including Iraq, provided the pretext to terrorist networks that portray the United States as a religious crusade, and endangered critical cooperation from U.S. partners—whether the leader of a mosque in the United States or the head of a Muslim country's intelligence service.[26]

Further, President Donald Trump's new counterterrorism strategy draft makes little mention of promoting human rights, development, good governance, and other "soft power" tools that Washington has embraced in the past to help foreign governments reduce grievances that feed extremism.[27] In contrast, critics say that the Obama counterterrorism strategy made "respecting human rights, fostering good governance, respecting privacy and civil liberties, committing to security and transparency and upholding the rule of law" the foremost of its guiding principles.[28]

In my view, the new administration of President Trump could very well change its policies over time and adapt to developments in its war against terrorism. After all, Trump has been known to change his positions. Also, the situation is fluid, especially in the first few months of the administration. However, based on his speeches during the election campaign and statements that he has made during the first few months of his presidency, Trump's strategy for counterterrorism is based on a few major principles I describe below.

Mistakes about Trump's Visit to Saudi Arabia

Trump's position on involvement in Iraq has appeared to waver. As early as 2006, Trump had condemned the Iraq war as "a total mess, a total catastrophe, and it is not going to get any better. It's only going to get worse." His prescription? "What you have to do is get out of Iraq." In an interview with CNN in March 2007, Trump elaborated: "You know how they get out? They get out. That's how they get out. Declare victory and leave."[29]

His position to stay out of Iraq did not seem to change by almost ten years later. As the war against ISIS raged in the fall of 2015, Trump lamented that in Iraq "We're nation-building. We can't do it. We have to build our own nation." Yet, in contradiction, during the course of the campaign in 2016, an integral part of Trump's critique of President Obama's foreign policy was his decision to withdraw all U.S. troops from Iraq in 2011.[30]

President Trump's position on Iraq is critical, given the presence of U.S. forces in the country. In what can be considered quite controversial, the president's first visit outside the United States in May 2017 included a visit to only one Arab country, namely, Saudi Arabia. Notably, he did not visit Iraq, where U.S. forces were fighting terrorist group ISIS alongside Iraqi Security Forces.

In my view, President Trump's decision to visit Saudi Arabia and not Iraq sent wrong signals to the Iraqi side about his priorities in the region. If the United States' number one priority in the region is to defeat ISIS, then a visit to Iraq should have been a top priority. This is an exceptionally important point, given that no country in the world has sacrificed more than Iraq in fighting and pushing back ISIS.[31]

As the saying goes, a picture is worth a thousand words. Thus, nothing would have illustrated that better if Air Force One had been on the tarmac at the Baghdad International Airport. At a time when the president needed to change breaking news headlines focused on accusations of Russian meddling in the U.S. elections, and the president's firing of FBI Director James Comey, a visit to Iraq would have done just that.[32]

Gulf Countries Crisis with Qatar

On June 5, 2017, three of the six members of the political and economic alliance of the Gulf Cooperation Council (GCC)—Saudi Arabia, the United Arab Emirates, and Bahrain (later followed by Egypt)—announced their decision to sever diplomatic relations with Qatar and install an air, land, and sea blockade of Qatar, citing their concern over the security and stability of their nations, claiming that Qatar works to support "terrorism" and to meddle in the internal affairs of its brethren in the GCC.[33]

Saudi Arabia and its allies published a list of individuals and organizations they claimed are involved in terrorism and mostly linked to Qatar, including Yusuf al-Qaradawi—an Egyptian-born cleric linked to the Muslim Brotherhood with ties with Qatari royals. It also blacklisted charity organizations including Qatar Voluntary Center and Qatar Charity, as well as some individuals sanctioned by the United States over links with Al Qaeda in 2011.[34]

The three Gulf countries also banned all flights from the Qatari capital Doha from entering their airspace. As the diplomatic stranglehold placed on the tiny gas-rich country by its neighbors intensified, in response, a Qatar Foreign Ministry statement fired back, "The State of Qatar has never seen such hostility, not even from a hostile state."[35]

President Trump called on Qatar to stop funding terrorism, claiming credit for and endorsing the decision of Gulf nations to ostracize their neighbor. This position was controversial, since some U.S. cabinet officials said the blockade is hurting—not helping—the campaign against ISIS.

For example, Secretary of State Rex Tillerson, speaking to reporters shortly before Trump's remarks, said the Gulf countries' land and air blockade of Doha is hurting the campaign against ISIS. Notably, Pentagon officials only partially corroborated this assessment. Even so, the divergent opinions highlighted the often mixed messages emerging from the Trump administration since the Qatar crisis began.

But President Trump defended his position. "We had a decision to make," he said, describing conversations with Saudi Arabia and other Gulf countries. "Do we take the easy road or do we finally take a hard but necessary action? We have to stop the funding of terrorism."[36] I must point out here that I agree with this statement, since stopping the funding of terrorism is a major step in my own strategy outlined in this book.

Understandably, those in the region disagreed with the President's position. The CEO of Qatar Airways, Akbar Al Baker, accused the United States of fanning the flames of a dispute between the country and its Gulf neighbors, saying that the decision by Saudi Arabia, the United Arab Emirates, and other states to sever diplomatic and transport links with Qatar amounted to an "illegal" blockade that the United States should be doing its best to resolve.[37]

The U.S. position regarding the Gulf crisis caused confusion and chaos in the Middle East. Despite the United States' negative position toward Qatar and Qatar's protest against the U.S. position, just days after Gulf nations accused Doha of funding terrorism and announced the air blockade, Qatar welcomed two U.S. Navy warships and said it firmly believes that its ties to the United States remain strong, despite the diplomatic crisis in the Middle East.[38]

In addition, amid this ongoing diplomatic crisis between Qatar and a number of its Gulf neighbors, the United States agreed to sell $12 billion worth of American F-15 fighters to the country. Pentagon spokesman Lt. Col. Roger Cabiness said in a statement, "Secretary of Defense Jim Mattis met on June 14, 2017 with Qatari Minister of State for Defense Affairs Dr. Khalid al-Attiyah to discuss concluding steps in finalizing the Foreign Military Sales purchase of U.S.-manufactured F-15 fighter aircraft by the State of Qatar. The $12 billion sale will give Qatar a state of the art capability and increase security cooperation and interoperability between the United States and Qatar."[39] This crisis among Gulf countries could have an impact on security and stability in the Middle East and could affect the campaign to fight terrorist groups such as Al Qaeda and ISIS.

Saudi Arabia Succession

Relations with Saudi Arabia are clearly important for the United States in the region. Two important steps in this regard took place by summer of 2017. In June 2017, Saudi Arabia King Salman, at 81 years old and reportedly in declining health, declared his son Mohammed bin Salman al Saud as next in line to the throne, replacing his 57-year-old nephew. This act handed his 31-year-old son sweeping powers at a time when the kingdom was seeking a radical overhaul of its oil-dependent economy and faced mounting tensions with regional rival Iran. The act was significant to the United States–Saudi relations and for President Trump's positioning in the region. President Trump telephoned bin Salman to congratulate him on the promotion.[40]

Upon his rise to power, Mohammed bin Salman embarked on major overseas visits, including a trip to the White House to meet President Trump in March 2017. That visit helped lay the foundation for Trump's visit to Saudi Arabia two months later, in May, with Saudi Arabia selected as the only Arab country for his first overseas visit. The trip was promoted heavily by the Saudi government as proof of its weight in the region and wider Muslim world.

On the U.S. front, the visit was debated. Given that there was a power struggle between the two princes—the son promoted to power and the nephew deposed of it and made to pledge allegiance to the son—one article (in *Politico*), using the provocative title alluding to the popular television show *Game of Thrones* entitled "Trump Drawn into Saudi Game of Thrones," speculated if Trump crossed some political line during the meeting.[41]

Other opinions considered positive outcomes. During the meeting, Trump and Prince Mohammad bin Salman reportedly agreed that Iran is a major threat. After the meeting, a senior adviser to the prince said in a statement that the meeting was a "turning point in relations between both countries." The Associated Press reported that warm ties forged between Riyadh and the Trump administration that then may have helped accelerate Prince Mohammed bin Salman's ascension as crown prince. The visit also helped lay the foundation for Trump's visit to Saudi Arabia in May 2017, during his first overseas trip.[42]

Although this promotion of his son to crown prince had long been expected, the timing was a surprise and put the kingdom's future in relatively untested hands. An all-but-certain takeover of the throne by a prince has implications on issues in the region. Notably, the crown prince has taken a hard line on rival Iran, ruling out dialogue. The kingdom, which has isolated Qatar as mentioned earlier, has also been criticized for facilitating a devastating war in Yemen that has killed thousands of civilians.[43] This has the dangerous potential to escalate conflicts, chaos, and turmoil in the Middle East, which will divert attention away from the major threat of terrorism and the war against ISIS.

Trump's affinity with Saudi Arabia has been criticized. Human rights groups are among the critics. Records of human rights in Saudi Arabia are very low. Women are forbidden from driving in the kingdom, an issue toward which Mohammed bin Salman has taken a cautious approach. "Society is still not convinced of women driving and believes it has very negative consequences if women are allowed to drive," he said in April, 2016. "This is up to Saudi society. We can't force something it doesn't want."

According to Freedom House, a U.S. government funded nongovernmental organization (NGO) that conducts research and advocacy on democracy, political freedom, and human rights, Saudi Arabia "restricts almost all political rights and civil liberties through a combination of oppressive laws and the use of force." In its most recent "Freedom in the World" report, the group listed Saudi Arabia as the ninth least free society in the world.[44]

Critics further purport that Saudi forces have killed scores of civilians and called on the United States, as well as the United Kingdom and France, to halt the sale of weapons to Saudi Arabia that could be used in the Yemen war. The war in Yemen has undercut the kingdom's traditional alliances. Pakistan refused repeated requests to send troops to fight the Houthis. Oman opted to stay out of it. Egypt provides only token assistance. For Yemenis, the war has brought mass starvation. Cholera has broken out. A child dies every 10 minutes as a consequence of the war, and 7 million people are at acute risk. The United Nations has called the crisis the worst humanitarian disaster since 1945.[45]

Saudi Arabia is an absolute monarchy and theocracy. The king has complete authority and control. His replacement of his nephew with his favorite son as next in line to the throne indeed may have been seen as controversial by the family and the clerical establishment, but the more important and worrisome issue was the longer-term costs of upsetting the legitimacy of the line of succession in the midst of low oil prices and regional tensions.[46]

Another major concern was that the young prince was following a hawkish policy in the region, evidenced by claims that he was behind Saudi Arabia's harsh policy against Qatar, the sanctioned neighboring country (and member of the Gulf Cooperation Council). This position contrasted with that of the removed nephew, Prince Mohammed bin Nayef, considered to have warm relations with the emir of Qatar and his father, that would make relations with the neighbors more accommodating.

Some analysts even wondered whether the young prince's assertiveness would further destabilize the region. "This is a time when we really need some quiet diplomacy," said Maha Yahya, the director of the Carnegie Middle East Center in Beirut. "We need coolheaded politicians who are able to defuse tensions rather than inflame them. There has been a far more aggressive stance in Saudi foreign policy under King Salman, and now it might get worse."[47]

Reactions of U.S. allies matter. In December 2015, a memo from Germany's foreign intelligence service was leaked to news outlets. It argued that Saudi Arabia's new leaders were destabilizing the Middle East. The memo said King Salman and his advisers had replaced the kingdom's decades-long, cautious foreign policy with "an impulsive policy of intervention."[48]

The German memo singled out the king's favored son, Mohammed bin Salman, who had quickly amassed tremendous power as deputy crown prince and defense minister, in addition to serving as something of an economic czar. It warned that the concentration of so much power in the hands of a young, relatively inexperienced prince posed a "latent danger that, in an attempt to establish himself in the royal succession while his father is still alive, he could overreach."[49]

In my view, actions regarding any region have to take into account the reactions of allies, with efforts to coordinate. As during the experiences I described in my introduction and my efforts to get the United States and United Kingdom to agree with my position regarding Iraq, the strongest of efforts need to be made to reach consensus. However, it cannot be ruled out, given sovereignty of states, that some situations will require individual positions.

Prince Mohammed bin Salman has taken a hard line in many cases in the region such as the war in Yemen, isolation of Qatar, and fighting Iran. In a television interview in May 2017 he said that dialogue with the country, a Shiite power, was impossible because it sought to take control of the Islamic world. "We are a primary target for the Iranian regime," he said, accusing Iran of aiming to take over Islamic holy sites in Saudi Arabia, home to Mecca and Medina. "We won't wait for the battle to be in Saudi Arabia. Instead, we'll work so that the battle is for them in Iran."[50]

Armed assailants, including some disguised as women, stunned Iran on June 7, 2017, with brazen attacks on the Parliament building and the tomb of its revolutionary founder, constituting the worst terrorist strike to hit the Islamic republic in years. At least 12 people were killed and 46 were wounded in the near-simultaneous assaults, which lasted for hours.[51] ISIS claimed responsibility for these terrorist attacks in Iran. Iran's Revolutionary Guards said that Saudi Arabia was behind the twin attacks in Tehran. However, Saudi Arabia denied any involvement in the attacks.[52]

These developments that occurred after the May visit of President Trump to Saudi Arabia could be seen to escalate the sectarian strife in the Middle East and could lead to a regional conflict similar to Iraq-Iran War between 1980 and 1988 in which millions of people were killed and injured and resulted in the destruction of economies and infrastructure of the region. Fareed Zakaria of CNN said, "The United States has now signed up for Saudi Arabia's foreign policy—a relentless series of battles against Shiites and their allies throughout the Middle East. That will enmesh Washington in a never-ending sectarian struggle, fuel regional instability and complicate its ties with countries such as Iraq that want good relations with both sides. But most important, it will do nothing to address the direct and ongoing threat to Americans—jihadist terrorism. I thought that Trump's foreign policy was going to put America first, not Saudi Arabia."[53]

It is also important to point out the complicated and ironic developments that evolved from the fact that the West supported Saddam Hussein during the Iraq-Iran War with sophisticated arms, intelligence, and technology. That support made Saddam act as a regional super power and encouraged him to invade Kuwait in 1990, which led to the second Gulf War and the United Nations sanctions against Iraq. Those developments led to the rise of terrorist groups Al Qaeda and its offshoot ISIS, as I explained in this book.

Possible War between the United States and Other Nuclear States

President Trump embarked on his election campaign and started his first few months in office with many fiery declarations, accusations, and controversial statements on various issues. This caused concern among many groups in the United States, including leaders of the Republican Party (his own party), lawmakers, journalists, and the public. Some of these involved statements about the world economy, and about relations with other superpowers, in the context of his campaign slogan, "Make America Great Again," and focus on America First. They also created tension with countries and governments in the world and raised concerns among allies in Europe and the Middle East.

The Germans were angry, the Chinese were downright furious, leaders of NATO were nervous, while their counterparts at the European Union were alarmed. No one knows where exactly Trump is headed.[54]

The situation regarding North Korea emerged of great concern. Tension between the United States and North Korea had risen by the time Trump was early into his term of office in 2017. In a dramatic move, the U.S. Navy fired 59 Tomahawk missiles at a Syrian airfield on April 6, 2017, in response to a deadly gas attack, a U.S. response that raised concerns about Trump's plans for North Korea, a country that was conducting missile and nuclear tests in defiance of the United Nations' and United States' unilateral sanctions. The United States warned that its policy of "strategic patience" was over.[55]

On April 13, 2017, NBC News reported that intelligence officials told them that the United States was prepared to launch a preemptive strike against North Korea with conventional weapons if it was certain that the reclusive nation was going to perform another nuclear weapons test. The officials reportedly said the United States had two destroyers capable of shooting Tomahawk cruise missiles into North Korea—the same type of weapon used to strike a Syrian airfield on April 6, 2017.[56]

Defense Secretary James Mattis offered a dark outlook of what war with North Korea would look like, hours before the rogue regime launched another ballistic missile. Mattis said, in a televised interview with the CBS News show *Face the Nation* on May 29, 2017, that a conflict with North Korea would be "probably the worst kind of fighting in most people's lifetime."[57]

President Trump talked to Taiwan President Tsai Ing-wen on the telephone and lashed out at China on his favorite social media site Twitter.

These tactics reportedly perplexed some leaders in Beijing and the White House, who feared that Trump would disrupt international relations, as he was domestic politics, no matter what conventions were broken in the process.[58]

Trump already had China in his crosshairs during the presidential campaign. He accused China, the world's second biggest economic power, of "raping" the United States by stealing trade secrets, manipulating its currency, and subsidizing its industries. "It's time America had a victory again," he has said. What kind of "victory," Trump did not say.[59] He vowed to institute tough new policies designed to crack down on the Chinese and extract concessions, such as by imposing higher tariffs on goods manufactured there.[60]

A senior Chinese military official reacted strongly by saying that war with the United States under Trump is "not just a slogan" but becoming a "practical reality." Certainly, Trump was taking a hard line on relations with China and what he thinks China's role should be in relation to the United States and to North Korea.

In truth, I have never shied away from controversial and strong positions that shake others up, even if I thought I was always on the right side of the fence and not subject to criticism (except by an agreed enemy, namely, a purveyor of terrorism). But in my roles in government, and at the UN, I have always had to take on political positions also. So I am sensitive to how a strong public position will always trigger critics.

To elaborate on the international context Trump faced, in the summer of 2017, the issue of United States–Russia relations came under intense scrutiny, focused on whether Russia had meddled in the U.S. elections. In this climate, President Trump reiterated his focus on what is best for the United States. Given the United States' involvement in Iraq, clearly, the developments regarding the controversy over the two superpowers' involvement has major implications for U.S. policy throughout the world, and specifically concerning Iraq. For this reason, it is of vast importance that I address this issue in my strategy in this book.

Given the intricacies of international relations, it is imperative to also consider involvement in other major fronts in the world, for a clear picture of the future of the United States–Russia relations, as well as for a successful strategy for the fight against terrorism. One of these areas, surely, is Syria, embroiled in a complex war involving the superpowers. Consideration of the situation in Syria further requires understanding the events involving Iran. This widening circle defines the intricate international interactions I am referring to, which must be taken into serious consideration for a successful strategy to fight terrorism.

During the first six years of the Syrian crisis, the United States supported rebel groups fighting Syrian President Assad but avoided direct conflict with his forces. That changed on April 6, 2017, when President Trump ordered a cruise missile attack on a Syrian air base in response to a chemical attack that killed more than 70 people, including civilians. That act engaged the United States in air-to-air combat in Syria for the first time. Specifically, the U.S. Navy launched 59 cruise missiles, targeting a Syrian air base from two destroyers in the Mediterranean following the chemical weapons attack.[61]

Two months later, in June 2017, three more incidents occurred. This time, the U.S. military—a U.S. F-15 fighter jet—shot down armed drones over southern Syria, supportive of the Syrian government regime. Days earlier, a Syrian fighter jet had been downed. Importantly, the two shoot downs represented an escalation in the conflict between the United States and forces loyal to Syrian President Bashar al-Assad, heightening tensions in the region.[62]

All of the strikes, the Pentagon maintained, were in self-defense for the United States, and legal under the Authorization for Use of Military Force passed after the 9/11 terrorist attacks in the United States. The drone was considered a threat to the United States, as it was detected approaching U.S. military forces in southeastern Syria. The shoot down of the manned jet was part of a steady escalation of the U.S. military's role in Syria. Hundreds of U.S. special operations forces were working alongside Syrian rebels fighting ISIS, while U.S. warplanes and a Marine Corps artillery unit provided firepower for the advancing forces on a daily basis.[63]

Yet, here is where tensions also escalated between the United States and Russia. Moscow considered the strengthening of U.S. forces in southern Syria unlawful, according to Russia's special presidential representative for the Middle East and Africa, Deputy Foreign Minister Mikhail Bogdanov. "It's utterly unlawful," Bogdanov said. "There is neither such a decision of the Security Council, nor a request by the legitimate authorities of the Syrian Arab Republic as a sovereign state."[64]

Russia, whose armed forces offer critical support to the Assad government, threatened retaliation. The downing of the Syrian fighter jet led Russia's Defense Ministry to declare that it would track any U.S. or other coalition partner aircraft in Syria that flies west of the Euphrates River.[65] The Russian Defense Ministry further said it would regard any U.S. coalition aircraft detected west of the Euphrates River in Syria as legitimate targets. The ministry called the downing of the Syrian jet "a cynical violation of Syria's sovereignty." Moscow also shut down the "deconfliction" channel designed to prevent midair contact between Russian and American warplanes in the skies over Syria.[66]

Syria also issued its reactions to the downed fighter jet. A Syrian army statement released on state television said the "flagrant attack was an attempt to undermine the efforts of the army as the only effective force capable with its allies . . . in fighting terrorism across its territory." The statement said, "This comes at a time when the Syrian army and its allies were making clear advances in fighting the [ISIS] terrorist group."[67]

For its part, a Pentagon spokesman, Navy Captain Jeff Davis, said the U.S. pilot saw the Syrian pilot eject and saw a parachute deploy, and the United States believed the pilot would have landed in ISIS-controlled territory in Syria. The question then arises about what was the intention of the jet and what danger it posed to U.S. troops. Further, the downing of the fighter jet was justified on the basis that U.S. troops were put at risk, given that the downed plane was flying too close to the U.S. aircraft.[68] After shooting the jet, the American-led task force said that it was not seeking a confrontation with President Assad or the Russian and Iranian forces or Shiite militias that are fighting to support the Syrian leader—but added that it would defend the Syrian fighters it has assembled to pursue ISIS.[69]

The Senate Foreign Relations Committee formally requested the Trump administration's legal justification for the U.S. military shoot down of the Syrian jet and other confrontations between U.S. forces and those loyal to Syrian President Bashar al-Assad.[70] Chairman of the Joint Chiefs of Staff Joseph Dunford suggested the 2001 authorization for the use of military force justified the jet downing, since that is what is providing the legal rationale for U.S. forces fighting ISIS. Yet, that explanation was subject to some question, since critics claimed that the target was the Syrian government, not ISIS or Al Qaeda, and the campaign should be directly against ISIS and Al Qaeda in Syria.[71]

From the U.S. perspective, the key question emerging from these three critical incidents is whether the Russians can control the Syrians and the Iranian-backed forces there, with the concern that the Russian may *not* be able to control the forces they say that they can. With tensions between Russia and the West at a post–Cold War high, perhaps the most serious concern is revealed in the comment from British General Sir Richard Shirreff, who served at the second highest NATO military office in Europe between 2011 and 2014, that a nuclear war with Russia over the Baltic nations in 2017 is "entirely plausible."[72]

I agree, and emphasize that serious consideration must be given to military actions as they impact the United States–Russian relations, and with assurances that any actions would comply with legal justifications. Yet assuredly, national security and sovereignty, as well as international relations on all sides, must be weighed.

On June 26, 2017, the White House has warned that there are "potential preparations for another chemical weapons attack" by the Syrian regime and told the country's president, Bashar al-Assad, he would face a "heavy price" if one is carried out. The announcement comes amid rising tensions in Syria between the United States–led coalition and Russia, which is backing the Assad regime.[73]

Russia, a key Syrian ally, dismissed the White House statement on June 27, 2017, and called Washington's threats against Syria "unacceptable." Any U.S. military action, however, could further deepen tensions with Russia.[74] On April 6, 2017, President Donald Trump authorized an early morning Tomahawk missile strike on Shayrat Air Base in central Syria in retaliation for what he said was a deadly nerve agent attack carried out by the Syrian government. U.S. investigative journalist Seymour Hersh revealed that Trump was "warned by the U.S. intelligence community that it had found no evidence that the Syrians had used a chemical weapon," to German news site Die Welt.[75]

CALLING TERROR "ISLAMIC RADICAL TERRORISM"

As I outline in my counterterrorism strategy in this book, terms that are used gravely impact the effectiveness of a counterterrorism approach. As one example, the terrorist group ISIS has called itself "Islamic States in Iraq and the Levant (Sham)" although many Western leaders have said it is not Islamic and it is not a state, which is important in order to avoid giving these terrorist groups any semblance of legitimacy. Nevertheless, Donald Trump has insisted on referring to the terrorism of Al Qaeda and ISIS as "Radical Islamic Terrorism." In contrast, many Western leaders including President Obama refused to call it "Islamic Terrorism."

Naming terrorist groups "Islamic" serves terrorist groups and supports their claim that they are Islamic and they represent Islam. But it also has the effect of characterizing all followers of Islam as terrorists. This is similar to referring to Christian and Jewish killers as Christian terrorists and Jewish terrorists. In stark contrast, Islam, similar to other religions, calls for people to live in peace and harmony, as I will explain in this book.

As an example of his use of the term, on August 15, 2016, in his speech on immigration and terrorism in Ohio, then-presidential candidate Donald Trump said, "Today we begin a conversation about how to make America Safe Again. In the 20th Century, the United States defeated Fascism, Nazism, and Communism. Now, a different threat challenges our world: Radical Islamic Terrorism."[76]

J.M. Berger, a fellow at the International Centre for Counter Terrorism in The Hague, said, "Everything that we've heard from this administration and all the appointments Trump has made really point to sort of expanding the idea that the ideology of terrorism is the ideology of Islam and that's extremely counterproductive . . . What I fear is that Trump administration is going to pour gasoline onto this fire."[77]

On the campaign trail, Trump also said, "One of my first acts as President will be to establish a Commission on Radical Islam—which will include reformist voices in the Muslim community who will hopefully work with us. We want to build bridges and erase divisions."[78]

In my view, as in the view of others, rebranding terrorism as "Radical Islamic Extremism" and establishing a Commission on Radical Islam could be counterproductive and could backfire on the American administration. Some advocates even fear that such rebranding could make it more difficult for the U.S. government to work with Muslims who are already hesitant to trust the new administration. Some Republicans in Congress said that branding the problem as "Radical Islam" would only serve to alienate more than three million Americans who practice Islam peacefully.[79]

Tragically, in my view, there are life-threatening consequences to a careless disregard for the proper use of language. In 2015, crimes against American Muslims *tripled*. Why? Because dozens of self-righteous non-Muslims equated believers in Islam with terrorists. That false equivalency resulted in hateful—and sometimes deadly—acts committed against innocent human beings. Such acts have been happening for too long.[80]

RENAMING COUNTERING VIOLENT EXTREMISM

As I am emphasizing here, names matter. So does understanding the enemy, another step in my strategy. In this regard, the White House needs to plan a program based on understanding the source of threats from terrorist groups and designing an appropriate program with an appropriate name and mission. For example, violent extremist threats can come from a range of groups and individuals, including domestic terrorists and homegrown violent extremists in the United States and abroad, in addition to the terrorist groups like Al Qaeda and ISIS.[81] In fact, this is what has been happening by the summer of 2017.

Regarding the government program, the White House hosted its Summit on Countering Violent Extremism (CVE) in February 2015, to highlight domestic and international efforts to prevent violent extremists and their supporters from radicalizing, recruiting, or inspiring individuals or groups in the United States and abroad to commit acts of violence.[82] The objective of CVE program is to prevent violent extremism by using measures such as social media campaigns and community partnerships to counter extremism in U.S. communities.[83]

According to a Reuters report, the Trump administration wanted to refurbish and rename a U.S. government program designed to counter all violent ideologies so that it focuses solely on Islamist extremism. The "Countering Violent Extremism" name would be changed to "Countering Islamic Extremism" or "Countering Radical Islamic Extremism" and would no longer target other groups (that incite terror) such as white supremacists who have also carried out bombings and shootings in the United States.[84]

This timing appears especially odd, with terrorist attacks by white supremacists in the news. For example, an attack on a mosque in Quebec killed six people on January 29, 2017, a few weeks after Dylann Roof was sentenced to death for the June 2015 attack that killed nine in a historically black church in Charleston, South Carolina.[85]

Some critics fear that the rebranding to focus on Islamics—even though qualified as violent and extreme—could make building relationships with the Muslim community more difficult, especially after the outcry over Trump's executive order to halt immigration from seven predominantly Muslim countries.[86]

TRAVEL BAN ON MUSLIM NATIONS

During his election campaign and the first few weeks of his presidency, President Trump talked a great deal about his intentions to change the United States policies regarding immigrations, refugees, and asylum procedures. In August 2016, he called for a ban on immigrants from countries with a "history of exporting terrorism," saying it is impossible to properly vet people coming from those places.[87]

We have to look at this contrast with President Obama's stance. Before he left office and just before the voting for the presidential contest between Trump and Hillary Clinton, Obama said that for terrorist groups like Al Qaeda or ISIS who have killed children and Muslims and taken sex slaves, there is no religious rationale that would justify in any way any of the things they do. He added, "But what I have been careful about when I describe these issues is to make sure that we do not lump these murderers into the billion Muslims that exist around the world, including in this country, who are peaceful."[88]

After Trump's victory, Obama rejected Trump's call for a ban on Muslims. "If we act like this is a war between the United States and Islam, we're not just going to lose more Americans to terrorist attacks, but we'll lose sight of the very principles we claim to defend," Obama said. He added the United States is not a place where some citizens have to prove they are not an enemy.[89] Obama compared using the term "Muslim" to a Christian being a murderer but claiming their religion in their actions. He said, "If you had an organization that was going around killing and blowing people up and said, 'We're on the vanguard of Christianity.' As a Christian, I'm not going to let them claim my religion and say, 'You're killing for Christ.' I would say, that's ridiculous."[90]

Just one week into taking the office of the President, and in the name of protecting Americans from terrorism, Trump signed an executive order to ban entry to the United States for people from seven Muslim-majority countries—Iraq, Iran, Libya, Somalia, Sudan, Syria, and Yemen—for at least 90 days. The ban included those who hold permanent residency in the United States (Green Cards). It banned all refugees for at least 120 days and banned refugees from Syria indefinitely.

Lawmakers and politicians from the Republican and Democratic parties expressed strong concern or objection. Human rights and freedom advocates, as well as lawyers and community people, objected, and demonstrations were organized all over the United States. Trump was so staunching standing by his decision that he promised to take the matter to the top court if necessary.

TRAVEL BAN EMBOLDENS TERRORISM

In my view, Trump's travel ban on the seven Muslim nations is counterproductive and poorly considered. Why? Because it gives the terrorists a good pretext to brainwash recruits, to mobilize Muslims against the United States, and to claim that the United States is against Islam and Muslims. My fear is that it could inspire terrorist throughout the world.

The travel ban could affect decisions of allies in the Middle East regarding sharing information and fighting terrorists. In Iraq, for example, while the Iraqi security forces are fighting ISIS and working alongside American advisers there, there was a backlash of emotions from the Iraqi population about this decision banning Iraqis from traveling to the United States. Fortunately, the order has since been rewritten to exclude Iraq from the list of banned countries. But substantial damage has already been done to the average Iraqis' perception of the United States.

The ban could also make Muslims in the United States stop cooperating with authorities regarding reporting suspicious activities of family members and fellow Muslims, if they feel that the U.S. administration is unfairly targeting Islam and Muslims. Such cooperation is important in my 12-step strategy as you will see outlined in this book.

"The whole travel ban order is and will be read as another anti-Islam, anti-Muslim action by this president and his administration," said Paul Pillar, a former top official at the CIA's Counterterrorism Center. "It is not targeted at where the threat is, and the anti-Islam message that it sends is more likely to make America less safe."[91] Democratic politicians were also strong in their criticism. U.S. Senator Charles Schumer (a Democrat from New York), called the ban "mean-spirited." Schumer said Trump's order only served to "embolden and inspire" terrorists around the world.

In the midst of all this criticism, I dare say that terrorists won. Supporters of ISIS quickly claimed the travel ban as a victory. Postings on social media sites linked to the terrorist group predicted that President Trump's order would galvanize Muslims, and claimed that it showed that the United States is at war with Islam.[92]

USING "ENHANCED INTERROGATION TECHNIQUES"

Trump's take on terrorism has suffered criticism on yet another important front, namely that of bringing back enhanced interrogation techniques.

This stems back to the Bush administration. Following the 9/11 terrorist attacks, President Bush authorized the use of "enhanced interrogation techniques" (EIT), which includes waterboarding, and authorized the CIA to detain suspected terrorists in detention centers around the world. Many terrorists were subjected to these enhanced interrogation techniques, including Al Qaeda leaders Khalid Sheikh Mohammed, Abd al-Rahim al-Nashiri, and Abu Zubaidah. The *Washington Post* newspaper exposed, in November 2005, the existence of a global CIA interrogation program that President Bush only publicly acknowledged a year later.

In stark contrast, President Obama said that enhanced interrogation techniques constitute torture and banned using them in interrogations. In January 2009, President Obama limited interrogation to techniques authorized by the Army Field Manual.[93]

Trump's stance stands in defiance of the Geneva Conventions and Detainee Treatment Act of 2005, which prohibited such abuses. The UN Convention against Torture, signed by the United States, defines torture as "any act by which severe pain or suffering, whether physical or mental, is intentionally inflicted on a person" in order to get information. The U.S. legal code defines torture as an action "specifically intended to inflict severe physical or mental pain or suffering," while the U.S. Constitution bans "cruel and unusual punishment." Human rights groups and many governments claimed that the CIA program amounted to torture.[94]

Former FBI agent Ali Soufan was among the critics. He said, "Many investigations were carried out into the efficacy of enhanced interrogation techniques. There were investigations done by the FBI, the Department of Justice, and the CIA's own inspector general, and there was a congressional investigation by the Senate Select Committee on Intelligence that started as a bipartisan investigation and later became only a Democratic investigation. . . . And there was one [common] thing among all these investigations that these techniques did not work, and these techniques hurt the national security of the United States."[95]

Then a leak to the press happened that created a public and political uproar. Pictures showed graphic scenes of tortured, humiliated, and naked prisoners at the hands of American military and intelligence at the Abu Ghraib prison in western Baghdad. The photos, and ensuing scandal, in my view, may have created outrage, but they served the cause of terrorist groups and insurgency groups, who used the scandal to recruit terrorists who were fighting the American forces and Iraqi government after 2003 and could point to the mistreatment of their comrades at the hands of the West, the enemy, and the infidels.

MISTAKES OF THE SPECIAL MISSION IN YEMEN

Part of President Trump's counterterrorism strategy is to continue the policy of using drone strikes and to capture leaders of terrorist groups to get data about terrorist networks and information about terrorist plans for future attacks. In a speech during the campaign, in August 2016, Trump said, "Drone strikes will remain part of our strategy, but we will also seek to capture high-value targets to gain needed information to dismantle their [terrorist] organizations. Foreign combatants will be tried in military commissions."[96] Only a week after he took office on January 27, 2017, following up on the strategy to step up operations targeting terrorists, Trump authorized the first special military mission, which was considered to be a success by Trump and his team but considered to be a failure by critics.

Specifically, a Special Forces raid was carried out in Yemen, resulting in the death of one U.S. Special Forces operative (a SEAL) as well as up to a dozen civilians, including children. Several anonymous officials said the objective of the secret mission was to capture or kill Qassim al-Rimi, the head of Al Qaeda in the Arabian Peninsula and one of the world's most wanted suspected terrorists, but this individual survived and was subsequently taunting Trump in an audio message being shared online.[97] That audio recording purportedly features al-Rimi's voice referring to Trump, who authorized the raid, as the "fool of the White House" who "got slapped" early on in his role as commander-in-chief. The operation resulted in a lengthy firefight during which air reinforcements had to be called in to ward off attacks on the ground troops.[98] Specifically, al-Rimi said, "The White House's new fool has received a painful blow at your hands in his first outing on your land." Al-Rimi also claimed that a larger number of people died—25, including 11 women and children—and that scores of U.S. soldiers were killed or wounded.[99]

In my view, President Trump was in a rush to implement his new counterterrorism strategy that seeks to capture leaders of terrorist groups to get information about terrorist plans for future attacks in Europe and the United States. The intention is good, but the implementation backfired.

Certainly, it is a sign of failure that the president's move to authorize a special military mission to capture a leader of Al Qaeda in Yemen led to the death of a U.S. Navy SEAL commander and civilians. Sadly, it was the first counterterrorism operation authorized by President Trump after he took office, and the SEAL commando was the first U.S. service member to die in the years-long shadow war against Al Qaeda's Yemen affiliate. Critics also claimed that the circumstances surrounding the attack were suspicious. The U.S. Navy SEAL Team 6 that carried out the attack, with forces from United Arab Emirates, faced fierce resistance, landmines, snipers, and a larger number of fighters than expected. Additionally, the defenders seemed to know they were coming, either by hearing aircraft in the area, flying lower than usual, or through an intelligence leak. This is tragic.

In the wake of this tragedy, President Trump tried to play the "blame game" that I mentioned in this book as a tactic other politicians use, by putting the responsibility on others—in this case, on President Obama or the military generals. In an interview broadcast on February 28, 2017, Trump said that the former president, Obama, was partly at fault for the raid in Yemen that resulted in that death of the Navy SEAL, even though it was he, Trump, who gave the order to carry out the raid.[100]

Making matters worse, after initially denying that there were any civilian casualties, American officials said they were assessing reports that women and children had in fact died in the attack. A Yemeni official said that at least eight women and seven children, ages 3–13, had been killed in the raid.[101]

In my mind, that action may not have been considered carefully enough. When Secretary of Defense James Mattis and Chairman of the Joint Chiefs Joseph Dunford presented the plan to Trump at a dinner with advisers Jared Kushner and Steve Bannon, Trump approved it immediately, without reportedly going through the usual process of consulting various agencies and cabinet departments. As a result, critics laid the costs of the raid at Trump's feet, accusing him of approving his first covert counterterrorism operation without sufficient intelligence, ground support, or adequate backup preparations.[102]

The raid, which marked the first use of U.S. ground troops in Yemen's two-year-old civil war also resulted in the destruction of a $70 million MV-22 Osprey helicopter. Even the American Senator John McCain, a Republican from Arizona, oft lauded as a war hero, called the action a "failure."[103]

POSITIVE POINTS IN TRUMP STRATEGY

As I have assured you, I must be fair, neutral, and rational in my assessment of President Trump's strategy of counterterrorism; therefore, I must point out the positive points in Trump's strategy. For example, ending ISIS caliphate, stopping support for opposition groups, launching ideological warfare, stopping funding and material support for terrorist groups, and fighting Internet and cyberwarfare, are essential points in Trump's strategy for counterterrorism. These are points I raise strongly in my strategy. They are valid and essential.

From past administrations, it is obvious that the U.S. policy of regime change in the Middle East has caused chaos as a result of political, military, and security vacuums. In his defense, I must point out that Trump has repeatedly said he is against a regime change policy. In all American attempts to change regimes in the Middle East, such as in countries like Afghanistan, Iraq, and Libya, there were mistakes, including lack of planning for post-regime change, lack of enough integration with local forces and advisers, and chaos that followed the change and power vacuum, which resulted in safe havens for terrorist groups to thrive.

ENDING ISIS CALIPHATE

A caliphate is a territory under the leadership of an Islamic steward known as a caliph. Muslims after the death of Prophet Mohammed divided into Sunnis who followed the caliphs and Shiites who followed the Prophet progeny called Imams. A counterterrorism strategy must end the territory controlled by ISIS that ISIS considers legitimately theirs.

ISIS tries to mislead Muslims that they are bringing back the old caliphate Islamic State which succeeded the Prophet. I describe this below.

In my view, President Trump is being more aggressive than President Obama in his strategy to fight ISIS, which in general is positive and necessary for world peace. This is especially valid in light of the many attacks by terrorists in so many forms (organizationally and by individuals) that are taking place in recent times in so many countries. In his speech on immigration and terrorism in Ohio on August 15, 2016, during the campaign, Trump said, "My Administration will aggressively pursue joint and coalition military operations to crush and destroy ISIS."[104] A tough stance is important to counterterrorism.

There is something to be said positively about Trump's tough stance on terrorism, tougher than the previous administration or, as he pointed out, tougher than his opponent in the presidential campaign, Hillary Clinton. Trump blamed both President Obama and his former Secretary of State Hillary Clinton for the rise of ISIS. "The Obama-Clinton foreign policy has unleashed ISIS, destabilized the Middle East." He also declared that Hillary Clinton "lacks the mental and physical stamina to take on ISIS and all of the many adversaries we face."[105]

In my strategy, the objective to pursue joint and coalition military operations to crush and destroy ISIS cannot be achieved without working with governments in the Middle East, including Iraq. Putting Iraq initially on the list of seven nations banned from entering the United States had negative consequences on relations with the Iraqi Army and other security forces where the United States is engaged. However, the subsequent move of removing Iraq from the travel ban list led to a positive outcome. President Trump invited Iraq's Prime Minister Haider Al-Abadi to visit Washington, D.C., and the prime minister said he found that President Trump is willing to engage more than his predecessor.

STOPPING SUPPORT FOR OPPOSITION GROUPS

On the U.S. election day in 2016, Trump said that he was likely to abandon the American effort to support "moderate" opposition groups in Syria who are battling the government of President Bashar al-Assad, saying "We have no idea who these people are."[106] I believe that this is another positive point in President Trump's strategy, as the strategy of supporting opposition groups in Libya resulted in rising terrorist groups such as Insar Al-Shari'a, which killed a U.S. Ambassador and three more Americans, in the case that became known as "Benghazigate" on September 11, 2012—and for which Hillary Clinton has been blamed.

In addition, the support of the Syrian opposition resulted in the rise of terrorist groups such as Al-Nusra Front, affiliated with Al Qaeda, and ISIS, which managed to get weapons, money, and fighters in Syria, crossed the border into Iraq, and controlled cities and towns in Iraq. ISIS declared its

Islamic State "caliphate" and committed atrocities throughout the world especially in Iraq and Syria, as well as Europe and the United States.

President Trump rejected these polices and said these policies have caused chaotic military and security vacuums. He said, "Our current strategy of nation-building and regime change is a proven failure. We have created the vacuums that allow terrorists to grow and thrive."[107]

On February 21, 2017, Reuters reported that the CIA-coordinated military aid for rebels in northwest Syria had been frozen since they came under major terrorist attack in January 2017. Rebel sources were raising doubts about foreign support key to their war against President Bashar al-Assad.[108]

However, in May 2017, Michael R. Gordon and Eric Schmitt reported in the *New York Times* that President Trump had approved a plan to arm Syrian Kurds so that they could participate in the battle to retake Raqqa from ISIS, a strategy that has drawn deep opposition from Turkey, a NATO ally. American military commanders have long argued that arming the YPG, a Kurdish militia fighting alongside Syrian Arab forces against ISIS, is the fastest way to seize Raqqa, the capital of the militants' self-proclaimed caliphate.[109] In my view, this will complicate the situation in Syria and in the Middle East and lead to conflict between Turkey and the Syrian Kurds, which will divert attention away from fighting ISIS.

LAUNCHING IDEOLOGICAL WARFARE

Ideology is the major motive behind extremism and especially for terrorists who carry out suicide attacks, as evidenced in the 9/11 attacks in the United States, attacks in Paris in November 2015, attacks in Brussels in March 2016, and attacks in the Middle East, especially in Iraq, since 2014, after the Iraqi security forces started to push back ISIS from territories they controlled.

ISIS managed to brainwash Muslims throughout the world through distorted, perverse, and deviant ideology. My counterterrorism strategy focuses on the war of ideology. The world must be united in fighting this destructive ideology by launching a war against that ideology, which explains the truth about terrorists' ideology, objectives, and malpractices.

Another positive point about President Trump's position on counterterrorism is that he believes that the United States should launch a war of ideology against terrorist groups. In his speech on immigration and terrorism in Ohio on August 15, 2016, Trump said, "We must use ideological warfare to defeat terrorism."[110] Invoking comparisons to the Cold War era, he argued that the United States must wage an unrelenting ideological fight, in order to defeat ISIS. He said, "Just as we won the Cold War, in part, by exposing the evils of communism and the virtues of free markets, so too must we take on the ideology of Radical Islam."[111]

In this context, the Trump administration needs to do a better job of communicating with and reinforcing the vast majority of peace-loving Muslims. At the same time, the administration needs to attack ISIS and other extremists' distorted beliefs and emphasize that their views are not just incompatible with Western ideals, but that they are also incompatible with the beliefs of ordinary Muslims as well.

STOPPING TERRORIST FUNDING AND MATERIAL SUPPORT

Terrorism requires money, so an important step in fighting terrorism is to stop the flow of funding. Trump has also recognized this. ISIS is the richest terrorist organization in the world, managing to make billions of dollars through many resources such as oil smuggling and selling oil products. ISIS managed to control oil fields and oil refineries in Iraq and Syria and smuggle crude oil and oil products to international market mainly through Turkey.

Other major sources of funding include donations, kidnappings for ransom, taxes, selling antiquities, and enslaving women and selling them. Unfortunately, the world has failed to stop the funding of terrorist groups, and some governments even helped in funding them both directly and indirectly.

I emphasize dramatically that it is imperative to cut off ISIS funding through all these sources. Thus, I will explain in detail in this book the sources of funding for terrorist groups, such as Al Qaeda and ISIS, and will also propose ways to stop the funding. President Trump has pledged to not only stop the funding of ISIS, but pursue criminal charges against those who lend material support for terrorism. Trump said, "We will pursue aggressive criminal or immigration charges against anyone who lends material support to terrorism. Similar to the effort to take down the mafia, this will be the understood mission of every federal investigator and prosecutor in the country." He added, "to accomplish a goal, you must state a mission: the support networks for Radical Islam in this country will be stripped out and removed one by one."[112]

FIGHTING THE INTERNET AND CYBERWARFARE

In my view, the future of terrorism will increasingly depend on the Internet to radicalize youth—especially in the West—particularly to inspire lone wolves to carry out terrorist attacks. Cyberwarfare will be used more and more to sabotage Western government facilities. Thus, I urge that the world needs to be more aggressive when it comes to preventing terrorists from exploiting the Internet and engaging in cyberwarfare. I will explain in this book about the dangers of the Internet and cyberwarfare used by terrorists groups and how to stop terrorists on this front.

During his election campaign, Trump repeatedly vowed to expand the offensive cyber capabilities of the United States. On October 3, 2016, he said, "I will make certain that our military is the best in the world in both cyber offense and defense." Trump also said in a campaign speech, "As a deterrent against attacks on our critical resources, the United States must possess the unquestioned capacity to launch crippling cyber counter-attacks." He added, "America's dominance in this arena must be unquestioned."[113]

However, there were concerns and worries about Trump's statements. The concern is that while a more aggressive U.S. cyber policy may deter some adversaries, it can also backfire and accelerate the emerging cyber arms race. Given the fact that cyber weapons programs originate from the world of intelligence and are cloaked in secrecy, their capabilities are largely unknown, thus fostering greater uncertainty for policy makers.[114]

Trump has repeatedly drawn attention to this issue, in pointing out, "Our institutions are under cyberattack, and our secrets are being stolen. So my question is; Who's behind it? And how do we fight it? We should be better than anybody else, and perhaps we're not."[115]

Working together with other nations is crucial. Can Trump do this effectively? Good relations with allies and sharing intelligence are important to defeat the terrorist organization. This is another step in my comprehensive strategy. All these issues I outline above are elaborated in the ensuing chapters about action steps in my strategy for counterterrorism.

CHAPTER 2

Why the World Failed to Stop Al Qaeda

At times in the book, I point out successes or positive approaches in the current fight against terrorism, as I did in the previous chapter by mentioning my approval of certain aspects of President Trump's approach, but I am being bold about pointing out mistakes, in order to take advantage of lessons learned, for a more strategic and successful counterterrorism strategy.

Notably, the United States had many opportunities to stop the Al Qaeda terrorist groups years ago—and even to kill its leader Osama bin Laden before they actually finally succeeded—but repeatedly failed to do so. The impact of this is being felt today. For example, when the United States started the war against the Taliban's regime in Afghanistan on October 7, 2001, they had a golden opportunity to capture or kill Osama bin Laden and other leaders of Al Qaeda. However, bin Laden and most of the leaders of Al Qaeda managed to escape and sneak across the borders from Afghanistan to Pakistan. From that position of relative safety, Al Qaeda continued to plan and execute attacks throughout the world, including in Western Europe and the United States. Osama bin Laden was not killed until almost 10 years after that invasion, when he was taken out by U.S. Special Forces in the daring mission in Pakistan on May 1, 2011.

Making matters worse, U.S. foreign policy in the Middle East was often not more than a reaction to certain events and circumstances. There was a lack of long-term planning, and there were no comprehensive strategies to collectively solve problems faced in the region and around the world. The reaction of the United States to the Soviet invasion of Afghanistan in December 1979 and the reaction to Saddam Hussein's invasion of Kuwait in August 1990 are just two examples of these failures. This reactionary approach, rather than implementing a proactive policy, could also clearly be seen in U.S. policies regarding counterterrorism. U.S. foreign policy was passive, and did not adequately respond to the activities of Al Qaeda and Osama bin Laden until the 9/11 attacks on the World Trade Center in New York City and the Pentagon in Washington, D.C. That tragedy was a wake-up call, when there should have been action long before.

After World War II and during the Cold War, concern regarding the spread of communism in the Middle East pushed the United States to adopt an ill-advised policy of supporting some Islamic movements, such as the Muslim Brotherhood, on the basis that these movements could act as an effective counterweight to communism in the Middle East. Fear of the spread of communism led the United States to support Arab fighters who launched a jihad or holy war in Afghanistan. This allowed Osama bin Laden to lead the Arab fighters and establish Al Qaeda, which became a very dangerous terrorist organization beginning in the 1990s and continuing through modern times, even past the death of its notorious leader.

Another example of a flawed reactionary policy was President George H.W. Bush's announcement that the liberation of Kuwait in 1991 was not going to be another Vietnam War. This analogy raised negativity. President Bush decided to go half way into the effort to stop the war after the liberation of Kuwait. He stopped short of ending Saddam's regime because, critics claimed, he was suffering from a "Vietnam Complex." He took this half-way step against advice of Iraqi people, some other countries in the region, and U.S. military experts such as General Norman Schwarzkopf, the commander of allied forces that liberated Kuwait. In his televised speech addressing the nation on January 16, 1991, President George H.W. Bush said, "I've told the American people before that this will not be another Vietnam, and I repeat this here tonight."[1]

This mistake of not finishing off the Saddam regime in 1991 cost the United States around 4,500 soldiers and billions of dollars to remove Saddam's regime later, in 2003. By that time, they had to face the radicalized and extremist Sunnis in Iraq. Between those crucial years of 1991 and 2003, Saddam put in place a policy designed to radicalize the Sunnis in Iraq so that they could fight the Americans and protect his regime. He launched the "Faith Campaign," through which he encouraged the spread of the extremist Salafi-jihadi ideology in Iraq. During the same period, Saddam's deputy, Izzat Al-Dori, was put in charge of the "Naqshbandi Order" which became a major insurgency group called "The Army of the Men of Naqshbandi Order." The terrorists were mobilized to belong to a strong-arm group. They had all that time to mobilize and strengthen their organization, while the United States stood back.

BACKGROUND OF INTERNATIONAL TERRORISM

The roots of contemporary international terrorism can be traced back to Afghanistan in 1979, when the Soviet Union invaded Afghanistan. Tribal fighters and Islamic mujahideen rose up against the Soviet occupation.

Tragically in retrospect, the United States assisted those fighters with money, training, and weapons.

President George W. Bush congratulated the United States with its allies when he described the situation, saying, "With assistance from the United States, Pakistan, and Saudi Arabia, the rebels inflicted fifteen thousand causalities and drove out the Soviets in 1989."[2] But, the negative side of the picture is the long-term consequences of U.S. support for Arab fighters in Afghanistan that resulted in the birth of Al Qaeda and other terrorist groups that grew to commit atrocities throughout the world.

Condoleezza Rice, then-National Security Adviser to President Bush, said, "Arab fighters joined local resistance forces that had set aside tribal and ethnic differences to form a loose alliance that became broadly known as the mujahideen. With the assistance of U.S. and Saudi funding and weapons funneled through Pakistan, the mujahideen succeeded in defeating the Soviet forces in the late 1980s."[3]

These self-congratulatory quotes from President George W. Bush and his National Security Adviser Condoleezza Rice reveal clearly how in reality this was a big mistake on the part of the United States and its then-allies, Pakistan and Saudi Arabia. As I noted above, the huge support for Arab fighters in Afghanistan provided money, weapons, and training that Osama bin Laden and the terrorists of Al Qaeda needed to launch an international holy war (jihad) against the West, especially the United States. Essentially, the terrorists effectively bit the hand that fed them. And, to use another common phrase, the United States and its allies shot themselves in the foot.

In my view, by contrast, the situation could have gone another way that would have been more constructive. The United States could have supported hundreds of thousands of Afghan resistance and tribal fighters to defeat the Soviet Union forces without the need to support the few thousand Arab fighters who became the Al Qaeda terrorist groups. After all, Afghan fighters and resistance movements managed to defeat many foreign invasions throughout history, and they could have defeated the Soviet invasion in 1979 by themselves without the assistance of Arab extremist fighters, who radicalized the Afghani fighters with Salafi-jihadi ideology.

Let us go way back in history to illustrate my point about the strength of the Afghan fighters. In 330 BC, Alexander the Great invaded Afghanistan and in the two years spent fighting, he faced repeated Afghani rebellions. Centuries later, in 667 AD, Arab armies swept into Afghan territory, but only partially subdued locals, and faced frequent revolts. In 1220 AD, Genghis Khan's Mongol armies swept through Afghanistan and faced fierce Afghani resistance. Further, Afghanistan defeated three British occupations, namely, the first Anglo-Afghan war from 1839 to 1842, the second Anglo-Afghan War from 1878 to 1880, and the third Anglo-Afghan war in 1919, which ended with Afghanistan effectively regaining its independence.[4]

With this in mind, the Americans made a mistake in the 1980s. They could have depended on Afghani resistance and tribal fighters, who had proven their strength throughout history, to defeat the Soviet forces. They did not need Osama bin Laden and his fighters, who numbered only a few thousand, to achieve their objective of forcing the Soviet forces to withdraw from Afghanistan. Injecting a Salafi-jihadist strain into the mix of hundreds of thousands of non-jihadist Afghan rebels, was both unnecessary and shortsighted, and ultimately backfired.

Another mistake made by the United States was to neglect Afghanistan after the withdrawal of Soviet forces in 1989. President George Bush Jr. admitted the mistake when he said, "Free of the communist occupiers . . . the U.S. government no longer saw a national interest in Afghanistan, so it cut off support."[5]

President Bush admitted another mistake when he said that noninvolvement of the United States in Afghanistan created a vacuum. "Ultimately, the Taliban, a group of Islamic fundamentalists, seized power. They imposed a fanatical, barbaric brand of Islam that prohibited girls from going to school, required men to grow beards of a certain length, and forbade women from leaving their homes without a male relative as an escort. The simplest pleasures—singing, clapping, and flying kites—were banned."[6]

MISTAKES IN DEALING WITH AL QAEDA

The United States made political, military, and intelligence mistakes in dealing with the situation in Afghanistan and the Taliban's regime, which allowed them to become the most fundamental and extreme terrorist regime in modern history. There were also political, military, and intelligence mistakes made in dealing with Al Qaeda and its leader Osama bin Laden and in responding to the terrorist attacks conducted by Al Qaeda, especially the 9/11 attacks in New York City and Washington, D.C.

When it comes to fighting terrorism, politicians have not taken responsibility but have blamed others. President George W. Bush blamed the intelligence community for the 9/11 attacks and considered the attack to be an "intelligence failure." President Barack Obama blamed U.S. intelligence for underestimating the power of ISIS during the time period when they were still gaining strength before they took control of the second largest city in Iraq, Mosul, on June 10, 2014.

However, U.S. intelligence had briefed President Bush and informed his National Security Adviser Condoleezza Rice about Al Qaeda's plan to carry out terrorist attacks inside the United States. The intelligence community also warned President Obama of the danger of ISIS, and the group's likelihood of taking control over parts of Syria and Iraq, which later enabled them to declare their Islamic State "caliphate."

We have to see through such "blame games." Policy makers were provided with the information that they needed in order to recognize and deal with the terrorist threat, but they failed to do so and tried to pin the blame on the intelligence community. Some mistakes were diagnosed by lawmakers, retired officials, and retired military officers or by academics, experts, journalists, and so on. I will shed a light on some of these mistakes in the following section.

POLITICAL MISTAKES

After the 9/11 terrorist attacks in the United States, President George W. Bush emphasized in his memoirs that the lack of a serious response on the part of the Clinton administration to the terrorist attack on the naval destroyer USS *Cole* in Yemen was misinterpreted by Al Qaeda and Osama bin Laden as a sign of U.S. weakness. This wrong impression about American weakness encouraged bin Laden to plan and carry out the 9/11 attacks. Bush wrote, "Al Qaeda messages frequently cited our withdrawal as evidence that Americans were, in the words of bin Laden, 'paper tigers' who could be forced to 'run in less than twenty-four hours'."[7] I have noted this point in the introduction to this book, but it is relevant to my various arguments throughout this book.

Bin Laden was obsessed with the idea that the United States was weak. He spoke of this weakness to his followers before and after the 9/11 attacks, giving examples of the U.S. withdrawal from Vietnam in the 1970s, from Lebanon in the 1980s, and from Somalia in the 1990s. Bin Laden explained how Al Qaeda smuggled fighters into Somalia in 1993 to help train the Somali mujahideen fighting U.S. forces. "Our boys were shocked by the low morale of the American soldier, and they realized that the American soldier was just a paper tiger," bin Laden exulted.[8]

In his memoirs, Secretary of Defense Donald Rumsfeld noted a comment that Israeli Prime Minister Shimon Peres once made to him: "If a problem has no solution; it is not a problem to be solved but a fact to be coped with over time."[9] That seems to be the approach that was being taken about terrorism at that time. The U.S. administration was coping with it, and was taking care of the damage inflicted by terrorism, instead of finding the ultimate solution to end it. Although admittedly there is no single simple solution to make terrorism go away entirely at this time, a comprehensive plan utilizing a wide range of strategies could have been effective—and needs to be implemented now, to drive a stake through the heart of the vampire, to kill the evil.

Rumsfeld also said, "Throughout my decades in public life, I have seen personalities come and go, but some degree of friction in the NSC's processes has remained a constant. . . . Just as there is no single successful model of management in business, there is no single correct model or approach for a president to use to lead his NSC."[10] The White House National Security Council (NSC) is the principal forum used by the president of the United States for consideration of national security and foreign policy matters with senior national security advisers and cabinet officials and is part of the Executive Office of the President of the United States. Rumsfled's observation does not lend optimism to ending terrorism, if, as he says, friction is so common. And if no model is available, then creative measures need to be devised.

Indeed, creative and multi-faceted approaches are required, since there are many terrorist groups in the world today. Though they seem to come from the same region, they are all different in some ways. So, to fight different groups, the United States and its allies need different approaches. Unfortunately, trial and error seems to work. But as lives are at stake, the trial and error method is not a reasonable plan.

I personally witnessed the dissention Rumsfeld referred to, between different U.S. departments, when I was invited to Washington, D.C., in June 2002, with three other Iraqi leaders representing three Iraqi opposition groups, namely, the Iraqi National Accord INA, Kurdistan Democratic Party KDP, and Patriotic Union of Kurdistan PUK. We met many U.S. officials, including Douglas Feith, Under Secretary of Defense for Policy and Marc Grossman, Under Secretary of State for Political Affairs. During those meetings, we received conflicting messages regarding Dr. Ahmed Al-Chalabi, the head of the Iraqi National Congress (INC). The State Department wanted us to criticize Al-Chalabi in the media, and we refused, explaining that our mission was to fight Saddam's regime and not to criticize any Iraqi personality. On the other hand, the Defense Department wanted us to work with Al-Chalabi. This was a direct conflict between administration departments.

When we complained about these conflicting positions and contradicting messages we received from the Defense Department and the State Department, the U.S. administration decided to invite a delegation of six Iraqi groups including Dr. Al-Chalabi of INC and Sharif Ali of the Iraqi Constitutional Monarchy. As I mentioned in the introduction to this book, I was part of the six Iraqi opposition groups that met with Vice President Dick Cheney, Secretary of State Colin Powell, and Secretary of Defense Donald Rumsfeld, in addition to many other officials in the National Security Council and the White House. Selected by the Iraqis to be the spokesman of the delegation, I read a statement to the media outside the State Department, rejecting the military occupation of Iraq. And I emphasized that the United States should set up an Iraqi government following the fall of Saddam's regime.

During our meeting with Rumsfeld, it was clear he did not know much about Iraq, the Iraqi people, or Saddam's regime. Rumsfeld asked if Saddam's forces would fight fiercely when U.S. forces come close to the capital Baghdad, simply because Saddam said that his forces will kill the Americans at the outskirts of Baghdad. That is an indication that Rumsfeld was not well informed; so we told him that Saddam's forces around Baghdad would not fight the American forces and would quickly collapse against the full force of the American military. That is exactly what happened when U.S. forces entered Baghdad. Saddam's elite forces ran away and did not fight.

Rumsfeld also asked if the Shiites in Baghdad were armed and if they would rise up against Saddam's regime if the Americans attacked Saddam's forces, as they did in the uprising of March 1991 that followed the liberation of Kuwait. What had happened back at that time is relevant here. After Saddam's invasion of Kuwait on August 2, 1990, President Bush made a speech targeting Iraqis, broadcast on Voice of America radio, in which he said, "There is another way for the bloodshed to stop: and that is, for the Iraqi military and the Iraqi people to take matters into their own hands and force Saddam Hussein, the dictator, to step aside."[11]

The Kurds in the north and the Shiites in the south responded to Bush's statements and rose up against Saddam's regime hoping that the United States would support them. However, the U.S. administration let them down and allowed Saddam's elite forces—called the "Republican Guards"—to withdraw from Kuwait with their heavy tanks, and Saddam was left free to use his helicopters and tanks to crush the uprising and to slaughter around 500,000 Iraqis.

So, the answer to Rumsfeld was that the Iraqis were frightened to rise up again as happened in 1991 because the United States let them down and allowed Saddam to crush that uprising in 1991. The political mistakes of President Bush undermined the U.S. credibility in Iraq and the region. The Iraqi people started to feel that Americans go half-way and do not finish the job. When the United States wanted to remove Saddam's regime in 2003, the Iraqi people did not rise up, since they were frightened that once the strategic goals of the United States were met, the Americans would let Saddam crush the uprising again, as happened in 1991.

My expectations were met when the British Forces entered the city of Basra in southern Iraq in 2003. I was asked in a News Night BBC program why the Iraqis did not welcome the British Forces. I answered by giving the same explanation that I had given to U.S. officials in 2002: the Iraqis were worried that the U.S. and U.K. forces would go half-way and not remove Saddam's regime, and that Saddam forces would slaughter them just like they did in 1991. The next day, Prime Minister Tony Blair was asked in the British Parliament why the Iraqis did not welcome British troops in Basra, and he said that if you listened to Dr. Hamid Al-Bayati yesterday on *News Night*, and his answer is worth repeating, that the Iraqi people are worried that we will go half-way and stop short of removing Saddam. Blair added that he wanted to assure the Iraqi people that this time the British would not stop until they removed Saddam from power. The Iraq desk officer at the Foreign Office called me the next day and told me that Blair mentioned my name in the Question Time of the Parliament and sent me the text from the records.

Another political mistake took place after the 9/11 attacks, when President Bush developed a strategy to protect the United States that came to be known as the "Bush Doctrine." This doctrine was based on the major principle to make no distinction between the terrorists and the nations that harbor them—and to hold both to account.[12] Nevertheless, in the immediate aftermath of the 9/11, the United States made it apparent (contradictory to my view) that Saudi Arabia and Pakistan, countries that do harbor terrorists, would not be targeted in the War on Terror.[13]

Excluding Pakistan and Saudi Arabia from accountability is a clear example of why the War on Terror was inherently flawed from its onset. It can be seen as an egregious error that two countries that arguably played the largest roles in the growth of fundamental terrorism were immediately excused from being held responsible for their actions. The extremist Taliban regime was the first U.S. target of the War on Terror for its role in hosting Al Qaeda and Osama bin Laden. Yet Pakistan escaped scrutiny in the War on Terror even though it had played a central role in creating and supporting the Taliban and had actively worked to help the group maintain control over Afghanistan. Even after 9/11 and the international war on terrorism and the war against the Taliban's regime in Afghanistan, Pakistan was left alone as a safe haven for Taliban and Al Qaeda leaders.

To support my point, it is relevant to mention here a few examples of how Pakistan operated as a safe haven for terrorists. On September 9, 2002, Ramzi Bin al-Shibh, an alleged planner of the 9/11 attacks, was arrested in Pakistan.[14] On March 1, 2003, Khalid Shaikh Mohammed, the mastermind of the 9/11 attacks, was captured in Pakistan.[15] On March 15, 2003, Yassir al-Jaziri, who oversaw communications among the terror network's operatives of Al Qaeda, was captured in Pakistan.[16] On May 4, 2005, Abu Farraj al-Libbi, believed by U.S. counterterrorism officials to be Osama bin Laden's No. 3 man, was arrested in Pakistan.[17] On May 2, 2011, bin Laden was found and killed by U.S. commandos in Abbottabad, Pakistan, close to the most important military academy in Pakistan that is equivalent to the famed U.S. West Point Military Academy. On May 17, 2011, Mohammed Ali Qasim, a key courier between Osama bin Laden and his deputy, Ayman al-Zawahiri, was arrested in Pakistan.[18] On September 5, 2011, Younis al-Mauretani and two Al Qaeda associates were arrested in Pakistan. Al-Mauretani was a senior Al Qaeda leader who sought to attack targets in the United States, Europe, and Australia.[19] Given all these examples, it is obvious that excusing Pakistan was a big mistake.

MILITARY MISTAKES

Militarily, the United States had the best chance to destroy the Taliban and to kill or capture its leader Mulla Omar and destroy Al Qaeda and kill or capture its leader Osama bin Laden in Afghanistan in 2001. However, the Americans failed to do that because military mistakes were made in the U.S. war against the Taliban's regime in Afghanistan.

Following the 9/11 terrorist attacks in the United States, the whole world was supporting the American war against the Taliban and Al Qaeda in Afghanistan. On September 12, 2001, the UN Security Council adopted a resolution to combat terrorist acts by all means. On the same day, NATO invoked Article 5 of the NATO charter which meant that the 9/11 attacks were treated as not just an attack against the United States but also as an attack against all 19 members of NATO. On September 14, 2001, the U.S. Congress passed an authorization for use of military force ("AUMF") against those nations, organizations or persons the president determines planned, authorized, committed or aided the terrorist attacks.[20]

President Bush wrote, "Our rapid success with low troop levels created false comfort, and our desire to maintain a light military footprint left us short of the resources we needed."[21] When the United States had the opportunity to capture Osama bin Laden after attacking Afghanistan in 2001, he escaped with other top Al Qaeda leaders by evading the few U.S. troops on the ground in Tora Bora, the cave complex in the mountains of eastern Afghanistan that is very difficult to navigate and easy to hide in, and that became so notoriously covered on American television news and news talk shows. This was just three months after the 9/11 attacks, when their trail should have been hot. There were only several dozen Delta operators, Green Berets, U.S. Air Force tactical air controllers, and CIA officers in Tora Bora when, in my opinion, there should have been hundreds more.

A military official said that they did not believe bin Laden would escape and hide out. They mistakenly believed that this would undermine his credibility. They thought he would stay and fight. Another military official said that the troops in Tora Bora were kept to a minimum in order to not create bad will with the Afghan villagers.[22]

Military officials came to regret allowing bin Laden and his men to escape, when he then took the opportunity to rebuild Al Qaeda and continue terrorist activities. It took ten years after bin Laden had escaped from Tora Bora for U.S. Special Forces to kill him. In my view, that was an excessively long time. It should have happened much sooner and the fact that it did not is evidence of significant military as well as intelligence mistakes.

Part of the reason for the U.S. failure, in their defense, was that leaders of Al Qaeda and the Taliban were at home in this treacherous territory. They easily moved across the border into Pakistan, out of range of the U.S. military. In a sense, Al Qaeda was just going home, since it was in the Pakistani city of Peshawar in 1988 that bin Laden founded the group, and several of their leaders had attended the Haqqania madrassa (school) just outside of Peshawar, known as the Harvard of the Taliban.[23]

U.K. Prime Minister Tony Blair admitted the Allies forces' mistakes in Afghanistan, in saying, "I am not saying we did everything well or could not have done many things better. But above all, I certainly misjudged the depth of the failure of the Afghanistan state; and the ability of the Taliban to plunge themselves into the local communities, particularly in the south, and to call upon reinforcements from across the border in the mountainous highlands."[24]

In March 2002, U.S. Vice President Dick Cheney claimed, erroneously, "The Taliban regime is out of business permanently." Indeed, more than seven years later, in December 2009, Admiral Mike Mullen, Chairman of the U.S. Joint Chiefs of Staff, said that the Taliban "have a dominant influence in 11 of Afghanistan's 34 provinces."[25] Clearly, military mistakes are even evident in contradictory statements made by U.S. leaders.

After the Taliban and Al Qaeda moved from Afghanistan to Pakistan, the long arm of the Taliban continued to carry out terrorist attacks in Afghanistan, and Al Qaeda continued to launch terrorist attacks in Europe and inspire many attacks that were carried out by lone wolves in the United States.

The terrorist attacks inspired or carried out by Al Qaeda and all its offshoots and derivatives are strong evidence that the world failed to stop Al Qaeda when it could have and are strong imperatives for the need for a new strategy for counterterrorism.

INTELLIGENCE MISTAKES

There were many intelligence mistakes made in dealing with Al Qaeda and Osama bin Laden. I will mention a few.

Sadly, the intelligence agencies missed many indications and clues that could have led them to predict or stop the 9/11 terrorist attacks in the United States. Osama bin Laden said many times publicly before the 9/11 attacks that Al Qaeda terrorists were going to attack the United States on its soil and follow in the steps of Ramzi Yousef who planned and executed the first terrorist attack on the World Trade Center in 1993. After that attack in 1993, Ramzi Yousef was arrested in Pakistan and brought to the United States, where he admitted that he received money from his uncle Khalid Shaikh Mohammed, the mastermind of 9/11. Yousef boasted to the FBI that he could have brought the entire World Trade Center down if he had more money to build a bigger bomb.

The 1993 attack was the culmination of events that started a year earlier. Consider these events that all spell mistaken opportunities for U.S. officials to stop him. In September 1992, Ramzi Ahmed Yousef arrived at JKF airport in New York holding a fake passport without a U.S. visa. When he was asked about the visa, he admitted the passport was fake and claimed that his real name was Abdul Basit Abdul Karim, and that he was an Iraqi, and requested political asylum. The immigration holding facility was full, so he was assigned a court date and released on his own recognizance. He took a taxi to New Jersey, went to a mosque, and soon recruited a makeshift crew to assist him in blowing up the World Trade Center. Yousef slipped away from immigration authorities even after he gave bomb recipes and diagrams to another terrorist traveling with him who was arrested. On top of all this, Yousef somehow managed to leave the United States after the attack and was only later arrested in Pakistan.[26] Granted, he was then tried in the United States and sentenced to two life sentences for his role in the 1993 bombing of the World Trade Center, but at so many junctures, he should have been flagged before this tragic attack.

After the 9/11 attacks, President Bush admitted that there were intelligence mistakes that prevented the intelligence community from discovering and putting a stop to the 9/11 attacks. However, he felt that he could not blame anyone during the crisis. In his memoirs, *Decisions Points*, President Bush wrote, "It was obvious the intelligence community had missed something big. I was alarmed by the lapse, and I expected an explanation. But I did not think it was appropriate to point fingers or fix blame in the middle of crisis."[27]

Bush's then-National Security Adviser Condoleezza Rice also admitted that she had not done enough before the 9/11 attacks and wrote in her memoirs, *No Higher Honor*, "I did everything I could. I was convinced of that intellectually. But, given the severity of what occurred I clearly hadn't done enough. . . . A part of me wanted to apologize, but the collective view of my advisors was that to do so would overwhelm anything else that I said. So instead I expressed regret."[28]

This reminds me of the U.S. administration position regarding President George H.W. Bush's encouragement of the Iraqi people to take matters into their own hands and remove Saddam following Saddam's invasion of Kuwait in 1990. As noted earlier, the Iraqi people rose up and liberated 14 out of 18 provinces in Iraq, but they were betrayed when the U.S. Army signed a cease fire agreement with Saddam, and let Saddam's elite forces—"the Republican Guards"—with their advanced weapons, crush the uprising. In one of my meetings in London with Under Secretary of State David Welch, he said just what Condoleezza Rice had said, "We are sorry for what happened to the Iraqi people in 1991, but we are not apologizing."

In fact, the major intelligence mistake is that prior to September 11, 2001, the U.S. intelligence community did not consider Al Qaeda as a threat to the United States. Paul R. Pillar, former deputy chief of the Counterterrorism Center at the Central Intelligence Agency (CIA), did not regard transnational Islamist terrorism as a strategic threat. In my view, that is almost inconceivable. The 9/11 attacks revealed that the transitional terrorist threat facing the United States and its partners was far more dangerous than most had previously recognized.[29]

Another intelligence mistake was in not recognizing that although Pakistan was a close ally of the United States, Pakistani intelligence services (ISI) played an important role in supporting terrorist groups such as the Taliban, Al Qaeda, and Osama bin Laden, with money, weapons, and training.[30] U.S. intelligence did not put enough pressure on Pakistani intelligence to stop their support to these terrorist groups. President Bush wrote in his memoirs, "On 9/11 Pakistan was one of only three countries that recognized the Taliban. Saudi Arabia and the United Arab Emirates were the other two."[31]

All three countries—Pakistan, Saudi Arabia, and the United Arab Emirates—are supposedly U.S. allies, but ironically they recognized the Taliban's regime in Afghanistan, a country that hosted Al Qaeda and bin Laden and facilitated the planning and execution of many deadly terrorist attacks between 1992 and 2001. In my view, there is a serious irony and mistake in that. Those attacks include attacks on American troops in Somalia, in Al-Khubar and Al-Riyadh, Saudi Arabia, as well as attacks on the U.S. Embassies in Kenya and Tanzania, the bombing of the USS *Cole* in Yemen, and the 9/11 attacks.

All in all, the United States did not put nearly enough pressure on its ally Pakistan to stop the ISI's support for the Taliban and Al Qaeda, when Pakistan was in fact harboring terrorists, as I pointed out in many examples earlier. After the war against the Taliban regime in Afghanistan in 2001, many leaders of Al Qaeda lived in Pakistan and were arrested there. Osama bin Laden lived in Pakistan between 2001 and 2011 and was ultimately killed there by a U.S. Special Forces operation.

The political, military, and intelligence mistakes made in dealing with Al Qaeda, and Osama bin Laden, enabled this terrorist group to continue its attacks and atrocities against military and civilian targets and were the reason for the world's failure to stop Al Qaeda over the course of three decades.

In the next chapter, I will explore why the world failed to stop ISIS.

CHAPTER 3

Why the World Failed to Stop ISIS/ISIL

THE WORLD FAILED TO STOP AL QAEDA AND ITS SPIN-OFF, ISIS

As I pointed out in the previous chapter, the world failed to stop Al Qaeda despite many opportunities. Although there were so many indications pointing to the rise of Al Qaeda and many terrorist attacks carried out by Al Qaeda between 1992 and 2000, the majority of Western officials, military commanders, and intelligence agents underestimated the rise of Al Qaeda, and considered it an unexpected development in the world.

In spite of Osama bin Laden's public threats to attack the United States on its own soil and to follow the steps of Ramzi Yousef, the mastermind of the first attack on World Trade Center, Western officials saw the 9/11 attacks as a surprise. They compared Al Qaeda's attacks on 9/11 with the surprise Japanese attack on Pearl Harbor in World War II. But I decidedly disagree with those who maintain that 9/11 came out of the blue. Some U.S. officials, including intelligence agents, agree with my view that these attacks were predictable, and also avoidable. I consider it a serious problem when leaders in various key positions in a country ignore or deny events and actions that allow terrorist organizations to thrive.

The problem is magnified when U.S. high-ranking officials seem surprised at the rise of ISIS and claim that their advance in Iraq and Syria was unpredictable. Many U.S. officials, even those who accept that 9/11 was predictable and avoidable, fail to accept that the rise of ISIS was also a foreseeable outcome of developments in the Middle East. In July 2014, then-Attorney General Eric Holder warned that the rise of ISIS is "more frightening than anything I think I've seen as attorney general," and that "9/11 was something that kind of came out of the blue. This is a situation that we can see developing."[1]

I for one, as you can tell from reading this book, am not surprised. For years, I have even warned about a new generation of terrorists who are more extreme and more brutal than Al Qaeda, because I could see it coming like the sun on a summer day. In 2013, I wrote about the fourth generation of terrorism arising from the civil war in Syria. The first generation came from Afghanistan, the second from chaos in Iraq, and the third from Libya.

Given these different generations and types of terrorists, no one approach is sufficient. This means a multi-dimensional approach is needed. It also means that a long term view has to be taken. That is the only way to think of stopping terrorism entirely. Some believe a complete end to terrorism is not possible. For example, President Trump's draft of new counterterrorism strategy, previewed on May 5, 2017, by Reuters news agency, acknowledges that terrorism "cannot be defeated with any sort of finality."[2] British Prime Minister Theresa May said following the London Bridge terrorist attack on June 3, 2017, in which at least seven people were killed and dozens more wounded, "Enough is enough." May also vowed to conduct a sweeping review of Britain's counterterrorism strategy after three knife-wielding assailants unleashed an assault, the third major terrorist attack in the country in three months.[3] Former British Prime Minister Tony Blair said, "We will defeat ISIS in the end. But defeating ISIS isn't going to defeat the problem. So you've got to go down and deal with the roots of it."[4] I agree, as you will see in a following chapter about rooting out the roots of extremism. The world, and particularly the United States in its role as a world superpower, failed to stop the emergence of ISIS. All of the signs of ISIS's rise were missed and U.S. intelligence estimates had not accurately predicted ISIS's advances through Iraq and Syria.

THE RISE OF TERRORIST GROUP ISIS

I have watched the rise of terrorism and the times when it could have been stopped from a first-hand perch. As I elaborate upon in several relevant places in this book, on May 10, 2003, a month after the fall of Saddam's regime on April 9, 2003, I returned to Iraq from my exile in London. More details about various incidents I point out in this book further develop my thesis and my strategy, which is why I return to certain events.

Concerning my return to Iraq after my exile, Paul Bremer, who was appointed as Administrator of the Coalition Provisional Authority (CPA) by President George W. Bush arrived two days later. Shortly after, he asked to meet with individuals in the Iraqi opposition to Saddam who had lived in exile. I was in that meeting.

As I noted in the introduction, but I elaborate here in this chapter, Bremer said he was the highest authority in Iraq and that he would appoint a "Political Council," which was later called the "Governing Council" to give it more weight. He also said that he would appoint a "Constitutional Council" to write a constitution.

Bremer issued CPA Order No. 1 calling for de-Ba'athification, which dismissed the four highest-ranking levels of Ba'ath Party members from their public jobs. When Bremer was asked about it, he said the concept of the de-Ba'athification decree was that the Ba'ath Party had been one of the major tools of Saddam's control over the Iraqi people. Saddam Hussein himself acknowledged that he built the Ba'ath Party on the model of the Nazi Party because he admired the way in which Hitler was able to use the Nazi Party to control the German people. I am sure you, as me, are outraged to read this, but it gives you a reminder of Saddam's evil, earning the name referred to in the media, "Butcher of Baghdad."

Bremer admitted he made mistakes in these orders, saying, "Just as in [the United States] occupation of Germany we had passed what were called 'de-Nazification decrees' and prosecuted senior Nazi officials, the model for the de-Ba'athification was to look back at that de-Nazification." However Bremer noted, "The implementation is where [he] went wrong."[5] Bremer compared Iraq with Germany and Japan after World War II in many places in his memoirs, *My Year in Iraq*. However, in my view, there is a huge difference between Germany and Iraq, and a big difference between 1945 and 2003.

CPA Order No. 2 was to dismiss the Iraqi Army, police forces, and all intelligence agencies in Iraq. But it is important to note that thousands of military officers lost their jobs and their families' income—so they joined terrorist organizations such as Al Qaeda and ISIS. Bremer wrote an op-ed in the *Washington Post* newspaper in 2007 that he was fed up with being a punching bag because everyone blamed him for mistakes in Iraq, especially the de-Ba'athification and dismissal of the Iraqi Army. He even used me, adding that to prove that dismissing the Iraqi Army was popular, Dr. Al-Bayati came to see him two days later and said, "We were worried that you will keep Saddamism without Saddam."

I was surprised that after serving for more than a year as the highest authority in Iraq, Bremer could not distinguish between Saddamism, which means people loyal to Saddam and military personnel, and regular Ba'ath Party members who had joined these institutions to make a living although they were not loyal to Saddam. Indeed, at one point we Iraqis were worried that the Americans would remove Saddam and keep his top aides to rule Iraq. However, they ended up going to the other extreme and dismantled the essential institutions of the state.

Thousands of Saddam's military officers and Ba'ath Party leaders, who ran the state of Iraq from 1968 to 2003, were dismissed by Bremer. They then joined the insurgency and terrorist groups and fought against American forces and the new Iraqi government. They would go on to become high-ranking military commanders of ISIS. How can this not be seen as an egregious error?

ISIS leader Abu Bakr al-Baghdadi, like many other terrorists, started his career after the U.S. occupation of Iraq. The occupation was the biggest mistake the United States made in Iraq. Although many high-ranking U.S. officials stated in their memoirs that they did not want to look like conquerors in Afghanistan, they decided to formally occupy Iraq. For example, President Bush said that "the plan for the war in Afghanistan called for deploying CIA teams to arm, fund and join forces with the Northern Alliance. Together they would form the initial thrust of the attack. By mating up [American] forces with the local opposition, [the United States] would avoid looking like a conqueror or occupier. America would help the Afghan people liberate themselves."[6]

In several meetings of the Iraqi opposition delegations that I attended with U.S. officials in Washington, D.C., London, Turkey, and Kurdistan in Northern Iraq before 2003, we emphasized the importance of setting up an Iraqi government immediately after the fall of Saddam's regime. We added that an occupation would face resistance from the Iraqi people and from some Arab nationalists and extreme groups such as Al Qaeda.

The most important meetings on U.S.–Iraqi relations were held in Washington, D.C., after we Iraqis received an official invitation to meet high-ranking U.S. officials including Vice President Dick Cheney, Secretary of Defense Donald Rumsfeld, Secretary of State Colin Powell, and officials in the White House in August 2002. At these meetings, we pointed out several misunderstandings and mistakes that the United States was doing in dealing with terrorists. For one, it is important to emphasize that the government approach to prisoners was only serving to radicalize Muslim. For example, Abu Bakr al-Baghdadi, the leader of ISIS, became more radicalized in prison when he was arrested by the U.S. Army. He started to lead prayers and teach other prisoners extremist ideology and built a network of terrorists and a reputation as an Islamic leader.

The revelations of torture in the Abu Ghraib prison in Iraq also radicalized prisoners and followers. This scandal started when a detainee died during an interrogation at the prison. I knew about this firsthand, since I had a relative who worked with the American forces in Iraq and he told me the full story of how one of Saddam's military officers was tortured to death. Then, photos were exposed of naked Iraqi detainees being humiliated, in a scandal that was one of the triggers for the insurgency in Iraq. The Abu Ghraib scandal served terrorist groups and the insurgency in Iraq who used the scandal to recruit fighters.

The CIA's internal think tank, the National Intelligence Council, concluded that Iraq had replaced Afghanistan as the training ground for a new generation of jihadist terrorists. My country had become "a magnet for international terrorist activity," according to the council's chairman, Robert Hutchings.[7] What is important from this information is to trace terrorism through the four generations I alluded to above, that is, from its first generation emerging from the war in Afghanistan, and the second generation, growing up after the war of 2003 in Iraq, and the third generation starting after the war in Libya in 2011, and the fourth generation rising as a result of the war in Syria in 2012. As ISIS claimed eastern parts of Syria and western regions of Iraq, the borders between these two states were eradicated. ISIS wanted to affirm the existence of a new, stronger, and more powerful Islamic State, or "caliphate," which defeated the infidels and nonbelievers.[8]

The civil war in Syria that started in 2011 attracted fighters from Iraq who were part of insurgency and terrorist groups such as Al Qaeda in Iraq (AQI). Fighters who joined ISIS traveled from Iraq into Syria to fight against Syrian President Assad. Those forces got heavy weapons including tanks and artillery from Syria, which they used when they crossed the borders to Iraq in 2013, seizing much of the province of Anbar, and eventually taking control of Mosul, the second-largest city in Iraq, in 2014.

Many experts on terrorism believe that Saddam's military officers and Saddam's Ba'ath Party leaders played an important role in making ISIS a strong military terrorist organization. American terrorism expert Peter Bergen supported this view, saying that a number of Saddam's regime commanders helped to make ISIS a fighting force.[9] Reporter Dexter Filkins of the *New Yorker* agreed, writing that "ISIS is run by a council of former Iraqi generals. Many are members of Saddam Hussein's secular Ba'ath Party who converted to radical Islam in American prisons."[10] In addition, ISIS played the sectarian and ethnic cards, and attracted Sunni tribes in western Iraq along with Arab nationalists who felt they were disadvantaged by the new government, and covered by Sunni-Salafi-jihadi ideology that is an ultraconservative branch and a movement within Sunni Islam. In addition to all these forces, Saddam's intelligence agents played an important role in making ISIS the most brutal and most feared terrorist group in the world. ISIS acted as both a mafia and a religious cult.[11]

The use of brutality and beheadings that were made public and flaunted on the gruesome sights engendered great fear and loathing throughout the world. The acts, and their successfully attracted attention, further fueled ISIS. The beheadings were used by terrorists strategically. For example, in retaliation for U.S. air strikes against ISIS, the terrorist group posted a video of American journalist James Foley being murdered. Another American journalist, Steven Sotloff, was also brutally murdered and recorded on video, and British aid worker David Haines was also slain. An American aid worker who converted to Islam became another victim. Two Japanese hostages, Haruna Yukawa and freelance journalist Kenju Goto, were murdered and displayed for the world to witness.[12] What is critical to note in this chapter in recounting these murders is that Mohammed Emwazi, a foreign fighter from Britain, revealed himself to be one of the most notorious members of ISIS who performed the horrific murders. ISIS was rearing its ugly head and taking the heads of nationals from not only the West but also from the East.

ISIS was brutal, as it knew no boundaries, and even murdered an Arab, Jordanian pilot, Muadh al-Kasabeh, by burning him to death in a locked cage. These murders demonstrate the ISIS brutality extended in the Middle East and ensured that the West was aware of how dangerous and how brutal the newly strengthened ISIS had become in just a short period of time.[13] I mention these murders to emphasize that the entire world was not paying attention despite this cruelty, made so brazenly public. What did Japan, Britain, the United States, and Jordan need in order to wake up?

ISIS justified the act of immolation by quoting a religious decree at the end of the video of the al-Kasabeh execution. This religious decree came from the 13th-century Salafi-jihadi scholar Taqi Al-Din Ahmed Ibn Taymiyyah (born in 1263 AD in Harran, Mesopotamia and died in 1328 AD in Damascus, Syria) who considered non-Muslims as infidels and other sects of Muslims as apostates.

Following this creed, ISIS published a penal code listing crimes punishable by amputation, stoning, and crucifixion, along with a vow to ensure the code is enforced in areas under its control. The document's release was followed by an unprecedented flood of violent executions that saw a woman accused of adultery stoned to death, 17 men crucified, and 2 men accused of homosexual acts thrown off a building within 48 hours.[14]

MISTAKES IN DEALING WITH ISIS

Safe havens in countries further fueled ISIS, and it did not stop. The safe haven in Afghanistan under the Taliban's regime enabled Al Qaeda to plan and execute worldwide terrorist attacks, and the safe haven in Syria helped ISIS to get fighters and weapons and to cross the borders to Iraq and take control of cities in 2013 and 2014.

Remember I said that the lack of a robust response to Al Qaeda terrorist attacks against U.S. troops in Somalia and in Saudi Arabia and the USS *Cole* in Yemen encouraged Al Qaeda to plan the 9/11 attacks. Similarly, the lack of an adequate response to ISIS helped it to continue its advance from Syria to Iraq.

In both cases, there were many political, military, and intelligence mistakes in handling the rise of these terrorist groups. The world did not predict the emergence of Al Qaeda and ISIS and did not deal with it in an early stage of growth. This allowed the terror groups to grow and become a real danger in that region and for the world.

POLITICAL MISTAKES

It was a mistake to support the Arab mujahideen in Afghanistan because they became the terrorists of Al Qaeda. The mistake was repeated in supporting the opposition in Syria with money, weapons, and training.

The majority of the Syrian opposition forces were fundamentalists and extremists, many of whom went on to join Al Qaeda and ISIS and turn against the West as well as their regional supporters.

In regard to training the Syrian opposition, on June 26, 2014, President Obama requested $500 million from Congress to train and equip what the White House was calling "appropriately vetted" members of the Syrian opposition. This reflected an increased worry about the spillover of the Syrian conflict into Iraq.[15] The goal was to train about 15,000 rebels in Jordan and other countries so that they could return to Syria and fight.[16]

The U.S. Congress authorized the White House to train and equip Syrian rebels. But many in the Republican Party said they were not persuaded that the administration's strategy would be forceful enough to eradicate the danger posed by the militants.[17] However, U.S. defense officials admitted in September 2015 that only four or five of the recruits in the program had actually returned to the battle. When speaking about this, Obama was reported to look frustrated as he described "failures" in the U.S. train-and-equip program.[18]

As for arming the Syrian rebels, another drastic mistake occurred. Most of the arms shipped to Syrian rebel groups fighting the government of Bashar al-Assad were going to extremist fighters and not to the more secular opposition that the West wanted to support. Reports indicated that the shipments organized from certain Gulf countries were largely going to hard-line extremists. American officials were trying to understand why extremists had received the lion's share of the arms shipped to the Syrian opposition through the mysterious pipeline with roots in friendly Gulf countries.[19] The CIA began delivering weapons to rebels in Syria, with the shipments streaming into the country along with separate deliveries by the State Department of vehicles and other gear—a flow of material that marked a major escalation of the U.S. role in civil war in Syria.[20]

The Syrian opposition interestingly complained that they were not receiving the materials. But then-Secretary of State John Kerry, under Obama, countered by saying that, "many of the items that people complained were not getting to them are now getting to them."[21] In fact, CIA-funded weapons began flowing to Syrian rebels. A U.S. official confirmed, "That is something we are not going to dispute, but we are not going to publicly speak to it," claiming that the weapons were not U.S.-made, but admitting they were funded and organized by the CIA.[22]

Lawmakers authorized an expanded mission to arm and train Syrian rebels, with President Obama's fiercest opponents in the House GOP (i.e., Republicans, on the opposite aisle to Obama's Democratic Party) prepared to consent—on condition that no U.S. ground forces were deployed in the fight against ISIS.[23]

At one high point for the Syrian opposition, rebel commanders were optimistic when the CIA decided to supply them with American anti-tank TOW (tube-launched, optically tracked, wire-guided or wireless) missiles to attack Syrian Army's tanks.[24] A Syrian rebel leader reportedly told his men that the crushing war of exhaustion they had been fighting against the Syrian government was about to turn in their favor. The reason was that he could now get nearly all the weapons he wanted and that "for the first time they [the United States] were not holding anything from us—except anti-aircraft missiles."[25]

Some of the U.S. allies in the Gulf also supported extremist Syrian opposition with weapons, such as Qatar, which did not completely ignore the concerns of its Western allies. When it transferred arms from Libya to rebels in Syria, Qatari officials cleared out any surface-to-air missiles, in obedience to the United States' demand to prevent the supply of this particular category of weapon. But Qatar's willingness to support extremists has caused disappointment for the West.[26]

Making matters worse, in my view, besides all this support of arms was supporting the Syrian rebels with money. Some officials recognized this, although it was not stopped. For example, Chairman of the Joint Chiefs of Staff General Martin Dempsey acknowledged in front of the Senate Armed Service Committee in a hearing about combating ISIS that the U.S.–Arab allies were funding ISIS, saying, "I know major Arab allies who fund them."[27]

Qatar deliberately sent weapons and money to extremist rebels, particularly a group calling itself Ahrar al-Sham. Qatari Foreign Minister Khalid al-Attiyah praised this movement as "purely" Syrian. But Ahrar al-Sham played a key role in transforming the Syrian opposition into an extremist uprising. Ahrar al-Sham men fought alongside Jabhat al-Nusra, an Al Qaeda affiliate, and were accused of sectarian massacres. This is important because this group helped ISIS to run Raqqa, an ISIS capital in Syria.[28] CIA funding was not inconsequential. Money fuels terrorism, and the source is critical. The CIA provided money to Syrian rebel leaders and at the end of each month, the commanders submitted payroll information, picking up money a few days later for salaries and administrative expenses. Monthly payments were made in American cash with $100 bills.[29]

MILITARY MISTAKES

One of the major military mistakes made in dealing with ISIS was the withdrawal of U.S. forces from Iraq completely by end of 2011. Military commanders suggested leaving some residual forces in Iraq, which in my view, could have made a big difference, even if it was just a small number of U.S. troops with a few jet fighters.

Iraqi former Prime Minister Nouri al-Maliki told me during his visit to the United Nations headquarters in New York in 2009, that after Iraq had bought weapons from Eastern European countries, and some of them were not very good quality, American officials advised him to buy more advanced American weapons. However, the Iraqi government paid $2.3 billion in advance to buy such advanced American weapons; but two years later, they had only received a small portion of these weapons. Iraq needed some weapons desperately, especially jet fighters—a desperate situation that led to the Iraqi government signing a deal with the United States in 2011 to purchase 36 F-16 fighters.

However when ISIS took control of major cities in Iraq in 2013 and 2014, Iraq had not a single one of the purchased 36 F-16 fighters. Masoud Barzani, leader of the Kurdistan Regional Government (KRG) in northern Iraq, said he opposed the sale of F-16 warplanes to Iraq while Nouri al-Maliki was in the position of prime minister, giving the reason that he feared the weapons would be used against the region.[30] What is ironic is that in my conversation with a former U.S. Ambassador to Iraq in 2014, he blamed al-Maliki for the failure to stop ISIS. I then countered that the Americans should take some blame, since it was the Americans who insisted that al-Maliki should stay for a second term in 2010; but he contradicted me, deflecting blame from the Americans and saying it was Masoud Barzani who insisted that al-Maliki stay. Barzani also insisted on bringing al-Maliki for the first term as an alternative to elected Prime Minister Ibrahim al-Jafari.

Nevertheless, the office of Iraqi Prime Minister Haider al-Abadi said that the Iraqi Air Force waited four years from this deal to receive the first batch of four advanced F-16 fighter jets from the United States.[31] This delay had a major deleterious impact, as the lack of airpower seriously hindered the Iraqi government's ability to stop ISIS's expansion into Iraq.

Timing, according to a popular saying, is everything. Debates stretch out and time is lost. There was a long debate about leaving some U.S. forces in Iraq after the end of 2011. Yet President Bush had signed a Status of Forces Agreement (SOFA) three years earlier with then-Iraqi Prime Minister Nouri al-Maliki, calling for the withdrawal of all American troops by the end of 2011.

After Obama took office in January 2009, Iraq and the United States renegotiated that agreement, but there was little consensus on whether a residual force should stay in Iraq. Some military leaders in Baghdad and the Pentagon pushed for as many as 24,000 troops to conduct counterterrorism work and train Iraqi security forces, but the White House rejected that amount[32] and was open to leaving up to 10,000 troops in Iraq. This was another mistake. The number was reduced to about 3,500 troops and half a dozen F-16s.[33] Obama's election campaign has been based on ending the so-called Bush wars in Afghanistan and Iraq, so he did not push to leave any U.S. troops in Iraq. Even more importantly, the withdrawal of troops allowed him to declare that he was "ending the war in Iraq." Later, during the 2012 presidential debates, Obama strangely denied that he had even attempted to keep troops in Iraq.[34] The disagreements and confusion over this action added to the failed strategy against ISIS.

U.S. Ambassador to Iraq James Jeffrey said in 2011 that Iraqi Prime Minister al-Maliki at times floated in private the idea that the SOFA could be extended through an executive agreement. Brett McGurk, who worked as an adviser to the U.S. Ambassador to Iraq at the time, was the one senior official who favored pursuing such an arrangement. But in the end, McGurk was overruled and the troops left.[35] McGurk currently serves as the Special Presidential Envoy for the Global Coalition to Counter ISIS at the U.S. Department of State, leading a global coalition of 68 members to help coordinate all aspects of U.S. policy related to the ultimate destruction of ISIS.

Former U.S. Defense Secretary Leon Panetta, who as former director of the CIA under Obama from 2009 to 2011 oversaw the operation that brought down bin Laden, said he disagreed with the moves to completely pull American troops out of Iraq. Panetta, who took over as Secretary of Defense about six months before the United States withdrew all troops from Iraq, said, "I don't think there's any question that, had we left 8,000, 10,000 troops there, plus our intelligence operations, plus a strong diplomatic presence, that that would've had an impact."[36]

Thus, in the ranks of the military, there were varied opinions. But in the end, in my view, the adopted exit strategy left the door open for ISIS. Some others would agree. U.S. Army Chief of Staff General Raymond Odierno said that had the U.S. military stayed in Iraq longer, the ISIS situation might be more under control. A number of military leaders who were in power when all U.S. troops left Iraq were saying that the complete exit left the door open for ISIS's land grab.[37]

Two months after ISIS managed to control Mosul, the second largest city in Iraq, the Obama administration started aerial bombarding against ISIS in Iraq. The administration did not take military action against ISIS in Syria for about three months. Again, time delays made for mistakes. The former commander of British forces in Iraq, Major General Jonathan Shaw, said ISIS "made their big incursion into Iraq in June of 2014 but the West did nothing, even though thousands of people were killed." He added, "What's changed in August was beheadings on TV of Westerners. And that has led us to suddenly change our policy and suddenly launch air attacks."[38]

INTELLIGENCE MISTAKES

Some experts believe that the intelligence mistakes could be a result of the decision to withdraw U.S. forces from Iraq by end of 2011. The administration decided to dismantle its intelligence stations in Iraq, but they could have provided information on ISIS's activities and its advance in Iraqi cities, such as Ramadi and Falluja, in December 2013, before the major sweep of Mosul in June 2014. So, it could be said that the United States' lack of intelligence in Iraq resulted in underestimating the capability of ISIS to fight the Syrian Army, opposition forces, and other terrorist groups in Syria such as Al-Nusra Front, and to get heavy weapons, tanks, and artillery.

The United States' lack of intelligence in Iraq could also have resulted in the United States mistakenly overestimating the power of the Iraqi Army on which they spent millions of dollars and trained for many years. Yet the United States relied on the hapless Iraqi Army to combat ISIS. Exacerbating the military mistakes in the situation, unmanned surveillance flights over Iraq that would have provided crucial overhead intelligence on areas where ISIS operated were limited to about one mission per month until about mid-June of 2014. In July 2014, there were 50 such sorties over Iraq per day. But the U.S. Air Force had carte blanche to fly its drones and planes over Iraq's skies and the 300 special operators Obama sent to Iraq were preparing target lists for U.S. aircraft.[39]

In September 2014, U.S. officials began getting warnings of the United States' limited intelligence-gathering capacity inside the countries where ISIS was expanding. After 2011, the Obama administration basically ignored Iraq. Adding to that mistake, when officials spoke about what was happening there, they were often ignorant of the reality. "This mistake shows all too clearly how the Obama administration came up short in badly underestimating ISIS' capabilities," said Paul Bremer. "Obama calling ISIS the 'jayvee' team of terrorists can help explain why there was never a strategy drawn up to respond to potential worst-case scenarios— which has certainly exacerbated the situation."[40] However, intelligence agencies said they had been warning the Obama administration of ISIS's danger for a long time.

I have to recount some of these warnings, so you can see from so many of them that the red lights were there. But action was not taken.

In August 2012, the Defense Intelligence Agency issued a classified report predicting that the chaos in Syria was creating conditions that could allow Al Qaeda in Iraq to make a comeback and declare an Islamic caliphate. The report accurately predicted much of what had come to pass in Iraq since Obama's withdrawal of American troops.[41]

David Shedd, then-Acting Deputy Director of the Defense Intelligence Agency, said in a conference that Al Qaeda–affiliated groups were gaining strength in Syria. "It is very clear over the last two years they have grown in size, grown in capability and ruthlessly grown in effectiveness," he said. "They will not go home when it is over. They will fight for that space. They are there for the long haul."[42]

A senior U.S. administration official also warned that ISIS was not going anywhere, when he told reporters that the danger from ISIS was intensifying. "This is really a major and increasing threat to Iraq's stability . . . and it's an increasing threat to us," said the official, who was previewing a visit to Washington, D.C., by then-Iraqi Prime Minister Nouri al-Maliki.[43]

When al-Maliki visited the White House, he made a rather stunning request. Maliki, who celebrated when the last U.S. troops left his country in 2011, asked Obama to quietly send the military *back* into Iraq and help his Air Force develop targets for air strike. That is how serious the threat from the insurgents, led by the extremist group ISIS, had become. Maliki's requests were rebuffed.[44]

Some in U.S. Congress were aware of impending danger regarding Syria. For example, Chair of the Senate Select Committee on Intelligence Dianne Feinstein (a Democrat Senator from California), said that because of areas of Syria that are "beyond the regime's control or that of the moderate opposition," a "major concern" was "the establishment of a safe haven, and the real prospect that Syria could become a launching point or way station for terrorists seeking to attack the United States or other nations."[45]

Lieutenant General Michael Flynn, Obama's Director of the Defense Intelligence Agency, who played a key role in shaping U.S. counterterrorism strategy and dismantling insurgent networks in Afghanistan and Iraq (and briefly served as President Trumps' National Security Adviser until forced to resign over communications with a Russian Ambassador), was also predicting danger, when he said in February 2014 before the annual House and Senate intelligence committees' threat hearings, that ISIS would likely make a grab for land. He said, "ISIS probably will attempt to take territory in Iraq and Syria to exhibit its strength in 2014,"[46] pointing out that ISIS had already taken the cities of Ramadi and Fallujah, so for him it was not difficult to think what ISIS would do next, and the prediction was not exactly hard to make.

In that hearing, Director of National Intelligence James Clapper warned that the three most effective jihadist groups in Syria—one of which he said was ISIS—presented a threat as a magnet for attracting foreign fighters. John Brennan, a Muslim who converted to Islam while stationed in Saudi Arabia, who served as CIA Director from 2013 to 2017 and was chief counterterrorism adviser to U.S. President Barack Obama with the title Deputy National Security Adviser for Homeland Security and Counterterrorism, said he thought both ISIS and Jabhat al-Nusra, Al Qaeda's formal franchise in Syria, presented a threat to launch external operations against the West.[47] Brett McGurk, a Deputy Assistant Secretary of State and the Obama administration's senior U.S. official in Baghdad since the ISIS crisis began in June 2014, presented to Congress a similarly dark warning that ISIS was launching upwards of 40 suicide bombers a month, encouraged by the weakness of al-Maliki's military, echoing ominous reports that American intelligence agencies had been delivering privately for months.[48]

The big mistake is that when ISIS threatened the capital of Iraq, Baghdad, Obama did not take action, and if ISIS had managed to take control of Baghdad, it would have controlled the whole of Iraq and could have gone on to take over Gulf Arab countries, which hold some of the richest reserves of oil and gas in the world. The world failed to stop ISIS because the mistakes in dealing with Al Qaeda were repeated, and the policies of the West and their regional allies helped in creating ISIS. These policies were providing money, arms, and training for Syrian opposition groups, the majority of whom are fundamentalist, extremist, and have joined Al Qaeda and ISIS. Support from the West and their allies to Syrian rebels helped ISIS gain a safe haven in Syria, get weapons, and cross the border to Iraq to control huge swathes of land, including Mosul, the second largest city in the country. Then ISIS declared itself a caliphate, which enables it to attract foreign fighters from all over the world.

In this chapter, I have shown how the world not only failed to stop Al Qaeda, as I noted in the previous chapter, but also failed to stop ISIS, early on, when there were so many signs about this terrorist organization. In the next chapter, I will expand on the funding of terrorism, since massive amounts of money are needed, and provided, to allow terrorists to continue their evil. Thus, methods of stopping this funding, which I will also present, are critical to my strategy.

CHAPTER 4

Funding Terrorism

Every terrorist group, regardless of its ideology, religion, or objective, cannot become influential and powerful without considerable financial support. The more money a terrorist group receives, the more followers, weapons, and attention it can get, and the more frequent and bigger are the terrorist attacks it can carry out. Terrorist groups need funds to run their operations. Funding covers not only terrorist attacks but also other expenses such as salaries for leaders and members who are not volunteers. Funding also pays for the expenses associated with running training camps, buying weapons, traveling expenses, propaganda campaigns, getting equipment, and other needs.

The importance and effect of successful fundraising is clear if we compare Al Qaeda with ISIS. Although Al Qaeda collected millions of dollars, they could not establish a state as ISIS did. ISIS had access to billions of dollars from sources to which Al Qaeda had no access. One major difference between the groups is that Al Qaeda depends mostly on donations whereas ISIS generates money for itself, which is used in small part to fund ISIS's war. The U.S. Department of Treasury recognizes ISIS's ability to collect huge wealth at unprecedented speed.[1] Abo Bakr al-Baghdadi, the leader of ISIS, put his brother Ahmed, other members of his family, and close aides in charge of financial matters to keep tight control of the organization.[2]

SOURCES OF FUNDING FOR TERRORISM

Having an effective financial strategy is a necessary tool to construct terrorist activities and fulfill their objectives. One suicide bombing may only cost a terrorist organization US$1,000; however, if that organization cannot pay for sophisticated training, cannot adequately maintain its international alliances, and cannot develop all the programs and operations it imagines, then its ultimate impact will be limited.[3]

Terrorist groups collect money using several different methods. Some funding comes from states; other funds come from private donors, non-governmental organizations (NGOs), companies that participate in illegal trade, and from criminal acts such as stealing money and kidnapping for ransom (KFR). Yet another source is forcing companies to pay unreasonable taxes and coercing them to fund social events and fundraisers.

Securing reliable funding is key to moving from a marginal radical group to becoming a recognized terrorist organization, in other words, moving from a hand-to-mouth existence to a more ordered and organized model. Successful groups are often defined as much by their skills and their capable financial managers.[4]

Charity is one of the fundamental principles of Islam. All Muslims who have a certain amount of money are obliged to pay zakat (2.5% annually of savings and assets). Apart from the obligatory zakat, the Quran and Islamic tradition also advocate sadaqah (voluntary contributions) to the neediest people. Most Muslims pay these contributions to Islamic charities or to their mosque, and the money is used to finance a variety of religious, humanitarian, and social activities.[5]

Terrorist groups cannot have bank accounts in their names or in the name of anyone affiliated with them, because it may expose both the organization and those affiliates. However, they can mislead intelligence agencies by putting money in the names of fake companies and not-for-profit organizations. They use a money laundering mechanism to transfer money in return for imported products and goods.[6]

This is why terrorist groups also use the so-called hawala, a trust-based informal banking system that uses couriers to move money or operate on the margins of the formal financial system. There are also other ways to transfer money with low risk of detection. The new methods of payment through new information technology enable terrorists to move money with total anonymity.[7]

AL QAEDA SOURCES OF FUNDING

Al Qaeda started its work with financial support from states, more than other sources, after the Soviet Union invasion of Afghanistan in 1979. However, following Saddam's invasion of Kuwait and bin Laden's declaration of war against the United States, Al Qaeda started to depend more on private donations and not-for-profit organizations.

Fundraisers collected money from donors, some of whom were aware that their money was funding terrorist objectives but others were not. Many Al Qaeda fundraisers, such as Khalid Sheikh Mohamed, the mastermind of 9/11, have been arrested. Funds also come from some Mosques where imams collect the money for almsgiving (zakat) that I referred to earlier, but especially at the end of the holy month of Ramadan, during which Muslims practice fasting like the Christian practice of six-week fasting for Lent before Easter Sunday. Fasting the month of Ramadhan makes Muslims feel the suffering of hungry people; therefore, they pay a charity by the end of the month.

Al Qaeda has managed to build a financial network in the Muslim world and among immigrants in exile through businesses and charities. Al Qaeda instructed its branches and affiliated groups to be financially semi-independent. Many of these branches and groups committed ordinary crimes to provide funding for terrorist activities, according to a CIA report.[8] Al Qaeda's financial needs before the 9/11 attacks were almost US$30 million per year. To raise this money, Al Qaeda and its branches relied heavily on a variety of illegal activities, ranging from drug trafficking to kidnapping for ransom, often in association with international criminal organizations. For example, Al Qaeda in the Islamic Maghreb (AQIM), an Islamist militant organization that aims to overthrow the Algerian government and institute an Islamic state, has sustained itself since 2003 primarily on revenues derived from the business of hostage-taking, mostly Westerners. It also engages in drug trafficking from which it receives money.[9]

Donations are also sometimes transferred between like-minded terrorist groups. In 2005, a letter from Al Qaeda's deputy leader, Ayman Al Zawahiri, asked Al Qaeda in Iraq for US$100,000 because many of its own funding lines had been cut, and the Nigerian group Boko Haram reportedly received US$250,000 from Al Qaeda in the Islamic Maghreb (AQIM) in 2012.[10]

Many lawmakers, politicians, and terrorism experts say that the major source of funding for terrorism comes from the oil-rich Gulf countries. Some believe that funding is provided by private donors and charities in these states. The Gulf States' support for terrorism was almost made public during the Soviet Union invasion of Afghanistan. However, after the withdrawal of these forces, many argue that these states began to support terrorist groups indirectly through private donors or through charities.

Rachel Ehrenfeld, Director of the American Center for Democracy and an expert on terrorism and corruption-related topics, said state sponsorship continues to be one of the major forces sustaining terror organizations.[11] Italian journalist and political analyst Loretta Napoleoni believes that Dubai was involved in the 9/11 attacks because of the fact that some of the money that was paid for the destruction of the twin towers in New York passed through the Emirate's banking system. The Arab Emirates is an important tax haven, where money transits free from control or regulation.[12] In 2002, Dennis M. Lormel, Chief of the Financial Crimes Section in the FBI said in his testimony before the House Committee on Financial Services that the investigation into funding of the 9/11 terrorist attacks showed that some terrorist-owned bank accounts opened in the United

States directly received and sent wire transfers to foreign countries, including United Arab Emirates (UAE), Saudi Arabia, and even Germany.[13]

London-based journalist Oscar Williams-Grut wrote that terrorist organizations can take the form of small operators who collect from local communities or set up operations in the Gulf States where big-ticket donations regularly occur. Private donations originating from the Gulf are a vital funding stream for Al Qaeda and its affiliated groups. In the case of small operators, there are some instances of fundraisers abusing the charity sector.[14]

Former Secretary of Defense Donald Rumsfeld pointed out, "There is a lot of money going into these so-called madrasa (religious schools) and they aren't training people in mathematics or language or science or whatever, humanities, they are training people to kill. In spite of U.S. requests to the Saudi government to stop funding terrorist organizations and madrasas that breed hate, the Saudis have taken only baby steps in that direction."[15] An example that demonstrates the lack of control in funding terrorism is seen in the International Islamic Relief Organization (IIRO), one of the largest Islamic charities, based in Jeddah (Saudi Arabia). IIRO and some of its subsidiary organizations have reportedly been used, knowingly or otherwise, to finance Al Qaeda.[16]

ISIS SOURCES OF FUNDING

As with Al Qaeda, evidence indicates that funding for ISIS started to pour in from states and private donors in oil-rich Gulf countries. Some Western officials, journalists, and writers argue the accusation that some states are funding terrorism is false and believe that the funds come from NGOs. However, there is agreement that Gulf States either turn a blind eye to private donations for terrorist groups or at least do not do enough to stop funding to terrorists from being supplied out of their countries.

In late 2010, the *Guardian* newspaper published a leaked cable in which former Secretary of State Hillary Clinton wrote, "Donors in Saudi Arabia constitute the most significant source of funding to Sunni terrorist groups worldwide."

Social media is a tool. ISIS attracts donations via Twitter and accesses them via Skype. Donors transmit the numbers of international prepaid cards to organization representatives. The images of Saudi individuals pledging support online shows that they are a key source of funding.[17]

In a speech to the Harvard Kennedy School of Government, U.S. Vice President Joe Biden said, "The Saudis, the Emiratis, etc. poured hundreds of millions of dollars and thousands of tons of weapons to anyone who would fight against Assad's regime in Syria, however the reality was that the people who were being supplied were Jabhat al-Nusra and al-Qaeda and the extremist elements of jihadis coming from other parts of the world."[18]

Malcolm Nance, author of the book *Defeating ISIS: Who They Are, How They Fight, What They Believe*, maintains that wealthy donors, often from the Gulf States, can find a sincere religious justification for their donations to the jihadis. Gulf State donors to ISIS may be more open to geopolitical rather than religious arguments; that is, they may wish, above all, to think they are countering the influence of Shiite Iran in the Levant by balancing it with Sunnah fighters, no matter how extreme.[19]

Patrick Cockburn, in his book *The Rise of the Islamic State: ISIS and the New Sunni Revolution*, wrote, "The foster-parents of ISIS and the other Sunni-jihadi movements in Iraq and Syria had been Saudi Arabia, the Gulf monarchies, and Turkey. This doesn't mean the jihadis did not have strong indigenous roots, but their rise was crucially supported by outside Sunni powers. The Saudi and Qatari aid was primarily financial, usually through private donations."[20]

Charles River, editor of *The Islamic State of Iraq and Syria: The History of ISIS*, said the continued funding received by ISIS from private donations of wealthy citizens and charities in the Gulf was alarming. Wealthy and influential Gulf States like Kuwait and Qatar remain careless about the flow of private donations into Syria, and many Gulf-based financiers and "charities" are openly fundraising and sending large sums of money to Islamist groups in Syria, including ISIS.[21]

ISIS is the richest terrorist organization in the history of terrorism, as I said. It has managed to get billions of dollars, and established its own State, which terrorist organizations call a "caliphate," as I mentioned in a previous chapter. As a result, ISIS has gained control of more territory than the governments of Israel and Lebanon. According to the *Long War Journal*,[22] ISIS controls nearly a third of Iraq alone. In Syria, according to the Syrian Observatory for Human Rights, a Britain-based monitoring group with sources inside the country, ISIS controlled half of the country's land area following gains in both the Homs province in the center of the country and the Aleppo province in the north.[23]

Mohammed Alwash, author of *ISIS and Its Sisters, from al-Qaeda to Islamic State*, wrote:

ISIS also had stable financial resources and was collecting money in several ways in the areas of Iraq and Syria. Revenues from Power Stations and other energy resources, confiscation of state factories and industrial institutions, money from Banks and all financial institutions were confiscated. ISIS got around $500 million from the Central Bank in Mosul.

Properties of the Iraqi and Syrian governments were seized by ISIS In addition, money was taken from the Shiites in Iraq, the Alawites in Syria and from all religious minorities. Properties and money of Sunnis loyal to the Iraqi and Syrian governments were also confiscated. ISIS accessed all assets belonging to companies that had contracts with the Iraqi and Syrian governments. They imposed monthly taxes on commercial stores and shops, and collected tax revenues on trade and commercial trucks in areas under ISIS control.[24]

SALE OF OIL AND OIL PRODUCTS

Getting funds from states in the Arab region and donations from private donors and NGOs was not enough to satisfy ISIS. Their plan was to control oil fields and oil refineries in Iraq and Syria. Most ISIS commanders are officers from Saddam's army and Ba'ath Party leaders. As such, oil smuggling and other illicit black market activities was nothing new for them. Saddamists perfected the art of smuggling in the 1990s as a way to work around UN sanctions.[25] U.S. intelligence agencies estimate that ISIS collected black market oil revenues of approximately US$100 million in 2014 after seizing major parts of Iraq and acquiring oil fields and pipelines in both Iraq and Syria. After a year of almost unimpeded operations, the U.S. Treasury Department intelligence estimates that these ISIS-controlled oil fields generated around US$500 million in 2015.[26]

When ISIS gained control of many oil fields in Syria and Iraq, it started selling crude oil to traders and middlemen who then sold the oil through international networks. The Kurdish Regional Government in Northern Iraq did nothing to stop ISIS from obtaining oil revenues from fields in Northern Iraq. In Syria, ISIS controlled all of the essential oil fields including the Omar field, the largest field in the country.[27]

Even as allies increased air strikes and began to target oil refineries, ISIS turned to a small, sophisticated network of refineries housed within mobile trailers that are able to change locations with ease and produce enough oil to meet the needs of regions under their control. ISIS continued to extract oil at an alarming rate, some reporting upwards of 30,000 barrels a day that are smuggled to black market buyers, often across the border of Turkey and Iraq.[28]

The ISIS Finance Ministry Report put the number of oil wells under control of ISIS in Syria at 253, with 161 of them operational. A total of 275 engineers and 1,107 workers were running the wells, quite an alarming number of people working for ISIS.[29]

CONTROL OF OTHER NATURAL RESOURCES

ISIS began by collecting funds from the states in the Arab region and donations from private donors and NGOs, but then expanded vastly. Its plan, as I mentioned, was to control natural resources, especially oil fields and oil refineries in Iraq and Syria. But the plan went beyond this. It also planned to control water resources by controlling dams on the Tigris and the Euphrates Rivers in Iraq and Syria. The most immediate concern among those under ISIS rule in Iraq and Syria is basic survival. According to the UN and various humanitarian and human rights watch groups, populations under ISIS control risk starvation and drought due to the group's control over natural resources. The production of basic commodities such as wheat and grain and water from the dams are controlled by ISIS. Controlling food sources is a major way to enforce control of a region and peoples.

In 2015, ISIS controlled large parts of five of Iraq's most fertile provinces, areas that produce approximately 40 percent of the country's wheat crop. The militants also seized a number of government grain silos in the north of the country estimated to contain between 40,000 and 50,000 tons of grain. ISIS also seized an additional 700 tons of wheat from western Iraq. The grain was transported to Syria for milling.[30]

Imagine if a group took over the agriculture of a state in the United States, such as Kansas, and controlled all the assets necessary to produce wheat and corn. What if the group then seized all property and equipment from the farmers, effectively cutting off their livelihood and their sustenance? The group's next step is to take all the wheat and sell it back to the very same people from whom they forcibly stole it. It is an effective technique to effect a stranglehold. Most people would agree that this is mafia-style behavior at its most extreme.[31]

KIDNAPPING FOR RANSOM

Taking hostages for ransom is another easy source of income for ISIS. Using this tactic, large amounts of money can be acquired in a short amount of time. It is believed that ISIS collected US$45 million in 2014 from kidnapping hostages.[32]

The United Nations' official policy is to oppose negotiating in hostage situations where terrorist organizations are involved. As a result, those who negotiate with terrorists are indirectly funding them, and hostage-taking will surely increase if the terrorist groups get the results they wish for.[33] Unfortunately, not all countries are on the same page regarding non-negotiating with terrorists. In fact, Germany, France, Italy, and Spain have a record of paying off terrorist ransoms, specifically to Al Qaeda. In this way, terrorist groups are able to profit from European countries that negotiate in hostage kidnapping.[34] ISIS has got millions of dollars from European governments in return for releasing hostages. For example, ISIS kidnapped French journalists Nicolas Henin, Pierre Torres, Edouard Elias, and Didier François, in 2013 in Syria, all of whom were released in April 2014 after ransoms were supposedly handed over—although this was denied by officials.[35] The militants supposedly threatened that there were 72 hours to deliver US$200 million in ransom money or a video will be released showing a tragic end of the men.

The United Kingdom and United States adopted a principle of not negotiating with terrorist groups, with the U.S. government going further, with a policy of punishing families of hostages if they paid ransom for the release of the hostage. The United States and the United Kingdom maintain that negotiating with, and paying ransom to, terrorist groups only encourages more kidnapping, and that citizens who enrich terrorist groups by paying ransoms contribute to future attacks and kidnappings. A 2014 *New York Times* investigation found that since 2008, Al Qaeda and its affiliates had received US$125 million from ransoms, including US$66 million in 2013 alone.

TAXATION AND EXTORTION

A wealthy Iraqi businessman in Mosul alleged that ISIS collected monthly taxes from businessmen, traders, and contractors, demanding 20 percent of all the profits generated from any contract with the government. Reports also spoke to the fact that ISIS managed to obtain large amounts of money through blackmailing and confiscating the properties of people in several provinces in Iraq.[36]

After the allies' aerial strikes against oil fields and refineries controlled by ISIS, the terrorist group got most of its funding by taxing Iraqi government workers in areas under ISIS control. They could be taxed up to 50 percent of their salary, bringing in more than one million dollars per day from extortion and taxation.[37]

ISIS also taxed commercial activities, and if companies did not comply, ISIS threatened them with murder. Business owners were obligated to pay a tax in order to receive basic necessities, like water and electricity.[38]

SELLING ANCIENT ARTIFACTS

Syria and Iraq have a large number of historical sites, some dating back 8,000 years. The governments in Syria and Iraq cared for these historical sites to save the heritage and culture of their countries and to attract tourists. ISIS members destroyed some of these sites, claiming that people worship the holy shrines and the holy people they represent as a form of idolatry, instead of worshipping god.[39] In a similar way, ISIS destroyed holy shrines of messengers such as Prophet Jonah in Mosul and grandsons of the Prophet Mohammed called imams by Shiites. Similarly, Al Qaeda in Iraq destroyed shrines of Imam Ali Al-Hadi and Imam Hasan Al-Askari in Samara in February 2006, in a failed attempt to bring a full-scale sectarian war between Sunnis and Shiites.

ISIS justified their destructions on the basis of religious fundamentalism, explaining that such sites were not in accordance to true Islam. As ISIS gained ground throughout Syria and Iraq, it realized that the sites were a prime source of income. Therefore, ISIS also grants licenses to excavate and explore ancient sites, thereby gaining control of access to these historical sites and artifacts.[40] As a result, ISIS has sold a large number of priceless artifacts and garnered large sums of money. Although it is difficult to estimate how much income is generated by selling artifacts, the arrest of an ISIS messenger in June 2014 led to the discovery that the sale of artifacts in one province in Syria added US$36 million to the treasury of ISIS.[41]

As in Nazi Germany, the confiscation of artwork serves to both deflate and humiliate the dominated owners, as well as add to the dominator's coffers. In addition, except for the enslavement and rape of women and young girls, no other ISIS activity threatens the cultural fabric of the region more than ISIS's complete destruction and complete lack of respect for historical and archeological treasures. In fact, the destruction diminishes the collective knowledge of humankind in a much larger scope. "Objects are not just stones," said Bulgarian diplomat Irina Bokova, Director General of UNESCO since 2009, the United Nations agency that oversees cultural heritage sites. "This is about the identity of the . . . people, and destroying the identity of people is a big blow to their communities."[42] These extensive sources of income and the amounts of money reported in this chapter form the basis for a later chapter in this book that discusses how to stop this flow of money.

In the next chapter, I explore how terrorists exploit the Internet.

CHAPTER 5

Terrorists Exploit the Internet

The Internet helps humanity achieve many noble human objectives in all fields of life including education, health, and communication. It has connected the entire world into a village. But the Internet is also used for evil, by terrorist groups to facilitate acts of violence against innocent people. Terrorist organizations exploit the Internet to spread their distorted, subversive, and perverse ideology and to radicalize vulnerable people, especially youth. The Internet also provides fertile ground for terrorists to encourage their followers to attack soft targets in the West, such as civilians, including women and children.

The world must address the challenge of radicalization through the Internet, which has spread like a computer virus or a contagious disease. It is difficult for peace-loving nations to accept and face this kind of evil. According to statements from high-ranking officials in the West and many global experts, terrorists are a step ahead of Western intelligence and successful in radicalizing many people who live in the Western countries who become willing to carry out terrorist attacks. Radicalized Westerners, often recruited through the Internet, have committed many atrocities.

According to Eben Kaplan, formerly assistant editor at the Council on Foreign Relations, terrorist websites can serve as virtual training grounds, offering tutorials on building bombs, firing surface-to-air missiles, shooting at U.S. soldiers, and sneaking into Iraq (and Syria) from abroad.[1]

It is true that intelligence agencies can monitor some suspects through online activities and can stop some potential terrorists. However, I think even if a few terrorists get through the cracks, it will be enough to cause catastrophic damage and cause causalities.

Examples that reportedly involved terrorists using the Internet include the attack in California on December 2, 2015, in which 14 people were killed; the attack in Florida on June 12, 2016, in which 49 were murdered; and the pressure cooker bombs that exploded in New York on September 19, 2016, injuring 31 people.

AL QAEDA EXPLOITS THE INTERNET

Terrorists use the Internet to communicate with each other. They also use it to broadcast their prowess to the world. They post propaganda videos on the Internet and quickly find ways to include news channels as part of their campaign. The Internet is a strong tool used by terrorists to exchange all kinds of messages, to share information, to recruit foreign fighters, and to inspire attacks. They also use social networks to collect donations especially from some Arab Gulf countries.

Concern over the use of imagery that helps terrorists identify targets was demonstrated immediately after the 9/11 attacks when several websites removed photos and data that suddenly appeared too sensitive. On October 18, 2001, the Pentagon purchased all rights to pictures of Afghanistan taken by Space Imaging Incorporated's IKONOS satellite, which can discern from space objects as small as 1 square meter on the ground.[2]

Terrorist websites host messages and propaganda videos, which help raise morale and further the expansion of recruitment and fundraising networks; the number of these increased dramatically after ISIS's rise. Al Qaeda's media arm, As-Sahab, may have been the most visible on the Internet, but the number of sites on the network of jihadist media outlets has jumped in the past few years.[3]

In the information age, terrorism expanded its scope, and found in technology a valuable tool to facilitate their efforts. The term "information terrorism" describes the process of exploiting the Internet for terrorist purposes, defining it as the link between criminal information, system fraud, and the physical violence of terrorism. Digital information systems are used and abused toward evil ends in terrorist campaigns.[4]

Abo Musaab al-Zarqawi, the leader of Al Qaeda in Iraq (AQI), pioneered the "marriage" of horrific ultraviolence and mass media. Al-Zarqawi shocked much of the world with televised and online videos of gruesome beheadings. His strategy evolved over time into the current professional quality media apparatus employed by ISIS as a powerful recruiting tool.[5] Al Qaeda has had an Internet presence for two decades using various platforms especially social media. A well-known online terrorist, "Irhaby 007" ("Terrorist 007"), impressed other online terrorists who were proud of his hacking skills and his ability to securely distribute information. Irhaby 007 shared his knowledge with other online terrorists through web postings such as his "Seminar for Hacking Websites," creating a network of technology-savvy terrorist disciples.[6]

ISIS EXPLOITS THE INTERNET

The Internet is the newest technology tool exploited by terrorist organizations and by extremist individuals such as lone wolves. Lone wolves have particular need for homemade weapons, like pressure cooker bombs and pipe bombs—information and instructions about their assembly of which is easily available and disseminated through the Internet.

ISIS had escalated its Internet efforts to the point where governments realize that winning the Internet battle is central to winning the fight against terrorism. The U.S. State Department launched its own Center for Strategic Counterterrorism Communications in 2011. European government officials met on October 9, 2014, in Luxembourg, with executives of technical companies including Twitter, Facebook, and Google to discuss ways to combat online extremism.[7]

Unfortunately, as state entities and technical companies grapple with the issues, ISIS is becoming increasingly sophisticated in its use of the Internet. Well-produced videos like the detainment of hostage British journalist John Cantlie provided chilling evidence of how knowledgeable the modern militant is in using the media. Bomb-making manuals written in English are freely available online to access English-speaking recruits, and terrorists are using chatrooms to openly discuss the best ways to make explosives.[8]

The Internet offers terrorists several advantages. Through the Internet, terrorists are able to operate remotely and anonymously, crossing national borders without being detected or regulated. Cyber attacks are cheaper and less dangerous than physical attacks and a computer attack would also reap significant media attention.[9]

ISIS has shown that it is able to use the highly complex Internet to its advantage. It has also been successful in controlling attacks and producing desired results even without direct communication between organizations and the individuals who end up carrying out attacks.

TERRORISTS EXPLOIT SOCIAL MEDIA

Terrorist groups exploit various platforms of social media networks to achieve their objectives. They disseminate their distorted ideology, radicalizing people, recruiting foreign fighters, and collecting donations. They also use social media networks for communication among themselves and with the leadership across borders. Social media networks have been used to launch propaganda campaigns and to demonstrate terrorists' power, brutality, and achievements. Social media postings display hostages being beheaded, military attacks, and car bombs, to spread fear among armies fighting them and among civilians they either control or seek to control.

Twitter and Facebook are popular platforms to recruit soldiers and spread ideology. Speeches from leaders and preachers that promote hate are easily accessible online, especially on YouTube. Extremists also use encrypted apps, for communication.[10] The Zello-encrypted app is used for sharing audio messages, propaganda sermons, and speeches.[11] The increasingly popular WhatsApp is useful to them, given that it is free with wifi access, and used by many people around the world. Tweets that are creatively worded to spread their message and incite fear are sent by ISIS, such as "Calamity will befall US, All Eyes on Islam, and World-Islam." These have created a steady following on Twitter; some followers are just curious and follow the online drama, and some are seriously interested in the message.[12] Tweets are accompanied with hashtags to further disseminate and spread the message. ISIS uses hashtags to boost the popularity of its material, accompanied by thousands of tweets a day, without triggering Twitter's spam controls.

ISIS is incredibly social media-savvy. The organization has its own social media team which, in coordination with the leadership, puts out content promoting the group and its ideology. This information is then picked up and spread all over the Internet by thousands of online supporters who often have no formal affiliation with the group itself.[13]

Online representatives of ISIS have delivered the following warnings in tweets distributed via Twitter:

"If the United States bombs Iraq, every citizen is a legitimate target for us."

"This is a message for every American citizen. You are the target of every Muslim in the world."

"For every drop of blood shed of the Iraqis, Americans will shed a river of blood."

"Every American doctor working in any country will be slaughtered if America attacks Iraq."

"Don't come to Iraq unless you want another 11th September to happen."[14]

Government agencies and social media companies, such as Twitter, YouTube, and Facebook, struggle to locate and remove social media accounts that disseminate jihadist propaganda. But for every deleted account, a new one is produced in its place. One complication of such deletions is that intelligence gatherers often allow certain accounts to remain active so that they can use them to collect information.[15]

On July 17, 2015, then-FBI Director James Comey said that ISIS has more than 21,000 English-speaking followers on social media. Because ISIS has so many followers on social media accounts, like Twitter and Facebook, the "lone wolf" strategy has been put into play by followers all around the world, like the attack on two military facilities on July 16, 2015, in Chattanooga, Tennessee.[16]

According to statistics provided by Steven Crown, Vice President of Microsoft Corporation, within 15 minutes of the Paris attacks on November 13, 2015, in which around 130 people were killed, there were 7,500 tweets. Within minutes of the Paris attacks, thousands praised the act, and within two weeks, there were one million views of videos on the Internet praising the attacks.[17]

This is not only tragic and outrageous, but also very alarming, and should be addressed seriously. Such usage of social media after a terrorist attack is one more wake-up call for the West—especially for those responsible for counterterrorism—about terrorist tactics and the urgency to counter them. Some terrorist sympathizers who praised the Paris attack live in Europe or in the United States; thus, it is vital that authorities figure out how many of these individuals are potentially planning to carry out their own attacks. This situation is a good proof that counterterrorism campaigns to date have failed to stop terrorism and that a more robust campaign is needed.

In tragic instances, intelligence fails to rout out the terrorist plan. On April 7, 2017, a terrorist killed 4 people and injured 15, in Stockholm, by driving a stolen beer truck into a crowd of shoppers and through the side of a department store. Rakhmat Akilov, 39, from Uzbekistan, was known to intelligence services.[18] Security services said that the terrorist was in intelligence reports but they had not viewed him as a militant threat. A Facebook page appearing to belong to him showed that he was following a group called "Friends of Libya and Syria," dedicated to exposing "terrorism of the imperialistic financial capitals" of the United States, Britain, and Arab "dictatorships."[19] Such examples cry out for ferreting out such terrorists who are posting on the Internet. Some experts maintain that such monitoring is too vast to be able to catch all potential terrorists in the Internet, while others say that technology is advanced enough to do a better job at present.

TERRORISTS USE PROPAGANDA VIDEOS

Visual presentations, such as videos on YouTube and pictures on Instagram, are becoming increasingly popular. Certainly, they are attractive and easy to view. Accordingly, terrorist groups are creative and produce very powerful pictures and videos to attract vulnerable young people, recruit them, and inspire them to carry out attacks. Influential producers of such material include the Al-Shabab terrorist militarist group in Somalia, which produced a 51:44-minute video in 2013, entitled *The Path to Paradise: From the Twin Cities to the Land of the Two Migrations* in English, that targeted Westerners by showing the story of Somali recruits from Minnesota (whose capital, St. Paul, and Minneapolis are known as the twin cities) and making comparisons to racism, to supposedly resonate with Westerners. The video showed three men who took the journey to Somalia in order to die in the "holy land." With this video, Al-Shabab is reported to have recruited up to 50 men.[20]

The recruitment video, posted on YouTube, featured recruits. According to the FBI, at least 15 Somali-American men left their homes in St. Paul, Minnesota, to join radical Syrian groups. One of them was Douglas McAurthur McCain, a 33-year-old man who grew up as a basketball-loving kid from Minneapolis who turned into a jihadi-fighting terrorist in Syria; he had communicated with family on Facebook, and once tweeted "pray for ISIS." Another ISIS recruit, 29-year-old Abdirahmann Muhumed, was a father of nine from Minneapolis. Both were found dead on the Syrian battlefield. One hypothesis is that these men were apparently looking to find their identity abroad.[21]

Another Minneapolis native, American jihadist Troy Kastigar (who adopted the name Abdirahman), a friend of Douglas McAuthur McCain, is seen in a video saying, "If you guys only knew how much fun we have over here, this is the real Disneyland. . . . You need to come here and join us, and take pleasure in this fun."[22] Kastigar, a Minnesotan who was not Somali, reportedly left for Somalia in November 2008 and was killed there in 2009.

The Al-Shabab terrorist group claims that its young are raised well, by providing health care and a decent education. Young recruits learn to speak English, obtain a high school degree, and even proceed on to junior college. Once they are older, stronger and healthier, they are sent to fight in Somalia or Syria, and join the forces of the terrorist group.[23]

Another American-turned jihadist, Alabama-born Omar Hammami, also known by the pseudonym Abu Mansoor Al-Amriki, or "the American," was raised in a Christian household with an American Protestant mother and a Syrian-born Muslim father. He joined the Somali Islamist militant group Al-Shabab, rose to become a leader, and earned a place on the FBI Most Wanted Terrorist List. He also became infamous for his two "jihad rap" songs. One song, called *Send Me a Cruise*, praised martyrdom at the hands of U.S. forces. The other song, *Make Jihad with Me*, was aimed at recruiting youth to join the Al-Shabab movement. Hammami supposedly turned against Al-Shabab, allegedly because the leaders lived extravagant lifestyles by taxes collected from ordinary Somalis, and sidelined foreign recruits. Hammami was active on Twitter and frequently tweeted with the well-known American counterterrorism scholar J.M. Berger.[24]

Al Qaeda originally contributed to large quantities of extremist online media contents. The leader of AQI, Abu Musab al-Zarqawi, spread propaganda videos such as the decapitation of American hostage Nick Berg, and the kidnapping of Egyptian and Algerian diplomats before their execution.[25]

When I was in Iraq, I watched videos produced by AQI and sold in the markets. A large number of Iraqis were watching these propaganda videos. There were even video games where users could pretend to be jihadist warriors fighting against U.S. soldiers in Baghdadi video shops.

Through the speed of the Internet, propaganda videos spread all over the globe. Thousands of people from the West have been filmed fighting alongside ISIS. These people pose a greater threat in the West because they are able to infiltrate Western civilization without being noticed by authorities.

ISIS promises Westerners that a great life is waiting for them when they move to Syria where they can practice the jihadist ideologies provided by ISIS. This propaganda reaches vulnerable people in Europe, Australia, Canada, and the United States. ISIS uses innovative technology like drones and GoPro cameras to attract the "modern man" of the West attracted to technology. The popular "mujatweets" are short videos that show a distorted view of ISIS by showing them handing out ice cream cones to Syrian children. Elliot Zewig, deputy director of the Middle East Media Research Institute, commented that, "The focus of these videos are much more on 'come and join us', it is not all difficulty and slaughter and suffering. It is 'come and join us, join me and we'll fight the good fight together.'"[26]

ISIS mixes extreme brutality with technical skill, using social media, making it one of the most feared organizations on earth. It releases well-edited and horrifying videos of beheadings of American and British hostages. One of its propaganda videos is three and a half minutes of the popular action-adventure video game Grand Theft Auto 5 (GTA), cut and edited to recruit new young members into joining the extremist organization. The video uses clips from Grand Theft Auto 5 in order to demonstrate that its fighters do in real life what Western youth do only in games. The video is meant to train teenagers to fight in the West, and implant terror into the hearts of opponents.[27] In the video, recruits imitate the video game characters, attacking a military convoy or killing police officers. This brings up familiar images of the 2014 "Occupy Gezi" protesters in Turkey, when many were harmed after Turkish police used tear gas and water cannons against protesters occupying a park in central Istanbul. The protesters championed the slogan, "You are messing with youth who grew up fighting police in GTA."[28]

One can understand why terrorists use the popular GTA 5 as a recruiting tactic, to attract young people. Many young people who have left the West to join up with ISIS have been influenced by such videos that appeal to their interests, pushing them toward believing that ISIS might be a good place for them. The appeal is that they can join a group that "loves GTA 5." This is consistent with research that has even shown that video games have the ability to desensitize young people to violence.[29]

ISIS has also used a British Muslim and ISIS militant, born as Muhammad Jassim Abdulkarim Olayan al-Dhafiri, and named later as Mohammed Emwazi, whom journalists called "Jihadi John," because he was featured on propaganda videos beheading Westerners. Such propaganda travels quickly across the world, aided in part by major broadcasting networks. Nowadays, propaganda is spread not only to ISIS and terrorist sympathizers[30] but also to everyday people who are just trying to get the news. Jihadi John was also nicknamed by journalists as "John the Beatle" (referring to Beatle John Lennon), as he was part of a terrorist cell called "The Beatles" because the cell members all had British accents.

Some ISIS fighters take advantage of the appeal of the culture of celebrity, like the French militant who goes by the name Guitone, and the

German rapper who calls himself Deso Dogg. They post pictures and videos showing their extravagant and relaxed lifestyles at the beach eating pizza. Rita Katz, of SITE, an intelligence agency that pressures social media companies to crack down on terrorist propaganda, warns that such approaches are silently inciting the killing of others by sharing extremist propaganda.[31]

TERRORISTS USE ENCRYPTED COMMUNICATION

Terrorist groups, like other criminal organizations, use encryption to keep their communication private and their plans secret, and to avoid detection and intelligence surveillance. Al Qaeda started by using very simple methods of encryption way back in the 1990s. The simple tools helped Al Qaeda to keep secret its communications regarding plans for the most devastating terror attacks in the history of the world on 9/11.

The Internet can be used to send messages secretly, much like the invisible ink that Al Qaeda promotes as a low-tech alternative to communications. Reports also indicate that Egyptian computer experts working in Afghanistan devised a communications network to enable extremists to exchange information via the World Wide Web without fear of being caught posting messages on e-mail and electronic bulletin boards.[32]

One of Al Qaeda's leaders, Khalid Shaikh Mohammed (KSM), a mastermind of the 9/11 attack, used a simple method of coded communication. He gave other terrorists simple words as codes. A "wedding" was an explosion, "market" was Malaysia, "souk" was Singapore, "'terminal" stood for Indonesia, and "hotel" for the Philippines. Thus, "planning a wedding at the hotel" would be "planting a bomb in Manila."[33]

Modern terrorists have manipulated the Internet as an efficient way to communicate. They access people and deliver their message through steganography, a special process that hides messages in pictures and graphic files. In this way, they communicate through thousands of saved e-mail drafts, which are available to anyone who has the password for the e-mail account.[34]

Cell phones' short message service (SMS) is a cryptic text. The message in cryptic form can be sent from one cell phone to another via an SMS center. Credible reports linked the use of SMS techniques to terrorist groups. SMS works by transmitting signals from a cell phone to the cellular operator's automatic SMS center. The center dials the SMS's destination number and puts the message in the queue. The effectiveness and simplicity of this technique may force governments to monitor SMS centers.[35]

When terror groups use encrypted communication, it can obstruct the surveillance process of intelligence agencies, but encryption also flags the communication as something the U.S. agency might consider listening to. The U.S. National Security Agency (NSA) considers any encrypted communication between a foreigner it is watching and a U.S.-based person as fair game to gather and keep, for as long as it takes to break the code and examine it.[36]

However, the problem arises when there is an encrypted communication between a foreigner who is not under NSA surveillance and an American person. This is why the U.S. intelligence service tried to solve this problem through a huge surveillance program to watch all communications and collect what is called "metadata," a strategy that could make it more difficult to find terrorists by expanding the search.

ISIS is much more sophisticated than Al Qaeda and other terrorist groups in exploiting modern technology, especially the Internet, social networks, and encrypted communications. It managed to evade European intelligence surveillance when planning the attacks in France, Belgium, and Germany in 2015 and 2016.

U.S. TERRORISTS RECRUIT VIA INTERNET

The ISIS brand is on the rise among aspiring and active American extremists. As of December 2015, 71 people have been "arrested, indicted, or convicted" for "ISIS-related activities" in the United States. These people are predominantly U.S. citizens and "the overwhelming majority of those charged (73%) were not involved in plotting terrorist attacks in the United States."[37]

On December 5, 2015, then-Director of the FBI James Comey warned that ISIS was trying to recruit followers in the West and that the FBI was tracking online activity of people attracted to ISIS; but, of course, the FBI cannot monitor Internet activity in the home of every potential militant. Comey said, "When you invest in a poisonous narrative that resonates with troubled souls, with unmoored people, and you do it in a slick way through social media, you buzz in their pocket 24 hours a day, saying come or kill, come or kill, that has an impact."[38]

In the same way that air travel sped the spread of viral outbreaks, the Internet provides tech-savvy organizations like ISIS with the means to spread mental poison. By flooding Twitter and Facebook with disgusting propaganda and extremist messaging, ISIS has easy access to those wavering on the edge.[39]

Some of the terrorists who were radicalized on the Internet by Al Qaeda and ISIS were successful in assembling homemade bombs, such as pressure cooker bombs and pipe bombs, that were used in terrorist attacks inside the United States. Other terrorists used handguns and rifles to shoot their victims.

American Army Major and psychiatrist Nidal M. Hasan, scheduled to be executed for killing 13 people at Fort Hood in Texas, was radicalized and inspired by Al Qaeda leader Anwar al-Awlaki in Yemen through the

Internet.[40] Intelligence agencies intercepted communications between Hasan and al-Awlaki. But federal authorities dropped an inquiry into the matter after deciding that the messages from Hasan did not suggest any threat of violence and concluding that no further action was warranted.[41] This oversight is shocking and turned out to be a drastic and tragic mistake.

In a widely media-covered tragedy, in April 2013, two brothers, 19-year-old Dzhokhar Tsarnaev and 26-year-old Tamerlan Tsarnaev, carried out what came to be called the "Boston Marathon bombing," killing three people and injuring a thousand more. Dzhokhar Tsarnaev had downloaded copies of books that advocate violence, glorify martyrdom in the service of violent jihad, and direct Muslims not to give their allegiance to governments that invade Muslim lands. He downloaded a copy of Volume 1 of Al Qaeda's *Inspire* magazine, which includes an article, "Make a Bomb in the Kitchen of Your Mom," and instructions on how to build IEDs using pressure cookers or sections of pipe, explosive powder from fireworks, and shrapnel.[42]

The FBI concluded that the brothers likely used the Internet to research bomb craft. The Tsarnaevs distinguished themselves by building four separate IED designs and used three types successfully, including pipe bombs and CO_2 "cricket" grenades.[43]

In another tragic incident, Chicago-born Syed Rizwan Farook, a devout Sunni Muslim, and his wife, Pakistani-born Tashfeen Malik (who grew up in Saudi Arabia), gunned down 14 people in San Bernardino, California. The FBI said that the shooters, who declared allegiance to ISIS on Facebook before their workplace attack, were radicalized through the Internet.[44] Farook had a profile on the dating website iMilap.com, in which he listed backyard target practice as a hobby, and met his wife over the Internet. The shooting was considered one of the deadliest terrorist attacks to occur in the United States since the 9/11 attacks. Malik was one of a small number of female mass shooters in the United States; women constituted only 3.75 percent of active shooters in the United States from 2000 to 2013. Interestingly, a dispute ensued between the FBI and Apple, relying on its security policy, until finally the couple's iPhone was eventually unlocked.

On June 12, 2016, in another mass murder that triggered tremendous public outrage, Omar Matten, a 29-year-old New York–born American citizen of Afghani parents, opened fire at the Pulse gay nightclub in Orlando, Florida, murdering 49 people. President Obama said the murders were "inspired" by violent extremist propaganda on the Internet. Obama acknowledged that while the United States continues to go after ISIS abroad by targeting the leadership and infrastructure, "one of the biggest challenges" is to combat ISIS's propaganda "and the perversions of Islam" generated on the Internet.[45] Shockingly, Matten had been investigated for connections to terrorism by the FBI in 2013 and 2014 and placed on the Terrorist Screening Database, but subsequently he was removed.

Ahmad Kahn Rahimi, a 28-year-old Afghan immigrant naturalized as an American citizen, planted bombs in the heart of Manhattan and in New Jersey. The bomb that exploded in Manhattan's Chelsea neighborhood injured over 30 people. Earlier that day, another improvised explosive device, also planted by Rahimi, detonated in the vicinity of Seaside Park, New Jersey.[46] Authorities arrested five people in connection with the Chelsea bombing along with their counterparts in New Jersey.[47] Investigators determined that Rahimi was not part of a terrorist cell, but was motivated and inspired by the ideas of Anwar al-Awlaki, a U.S.-born leading propagandist and recruiter for Al Qaeda who was killed in a U.S. drone strike in September 2011.[48] The criminal complaint filed against Rahimi stated that he had a YouTube account listing two jihadist propaganda videos as "favorites."

Students regularly use the Internet, making them vulnerable to terrorists through this means, or able to use it to the advantage of their terrorist intent. A student at Ohio State University intentionally rammed a car into pedestrians on a busy campus sidewalk and then began slashing passers-by with a butcher knife, injuring 11 students, faculty, and staff members, and setting off panic at one of the nation's largest public universities. A university police officer fatally shot him.[49] Although in this case there was no clear connection between the attacker and ISIS or any other terrorist group, ISIS claimed that Abdulrazzaq Artan was as one of its soldiers. ISIS loosely uses the term "soldier" to describe those who have no formal connection with the group, but have been radicalized through the Internet where their ideology inspires some to attack civilians in the west.

Sadly, ISIS and Al Qaeda can remain with us for a long time, and new terrorist groups that may be even more brutal and extreme can surface. Whether the group is old or new, it will use the Internet to disseminate extremist ideology and to convince people, especially vulnerable youth, in the West to continue the attacks. My proposed strategy to counter terrorism addresses how to face and defuse Internet tools in a later chapter.

The next chapter addresses "lone wolf" terrorism, perpetrated by young or vulnerable people who are tempted through the Internet. The number of "lone wolf" terrorists is increasing, and the dangerous acts they commit are becoming more frequent.

CHAPTER 6

Lone Wolf Terrorists

This chapter addresses the emergence of "lone wolf" terrorists, whose numbers are on the rise in Western democracies, and who are more dangerous because they are more difficult to detect than cells directly connected to terrorist groups and organizations. They are also free to decide what to do, as well as where and when to do it. Initially, lone wolves were considered by many officials and terrorism experts to be less lethal than cells and clusters of terrorist groups. The belief was that they did not have the ability to plan devastating attacks and lacked the experience to fight.

However, that misconception was altered after attacks by lone wolves in Europe and the United States during 2015, 2016, and the first half of 2017. These attacks demonstrated that lone wolves could be lethal, plan horrific attacks, and cause large numbers of causalities. It also showed that these individuals can follow recipes on the Internet to produce explosives from basic material to assemble powerful homemade bombs, plan devastating attacks, and carry them out. Lone wolf attacks revealed that terrorist organizations are capable of recruiting and inspiring vulnerable people to accept their ideology and to justify injuring and killing innocent people.

Governments sometimes use the point that lone wolves act individually and alone to downplay the capabilities of terrorist groups to act in their countries. But, I believe that the facts point to the contrary, that a lone wolf attack is an indication that terrorist organizations have managed to achieve their evil goals by inspiring and recruiting lone wolf actors using their warped ideology to justify killing other people.

The number of lone wolf attacks has spiked in recent years, unlike huge terrorist assaults, like those on September 11, 2001, which seem to have decreased. After 9/11, the United Sates established an enormous homeland-security apparatus. Sharing intelligence with other nations has foiled a number of terrorist plots, so has an effort to overcome the American tradition of federalism and to coordinate federal, state, and local law-enforcement information.[1]

THE TERM "LONE WOLF"

As with most terminology used in the war against terrorism, the term "lone wolf" needs to be clearly defined. We must determine if a lone wolf is an individual with no connection to terror groups, or if the "lone wolf" is connected through the ideology but not necessarily by organizational connection. A definition of lone wolf terrorism must be extended to include individuals who are inspired by a certain group but who are not under the orders of any other person, group, or network. They might be members of a network, but this network is not a hierarchical organization in the classical sense of the word.[2]

Fred Burton and Scott Stewart of Stratfor intelligence think tank, define a lone wolf as "a person who acts on his or her own without orders from—or even connections to—an organization." They stress the difference between lone wolves and sleeper cells, arguing that sleepers are operatives who infiltrate the targeted society or organization and then remain hidden until a group or organization orders them to take action.[3]

Washington Post columnist Charles Krauthammer said there are two kinds of lone wolves: the crazy and the evil. Perhaps the most dangerous terrorists are actually rational. Major Nidal Hasan, the Fort Hood shooter, can be seen as one example. Hasan—who had a business card listing his occupation as "S of A," standing for "Soldier of Allah" and shouted "Allahu Akbar" as he shot dead 13 fellow soldiers—sits in jail after being sentenced to death, but to this day, speaks coherently and proudly of the massacre.[4]

In contrast, Haron Monis, who was responsible for a hostage-taking attack in Sydney, Australia, was a marginal, alienated Iranian immigrant with psychopathologies. Described by his own lawyer as "unhinged," Monis grew increasingly paranoid. His religiosity was both fanatical and confused. A Shiite converted to Sunni Islam, his Internet postings showed the zeal of the convert but also reportedly a remarkable ignorance of Islam and Islamism.[5]

For people like Monis, the terrorist group provides not just an ideology, motive, and plan to act, but a chance for a lonely and disturbed individual to belong and to become a "hero" whose actions become well-known in the world through media coverage.

Jeffrey Simon, a visiting lecturer in the Department of Political Science at UCLA and author of *Lone Wolf Terrorism: Understanding the Growing Threat*, said, "Basically the lone wolf is an individual—or it even could be two individuals—working alone without any significant outside logistical or financial support given to them. They are basically working by themselves."[6]

TV host Greg Gutfeld of Fox News argued against calling these individual terrorists lone wolves. He said that a lone wolf is not only an inaccurate description; it is also a harmful one because it sounds "cool." He added that these fiends are not lone wolves because that term suggests independent thinking; but rather they are simply bitter sheep in the grip of a death cult. Calling them lone wolves untethers their acts from the murderous ideology behind it, making it increasingly difficult to identify evil as it grows. If you deny the link, you are less likely to catch it early on and crush it.[7]

The U.S. government associated the term "lone wolf" with the terrorist attacks that took place during 2015–2016 in California, Florida, New Jersey, New York, and Ohio. This association can be seen as misleading, as it implies falsely that terrorist groups such as ISIS could not infiltrate the country and send their terrorists to America, like they did in France, Belgium, and Germany. In fact, although some supposed lone wolf terrorists were not directly connected to ISIS, they are in fact connected, indirectly, because they were radicalized and inspired to attack by ISIS.

CALLS FOR LONE WOLF ATTACKS

The lone wolf attacks carried out in recent years were inspired by extreme Salafi-jihadi groups. The idea of support for small-scale, loosely organized terrorist attacks can hardly be called new. Terrorist groups such as Al Qaeda and ISIS have long called for lone wolf attacks in Europe, the United States, Canada, and Australia. In 2003, an article was published on the extremist Internet forum, *Sada al Jihad* (Echo of Jihad), in which Osama bin Laden sympathizers were encouraged to take action without waiting for instructions.[8]

Abu Musab al-Suri, once an ally and internal critic of bin Laden, released a 1,500-page *Call for Global Islamic Revolution* on the Internet, spreading this concept all over the world, and referring to the concept as "nizam la tanzim," or "a system not an organization."[9] Al Qaeda leader Abu Jihad al-Masri followed suit with a call to arms entitled "How to Fight Alone" circulated widely in jihadist networks.[10]

Al Qaeda's media arm As-Sahab released a videotape praising the Fort Hood, Texas, shooter, Major Nidal Hasan, who shot dead 13 fellow soldiers, calling him an "ideal role model" whose solitary action should be emulated by other jihadists in America. Another video urged Muslims in America to take advantage of lax firearm laws to purchase guns and carry out attacks on their own initiative.[11] Abu Muhammad al-Adnani, an ISIS spokesman, who was killed in August 2016, called for sympathizers of the terrorist group throughout the world to respond to Western aerial bombardment by attacking any citizen of any country that participated in air strikes against ISIS. In fact, ISIS encourages supporters to commit attacks on their own.[12]

In June 2016, Al-Adnani called for attacks during the lunar month of Ramadan, when Muslims fast for a month similar to Lent for Christians, claiming this is an especially honored time to take action. Only a small percentage of people to take the bait is needed for ISIS to be effective in spreading terror. Even if only a small number of lone ISIS terrorists express certain things openly or on the Internet, they reach masses in the United States and the Western world, where people have freedom to express themselves publicly in an open democracy.[13]

Lone wolf attacks are changing aspects of international terrorism and forcing the world to change its thinking about terrorism. The world should not only focus on terrorist organizations and watch actions of their members but should also shift the focus to the lone wolf paradigm, which may be more dangerous and is much harder to detect. Lone wolves must become known wolves.

As I noted in the previous chapter, modern technology played an important role in using lone wolves effectively. The Internet became the easiest and best way to radicalize people who live thousands of miles away, to provide instructions for making bombs, and to encourage them to carry out attacks on soft targets such as malls, clubs, and celebrations.

LONE WOLF ATTACKS IN THE UNITED STATES

During 2015 and 2016, the United States witnessed several lone wolf attacks in California, Florida, Minnesota, New Jersey, New York, and Ohio. Some suspicion exists that some lone wolf attacks may even be reported as workplace violence, to decrease public panic from thinking about a large number of terrorist attacks being carried out. However, lone wolf terrorist attacks are carried out at workplaces because terrorists have easy access to places where they work, and because it is not unusual to hold a party or a celebration in such places where large numbers of people gather who can be targets. An example is Major Hasan who opened fire on the Fort Hood military base where he used to work, and Syed Rizwan Farook and Tashfeen Malik, the married couple who targeted a Christmas party of about 80 employees at a place where one of them used to work.

The FBI called Alton Nolen's attack on two employees at the Vaughan Foods food-processing plant in Moore, Oklahoma—where one woman was beheaded with a knife—a case of workplace violence. Nolen had recently been suspended from his job at the plant. But in fact, prosecutors noted that Nolen had demonstrated an "infatuation" with beheadings, and the case came to national attention due to its gruesome nature and its timing coincident with well-publicized beheadings carried out by ISIS. Nolen's Facebook page contained a picture of him giving the ISIS salute, multiple pictures of Osama bin Laden, and a screenshot of the 9/11 attacks on the World Trade Center and the Pentagon.[14]

Daniel Byman, a researcher at the Center for Middle East Policy at the Brookings Institute, noted that the attack in San Bernardino, California, at a County Health Department where the attacker was employed, might have been considered workplace violence had the husband and wife perpetrators not made a last-minute pledge to the Islamic State on Facebook.[15]

The Obama administration has treated "lone wolf" terrorist attacks inside the United States as though they were non-terrorist crimes.[16] But the connections are hard to overlook, as in another military base–related crime, where Mohammod Youssuf Abdulazeez, a 24-year-old Kuwaiti-born man, opened fire on a military recruiting station, then raced to a second military site where he killed four U.S. Marines, prompting a federal domestic terrorism investigation. Three other people, including a Marine Corps recruiter and a police officer, were wounded, according to law enforcement officials.[17]

Public places are common sites for attacks. That point is clear from the case of Omar Mateen, the 29-year-old security guard who opened fire inside the Pulse nightclub in Orlando, Florida. In another case, Ahmad Khan Rahimi tried to detonate four bombs on streets in New York and New Jersey. Mohamoud Mohamed went on a knife rampage at a Minnesota mall, injuring nine people, and Abdulrazzaq Artan attacked innocent people at Ohio State University with a knife, injuring 11 students, faculty, and staff members.

STOPPING LONE WOLVES

It is more difficult for intelligence agencies to detect lone wolves. They are more difficult to identify and capture because they do not communicate with each other and they do not need to contact the leaders of any terrorist groups, because they act alone. According to reporters Jay Weaver and David Ovalle, in a lone wolf attack, there are usually no complicated plots for agents to uncover, and no communications chatter to provide clues of what might be coming. Instead of large-scale attacks on landmark targets, there are now mass shootings by one person or a few acting together. The perpetrators commit the crime in a short amount of time, without long preparation that could be uncovered. By the time the act is in motion, it is too late to prevent, or stop, them.[18]

Lone wolves are a challenge for intelligence agencies and the FBI because typically they are local and their activities are local. Some of them manage to slip through the cracks by taking advantage of the shortfalls and gaps of the homeland security apparatus. For all these reasons, I predict that lone wolf attacks will be an increasing trend, and we will see more of them in the future.

Compared to group terrorism or network-sponsored terrorists, lone operators have a critical advantage in avoiding identification and detection, since most of them do not communicate with others with regard to their intentions. Some experts believe lone wolves might be disadvantaged because they lack the means, skills, and "professional" support of terrorist groups, yet some of them nonetheless have proven to be very lethal.[19]

When an individual travels to Syria to fight or is in contact with ISIS handlers, U.S. intelligence agencies can pick up on the communication and interaction. And by going abroad to fight for a terrorist group, an individual is committing a crime and can be arrested. Lone wolves, by definition, lack such links.[20] After the shooting of Omar Mateen in Orlando, President Obama said, "it is increasingly clear" that the killer, a U.S. citizen, became "radicalized" by "extremist information and propaganda over the internet"—noting that such lone wolf attacks are "the hardest to detect."[21]

Lone wolves can be more dangerous than classic terrorists when they are creative and innovative. Since these lone wolves work alone, they do not have instructions from any organization or leader that could slow the actions of enthusiastic and reckless young people. A terrorist organization may prefer formulating plans, operations, and attacks that might squash and discourage the creativity and impulsivity that characterize the lone wolf.

Terrorist expert Jeffery D. Simon, who runs a security and terrorism research consulting company, argues that lone wolves are free to think up different scenarios and then to try to act upon them. Because they are not part of a group, lone wolves, unlike other terror groups, are not concerned about potential government and law-enforcement crackdowns following an incident that could lead to the virtual elimination of the group through arrests and other measures.[22]

Some experts argue that a lone wolf approach is bound for failure. Lone wolves may kill, but they do not win notoriety or status in some group cause. Because lone wolves like Omar Mateen are not usually trained, they often fail in their objectives, and even if they succeed, they are less lethal than "professional" terrorists. Daniel L. Byman, a senior fellow at the Center for Middle East Policy in the Brookings Institute, made a sharp distinction between the attacks in Paris, Madrid, and London where Al Qaeda- or ISIS-linked attackers worked together to bomb and shoot victims, and the individual-generated attacks in Orlando, San Bernardino, and Fort Hood, according to the locations and circumstances in which these attacks took place. Additionally, following 9/11, professional, organized attacks were easier to organize in Europe than attempting similar attacks in the United States.[23] Circumstances became different over the years from 2001 to 2014 after ISIS's rise. After 9/11, it became more difficult to plan a large-scale organized attack without being detected by intelligence agencies, especially in the United States. This was the reason ISIS called for lone wolf attacks.

The lone wolf was traditionally really a loner. But now, by pledging allegiance to ISIS, lone wolves feel they are carrying out the work of a particular group, even if they have never met with the leaders or members. This arrangement seems perfect for the group, as well, that gets the publicity and the gruesome rewards for the act without any risks or spending any money.[24]

MOTIVES BEHIND LONE WOLVES

Different motives drive different people. Some lone wolves would like to join a terrorist group but are prevented from doing so perhaps because of security scrutiny, especially in the United States. Other lone wolves may have personal problems such as social, financial, and psychological problems, or suffer from substance abuse, like drug addiction and alcoholism. Like their organized brethren, they convince themselves that they can change their future by conducting holy war (jihad) against disbelievers, infidels, and apostates. Some lone wolves in the West blame society for their situation, claiming that society is responsible for their bad behavior, which may include using drugs or committing petty crimes. These are motivated by a desire for revenge, or are driven to punish the society they believe encouraged them to be criminals.

An analysis of the background of dozens of young men who have embraced militant ideology and who have planned or carried out acts of violence shows that many have had a troubled upbringing. Although some come from comfortable backgrounds, they get involved with drugs and petty crime in their late teens or early 20s, and often cut off contact with their families. Some fall under the influence of radical preachers, and others become radicalized online.[25]

Many lone wolves might have had trouble trying to get into a group, but acting alone, they do not have to try, since using the Internet and social media allows them to feel part of a group anyway, through virtual reality.[26] Syed Rizwan Farook's attack in San Bernadino was partly tied to personal problems in work. Omar Mateen, who attacked the gay club, was homophobic; his father claimed that Mateen became upset when he saw two men kissing. ISIS claims to despise gays, but it desecrates many others, including Christians, Jews, Westerners in general, Shiite and other Muslim minorities, and Sunni Muslims who do not agree with it.[27] For many so-called lone wolves like Mateen, their "very strong personal agendas" intersect with Islamist extremist ideology trumpeted by social media. Acting alone, but still identifying with, or having loose ties to, a brand—like ISIS—as well as an organization that has power, makes the lone wolf feel bigger and more important.[28]

Reporter Isaac Chotinerm of *Slate* believes many lone wolves have personal issues, may be mentally unstable, and may have financial problems, leading them to latch on to an ideology to justify their actions. Their terrorist acts are both a personal grievance and a self-identification with a cause.[29] Journalists Jay Weaver and David Ovalle described a lone wolf as someone beset by some mix of mental and personal issues, who "self-radicalizes," proclaiming an affinity for militant extremists but acting on their ideology alone given easily accessible high-powered weapons.[30]

Interpretation of the motives of lone wolves to attack is not accurately solely individual in all cases. For example, Syed Rizwan's wife, and Omar Mateen, in separate lone wolf terrorist incidents, announced allegiance to ISIS. Some lone wolves can be motivated by ideology, and respond to calls by ISIS to attack for some reason, for example, in retaliation for U.S. air strikes against what they consider a pure Islamic State "caliphate"— which as I have said, is neither Islamic nor a state.

Tim Lister of CNN correctly noted that some lone wolves are motivated by the misleading ideology of extreme and terrorist groups, the Salafi-jihadi ideology. They may see radical ideology as a form of redemption for past misdeeds. Or their terrorist act may feed an existing animosity toward authority and a resentful sense of being "on the outside." Or they blame "kuffar" (nonbeliever) societies for corrupting them in the first place.[31]

LONE WOLVES AND THE INTERNET

Modern technology, especially the Internet and social networks, plays an important role in the rise of lone wolves, even though they existed before the Internet was invented. Social networks and the Internet make it easier for lone wolves to learn how to commit terrorist attacks, including how to make homemade bombs and other weapons.

An example of a lone wolf who used the Internet was American citizen Colleen LaRose, known as "Jihad Jane." She was attracted to the global reach of the Internet and hoped it would aid her in forming a terrorist network in 2008 and 2009 for high-profile attacks in Europe and South Asia. LaRose, who once tried to commit suicide after family deaths, was an American citizen convicted and sentenced to 10 years for terrorism-related crimes, including trying to recruit terrorists and solicit funds over the Internet to wage violent jihad and plotting to murder the Swedish artist Lars Vilks, who had drawn a cartoon of Prophet Mohammed. LaRose read Muslim websites, was fixated with YouTube videos of attacks on Muslims, and signed up at a Muslim dating site. ISIS perfected using the Internet, so when a lone wolf pledges allegiance to ISIS, ISIS gets their desired global publicity. And, when a lone wolf attacks, ISIS can claim that an ISIS fighter or one of its soldiers perpetrated the attack.[32]

One shocking example of a terrorist using Internet and social media network is the following.

On June 14, 2016, a lone wolf stabbed an off-duty police officer in Magnanville, about 35 miles from Paris, and left him bleeding to death on his own doorstep. He forced his way inside the home where he stabbed and killed the officer's female companion. He then sat down and videotaped himself live on Facebook declaring allegiance to the ISIS. Sitting just behind him was the couple's son, a terrified 3-year-old boy.

Larossi Abballa's Facebook post made clear that he wanted to terrify and destroy those he deemed "unbelievers," people he had come to hate. He also wanted to encourage other lone wolves to do the same. "It's super simple," he said, looking into the camera. "It's enough to wait for them in front of their offices; don't give them any break. Know this, whether you are a policeman or a journalist, you will never feel calm again. One will wait for you in front of your homes. This is what you have earned." Boasting that he had "just killed a policeman and I just killed his wife," he called on fellow believers to give priority to killing "police, prison guards, journalists." He specifically named several writers and journalists, adding rappers to the list because, he said, they "are the allies of Satan."[33]

The Internet has allowed individuals to build a sense of collective identity, even without formal connections to terrorist movements. Online representatives of extremist movements exhort sympathizers to operate on their own initiative, without direction from a formal organization.[34] The Internet is a game-changer for lone wolves, providing opportunities for them to learn about terrorist tactics and targets and to become radicalized by reading ideological web pages, tweets, and blogs. On the other hand, it can be helpful to authorities, providing them with a way to learn about lone wolves since they like to "talk" using the Internet. Many lone wolves blog or send out messages before an attack.[35]

What makes ISIS more successful than Al Qaeda in inspiring lone wolves and other terrorist groups is their ability to use the Internet and social media effectively. They use the Internet to send strong messages and attractive videos to attract lone wolves. In addition, ISIS's 2014 announcement to establish an Islamic State "caliphate" fulfilled the dreams of a large number of extremist Muslims of returning to the golden age of caliphs, even though some caliphs were corrupted leaders and implemented a misleading version of Islam.

Terrorist groups inspire and influence because of their prestige, which depends on their successes, which is measured in growing power, territorial conquest, and persuasive propaganda. As such, more terrorists now identify with ISIS, flying the flag of the Islamic State, than with Al Qaeda.[36] After the attack when Omar Mateen killed 49 people and wounded 53 others inside the Pulse nightclub in Orlando, Florida, then-FBI director James Comey said that there were strong indications that Mateen "was inspired by foreign terrorist groups," besides being partly "radicalized" individually over the Internet.[37]

Charles Krauthammer wrote in the *Washington Post* that lone wolves are limited in what they can carry out. They are too disorganized to do more than localized, small-scale damage. The larger danger is someone with mental faculties intact and purpose unwavering. Krauthammer said the still-greater threat is organized terror, such as the Taliban's attack on a school in Peshawar that killed at least 148 people, mostly children; that is evil in its purest form.[38] Personally, I object to comparing the attack of lone wolves with the Taliban's attack on a school in Peshawar. In Peshawar, Pakistan, there are many supporters and sympathizers of terrorist groups such as al-Taliban and Al Qaeda; because of that, it becomes easy for terrorist groups to get access to weapons, and then plan and execute an attack.

Obviously, it is much more difficult now for a terrorist group to plan and execute similar attacks in the United States, given precautions and security measures put in place after the 9/11 attacks. Thus, the attacks by lone wolves like Omar Mateen served the terrorist groups more than an attack in Pakistan, particularly for media purposes and propaganda campaigns, to show that they can reach out to people in the United States.

Given the dangers that lone wolves present, my proposed strategy includes ways to stop these violent characters and is outlined in a chapter in part II of this book. The following chapter describes how foreign fighters contribute to terrorist scourge.

CHAPTER 7

Terrorist Groups Attract Foreign Fighters

Besides lone wolves described in the previous chapter, another danger, and rising group of terrorists, is foreign fighters, which I address in this chapter. A "foreign fighter" is someone who travels to a foreign country to fight for a cause. This is a term that applies way back in history to the Crusades. When foreign fighters from all over the world join extremist groups, they present a very serious danger to the safety of civilians everywhere, especially in the United States and Europe. They are a very real threat to international peace and security. Foreign fighters and their networks pose both an immediate and a long-term threat and have become an urgent global security problem. Globalization has made international travel very accessible, and this creates opportunities for terrorists to move around the world to target hotels, public spaces, and venues.[1]

Militants from around the world have been drawn to Iraq and Syria after 2011 in much greater numbers than they were to the fighting in Afghanistan in the 1980s and post 9/11, as well as in the Balkans in the 1990s, in Iraq after 2003, or to the conflicts in Somalia or Yemen. Experts said in all of these cases, radical ideologues appealed to Sunni Salafi-jihadi Muslims to mobilize and join a jihad (holy war) in defense of fellow Sunni Muslims who were allegedly threatened by Shiites, non-Muslims, or by secular dictatorships.[2]

AL QAEDA ATTRACTS FOREIGN FIGHTERS

The phenomenon of extremist groups attracting foreign fighters is not new even in modern times. After the Soviet invasion of Afghanistan in 1979, thousands of foreign fighters traveled to Afghanistan to join Al Qaeda and its leader Osama bin Laden, to fight against the invaders. As the instigator of global jihad, Al Qaeda became a brand unlike any other terrorist organization in history. From Saddam's invasion of Kuwait in 1990, until Special Forces killed bin Laden on May 2, 2011, Al Qaeda attracted significant numbers of foreign fighters. Hundreds of young Westerners joined rebel forces affiliated with Al Qaeda and other militant groups, often doing turns in more than one battleground nation.[3]

After the U.S. military intervention and occupation of Iraq, foreign fighters traveled to Iraq and joined Al Qaeda and insurgency groups to fight American forces and the new Iraqi government. They killed civilians to cause chaos, instability, and insecurity. Many of the foreign fighters joined Abu Musaab al-Zarqawi's group Al Qaeda in Iraq (AQI). After the U.S. forces killed al-Zarqawi in June 2006, his group AQI evolved to become the Islamic State in Iraq (ISI), then the Islamic State in Iraq and Syria (ISIS) or Islamic State in Iraq and Levant (ISIL), and then the Islamic State (IS). During the Syrian civil war, started in 2011, many foreign fighters joined terrorist groups in Syria such as ISIS and Al-Nusra Front, which is affiliated with Al Qaeda. Many of these foreign fighters died in the conflict, some of those from the Gulf Arab states, Tunisia, Libya, Bosnia, China, Russia's Chechnya and North Caucasus region, as well as Europe, the United States, Canada, and Australia.

The phenomenon causes concerns in home countries of foreign fighters, not only because of potential attacks on home turf but also because some of these countries are being used as transit countries or as a departure base for fighters. The size and widespread origins of the fighters in this case is unprecedented. Between 2003 and 2011, terrorist and insurgent groups established sophisticated networks in Syria to facilitate the movement of foreign fighters into Iraq. These networks are worth closer scrutiny since foreign fighters, facilitated through Syria, have been responsible for some of the most devastating attacks on Iraqis and coalition forces.[4]

ISIS ATTRACTS MORE FOREIGN FIGHTERS

After declaring his Islamic State based on Sharia law "caliphate," ISIS's leader Abu Bakr al-Baghdadi in his first speech as a caliph (Islamic leader), shared his new direction, calling on Muslims everywhere to make immigration (*hijra*) "to the land of Islam" as a religious obligation. He said, "We make a special call to the religious scholars, and preachers, especially the judges, as well as people with military, administrative, and service expertise, medical doctors and engineers of all different specializations and fields."[5]

ISIS was more successful than any other terrorist group in attracting foreign fighters from all over the world. There were many factors that added to the attraction; one is establishing an Islamic State (caliphate) in Iraq and Syria and declaring ISIS's leader as a caliph (leader) for all Muslims in the world. The caliphate represents the golden age of Islam for the majority of Sunni Muslims, the successor leadership after the death of Prophet Mohammed, and a lost heritage of an era of Islamic history that ended when the Ottoman Empire's caliphate collapsed because it sided with Germany during World War I. For the Shiites however, the caliphate does not represent the proper line of succession in Islam as they believe that Prophet Mohammed appointed 12 leaders after him from his progeny, called *imams*.

ISIS also attracted a large number of foreign fighters and was successful in launching a propaganda campaign, through statements and videos and exploiting the Internet and social media networks. Sunni Salafi-jihadi extremists believed that ISIS brought them back the dream of living in an Islamic State under Sharia law.

ISIS had avoided the Al Qaeda model of attracting fighters first and radicalizing them later. With its media mix of graphic violence and attractive ideals, ISIS sought recruits and supporters who were further down the path toward ideological radicalization. Once these partially radicalized fighters and their families arrived in Iraq and Syria, they were exposed to an environment boiling with traumatic stress, sexual violence, slavery, genocide, death, and mutilation as public sights.[6]

Some of the foreign fighters were instructed to go back to their home countries to conduct ISIS-related operations there. Countries like Turkey and Saudi Arabia who opposed the Assad's regime in Syria have an interest in supporting the Syrian rebels, so experts believe Turkey allowed a free flow of foreign fighters from all over the world to enter the country and then cross its borders into Syria.[7]

Most foreign fighters join terrorist groups in Syria, including ISIS, Al-Nusra Front, and to a much lesser extent, other extreme Salafi groups like Ahrar al-Sham. There are also front groups and affiliates of ISIS and Al-Nusra Front, including the Muhajirin wa-Ansar Army, the Suqour al-Ezz Battalions, the Sham al-Islam Movement, the Green Battalion, the Umma Brigade, and Jund al-Sham.[8] International attention given to foreign fighters within the ranks of ISIS is largely focused on militants from Europe and the United States. These Western fighters have had a high media profile, especially since the beheading of U.S. and British hostages by a British terrorist.[9]

In October 2014, top U.S. and British counterterrorism officials said that the growing number and variety of foreign fighters streaming into Syria is unprecedented in recent history. The rate of travel into Syria by foreign fighters is greater than that of Afghanistan, Yemen, Somalia, and Iraq. Law enforcement sources said that several law cases working their way through the system in various jurisdictions include American citizens who have actually made their way to Syria.[10]

Although many Westerners have gone to Syria to fight with groups like Al-Nusra and Ahrar ash-Sham, the success of ISIS and the establishment of the caliphate drew fighters away from those groups to ISIS, according to U.S. intelligence officials. At least three Americans who went to Syria to join those groups were later killed while fighting on behalf of ISIS.[11]

NUMBERS OF FOREIGN FIGHTERS WITH ISIS

ISIS attracted the largest number of foreign fighters in the history of terrorism. Thousands of foreigners from Europe and hundreds from the United States, Canada, and Australia traveled to Syria to join the caliphate. There were many others who were turned back or arrested on their way to Syria or who failed to make it there.

As usual, when data is incomplete, the authorities must guess. The number of ISIS's foreign fighters was underestimated by officials and intelligence agencies in the United States, Europe, and regional countries including Iraqi officials. Iraq's Foreign Minister Ibrahim Al-Jafari mistakenly claimed in my presence, in a meeting held on September 2014 in New York, on the margins of the United Nations General Assembly, that ISIS members who took control of Mosul, the second largest city in Iraq, were only 400–500 fighters. The total number of ISIS fighters was also underestimated. In 2013, Aaron Y. Zelin of the Washington Institute proposed a conservative estimate of the Sunni Arab rebels fighting in Syria, identifying the number of foreigner fighters as 5,000 individuals, while a more liberal estimate could be around 10,000.[12]

I am going to go through the estimates in a time line to show you how the numbers stack up. In August 2014, the United Kingdom estimated to reporters that 500 British citizens were affiliated with ISIS in Syria and Iraq. French- and German-speaking fighters have also been observed in large numbers on social media, and low-end estimates point to more than 550 fighters from Germany and more than 1,000 from France. Significant numbers of Canadian fighters have also made their presence known on social media.

In September 2014, the New York-based Soufan Group and the London-based International Centre for the Study of Radicalization suggested that the total number of foreign fighters in Syria is between 11,000 and 12,000, with only about 3,000 of them from the West. Of the remainder, Tunisians make up the largest group, estimated at about 3,000, followed by those from Saudi Arabia, estimated at about 2,500, and Morocco, estimated at about 1,500.[13]

At the same time, French Interior Minister Bernard Cazeneuve said in an interview published in *Le Journal du Dimanche* that 930 French or French residents are in Syria and Iraq, preparing to go, or en route. He said 36 have been killed.[14] The *New York Times* reported the U.S. intelligence officials estimate that 15,000 citizens from 80 countries were with ISIS in Iraq and Syria. They include more than 2,000 Europeans and 100 Americans, all presumably with passports that would permit them to return to their home countries to carry out lethal attacks.[15] Randy Blake, a senior adviser in the U.S. Office of Director of National Intelligence said that "there are about 16,000 foreign fighters who have traveled to Syria from over 80 countries," and that roughly 2,000 of those fighters hail from Western countries including "at least 500 from the United Kingdom, 700 from France, 400 from Germany, and more than 100 Americans who have traveled, or tried to travel into Syria."[16]

In February 2015, U.S. intelligence officials said foreign fighters are flocking to Syria at an "unprecedented" rate. The foreign fighters traveled to Syria from more than 90 countries, including at least 3,400 from Western states and more than 150 Americans. The estimate of the total number of foreign fighters flocking to Syria was up from a previous estimate in January of roughly 19,000.[17]

In the next month, Nicholas Rasmussen, the Director of the National Counterterrorism Center in Washington, D.C., stated that so far nearly 20,000 foreigners, including about 3,400 Westerners, have joined the Islamic State in Iraq and Syria. The majority of them have traveled through Turkey, underscoring, Western officials said, both the difficulty of patrolling a porous border and a degree of ambivalence among Turkish officials who do not see ISIS as a primary enemy.[18]

By December 2015, the French press agency, AFP, reported that the number of foreign fighters in Iraq and Syria had more than doubled between 2014 and 2015 to at least 27,000. Around 5,000 made their way from Europe, with a further 4,700 from former Soviet republics.[19] In January 2016, a study for the Heritage Foundation said ISIS has been able to attract more than 25,000 fighters from outside ISIS's territory to join its ranks in Iraq and Syria. These foreign fighters include over 4,500 citizens from Western nations, including around 250 U.S. citizens who have either traveled to the Middle East to fight with extremist organizations or attempted to do so.[20] In 2017 a UN official at the Counter Terrorism Committee Executive Directorate (CTED) said the number of foreign fighters who joined ISIS was estimated between 30 and 38 thousand.

By April 2016, then-FBI Director James Comey said that the number of people attempting to leave the United States to join ISIS has been down for the last nine months. Comey said there are a few reasons in addition to the group's battlefield losses. The aura and fashion that came with the group has faded, prison sentences for supporters are piling up, and people are realizing how hellish it is to live in the ISIS territory.[21] In September 2016, the *Washington Post* reported that according to U.S. intelligence officials, from a peak of 2,000 foreign recruits crossing the Turkey–Syria border each month, ISIS and other extremist groups operating in Syria are down to as few as 50. Governments from Britain to Tunisia say their citizens are less likely than they have been in years to heed ISIS's calls for front-line volunteers.[22]

The West realized the real danger of foreign fighters with ISIS after the attacks of Paris in November 2015, which resulted in the killing of around 130 people, and the Brussels attacks in March 2016 in which more than 30 people were killed and more than 200 wounded. U.S. and European intelligence agencies should have been able to calculate the danger inherent in the process that allowed foreign fighters to travel to Syria, join ISIS, and fight against the Bashar Al-Asad's regime. In my view, they should have implemented faster and stronger measures to stop the flood of foreign fighters. Clearly, foreign fighters constitute a serious threat.

WHERE DO FOREIGN FIGHTERS COME FROM?

The majority of foreign fighters with ISIS come from the Arab world, with Tunisia, Saudi Arabia, and Morocco, in the lead, although the number of Iraqis may be higher than is publicly known. The second largest group is Western Europeans, especially from the United Kingdom, France, Belgium, and the Netherlands. Additionally, there are some from the Balkans, the Caucasus, and other places. There are foreign fighters from more than 60 countries.[23]

In August 2014, ISIS marked Eid al-Fitr, the end of Ramadan, with a 20-minute, high-definition video offering its greetings to the Muslim world. Nice images of smiling worshippers embracing at a mosque and children passing out sweets to break the Ramadan fast were shown. These scenes were interspersed with shots of the *muhajireen* (Arabic for "emigrants")—British, Finnish, Indonesian, Moroccan, Belgian, American, and South African—each repeating a variation on the same message.[24] "I'm calling on all the Muslims living in the West, America, Europe, and everywhere else, to come, to make immigration (*hijra*) with your families to the land of Khilafah [Caliphate]," said a Finnish fighter of Somali descent. "Here, you go for fighting and afterwards you come back to your families. And if you get killed, then . . . you'll enter heaven, and Allah will take care of those you've left behind."[25]

Between June 2014 and December 2016, the stream of fighters from Western Europe, had doubled to approximately 5,000. Three-quarters of Western European fighters came from just four countries: France, the United Kingdom, Germany, and Belgium, each of which contains a handful of isolated hotbed communities that have contributed disproportionately high rates of fighters. The Molenbeek neighborhood of Brussels, from which several of the Paris attackers came, is perhaps the best known.[26]

In July 2014, ISIS's Al Hayat Media Center released an 11-minute video, *The Chosen Few of Different Lands*, which drove this point home. A masterpiece of extremist propaganda, it showed a Canadian fighter named Andre Poulin, a white convert known to his comrades as Abu Muslim. The video opened with stunning high-definition stock footage of Canada as Poulin described his life back home. "I was a very good person, and you know, *mujahideen* are regular people too. . . . We have lives outside of our job. I was like your everyday regular Canadian before Islam," he said. "I had money, I had family. I had good friends."

The barbaric nature of ISIS can lead observers to conclude its adherents are simplistic, violent, and stupid. *The Chosen Few* displayed a keen self-awareness of this perception and actively argued against it, with Poulin as its telegenic exemplar. In reality, Poulin was not quite the model of social integration that he portrayed in the film. He developed an interest in explosives early and had dabbled in communism and anarchism before settling on radical Islam as an outlet for his interests. He had been arrested at least twice for threatening violence against a man whose wife he was sleeping with.[27]

According to The Soufan Group, the largest number of foreign fighters with ISIS came from Tunisia, Saudi Arabia, Turkey, and Jordan, each of which in the early days of Syria's uprising were accused of turning a blind eye as their nationals streamed into Syria to fight their regional rival, President Bashar al-Assad. To Soufan, this concentration underlines that ISIS, at its core, remains "essentially a local and regional phenomenon."[28]

MOTIVATIONS OF FOREIGN FIGHTERS

There is no single reason that makes a lone wolf carry out a terrorist attack and there is no single explanation for what drives a person to adopt extremism. It is a process driven by a complex mix of personal and environmental factors triggered by certain circumstances and events. Some of those fighting with ISIS are pragmatists. They are generally Syrians or Iraqis who joined the fight on behalf of ISIS for nonideological reasons, to get a salary, to advance tribal interests, or to fight a common enemy. This was the case when Iraqi Ba'athists and members of the remnants of Saddam Hussein's military and security organizations joined the fight. Motivation for foreign fighters could be amplified by extremist Salafi-jihadi ideology of living in the long dreamed of Islamic State of Caliphate. For others, it may be an escape from personal problems like a history of petty crimes, alcohol abuse, or drug addiction.

Lisa Curtis and seven other experts wrote a detailed study for the Heritage Foundation in which they said, "Former CIA case officer Patrick Skinner says that Foreign fighters are either the Psychopaths or Pious. Some Western recruits fall into the category of Psychopath. They are seeking adventure and violence, and they are used for violent propaganda and suicide missions. The Pious are drawn to join ISIS for religious reasons. These fighters believe they are fulfilling a religious obligation by undertaking a *hijra* (a religious migration) to the self-proclaimed caliphate."[29]

Andrew McCabe, assistant director in charge of the FBI's Washington field office said, "To me, the instant appeal of participating in the caliphate is compelling. Al Qaeda's message has historically been, 'This is a long war, we'll fight the Great Satan and we'll try and establish a caliphate sometime in the future.' ISIS has come forward. . . . The time is now, it's happening now. We have our own territory, come join us. And I think that's one of the reasons [ISIS] has such appeal for this at-risk population."[30]

Some foreign fighters believe they are fulfilling a religious obligation by undertaking a religious migration (*hijra*), but they also feel they are fulfilling another religious duty, which is jihad or holy war in the name of God against infidels and disbelievers. Ahmed Khan Rahimi who planted pressure cookers bombs in New Jersey on November 17 and in Manhattan on November 18, 2016, wrote in his notebook, "In my heart I pray to the beautiful wise ALLAH [God]," and added a plea, "To not take JIHAD away from me, I beg."[31]

Converts to Islam are usually brainwashed and misled by the extremist ideology of terror groups like ISIS. They believe that jihad in the name of God is the path to heaven and that jihad is the forgotten duty of Muslims. Converts and naïve Muslim youth are convinced that the best way to be a good Muslim and to repent for previous sins is to practice jihad.

John Horgan, the Director of the Center for Terrorism and Security Studies at the University of Massachusetts Lowell, who has studied the subject intensively, said, "With the emergence of large numbers of foreign fighters on social media, it became possible to gather more about their internal motivations, which frequently went beyond the promise of heaven and turned instead to the theme of adventure. One British fighter, 23-year-old Ifthekar Jaman, coined the phrase 'five-star jihad' to describe the fun he was having fighting in Syria." Jaman was killed in December 2013.[32]

Michael Pizzi, a reporter covering the Middle East, U.S. foreign policy, refugee crises, and Internet policy, states, "the decision to go abroad tends to come through interpersonal networks, hence, the alarmingly high concentration of recruits from certain 'hotbed' countries, cities, and towns. The use of social media prepares the ground for persuasion, rather than to force the decision. As hotbeds develop, recruitment through social media becomes less important than via direct human contact, as clusters of friends and neighbors persuade each other to travel separately or together to join [ISIS]."[33]

Another important motive for foreign fighters to immigrate to the caliphate and join ISIS to fight in Syria or Iraq is to have an opportunity for martyrdom. To be killed in a holy war (jihad) for the cause of God is a part of the ideology of extremist groups which they disseminate on the Internet. For foreign fighters, it is a win-win situation. They practice their duty to wage a holy war against disbelievers and achieve victory which is the best they can hope for, and if they are killed while doing it they will become martyrs and this is the best possible ending for their life they can hope for.

Michael Zehaf-Bibeau, a lone wolf terrorist, carried out an attack on Canadian soldier Nathan Cirillo and the Canadian Parliament on October 22, 2014. A Muslim convert, he embraced extremist ideas and intent to travel to Syria. Zehaf-Bibeau was also angry that Canada actually supported the American bombing of ISIS in Syria and Iraq, an indication of extremism.

Martin Couture-Rouleau, who ran down two Canadian Armed Forces personnel with his car, killing one of them on October 20, 2014, spent hours on the Internet and devoured jihadist literature, adding that he dreamed of dying as a martyr. The Commissioner of the Royal Canadian Mounted Police (RCMP), Bob Paulson, confirmed that Couture-Rouleau's passport had been seized and that he was one of 90 suspected extremists who the RCMP believed intended to join militants fighting abroad.[34]

William McCants and Christopher Meserole, both from the Brookings Institute, wrote in *Foreign Affairs* about a project to test many proposed explanations for "Sunni militancy" around the globe.

The goal was to take common measures of the violence, namely, the number of Sunni foreign fighters from any given country as well as the number of Sunni terror attacks carried out within it, and then crunch the numbers to see which explanations best predicted a country's rate of Sunni radicalization and violence. The best judge of foreign fighter radicalization was whether a country was Francophone; that is, whether it currently lists (or previously listed) French as a national language. As strange as it may seem, four of the five countries with the highest rates of radicalization in the world are Francophone, including the top two in Europe, France and Belgium.

So, what could the language of love possibly have to do with Islamist violence? Researchers suspect that it is really a proxy for something else: French political culture. The French approach to secularism is more aggressive than the British approach. France and Belgium, for example, are the only two countries in Europe to ban the full veil in their public schools. They're also the only two countries in Western Europe not to gain the highest rating for democracy in the well-known Polity score data, which does not include explanations for the markdowns.[35]

The French approach to secularism is aggressive. Banning the hijab in public schools and instituting a complete ban on veils that cover an individual's face served terrorists well. It helped spread the idea that the West is against Islam and has launched a war against Muslims and their beliefs. The slogans that were raised by terrorists who attacked *Charlie Hebdo* magazine in Paris in January 2015 and other terrorist acts reflect those ideas. The same sentiments of persecution surfaced when Donald Trump said we should ban Muslims from entering the United States. ISIS immediately used that in its propaganda and presented it as a proof that the West, and especially the United States, is against Islam and against Muslims.

CHARACTERISTICS OF FOREIGN FIGHTERS

Since foreign fighters came from different countries, it is important to address their characteristics as we highlighted their motivations. These characteristics could be helpful to authorities and counterterrorism intelligence agents. The age, nationality, and country of foreign fighters could provide indications of the type of person that could join a terrorist group or travel to fight in Syria and Iraq.

In this conflict zone, "foreign fighters run the range in terms of age," said John Adams, the FBI's Deputy Director for Counterterrorism. "We're currently age-ranged from minors of 15 years old, which is our youngest traveler, up to 63 years old, which has been our oldest traveler. It's very, very difficult to try and identify a particular age group that this particular foreign fighter message resonates with," Adams said.[36]

There is also evidence that the jihadist foreign fighter message continues to resonate with European youth and with women, despite counter-messaging efforts. "It's still a profile that tends to be quite young," said David Sterman, from the New America International Security program. "The average age is 24 with many teenagers within the sample," he said. "Women continue to be quite well represented."[37]

A typical jihadist foreign fighter is a male between 18 and 29 years old, although there are exceptions. Some are well over 30, and it is not uncommon to see fighters between 15 and 17. Beyond age and gender (with terrorists being very predominantly male), there are few consistent patterns and no reliable profile to use when determining who the next foreign fighter might be, although a disproportionate number of converts can be typically found among Western recruits.[38] When recruiting Western fighters, ISIS often looks for recent converts or those with little knowledge of Islam. According to a study by the Heritage Foundation, as many as one in six fighters from Europe is a convert to Islam, many looking for answers to the basic questions of life and finding purpose in the mission of ISIS.[39] Leading experts on terrorism and authors of the book *ISIS: The State of Terror*, Jessica Stern and J.M. Berger believe, "Converts are often especially vulnerable to fundamentalist ideas, often combining wild enthusiasm with a lack of knowledge about their new religion, making them vulnerable to recruiters. This approximate profile has endured for decades, through multiple jihadist conflicts."[40]

There is an unequal level of combat readiness among foreign fighters. "The Chechens were older, taller, and stronger and wore hiking boots and combat trousers. They carried their weapons with confidence and distanced themselves from the rest, moving around in a tight-knit unit-within-a-unit. One of the Turks was a former soldier who wore western-style webbing and equipment, while the three Tajiks and the Pakistani were evidently poor. Their trousers were too short, their shoes old and torn."[41]

The fighters are also "secretive, especially when dealing with the Free Syrian Army. When the Syrians asked them where they were from, a blond French-speaker said they were Moroccans, the Chechens said they were Turks and the Tajiks said they were Afghans."[42] This situation does not portray a stable environment. The good thing is that when fighters do not trust each other and do not trust their leaders, it can open the door through which intelligence agencies can access valuable information.

Because foreign fighters are so much a part of the danger of terrorism today, I have included ways to combat the impact in my proposed strategy, which I will discuss in a chapter in Part II of this book.

CHAPTER 8

Terrorists Groups' Ideology

In September 2002 in Karachi, Pakistan, Yosri Fouda, a correspondent for Al Jazeera—a television network based in Qatar—interviewed Kahlid Shaikh Mohammed (KSM), who was the mastermind behind the 9/11 attacks. KSM told Fouda that they had planned the attacks of 9/11 to be a big slap in the face of the United States on its lands.[1] This is a powerful example of the concept of terrorist ideology that I address in this chapter.

When Fouda asked KSM who would carry out the attacks, KSM answered, "We never lack martyrs and in fact we have an administration called the martyrs administration." Fouda asked, "Is the martyr administration still active?" KSM answered, "Yes, and it will continue to be active as long as there is jihad (holy war) against infidels and Zionists," which points toward Christians and Jews.[2]

The interview demonstrates that the real motive that drives terrorists to practice holy war and to seek martyrdom is the Salafi-jihadi ideology, which is based on a subversive version of Islam. This ideology considers non-Muslims and all other Muslims who are not Salafi-jihadi as disbelievers and justifies killing anyone who is not one of them and those who do not submit to their rule.

There are websites that misrepresent the Quran and provide incorrect religious decrees (fatwas) to consider followers of any religion except Islam as disbelievers. For example, a Sunni-Salafi website, Islamweb.net, shows a religious decree number 2924, answering a question about the position of Muslims regarding followers of the holy books, such as Jews and Christians, and whether they should be considered as believers or disbelievers. The answer is "consensus among [Muslim] religious scholars indicates that whoever believes in any religion except Islam is infidel, his religion is rejected, and he is a loser in the hereafter."[3]

This Fatwa is misleading because there is no such consensus among Muslim religious scholars, and some of them even believe that the Jews and Christians are believers. This is also a misinterpretation of the Quran which really states that the Jews and Christians are not infidels, and that they are followers of the holy book.[4] The Quran also ordered Muslims to believe in all Prophets and Messengers sent by God before Prophet Mohammed, such as Abraham, Isaac, Jacob, Moses, and Jesus.[5]

The Quran states, "God revealed the Torah to Moses as guidance and light. By its standard has been judged among the Jews, by the prophets who submitted to God's will, and by the rabbis and believers in God, for to them was entrusted the protection of Allah's book, and they were witnesses thereto."[6]

The notion of jihad has been exploited by a series of extremist organizations and has been the subject of considerable propaganda to support various ends. But the word *jihad* means "effort in the cause of God." Such efforts can be of nonviolent means, but extremists tend to think of it only as fighting for religious purposes.[7]

Saudi author Ali Awadh Asseri has in fact said that terrorism is only using, or rather abusing, the name of religion. Terrorism's ultimate goal is essentially political and motivated solely by power ambitions. Religious terrorism can be more logically and fairly defined as the deliberate use of organized violence against unarmed civilians for achieving political ends by using a bigoted religious creed as a means.[8]

THE ROOTS OF EXTREME IDEOLOGY

Islamic ideology is based on two major sources, the holy Quran and Prophet Mohammed's Sunna, which is the Prophet's sayings and deeds, as well as what he has approved with respect to other people's deeds. All Muslims believe in one copy of the Quran that they believe was revealed to Prophet Mohammed 14 centuries ago. The Sunna is not as perfect as the Quran because many of the prophet's sayings were diverted to serve the interest of rulers who built their caliphate as an Empire ruled by the Umayyad, the Abbasid, and the Ottoman dynasties.

Throughout history there were many Muslim sects. The majority of them are now dead and extinct; however, a few are still alive. The Muslim sects that are still alive are the four Sunnis sects (Hanafi, Shafi'i, Maliki, and Hanbali), as well as the Shiites, Zaidis, Alwites, Abadites, Ismaili, and Durze. The majority of Muslims who follow these sects are moderate and believe that Islam, like Judaism and Christianity, is a religion of peace. They also believe that the Quran ordered Prophet Mohammed and Muslims to respect followers of other religions such as Jews, Sabians, Christians, and Magians who are different from polytheists and infidels.

The Quran states, "Those who believe [in Islam], Jews, Sabians, Christians, Magians, and Polytheists, God will judge between them on the Day of Judgment: for Allah is witness of all things" (Quran 22:17). The best proof of that ideology is reflected in the fact that Jews, Christians, Sabians, Magians, and members of other religions lived among Muslims from

Prophet Mohammed's time 14 centuries ago until today in most Arab and Muslim countries.

Prophet Mohammed was born in Mecca in the Arabian Peninsula (Saudi Arabia today) in AD 570. At the time, Arabs lived in a time of ignorance called (Jahiliya), in a tribal society where tribes attacked each other to kill men, steal what they could, and take women and girls as slaves. Women were deprived of all human rights such as inheriting wealth from their parents. As a result, fathers started to kill their young daughters just because they could be attacked and taken as slaves when they grew up. Fathers used to bury their daughters alive in the sand until the Quran forbade killing girls and gave women their rights.

The society worshipped idols and statues, and the holy mosque of Mecca built by Prophet Abraham was filled with metal, stone, and wooden idols that they called Gods. Prophet Mohammed rejected this behavior and wrong-doing. He called his people to worship God instead of the idols.

The Quran ordered Prophet Mohammed to preach his people gently and wisely, to lead his people to believe in God, to stop worshipping idols, to stop killing their daughters, and to give the women their rights and the slaves their freedom.

However, the heads of tribes and rich people who were ruling the society, including two of the Prophet's uncles, argued that by doing those things, the slaves would be encouraged to rise up against their masters; so they fought the Prophet and those who believed with him. Prophet Mohammed ordered his followers to be patient, to have the strength to tolerate the hurt, humiliation, and torture that continued for 13 years. For three of those years, the society imposed sanctions, isolation, and siege against the Prophet and those who believed with him. Nobody was allowed to buy anything from them and to sell anything to them, including food. The Prophet and his followers were starving, and many of them died including the Prophet's uncle, Abu Talib, and His wife, Khadija. The rest survived by eating grass and leaves of trees. When people saw that Muslims responded to hardship and torture with patience and pleasant words, more and more started to believe in Islam.

The heads of tribes and the rich masters started to kill weak, poor Muslims and slaves. Initially they were thinking of killing the Prophet himself, but they feared that his tribe "Quraish" would take revenge. Eventually they developed a plan to kill the Prophet by using 10 people, each one from a different tribe so that the Prophet's tribe could not go against all of the tribes.

The Quran ordered the Prophet Mohammed to emigrate from Mecca to Medina, and ordered Muslims to defend themselves against those who attack them, but not to commit aggression. The Quran states, "Fight in the cause of God those who fight you, but do not commit aggression; for Allah don't love transgressors" (Quran 2:190).

Extremists misinterpret this verse and similar verses in the Quran to conclude that God ordered them to launch a holy war (jihad) against the disbelievers such as Jews and Christians, as well as apostates Muslims such as Shiites and Alwites as well as moderate Sunnis. Jihad is a much-contested issue among Muslims. It emerged in the time of Prophet Mohammed as a means of defending the new Muslim community against its powerful enemies. In the periods that followed, a number of Muslim military leaders used it against Muslims for political and economic gains. It was also adopted against colonial forces in the 18th and 19th centuries. After gaining independence, the propaganda of certain leaders in the Middle East reinterpreted jihad within national contexts as an economic war against their country's state of poverty.[9]

After the death of Prophet Mohammed in AD 632, Muslims separated into two major sects, Sunnis and Shiites. The Sunnis followed the "caliphs" who established the "caliphate," and the Shiites followed the 12 leaders of the Prophet's progeny called *imams*. The Shiites believe that Prophet Mohammed appointed 12 members from his family to guide Muslims when he was gone. The first, his cousin and son-in-law Ali Ibn Abi Talib, was named as his successor, the second Imam was Ali's son Hasan, followed by Ali's second son Hussein. Then came Hussein's son, and eight of Hussein's grandsons.[10]

The Sunnis follow four jurisprudence sects: (1) the Hanafi school of thought, with its founder, the Persian scholar Imam Abu Hanifah al-Nu'man ibn Thabit (AD 699–767); (2) the Shafi'i school of thought with its founder Abu Abdullah Muhammad Ibn Idris al-Shafi'i (AD 767–820); (3) the Maliki school of thought with its founder Malik Bin Anas (AD 711–795); and (4) the Hanbali school of thought with its founder Ahmad Ibn Hanbal (AD 780–855).

There are other Muslim sects, such as Zaidis, Abadites, Ismaili, and Druze, but they are smaller in numbers than the Sunni and Shiites.[11]

The majority of Muslims, who are either Sunni or Shiite, neither consider other Muslims apostates nor do they consider Jews and Christians disbelievers (infidels). In the Quran, they were called "followers of the book" while the Quran described the worshippers of idols as disbelievers. There are, however, a minority of Muslims over history who consider Jews and Christians as disbelievers and who consider other Muslims as apostates, and they justify killing them on these grounds. In contrast, all Muslims, Sunnis, Shiites, and other sects lived in peace and harmony for centuries in many Arab and Muslims countries as they did with other religious groups such as Christians and Jews.

THE IDEOLOGY OF TERRORISTS

Terrorist organizations such as Al Qaeda, ISIS, Al-Shabab, Al-Nusra Front, Ansar al-Sharia, and many other terrorist organizations follow the extremist Salafi-jihadi ideology. This ideology started during the

Umayyad Caliphate (AD 661–750) and has continued to exist until today. The Umayyad dynasty transformed the Islamic state into an Arab oppressive and brutal kingdom. The Umayyads relied largely on the traditional political ideas of Arabs before Islam, but also claimed to uphold Islam. They were overthrown by the Abbasids in AD 750.[12]

In the 13th century, Taqi Al-Din Ahmad Ibn Taymiyyah, who was born in AD 1263 in Harran, Mesopotamia, and died in AD 1328 in Damascus, Syria, brought about a revival of the Salafi-jihadi movement. He was one of Islam's most forceful theologians, who claimed to return the Islamic religion to its sources: the Quran and the Prophet's sayings. He is also the source of the Wahhabism, a mid-18th-century extremist movement of Islam established by Mohammed Bin Abdul Wahhab.[13]

In contemporary history, many Islamic movements have followed the extremist ideology of Ibn Taymiyyah or Ibn abdul Wahhab. One such major movement was the Muslim Brotherhood established in Egypt by Hassan al-Banna in 1928. It started as a reformist movement but evolved into a violent organization. Al-Banna was assassinated in February 1949 following his organization's assassination of the Egyptian Prime Minister Mahmoud Fahmy Elnokrashy Pasha in December 1948 after he outlawed the Brotherhood.

In Egypt in the 1960s, a new leader of the Muslim Brotherhood emerged who was even more radical and extreme than his predecessors. This leader, Syed Qutb, wrote many books, and one of them, titled *Milestone in the Road*, set the Salafi-jihadi ideology for members of the Muslim Brotherhood. Qutb considered members of the Muslim society in Egypt and other Muslim societies as infidels and this lent legitimacy to the assassination of many Egyptian officials.[14] Qutb believed that the members of Egyptian society were infidels and that the Muslim Brotherhood should transform Egypt it into a *real* Muslim society that practiced restrictive Islam.[15] The ideology of Qutb influenced the majority of Islamic movements in Egypt and the Muslim world. They believe that a Muslim society that does not observe Islamic Sharia Laws is an infidel society and not truly Islamic even though Islam accepted many sects within a single Muslim society and accepted other religions such as Christian and Jews.[16]

Many Salafi-jihadi scholars follow the extreme ideology of Qutb, which considers non-Muslims as disbelievers and Muslims who don't practice Islamic rituals such as praying and fasting as infidels. Among them are major terrorists: Osama bin Laden, his successor as the leader of Al Qaeda Ayman Al-Zawahiri, Abu Mussab Al-Zarqawi, the leader of Al Qaeda in Iraq (AQI) which evolved into ISIS, and ISIS leader al-Baghdadi.[17]

The Saudi writer Hasan Farhan al-Maliki said that Wahhabism considers those Muslim countries to be disbelievers and not truly Muslim countries where Muslims respect the holy shrine and supplicate holy people such as the prophet's grandsons (Imams) as Shiite do. Wahhabism considers the religious scholars and people of these countries as infidels.[18]

Sunni writer Mohammed Al-Oamr argues that modern day Nazism extends to any extremist group that functions along the same principles as did Hitler and the Nazi Party. Following his argument, terrorism follows the same structure. In a very short amount of time, extremist groups such as ISIS have exploded as a more brutal, destructive terrorist group, that commits massacres, kills innocent people, mutilates dead bodies, and takes women as slaves.[19]

Consistent with this analogy, in July 2014, British journalist and author Patrick Cockburn said that an MI-6 boss hinted that a plan using a Nazi structure was developed dating back over a decade. In some areas, being Shia is similar to being a Jew in Nazi Germany. Since the capture of Mosul by ISIS on June 10, Shia women and children have been killed in villages south of Kirkuk and Shia air force cadets have been machine-gunned and buried in mass graves near Tikrit.[20] In Mosul, Shia shrines and mosques have been blown up, and in the nearby Shia Turkoman city of Tal Afar, 4,000 houses have been taken over by ISIS fighters as "spoils of war." Simply to be identified as a Shia or a related sect, such as the Alawites, in Sunni rebel-held parts of Iraq and Syria, has become as dangerous as being a Jew was in Nazi-controlled parts of Europe in 1940.[21]

ISIS's ideology is based on accusing everyone against them, Muslims and non-Muslims, of being disbelievers who deserve to be killed. This includes innocent civilians, elderly people, women, and children. This ideology started with the idea of the leader of Al Qaeda in Iraq, Abo Musaab al-Zarqawi, who considered everybody as infidel and justified killing almost every one to achieve his objectives. It is a more extreme order than the school of extremism in Afghanistan, Egypt, and Algeria.[22]

SAUDI ARABIA AND WAHHABISM

Saudi Arabia adopted Wahhabism, the ideology established by Mohammed Bin Abdul Wahhab, a mid-18th-century scholar, as the official sect in the oil-rich kingdom and supported its dissemination all over the world with huge amounts of money from oil revenues. Mohammed Abdul Wahhab considered Wahhabism as the correct sect in Islam and tried to impose it on people by force. The Saudis tried to make Wahhabism the Muslims' only sect in the world by spreading it through schools, mosques, books, and their scholars.

The Saudis invited Muslims to study Wahhabism in Saudi religious schools and then to go to mosques and schools they built all over the world to disseminate Wahhabism. In addition, they supported a large number of nonprofit organizations and other projects worldwide, to spread their word.

The leader of Al Qaeda, Osama bin Laden, was from a wealthy Saudi family because his father, who emigrated as a poor person from Yemen, became a close friend of King Abdul Aziz Bin Saud who gave him contracts to build many infrastructure projects throughout the kingdom. The majority of fighters with Al Qaeda, especially the suicide bombers, were from Saudi Arabia. Notably, 15 out of the 19 suicide terrorists in the 9/11 attacks in America were from Saudi Arabia.

Officials in Saudi Arabia do not deny their support for Wahhabis, and the Wahhabi extreme rules are enforced strictly in Saudi Arabia—interestingly, the only country in the world that forbids women from driving cars or traveling without a male member of their family. However, officials in Saudi Arabia deny any support for terrorism, and say instead that Saudi Arabia is a target for terrorist attacks by Al Qaeda and other terrorist groups.

Many experts and authors in Islamic ideology, extremism, and terrorism believe that Wahhabism was behind the sectarian strife in the Middle East because Wahhabism in the 18th century revived the 13th-century extreme Salafi-jihadi ideology of Ibn Taymiyyah.

British journalist Patrick Cockburn, author of *The Rise of the Islamic State: ISIS and the Sunni Revolution,* said Wahhabism's hostile takeover of Sunni Islam is the root of sectarianism in the Middle East.[23] Foaud Ibrahim, author of *From Najdi to Baghdadi,* said that although Western media likes to portray the narrative that the rivalry between Sunni and Shiite Muslims is just a part of the status quo that goes back to the early days of Islam, these different sects actually have a long history of peaceful coexistence. One only needs to take a look at the Gulf Arab Sultanate of Oman as proof that sectarianism is not an inherent characteristic of Islam.[24] Ibrahim added that the conflicts that we are seeing in the present day are a direct result of several decades of concerted efforts by the Saudi Arabian government and its religious establishments to export Wahhabism to other countries in the Muslim world. As Wahhabism has become more prominent in Sunni Islam, sectarian tensions have arisen as a direct result.[25]

Mohammed Alwash, author of *ISIS and Its Sisters, from Al Qaeda to Islamic State,* says that the Saudi kingdom was built to spread the Wahhabi ideology to the world. Evidence of this are the pilgrims who venture to Saudi Arabia for pilgrimage and return to their countries with books of Wahhabi ideology. This is a continuation of the schooling of Ahmad Bin Hanbal in the ninth century and of Muslim scholar Shaykh Ahmad Ibn Taymiyyah who lived centuries later.[26]

Juan C. Zarate, author of *Treasury's War: The Unleashing of a New Era of Financial Warfare,* wrote, "the Saudis had built an extensive global network for spreading a certain brand of religious thought, but in so doing they provided a platform for Al Qaeda and its like-minded supporters, who benefited greatly from this network both financially and in terms of growth. The Wahhabi ideology and Saudi preaching around the world provided an ideological baseline for Al Qaeda and the recruitment of like-minded believers."[27]

In Iraq, Sunnis and Shiites lived in peace and harmony for centuries until Saddam Hussein became president in 1979 and played the sectarian card during the Iraq–Iran war of 1980–1988, by attacking Shiites ideology and killing many Shiite religious scholars such as Grand Ayatollah Mohammed Baqir Al-Sadr and his sister in 1980. After the liberation of Kuwait and popular uprising of March 1991, Saddam killed half a million Iraqis, mostly Shiites. In the 1990s, Saddam allowed the Wahhabi-Salafi-jihadi ideology to spread in the country because he hoped that this ideology would stand against the United States. He also launched the "Enhancement of Islamic Belief Campaign" to advocate such extremist ideology.

Historically, Saudi Wahhabis launched raids on urban and tribal rural areas on the edges of desert between Iraq and Saudi Arabia. One example is the raid of April 22, 1802, against the holy city of Karbala, when the Wahhabis entered Karbala secretly and slaughtered everyone they saw on their way including elderly people, women, and children. The estimated number of people killed is 8,000.[28]

The Wahhabis launched another raid against the holy city of Najaf, but it failed because the people of the city were ready and defended the city. The Wahhabis continued their raids, and in 1922, they launched a surprised attack on Nasiriya province in Southern Iraq and massacred civilians, attacking a group of unarmed shepherds, gathering them with their wives and children, and killing them all.[29]

Former MI-6 agent Alastair Crooke, author of *Resistance: The Essence of Islamic Revolution*, said the world was troubled by contradictions and double standards dealings with ISIS in Saudi Arabia. Some ruling elites praised ISIS as Sunni "Fire" fighting the Shiites "Fire." Other Saudis were frightened, remembering the uprising against Abd-al Aziz bin Saud by the Salafi–Wahhabist movement in the late 1920s.[30]

Celebrations abounded of the Wahhabi current in Saudi Arabia as well as in other Sunni communities, and the Muslim Brotherhood currents, especially in the Gulf, when ISIS announced its control of Mosul. ISIS control raised questions regarding what ISIS represents in the Wahhabi popular awareness, in religious identity, and the expectations of Sunnis in general. Along with the uproar of ISIS that accompanied the invasion of huge swathes of Iraq, ISIS emerged as the pure ancestry of the generation which established Wahhabism.[31]

On June 29, 2014, the day of announcing the Islamic caliphate and the coronation of Abo Bakr al-Baghdadi (whose real name is Ibrahim Awad al-Badri) as a caliph for Muslims, followers of the Wahhabi sect in Saudi Arabia announced loyalty to him. That raised the question of the relations between ISIS and the followers of the official sect in Saudi Arabia.[32]

Hillary Clinton and Donald Trump did not agree on much, but Saudi Arabia was an exception. Clinton deplored Saudi Arabia's support for radical schools and mosques around the world that have set too many young people on the path toward extremism, and Trump called the Saudis "the world's biggest funders of terrorism."[33] President Obama described how he watched Indonesia gradually move from a relaxed, syncretistic Islam to a more fundamentalist, unforgiving interpretation. "Large numbers of Indonesian women have now adopted the hijab, the Muslim head covering. . . . The Saudis and other Gulf Arabs have funneled money, and large numbers of imams and teachers, into the country. In the 1990s, the Saudis heavily funded Wahhabist madrassas, seminaries that teach the fundamentalist version of Islam favored by the Saudi ruling family. Today, Islam in Indonesia is much more Arab in orientation than it was when he lived there."[34]

The former Saudi highest religious authority, Mohammed Bin Ibrahim Aal Al-Shaikh, considers the majority of Muslims and Muslim countries as disbelievers. He asserted that the apostate is any Muslim who is not a Wahhabi, and whoever converted to Wahhabism is converted to Islam. He also believes that the Wahhabis were right in taking Muslim women as slaves and to confiscate their money, based on the fact that these Muslims were considered nonbelievers.[35]

Aal Al-Shaikh described the Muslim Abadites sect in Oman as heresy, the Asha'ra sect as immoral, the Shafi'i sect as worshippers of graves, and the Shiites as apostates, worshippers of idols, and nonbelievers. He cursed all the Christians and Jews, whether they fight Muslims or not. He issued a religious decree (fatwa) that the earth is still and not moving, and that photography, smoking, selling radios and TVs, and blood donations are forbidden.[36]

Terrorism expert Rachel Ehrenfeld from the Hebrew University of Jerusalem believes the sources that feed terrorist organizations are much more varied than one might assume. The Saudi government has admitted to spending more than $87 billion over a decade of 1993–2003 in an effort to spread Wahhabism. This money has been spent on the creation of mosques, schools, and other institutions that have constituted the breeding grounds for the foot soldiers of the global Islamic terrorist movement.[37] This understanding of religion and sects within Islam, and the conflicts among the various factions, is crucial to determining a successful antiterrorist strategy.

PART II

A New 12-Step Counterterrorism Strategy to Defeat Terrorists

This part builds on the preceding chapters in Part I that outline the background of terrorism and the factors that contribute to its prevalence. The chapters in this part build on that information and present the elements of my 12-step strategy to defeat terrorism through action about those various factors.

CHAPTER 9

Strategy to Stop Terrorists' Funding

In Chapter 4, I described in detail the sources and methods of funding terrorism. In this chapter, I present the strategy to combat this issue. It is impossible to stop terrorism if the world cannot prevent funds from reaching terrorist groups. There are many obstacles and complications facing any entity that attempts to prevent funds from reaching terrorist groups. In some countries, there are no regulations in terms of registration, accountability, and transparency, and accounts held by NGOs and other charitable foundations are not audited. In other countries, there is only limited regulation for NGOs and charitable foundations. Accounts are easy to establish even if there is no initial capital, and background checks are not performed on the person who opens an account or on the employees who service the accounts.

In one case in 2013, two men were convicted because they were caught lying when they claimed that they were raising money for a charity called "Muslim Aid." In actuality, the money they raised was distributed to a network of fundraisers who sent the money to terrorist groups. The money was moved through currency exchange agencies and money transfer shops, gradually and in small amounts, so that ID documents were not required. They also used couriers to transport money across borders.

The U.S. State Department has long been aware that some Gulf monarchies funded Sunni extremist groups. It has never been held secret from Washington's policymakers. In 2009, a leaked action request cable from U.S. Deputy Assistant Secretary for Energy, Sanctions and Commodities, Douglas C. Hengel pointed out the necessity of cutting off "terrorist fundraising in the Gulf by Al Qaeda, the Taliban, Lashkar-e-Taiba (LeT), and other Afghanistan/Pakistan-based violent extremist groups, all of which undermine the security of the entire international community."[1]

Tracking financial information is one logical step, but it is not sufficient to detect how terrorist groups and affiliates are funded. However, if combined with other information held by intelligence services, it would help financial institutions detect signs of suspicious activity. In this sense, the development of intelligence-led indicators based on the study of evolving terrorist operating methods and the exchange of information between public and private sectors should be one of the pillars for the development of a more risk-based focus that can improve the detection of terrorist financing operations.[2]

Identifying, tracking, and dismantling the financial structure that supports terrorism is critical to successfully dismantling terrorist organizations and preventing future attacks. As is the case in many types of criminal investigations, "following the money" plays a critical role in identifying those involved in criminal activity, to establish links among them, and uncover evidence of their involvement in the activity.[3]

THE UNITED NATIONS AND TERRORISTS' FUNDING

After the 1998 Al Qaeda terrorist attacks against U.S. embassies in Kenya and Tanzania, the United Nations Security Council adopted Resolution 1267. The council designated Osama bin Laden and associates as terrorists and established a sanction regime that includes entities associated with Al Qaeda or the Taliban wherever their location is. The regime has since been reaffirmed and modified by a dozen further UN Security Council Resolutions.[4]

The 9/11 attacks in the United States brought an international sense of urgency to disrupting terrorists' financial networks. The United Nations and the United States took measures to prevent funding terrorists, and imposed sanctions on Osama bin Laden, the Taliban regime, Al Qaeda, and other entities associated with terrorists. In the immediate aftermath of 9/11, the United Nations also drew up a list of designated individuals and entities thought to be financing terrorist activities.[5] Within a few weeks after the attacks, the UN Security Council adopted a wide-ranging resolution demanding that countries take action to suppress terrorist financing.

Defining terrorism, however, poses a challenge. The United Nations General Assembly has for more than two decades tried to reach an agreement on a definition for terrorism. A clear definition would help underpin and strengthen a comprehensive treaty banning the practice of funding terrorism.

In spite of efforts to prevent terrorist funding, states and private donors continue to support terrorist groups financially and the international community has been unable to implement the proper actions to stop them. Even when the United States adopted a new military doctrine, called the Bush Doctrine, and built a wide alliance of friendly states that declared international war on terrorism, terrorist organization continued to receive money and financial support.

There are many stories regarding the failure of the world powers to stop financing terrorist. One of these stories was written by an eye witness Nidhal Hamada, who said:

After 9/11 attacks, the U.S. Treasury put Yassin al-Kadi on the list of International Terrorists in October 2001. Kadi was financing terrorist groups through fake companies and NGOs that belonged to Osama Bin Laden. The United States asked the United Nations to freeze all Kadi's assets in accordance with Security Council resolutions 1267 and 1333. Like Osama bin Laden, Yassin al-Kadi was a Saudi multi-millionaire and was a financier of Al Qaeda and ISIS. Yassin al-Kadi was forbidden from entering Turkey before the Justice and Development Party came to power in 2002 and all his money and companies were frozen.

However, when the Justice and Development Party, which is part of Muslim Brotherhood movement, came to power, it tried to cover the activities of Kadi using nonprofit organizations in Turkey. According to UN Security Council resolutions, Turkey should have frozen Kadi's assets but the Turkish Treasury of the Justice and Development Party turned a blind eye and allowed a person under international sanctions to continue to run his properties. The fact that names were changed to facilitate transfer of assets was mentioned in U.S. newspapers in 2004 and was a part of U.S. investigations into Al Qaeda money activities around the world. During a 2013 investigation into corruption and bribes which had overrun Turkey, reports of the Anti-Corruption Commission were leaked regarding the relationship between the Justice and Development Party and Yassin al-Kadi.[6]

OBAMA AND TERRORISTS' FUNDING

The Obama administration tried to cut off millions of dollars in oil revenue that made ISIS one of the wealthiest terror groups in history. The United States was unable to persuade its ally Turkey, where much of the group's oil was traded on the black market, to crack down on an extensive sales network. Western intelligence officials say they can track ISIS oil shipments as they move across Iraq and into Turkey.[7]

In October 2014, David Cohen, the Under Secretary of the Treasury for Terrorism and Financial Intelligence—responsible for directing the Treasury's efforts to cut the lines of financial support for terrorists, fight financial crime, enforce economic sanctions against rogue nations, and combat the financial support of the proliferation of weapons of mass destruction—outlined measures the U.S. government would take in the future to punish anyone found to have bought ISIS-extracted oil. "The middlemen, traders, refiners, transport companies, and anyone else that handles ISIS's oil should know that we are hard at work identifying them, and that we have tools at hand to stop them," he said.[8] "We will target for financial sanctions anyone who trades in [ISIS's] stolen oil. We not only can cut them off from the U.S. financial system and freeze their assets, but we can also make it very difficult for them to find a bank anywhere that will touch their money or process their transactions," he added.[9]

In November 2014, lawmakers expressed concern about the U.S. government's ability to dry up funding for ISIS. A treasury department official acknowledged several unique challenges inhibiting the Obama administration's offensive against deep-pocketed terrorist groups but urged patience as efforts continued. "Our efforts to combat its financing will take time," Cohen said. "We have no silver bullet, no secret weapon to empty ISIS's coffers overnight."[10]

A year after President Obama launched an international coalition to fight ISIS, the active trade at al-Omar oil field and at least eight other fields came to symbolize the dilemma faced by the campaign. Interviews with Syrian traders and oil engineers as well as Western intelligence officials and oil experts revealed a sprawling operation almost similar to a state oil company that has grown in size and expertise despite international attempts to destroy it.[11]

ISIS's oil company is carefully managed, and it actively recruits skilled engineers, trainers, and managers. In an appeal to sympathizers throughout the world, ISIS leaders asked doctors, engineers, and skilled people to immigrate to the caliphate state to run it as a state enterprise.

STOP ISIS'S OIL SMUGGLING

ISIS manages and controls oil fields in territories under its control. Coalition air strikes had an impact, but various states, such as Turkey and some member states in the European Union, were playing a duplicitous game by buying smuggled oil. A more concerted effort was needed by all nations not to allow one hand to pursue a policy of containment while the other opens up their government and private businesses to encourage ISIS by profiting from oil.[12]

In July 2015, a report on illegal oil sales by ISIS ordered and compiled in Norway revealed that most of the ISIS-smuggled oil was destined for Turkey, where it has been sold off at bargain prices. The Norwegian daily *Klassekampen* leaked details of the report, which was put together by Rystad Energy, an independent oil and gas consulting firm, at the request of the Norwegian Foreign Ministry.[13] "Large amounts of oil have been smuggled across the border to Turkey from ISIS-controlled areas in Syria and Iraq," *Klassekampen* cited in the report, adding, "The oil is sent by tankers via smuggling routes across the border and is sold at greatly reduced prices, from $25 to $45 a barrel."[14]

In November 2015, at a G20 summit—an international forum for the governments and central bank governors from 20 major economies—Russian President Vladimir Putin spoke of the urgent need to curb illegal oil trade. "I've shown our colleagues photos taken from space and from aircraft which clearly demonstrate the scale of the illegal trade in oil and petroleum products," Putin said, adding, "The motorcade of refueling vehicles stretched for dozens of kilometers, so that from a height of 5,000 meters they stretch beyond the horizon."[15]

On November 16, 2015, in a highly publicized effort, U.S. warplanes destroyed 116 ISIS oil trucks in Syria. Forty-five minutes earlier, leaflets were dropped advising drivers to "get out of [their] trucks and run away." The peculiar thing about the U.S. strikes is that it took the Pentagon nearly 14 months to figure out that the most effective way to cripple ISIS's oil trade is to bomb the oil.[16]

Before November, the U.S. strategy revolved around bombing the group's oil infrastructure. As it turned out, that strategy was minimally effective at best and it is not entirely clear that any effort was made to inform the White House, the Congress, and/or the public about just how little damage the air strikes were actually inflicting.[17]

The important point is that ISIS was producing, smuggling, and selling oil. In my view, the United States, the United Nations, and the international community should have much earlier put a stop to the major source of income for ISIS that they receive from producing, smuggling, and selling oil. Given my familiarity with the United Nations, having served as Ambassador of Iraq to the UN, I assert that the early adoption of a Security Council resolution under chapter VII authorizing UN member states to impose sanctions could have been very effective. Additionally, the Security Council should have referred some of those who helped fund ISIS to the International Criminal Court. The oil field, refineries, and trucks that smuggled oil and oil products should have been targeted right from the beginning in the international war against terrorism.

PREVENT KIDNAPPING FOR RANSOM

Many European countries paid millions of dollars in ransom to terrorist groups such as Al Qaeda and ISIS for the release of hostages. In contrast, other countries such the United Kingdom, United States, and Japan had a policy of not negotiating with terrorists and hostages from those countries were beheaded. Moreover, the United States used to have a policy of prosecuting families of hostages who negotiated with terrorists and paid ransom for the release of their family members. When ISIS beheaded British and American hostages in August 2014, and released hostages from other European countries after their governments paid ransoms, President Obama decided to change the U.S. policy. In June 2015, the White House announced changes to the way in which the government handles hostage situations involving U.S. citizens. President Obama directed the U.S. government not to threaten the hostages' families with prosecution if they attempted to pay ransom. This policy shift raised questions about whether U.S. citizens would become more lucrative targets for hostage takers.[18]

However, it remains illegal for the U.S. government to pay ransom directly to terrorists. Obama affirmed that there will be no change to existing laws that make it a crime to provide money or other material support to terrorists. He said, "I am reaffirming, the United States will not make concessions, such as paying ransoms, to terrorist groups holding hostages." However, as noted, the Justice Department will not prosecute anyone for paying ransom to a terror group.[19]

I believe all UN member states (i.e., governments) should adhere to the UN Security council declarations and policies to prevent ransom payments to terrorist groups like ISIS. Each country approaches this issue in a myriad of ways, as we have seen. Realistically, there must be international consensus and enforcement concerning a prohibition on ransoms paid to ISIS, and pressure should be applied not only on governments but also on individuals and private businesses/organizations to abide by the policies.

END STATE AND PRIVATE FUNDING

In his testimony before the Senate Committee on Governmental Affairs in 2003, John Pistole, Deputy Assistant Director of the Counterterrorism Division of the FBI, reported that following the 9/11 attacks, it became apparent that the role of NGOs as a source of funding for terrorist groups needed closer scrutiny. This included the role of Saudi Arabia and its citizens in the support of terrorism, both directly and indirectly, through the financial support of these charitable organizations.[20]

The Saudis have backed many extreme groups such as the Taliban. And the most pro-ISIS tweets come from Saudi Arabia, which is the hotbed of the most radical Muslims in the world, namely the Salafi-jihadi. The Saudis also back the radical schools called "madrassas" through which Islamic radicalism was spread. The largest number of terrorists who carried out suicide attacks in Iraq was from Saudi Arabia, and as I noted earlier, 15 out of the 19 terrorists involved in the 9/11 attacks were also from Saudi Arabia.[21]

ISIS changes its strategies of getting funds and adapts well to changes in the world, especially with respect to modern technology. The United States and the international community must also adapt. Instead of relying on national and multilateral regulatory tools, the focus must shift to developing and using targeted human intelligence.

No regulation can deter or detect small sums of money going to individuals. The only way to make a difference is to gather intelligence on such movements. By shifting resources from regulation to intelligence, we have a chance to understand changes in terrorists' strategies as they occur, and to adopt a more flexible, realistic response to money flows. It will be a far more effective strategy as we enter the next phase of confronting an intelligent, adaptable enemy.[22]

In my strategy, the international community must also take serious steps to prevent ISIS from getting state funding and private donations. Terrorist groups should be prevented access to international banking and financial systems. Donations sent from complicit states and donors should be stopped and donors should be prosecuted for their financial support of terrorism. The United States and allies should put sanctions on states, banks, and financial institutions that help ISIS transfer money. Governments in the region should tightly regulate and restrict all bank and wire transfers to and from any ISIS-controlled territory.

STOP TAXATION AND EXTORTION

After ISIS took control of big provinces and cities in Iraq such as Ramadi and Falluja in 2013 and Mosul, the second largest province in Iraq, in 2014, the Iraqi government continued to pay salaries and pensions to government employees in these cities for humanitarian reasons. The government employees were under ISIS control unwillingly, had families to support, and needed a salary to survive.

Before long, ISIS started to take taxes from these salaries before the people got paid. The Iraqi government was aware of this, and should have exercised control over the salaries and pensions paid to their government and state workers in ISIS-controlled territory. In addition, ISIS imposed taxes and levies on goods and services provided by businesses and individuals. This is clearly showing that ISIS manipulated regulations and restrictions on the financial and banking systems in the territories they control.

Taxation and extortion are a major source of ISIS money in areas it controls. This was reported by Patrick Johnston, a RAND Corporation researcher who worked on a top-to-bottom study of ISIS's financing and organization, and examined declassified documents that detailed the group's funding streams. ISIS demands between 10 and 20 percent of the revenues generated by businesses in its territories and operates other *mafia-style* rackets that yield as much as $1 million a day.[23]

ISIS created civil and administrative entities just like any legitimate state. To get anything done in ISIS-controlled areas, people are required to pay a fee to the terror group. Businesses are taxed if they want to secure essential things like electricity and security. Drivers who want to move through a checkpoint must hand over cash. When extortion is used as a control mechanism, it can appear to a terrified and traumatized populace as a normal tax system.[24]

ISIS has also stolen money. In June 2014, according to global intelligence firm Stratfor, the group raided several banks in Mosul and stole an estimated $500 million although the full amount is unconfirmed. In Syria, ISIS seized control of oil facilities from the rebel group Jabhat al-Nusra, which did not fight back.[25]

The international community, especially the United States and Europe, could have stopped ISIS's collection of taxes from some sources such as cross border trades, especially across the border of Syria and Iraq with Turkey. They could have imposed sanctions on individuals and entities that traded with the terrorist group. Attaching the name of an individual or company on a sanctions list could have stopped thousands from doing business with ISIS. Unfortunately, no such action was taken because there was no strong political incentive to do that. In my strategy, such actions should be taken.

HALT LOOTING AND SELLING OF ARTIFACTS

Following the U.S. occupation of Iraq in 2003 and Paul Bremer's orders to dismiss the Iraqi Army, which I discussed in Chapter 3, the police force and intelligence agencies in Iraq suffered a major blow. The chaos and looting that followed the toppling of Saddam's regime allowed people to torch buildings and to run off with treasures from Iraqi museums and historical sites that were thousands of years old. The situation became even worse when ISIS took over huge swathes of Iraq filled with holy shrines, historical sites, and museums. ISIS militants, whose strict Salafi interpretation of Islam deems the respect of tombs and non-Islamic remnant to be idolatrous, destroyed tombs, mosques, and churches and burned precious manuscripts and archives.

In September 2014, Béatrice André-Salvini, Director of Near Eastern Antiquities at UNESCO, stressed the need to recover and save Iraq's treasure from ISIS's hands before more artifacts were torched or sold off by the "artifacts mafia" that turned Iraq into a black market for stolen antiquities.[26] According to a *New York Times* opinion piece, ISIS allows locals to dig at ancient sites as long as those people give ISIS a percentage of the monetary value of anything found. The article was written by three people who had returned from southern Turkey and interviewed people who live and work in ISIS-controlled territory. They reported that the ISIS system of profiteering from antiquities thieving is very complicated.[27] In my strategy, this practice cannot be allowed to continue.

Smuggled Iraqi antiquities have traveled as far as France, Switzerland, and even California, where the FBI seized a series of ancient Mesopotamian tablets. Although ISIS uses a particularly organized mode of looting, the fact that terrorist groups profit from stolen artifacts is nothing new. Both Al Qaeda and the Taliban looted antiquities for the purpose of funding their operations.[28]

In March 2015, the *Daily Mail* reported that 2,000-year-old artifacts looted from ancient sites in Iraq and Syria by ISIS were being sold on eBay. Jewelry, ceramics, and coins plundered from museums are known to pass between criminal gangs before turning up in Gulf States and later appearing on trading websites. Two coins from Apamea that date back to Ancient Greece have appeared on eBay with price tags of £57 and £90.[29] In my strategy, these sites cannot be allowed to continue to support such activity.

A solution that I endorse, suggested by Hugh Eakin, Senior Editor at *The New York Review of Books*, is to extend the doctrine of "responsibility to protect." This traditionally was used to justify military intervention to stop genocide and massacre, but in my strategy, it should be extended to the protection of nonliving cultural heritage as well. A few well-placed air strikes on an ISIS convoy headed to loot an archaeological site could dissuade ISIS from gathering at such sites.[30]

A similar course of action that I support in my strategy was advocated by the Iraqi Tourism and Antiquities Minister Adel Shirshab, when he told a group of reporters, "I am calling on the international community and coalition to activate its air strikes and target terrorism wherever it exists." He further commented, "It was possible to carry out surveillance. Why didn't this happen?"[31] Another similar proposal I support was advanced by Italian Culture Minister Dario Franceschini, who called for the creation of an "international rapid response force to defend monuments and archaeological sites in conflict zones." This proposal needs to expand throughout the world in a manner similar to UN peacekeeping mandates, such that "A sort of 'blue helmets of culture' are needed, as there are blue helmets (the peacekeeping forces of the United Nations who are identified by wearing helmets colored blue) that intervene to protect in situations of war."[32] These efforts should be coordinated with UNESCO, the UN agency already engaged in protection of cultural sites and objects.

RETURNING STOLEN ARTIFACTS TO IRAQ

When I served as Ambassador of Iraq to the United Nations from April 2006 to April 2013, I participated in returning some Iraqi artifacts that were stolen, smuggled out of Iraq, and sold in the black market. In July 25, 2006, I participated in a ceremony at the Iraqi Embassy in Washington, D.C., during which a 4,400-year-old artifact that was stolen from the Iraq National Museum in April 2003 was returned after a 3-year search.

U.S. Secretary for Homeland Security Michael Chertoff, Iraqi Prime Minister Nuri al-Maliki, and U.S. Ambassador to Iraq Zalmay Khalilzad participated in the repatriation ceremony for the ancient diorite statue of King Entemena. U.S. Immigration and Customs Enforcement, an agency in the Department of Homeland Security, worked with the international police organization Interpol to find the statue.[33]

In 2008, the Mission of Peru to the United Nations sent me a letter saying that the customs authorities at the airport of Lima confiscated several pieces of Iraqi artifacts when a smuggler tried to get them in the country.

The letter explained how the Peruvian authorities contacted an antiquities expert in Spain who confirmed that those artifacts were stolen from Iraq after the chaos of 2003. I wrote to the Iraqi government who sent a delegation from the capital to New York and then to Lima. They received the artifacts in an official ceremony and then took them back to Iraq. This was an excellent cooperative action by Peru. In my strategy, such examples need to be well known so other countries will do likewise, and be on the alert. Such proactive steps have to be taken.

On December 7, 2011, I came across a strange piece of news that Park Avenue Autumn, a New York restaurant that changed its name to align with changes in the seasons, was offering a new dish, served on gold-painted plates looted from Saddam Hussein's palaces. I contacted the attorney of the Mission of Iraq to the United Nations, Jack Shakarchy, an Iraqi Jew and a good friend, who wrote a letter to the restaurant's owner. In his letter, he explained that the dishes were the property of the Republic of Iraq and that the restaurant should stop using them and promptly return them to the Iraqi authorities. The United Nations Security Council had adopted a resolution that stolen properties after the invasion of 2003 should be returned to Iraq.

Jack also contacted the State Department and the Justice Department, and they worked together to bring all 19 dishes to the Mission of Iraq. Originally, the dishes were sent in bubble envelopes from Iraq by mail with Iraqi stamps on them. After they reached the United States, they had been sold on eBay and the restaurant bought them. In the end, a U.S. official from the State Department and another official from the Justice Department brought the dishes in their bubble envelopes to the Mission of Iraq to the United Nations. This is another example in my strategy of both international cooperation and also stopping Internet sites from participating in such activities.

I handed the 19 dishes to the Prime Minister Nouri al-Maliki who was visiting the United States as that time and he took them back. In my first trip to Iraq after that, I checked with deputy director of the Baghdad Museum who told me that the prime minister handed over the dishes to them.

In 2012, I visited the Iraqi Ambassador to the United States at his residence in Washington, D.C., and he showed me a few ancient golden jewelry pieces which were handed to him by the U.S. authorities. He said the U.S. government handed over more than 4,000 artifacts to the Iraqi Embassy in Washington, D.C.

STOP THE SELLING OF WOMEN AS SLAVES

Non-Muslims such as Jews, Christians, Yazidiz, and Sabians lived in Iraq for centuries. However, ISIS considers people that belong to these religious groups to be disbelievers and they use this philosophy to justify killing their men and taking their women and children as slaves.

Shockingly, these "slaves" were then sexually abused and sold in open markets, while the whole world was watching. Some women who were sold had children, but the buyers refused to allow them to take the children with them. These women were separated from their children who were then taken by ISIS to special orphanages and schools to raise them as ISIS fighters and terrorists.

It is a shame on humanity to allow this kind of slavery, sexual abuse, and the sale of women by the most backward, brutal, and extreme terrorist group in the 21st century. Other than expressing outrage, dismay, and condemnation, the international community, the United Nations, and other international organizations such as UNESCO did not do much to stop these shameful atrocities. In my strategy, this inaction is not acceptable, as clearly it should not be tolerated.

To truly understand what was going on in ISIS-occupied lands, one should listen to a report from an aid worker who was helping rescued ISIS sex slaves, who says that ISIS "would offer people a choice: you either die or convert to Islam and swear allegiance to ISIS. Women and children were taken away as slaves."[34]

British extremists fighting in Syria and Iraq have boasted on Twitter that Yazidi women had been kidnapped and used as "slave girls." (Yazidi refers to a religious minority found primarily in northern Iraq and also in southeastern Turkey, northern Syria, the Caucasus region, and parts of Iran, and whose religion includes elements of ancient Iranian religions as well as elements of Judaism, Nestorian Christianity, and Islam.) A 17-year-old female from the Yazidi minority captured by ISIS described the horror of being kept as a sex slave, as one of a group of about 40 Yazidi women being held captive and sexually abused on a daily basis by ISIS fighters.[35]

In August 2014, United Nations Secretary-General Ban Ki-moon said he was "profoundly dismayed" by the barbaric attacks carried out by the ISIS group, including summary executions and the degradation of women where girls are abducted or trafficked as sex slaves. He urged the international community to do even more to help rescue members of Iraq's Yazidi community trapped on Mount Sinjar, saying, "The plight of Yazidis and others on Mount Sinjar is especially harrowing."[36]

Thousands of women and children in Iraq were forced into marriage and sexual slavery by members of ISIS. Slavery is such a significant part of ISIS's agenda that the group has published a pamphlet on the subject, which includes instructions such as, "It is permissible to buy, sell, or give as a gift female captives and slaves, for they are merely property, which can be disposed of."

In October 2014, Under Secretary for Terrorism and Financial Intelligence David Cohen said, "With time, patience, and close international cooperation, the steps I have outlined today will help undermine ISIS's financial foundation. I must stress again, however, that the campaign against ISIS's finances will require more than just financial tools."[37] Cohen added, "So, while we work toward lasting solutions, Treasury will continue to deploy innovative strategies to disrupt ISIS's financing. Together with our partners in the U.S. government and across the globe, we will degrade and ultimately defeat ISIS."[38]

Several months later, the Office of the United Nations High Commissioner for Human Rights (OHCHR) released a report on ISIS crimes in Iraq. One of the recommendations was that the situation should be referred to the International Criminal Court. This was important progress, along with the need to keep up the pressure until the Security Council takes action.[39] However, to date, in spite of the unprecedented kinds of crimes, painful violation of human rights, and huge abuses of women and children, the world has yet to see any leader or member of ISIS referred to the International Criminal Court. Action in this direction is a crucial part of my strategy.

I believe that U.S. officials were very good at developing theories and discussing plans to disrupt funding terrorist groups, especially Al Qaeda after the 9/11 terrorist attacks and ISIS after declaring their Islamic State "caliphate" and following the heinous crimes. However, practically speaking, theories and plans have not stopped those terrorist groups that continue to receive adequate funds to carry out and inspire all kind of atrocities in the Middle East, Europe, and the United States. The U.S. administrations should have been more serious in tracing, arresting, and indicting those who support terrorism in the same way they did with terrorists. In my strategy, these actions would be priority and tracking progress would be strict.

The U.S. government did arrest and indict some people in the United States, but if they bring just one terrorist financier to justice from oil-rich Gulf countries, they would deter thousands who act with impunity when they provide the financial lifeline for brutal extremists to continue their acts in Afghanistan, Iraq, Libya, and Syria. Stopping funding terrorism as described above is critical in my strategy to defeat terrorists.

Another essential tactic is to interfere with, and break, the Internet connections and exploitation of technology used by terrorists, as I describe in the next chapter.

CHAPTER 10

Strategy to Stop
Internet Terrorism

As described in Chapter 5, one of the reasons why the world failed to stop terrorist groups Al Qaeda and ISIS is that they could not prevent or curtail the exploitation of the major tools used to radicalize people, recruit youth, and inspire terrorist attacks, namely the Internet and social media networks. Terrorists have used unique tools such as using airplanes as missiles on 9/11 and anthrax letters to achieve their objectives. The Internet is another unique tool available for their use. This chapter outlines how the Internet is addressed in my counterterrorism strategy.

Terrorist groups exploit the Internet and the social media networks for encrypted communications to launch propaganda campaigns and collect donations. ISIS terrorists used the Internet and social networks to coordinate attacks in France, Belgium, Germany, and other countries. Thus, it is imperative to have a comprehensive and long-term strategy to fight Internet terrorism and to have a countercampaign to terrorist groups' misuse and abuse of Internet and social media networks. Furthermore, the world needs to unite in order to guide people away from extreme ideology on the Internet and to counter terrorist misinterpretation of Islam.

Terrorists fight their wars in cyberspace as well as on the ground. Cyber terrorism is a term that refers to the politically motivated use of computers and information technology to cause severe disruption or widespread fear in society. Not much was known about the threat posed by terrorists' use of the Internet until a few years ago when the dangers that cyber terrorism poses through use of the Internet came to light. The impact has also reflected on technology itself, making sources subject to mistrust. Today, terrorist organizations and their supporters maintain hundreds of websites, exploiting the unregulated, anonymous, and easily accessible nature of the Internet to target a selection of messages to a variety of audiences.[1] Terrorists can choose whether to remain hidden in the technological world, or to openly advertise.

THE SOLUTION FOR INTERNET TERRORISM

Some high-ranking U.S. officials, directors of intelligence agencies as well as managers of tech firms and social networks companies believe that there is no solution to prevent terrorists from exploiting the Internet, and that it is going to be very difficult to find terrorists before they strike especially when they are self-radicalized individuals and lone wolves that I described in earlier chapters. Some experts describe the process of finding a terrorist like finding a needle in a haystack. Other officials state that they cannot legally take down websites, even those used by ISIS and other terrorist groups.

I maintain that such statements encourage terrorist groups to continue their Internet campaigns and help sympathizers in the West continue their efforts to carry out attacks. Such statements are just an excuse for mistakes committed by those in important positions who miss the signs and cover up their failure to stop terrorists. Mattathias Schwartz of the *New Yorker* magazine believes, "It is unreasonable to assume we can stop the terrorist attacks 100 percent of the time—because of many factors, including their inventiveness—but in retrospect, every terrorist attack leaves a data trail that appears to be dotted with missed opportunities."[2]

For example, following the terrorist attack of Omar Mateen at the gay nightclub in Orlando in June 2016, President Obama said that the massacre raised the issue of terrorism. He also mentioned the issue of gun control, saying, "If we have self-radicalized individuals in this country, then they are going to be very difficult to find ahead of time, and, how easy it is for them to find weapons is, in some cases, going to make a difference as to whether they are going to be able to carry out attacks like this."[3]

In my counterterrorism strategy, gun control must be addressed. Of course in the United States, the gun lobby is strong, a fact that interferes with controlling the use of those weapons in terrorist attacks. In other countries, the issue may be resolved more readily. Former Director of the FBI James Comey was realistic in his warning that ISIS, trying to recruit followers in the West, is using the Internet extensively. Even though the FBI is tracking people attracted to ISIS, they cannot turn off the Internet in the home of every potential militant.[4]

Vice President of Microsoft Corporation Steven Crown told the United Nations Security Council that for the Internet industry, the challenge of terrorist propaganda and communication is daunting. "If there were an elegant solution, industry would have adopted it," Crown said at a Security Council debate on counterterrorism. "There is no single answer; there is no silver bullet that will stop terrorist use of the internet."[5]

Crown's statement that there is no single answer and there is no silver bullet to stop terrorists' use of the Internet is a classic and ready-made answer for any political, military, and security complicated problem. Some British and American officials used to say the same thing when Saddam Hussein's regime committed atrocities against the Iraqi people: "We wish we have a silver bullet or a magic stick to remove Saddam's regime, but we don't." I did not give up, as you can tell from reading about my background and life. My approach is to sit with a group of stakeholders and come up with solutions.

Terrorists cross borders, so solutions in my strategy require collective actions by international actors. I believe the international community has to respond, and collectively brainstorm solutions to combat the terrorists' use of Internet that inspires budding terrorists to kill innocent people. My strategy would follow the suggestion Obama made in addressing the nation after the 2015 attacks in Paris and San Bernardino, California, that left many dead. First, he recognized how the Internet can be partly responsible for acts of local terrorists. "As the Internet erases the distance between countries, we see growing efforts by terrorists to poison the minds of people like the Boston Marathon bombers and the San Bernardino killers," he said. Then, he suggested something I include in my strategy, saying that the solution to terrorism involves "urg[ing] high-tech and law enforcement leaders to make it harder for terrorists to use technology to escape from justice."[6]

In my strategy, governments, intelligence agencies, and tech firms need to do more to stop terrorism. They *can* do much more, if they exert what's referred to as political will. As the popular saying goes, "If there is a will, there is a way." There are many cases to prove this, so here I will give two examples of determination of broadcast media that led to successfully uncovering a terrorist.

On December 13, 2014, Indian police arrested a 24-year-old man named Mehdi Masroor Biswas whose carefully hidden true identity was discovered by British Channel 4 TV. He was the best-known follower of ISIS jihadists on social media. His Twitter site, "ShamiWitness," had 17,000 followers, with his commentaries and insights into jihadist behavior drawing a worldwide audience.[7]

In November 2015, an undercover investigation by Channel 4 uncovered some British women who were supporting ISIS in the United Kingdom. The undercover footage in the Channel 4 broadcast showed female ISIS sympathizers who, in weekly two-hour lectures in London, were using racially abusive language to describe Jews and Israelis, telling young Muslim women that Britain is waging a war against them, and urging them to abandon democracy and travel to Syria to join ISIS.[8]

If a TV channel can discover supporters and sympathizers of terrorist groups, the police, law enforcement forces, and intelligence agencies should be able to discover more of these supporters and sympathizers, because they have more resources, experience, and technology to do that.

IS NSA'S METADATA GOOD OR BAD?

In June 2013, it was revealed that the National Security Agency (NSA) has a surveillance program to collect huge quantities of information, called metadata, for all telephone calls and communications in the United States. This information will be stored for five years. I applaud this system and implore that it should be stored for more years since it can take a lot of time to uncover some terrorists.

Edward Snowden, the American computer professional, former CIA employee, and former government contractor for the NSA who copied and leaked classified NSA information in 2013 without authorization, revealed the secret programs and huge information bank of U.S. phone calls—who called whom, for how long, and from where. The information included Internet searches, social media content, and, most controversially, recordings. Snowden's leaks revealed that the NSA was scanning the worldwide use of nine U.S.-based Internet service providers, including Google, Yahoo, Skype, and YouTube. "After the leak, terrorists posted Arabic news articles about it and recommended fellow terrorists be very cautious, and not to give their real phone number and other such information when registering for a website. They also recommended that jihadists use privacy-protecting e-mail systems, like TOR."[9]

U.S. intelligence agencies struggled to save their surveillance of Al Qaeda and other terrorists, who were at the same time working to change how they communicate after Snowden leaked the details of two NSA spying programs. Such an electronic game of cat-and-mouse could have deadly consequences if a plot was missed or a terrorist operative managed to drop out of sight.[10]

Mass media, policymakers, and even security agencies have tended to focus on the exaggerated threat of cyber terrorism and have not paid sufficient attention to the more routine uses of the Internet. Those uses are numerous and, from the terrorists' perspective, invaluable.

After Snowden leaked documents about secret NSA surveillance programs, people demanded privacy from tech firms. The balance between privacy and security is a delicate one, and there is long debate and hard discussion regarding the fine line between privacy and security. Western governments should show more transparency about their programs on data requests, and should use better surveillance programs.

As you can tell by now, my strategy compromises some privacy in the interests of safety, prevention, and protection of citizens. Yet I understand that while we must better defend our societies against cyber terrorism and Internet-savvy terrorists, we must also consider the costs of applying counterterrorism measures to the Internet.[11]

Reporter Mattathias Schwartz of the *New Yorker* magazine wrote:

The N.S.A. asserts that it uses the metadata to learn whether anyone inside the U.S. is in contact with high-priority terrorism suspects, referred to as "known bad guys." The N.S.A.'s surveillance programs have stopped "fifty-four different terrorist-related activities." Most of these were "terrorist plots." Thirteen involved the United States. Credit for foiling these plots was partly due to the metadata program, intended to "find the terrorist that walks among us." President Obama also counted the benefits of the metadata program. In June 2013, in a press conference with Angela Merkel, the German Chancellor, Obama said, "We know of at least fifty threats that have been averted because of this information." He continued, "Lives have been saved."[12]

Schwartz' view has been criticized. At a Senate Judiciary Committee hearing in October 2013, Senator Patrick Leahy of Vermont called the fifty-four-plots statistic "plainly wrong . . . these weren't all plots, and they weren't all thwarted." He cited a statement that "there's only really one example of a case where, but for the use of Section 215 bulk phone-records collection, terrorist activity was stopped."[13] The terrorists could have switched e-mail accounts or cell phone providers or adopted new encryption techniques. Al Qaeda in the Arabian Peninsula has been among the first to alter how it reaches out to its operatives. Chat rooms and websites used by like-minded extremists and would-be recruits advise users how to avoid National Security Agency detection.[14]

A mass surveillance program is admittedly dangerous as it may give intelligence agencies a false feeling of security. If tracking a terrorist is like finding a needle in a haystack, then, as former FBI Director Comey said, "If the haystack is bigger, it would be harder to find the needle. In other words, if intelligence watches everybody, they are watching no body. Criteria have to be more discerning to detect potential attackers to surveil."[15]

As Thomas Drake, a former NSA executive and whistle-blower who has become one of the agency's most vocal critics, said, "If you target everything, there's no target." Drake favors what he calls "a traditional law-enforcement" approach to terrorism, gathering more intelligence on a smaller set of targets. Decisions about which targets matter, he said, should be driven by human expertise, not by a database.[16]

It seems obvious to me, and is included in my strategy, that both resources should be used—databases and human expertise. It is not easy to know if the NSA missed the terrorist attacks in the United States during 2015 and 2016 because they were watching too many people and collecting metadata made it more difficult to find a needle in a haystack instead of focusing on smaller numbers of people who were strong suspects and who posed real threats.

COUNTERPROPAGANDA CAMPAIGN

Terrorist groups are competitive, not cooperative, with each other. There are problems, conflicts, and fights among different terrorist groups. ISIS had problems with Al Qaeda, Al-Nusra Front fought ISIS, Ahrar al-Sham fought Al-Nusra, and so on. Competition extends to the Internet and social media.

Thus, it is imperative to have a countercampaign to defeat and to undermine their propaganda campaign. In my strategy, this counterpropaganda campaign would focus on the distorted ideology of terrorism, the unjustified bloodshed, and violations of human rights, especially abusing women and children.

The campaign would focus on divisions among the groups, to weed them out, and foster infighting so that they end up killing each other. This would also expose their hypocrisy when they claim to be on the right path of God, but are not. Thus, in my strategy, competition among terrorist groups in the media, Internet, and on social networks would be highlighted.

These divisions could be used to influence members of the terrorist organizations and to bring doubts about the motives and intentions of their leaders, revealing them to be obsessed with their personal interests and benefits, such as money, influence, and power. When such issues are raised, members of terrorist groups would be encouraged to reflect more objectively and possibly defect.[17] The counterpropaganda campaign could include engaging militants and their sympathizers while also allowing intelligence agencies to track and even interact with them. In this way, my strategy differs from a more traditional approach that does not engage in any way. This was happening when I was in Iraq with terrorist and insurgency groups. A State Department spokesman agreed with me when he said that nowadays, "the goal is to engage with and change the conversation, because it is happening."[18]

In May 2016, the United Nations Security Council requested a "comprehensive international framework" to counter propaganda by terrorist groups that motivates others to commit terrorist acts. In a statement adopted in the United Nations, the Security Council noted the urgent need to understand how these groups, such as ISIS and Al Qaeda, recruit others, and to develop a counternarrative campaign to amplify active denouncers of these groups.[19]

The Security Council asked its Counter-Terrorism Committee to present a proposal on the framework, with recommended guidelines and good practices by April 30, 2017. At the meeting, then-UN Deputy Secretary-General Jan Eliasson also called for further study and research on how violent extremists are using the Internet and social media.[20]

THE FBI NEEDS MORE LINGUISTS

In July 2000, the National Commission on Terrorism recognized that a shortage of trained linguists was undercutting U.S. security. In its final report, the commission stated, "All U.S. government agencies face a drastic shortage of linguists to translate raw data into useful information. This shortage has a direct impact on counterterrorism efforts." Because the FBI does not properly prioritize surveillance recordings, translators often tackle lower-value recordings even as some crucial ones are not translated.[21]

On September 11, 2001, the FBI had only one Arabic-speaking agent in the entire New York area, Ali Soufan, who left the FBI and wrote a book, *Black Banners*, in which he talked about the mistakes that led to the 9/11 attacks. In fact, he was one of only eight Arabic-speaking FBI agents in the whole United States. Soufan believes if the CIA cooperated with the FBI, they could have uncovered the 9/11 plot, although other intelligence agents believe that the 9/11 attacks were unavoidable.

In my strategy, it is essential to employ Arabic-speaking persons. Arabic is the language of major terrorist groups. Al Qaeda, its leaders and most of commanders, speak only Arabic. Important statements on audio and video tapes are in Arabic. Most Al Qaeda websites and Internet materials are also in Arabic—though clearly many materials are in other languages to appeal to recruits with other native tongues. Foreign fighters speak their native tongue as their first language even if they know Arabic, but they are less in number and importance than Arabic-speaking leaders.

In my strategy, I recognize the importance of employing native Arabs, along with experts or team members who have learned Arabic, even if they don't speak the language well. Staff in regions should be fluent in the local dialect, of which there are many throughout the Arab region.

ISIS also depends on Arabic language more than other languages although it has more foreign fighters than Al Qaeda. Its leader, Abo Bakr al-Baghdadi, speaks only Arabic, and all his statements and preachings are in Arabic. Therefore, it is necessary to know Arabic to monitor terrorist websites, Internet activities, and communications so as to understand what they are thinking, discussing, and planning in more accurate ways.

A lot of information could be collected from public statements, speeches and communiqués. It is well-known that during the Cold War, the United States and the Soviet Union were dependent on public information, newspapers, magazines, radios, and TV, to collect information about each other.

In 2005, while congressmen, journalists, and experts focused on the 9/11 Commission Report, the Office of the Inspector General at Department of Justice quietly released another report, highlighting the FBI's continuing difficulties with speedy and tactically effective foreign language translation.[22] In 2009, the FBI Inspector General's audit showed a backlog in translating critical documents, an increasing shortfall in reviewing counterintelligence and counterterrorism audio intercepts, and its difficulty in hiring linguists.[23]

Six years later, the 9/11 Review Commission, created to monitor federal law enforcement changes after the 9/11 attacks, issued a report stating that the FBI needs to improve its intelligence capabilities and hire more linguists to counter the evolving threats to the United States.[24]

FBI director Comey said the report has been "a tremendously valuable thing to me as director. Issues identified in the report—which would serve as a blueprint for the FBI over the next quarter century—are the recruitment of people with the necessary skills to deal with complex missions, such as cyber threats, and hiring linguists."[25]

In my counterterrorism strategy, speakers of all languages would be engaged, as the arm of terrorist groups and their use of Internet tools reaches into all countries, as I predicted. Comey said that ISIS has more than 21,000 English-speaking followers through social media. It is necessary to engage all language speakers since ISIS has so many followers on its social media accounts like Twitter and Facebook that reach a broad audience. This reach has resulted in the "lone wolf" effect that includes individuals of various backgrounds, cultures, and languages, as I described in previous chapters.[26]

If we compare the capabilities, budget, and resources of the FBI with that of ISIS, and compare the number of FBI agents speaking Arabic with ISIS's 21,000 English-speaking followers through social media, ISIS will come out on top. Thus, the FBI needs to do more to match ISIS in the number of linguists it employs.

SHUT DOWN TERRORIST WEBSITES

Terrorists groups are good at setting up a large number of websites to disseminate extreme ideology, radicalize people, and mobilize support for terrorism. They also encourage their sympathizers to attack military personnel, police officers, and intelligence agents. The terrorist organizations radicalize people through the Internet, and inspire them, to use all available means to kill innocents, such as using cars and trucks to mow down civilians and then to use kitchen's knives, axes, and machetes to kill more people when their vehicles crash.

Following deadly terrorist attacks in Europe and the United States, a strong argument emerged about terrorist websites and if authorities can shut them down. And if they can, why have they waited so long, until these websites were disseminated throughout the world and inspired terrorists to kill innocent civilians. It is hard to control terrorist messages when they are online because they are so easily accessed on the Internet. Shutting them down is difficult. But there are steps that governments and tech firms can take, to use systems that censor anything that looks like terrorism.

In December 2012, the Bipartisan Policy Center, a Washington, D.C., think tank, issued a report called "Countering Online Radicalization in America." The report issued a number of suggestions to lawmakers on how to curb the rise in terrorism online and offline. The report featured a number of common sense strategies. Their strategy is in three sections: reducing the supply, reducing the demand, and exploiting cyberspace.

The first, reducing the supply, says that current approaches to reducing radical content on the Internet is "neither feasible nor desirable." The group also offers some basic recommendations on how to cut down on violent rhetoric. The report suggests that Government should refrain from establishing nationwide filtering systems. Government needs to retain its capability for aggressive takedowns of foreign-based websites but only use it when doing so is absolutely essential to stop a terrorist attack and/or prevent the loss of life.[27]

Admittedly, it is difficult to know for sure if taking down a particular foreign-based website is enough to stop a terrorist attack and/or prevent the loss of life before such a terrorist attack takes place. Therefore, establishing a nationwide filtering system is best. In my strategy, the U.S. government should establish informal partnerships with large Internet companies to brief and guide them about national security threats, as well as trends and patterns in terrorist propaganda and communication.

After the Paris terrorist attacks in 2015 in which around 130 people were killed, U.S. Republican Representative Joe Barton from Texas had a plan to stop terrorists: shut down websites, including social media networks. Barton asked Federal Communications Commission (FCC) Chairman Tom Wheeler if the commission can shut down websites used by ISIS and other terrorist groups. Barton replied, "I'm not sure our authority extends to [shut down the websites]."[28] Wheeler similarly told Democrat Representative Bobby Rush from Illinois, "We do not have jurisdiction over Facebook and all the other edge providers. We do not intend to assert jurisdiction over them." But he said that he can use the FCC bully pulpit to press tech CEOs on the issue, such as Facebook's Mark Zuckerberg, saying, "I will call Mark Zuckerberg to raise the issue you've raised and I'm sure he'll have some thoughts."[29]

In my view, the big question is why FCC Chairman Wheeler waited until after the terrorist attack in Paris, and until after Congressmen Barton and Rush asked their questions, to use the FCC bully pulpit to press tech CEOs on the issue and to call Facebook's Mark Zuckerberg.

The answer includes that American democracy allows freedom of speech, and in a democracy, you cannot punish people for their political views. Some argue that there are a lot of ISIS sympathizers and that the law cannot stop them unless they commit a crime. However, I would argue that even in a democracy, whenever there is a clear threat, as when ISIS declared war against the United States, the United States should take action with respect to the Internet and social media.

REMOVE RECIPES TO MAKE BOMBS

Homemade bombs such as pressure cooker and pipe bombs are favored weapons of terrorist groups such as Al Qaeda and ISIS, because they are cheap, components are available in markets and on the Internet, and they are easy to assemble and very powerful. Extensive damage and injuries result, especially when nails and ball bearings are added.

Pressure cooker bombs were used in terrorist strikes in India, Afghanistan, Nepal, and Pakistan. The bomb shrapnel, consisting of metal fragments, ball bearings, and nails, are packed into pressure cookers and designed to look like discarded items. Cars have also been used as weapons. In May 2010, Al Qaeda inspired Faisal Shahzad to drive to Manhattan in a Nissan Pathfinder SUV, loaded with an improvised explosive pressure cooker bomb and incendiary devices consisting of propane tanks, and to park the car in busy Times Square.[30]

In April 2013, the brothers behind the horrific Boston Marathon carnage detonated two bombs made from kitchen pressure cookers packed with metallic pieces and nails. Instructions on how to build a pressure cooker bomb were featured in the infamous *Inspire* article, "Make a Bomb in the Kitchen of Your Mom." Doctors say that numerous sharp metal objects were extracted from victims of the blasts.[31] A post on a blog demonstrates how to make nitroglycerin, a main ingredient of dynamite. Also, a terror fugitive video, posted on YouTube, illustrates the contemporary methods used by terrorist cells to employ cyberspace and social networking in particular to incite hate.[32]

By 2014, members of ISIS forums started encouraging "lone wolf" bomb attacks in some of America's most high-profile tourist locations. A posting on the Internet entitled, "To the Lone Wolves in America: How to Make a Bomb in Your Kitchen, to Create Scenes of Horror in Tourist Spots and Other Targets," suggests attacking well-populated tourist sites, like Times Square in New York City, Las Vegas, and tourist sites in Texas, as well as metro train stations throughout the United States.[33]

In the attack that injured 31 people in a neighborhood of Manhattan in New York in September 2016, pressure cookers were used as bombs filled with "fragmentation materials," namely, small bearings or metal ball bearings. A second device that did not explode appeared to be filled with the same material.[34] Five people considered responsible for making the homegrown devices were arrested in connection with this bombing, including a citizen of Afghan descent born in Afghanistan.[35]

In contrast to those simple devices, an expert in IEDs used by terrorists around the world notes that constructing IEDs would require higher-than-average competence in these activities than is usually found in the United States. "Most of what we see in the United States is a pipe bomb with black powder or smokeless powder or a simple hobby fuse," said the expert.[36] It is clear, from the 2015–2016 terrorist attacks in California, Florida, New Jersey, and New York, that homegrown devices are becoming more popular, making terrorists a step ahead of experts and detectors, and proving that Al Qaeda and ISIS are successful in radicalizing people informally through the Internet, teaching them how to make bombs, and inspiring them to use those simplified weapons to attack innocent people.

The government and intelligence community in the United States and internationally need to do everything possible to remove instruction on the Internet, especially about how to make simple devices, like a pressure cooker bomb or a pipe bomb. Otherwise, we are going to see more lone wolves carrying out terrorist attacks with explosives they make in their kitchens from materials they buy through the Internet or get in neighborhood hardware stores.

In the next chapter, I will explain specifically my counterterrorism strategy to deal with lone wolf terrorists.

CHAPTER 11

Strategy to Stop Lone Wolf Terrorists

In this chapter, I will expand upon how to deal with the phenomenon of the lone wolf terrorist in the context of my counterterrorism strategy. Even though Western intelligence agencies managed to thwart many terrorist attacks, terrorist groups, especially Al Qaeda and ISIS, continue to inspire lone wolf attacks in the United States, Europe, Canada, and Australia, among other places.

The lone wolf terrorists have increased in numbers at the same time when ISIS lost some ground; for example, in Iraq in 2017, ISIS lost most of the territories that were under its control during 2014–2016 as a result of actions by the Iraqi Army, federal police, Kurdish fighters (Peshmerga), and popular mobilization forces, with the support of U.S. forces and their allies. Contributing to this decline was the focused intention of President Trump to see Mosul, the second largest city in Iraq and the major base of ISIS, liberated. The operation to liberate Mosul started in mid-October 2016, and as of June 2017, the city was not yet completely liberated. This is being accomplished slowly because ISIS uses the drastic and horrific practice of using civilians as human shields.

In retaliation to the U.S. action, ISIS sent fighters to infiltrate Western countries disguised as refugees who used fake passports, as happened in some of the terrorist attacks in France, Belgium, and the U.K. in 2015–2017. Another powerful weapon used by ISIS was to inspire individuals in the West to act on their own and to attack "soft" targets, especially gathering places for civilians such as malls, subways, and theaters, to kill as many people as possible.

As I pointed out, some women as well as men became these lone wolves. In Iraq, ISIS used women and children as suicide bombers to stop the advance of the Iraqi Security Forces. There was widespread use of female suicide bombers as part of the organization, but in addition women were asked to act on their own, reflecting the tactical advantage that women provide for terrorism.

First, women look less suspicious than men and thus are less likely to attract attention from security personnel. Second, in many conservative societies of the Middle East and elsewhere, there is hesitation to perform a full body-search on a woman. And third, a woman can wear a suicide device beneath her clothes, appear to be pregnant, and thus easily bypass security while approaching her target.[1] The advantages of females in creating terror was explored in the book, *Terror in the Holy Land: Inside the Anguish of the Israeli-Palestinian Conflict*, edited by Dr. Judy Kuriansky, who wrote the foreword for this book.[2]

CAN THE UNITED STATES STOP "LONE WOLVES"?

Several lone wolf attacks in the United States, I believe, were inspired by ISIS even if ISIS did not claim responsibility and credit; for example, in the attacks in California, Florida, Minnesota, New Jersey, and New York, U.S. intelligence agencies have shifted focus from sleeper cells connected to terrorist groups like Al Qaeda and ISIS to lone wolf actors inspired by terrorist groups. A focus on lone wolves is essential if the United States is going to accomplish what former New York Police Department Commissioner William Bratton said, "This is a new world, if you will, the evolving world of terrorism—and we are staying ahead of it."[3]

Lone wolf terrorism must be stopped. According to a *Washington Post–ABC News* poll conducted in December 2015, the majority of Americans believe that the United States cannot stop lone wolf terrorist attacks. The results show that 77 percent of respondents had only a "fair amount" or no confidence that individual attackers can be stopped. Amid growing national security concerns, Americans doubt the government's ability to stop these "lone wolf" terror attacks.[4] In contrast, 43 percent have at least a "good amount" of confidence in the U.S. government's ability to stop a large-scale, organized attack by a foreign group. When asked about these larger-scale attacks, most Democrats said they are confident in federal prevention measures, while most Republicans are doubtful.[5] Another poll carried out in June 2016 showed an even greater lack of confidence that the government could stop lone wolf attacks; with two-thirds reporting they are not confident. A high number of respondents, 8 out of 10, said they are concerned about lone wolf attacks.[6]

President Obama continued to get negative feedback for his handling of terrorism and dealing with ISIS militants.[7] As the number of apparent lone wolf attacks increased in the United States, it was evident that terrorist groups were developing tactics and misusing technology to recruit and brainwash people, especially vulnerable youth and women. Thus, developing a new comprehensive strategy is urgent to address these disturbing trends, including new recruitment tactics and new brands of terrorists.

INTELLIGENCE SHOULD FOLLOW LEADS

Carrying out a terrorist attack requires some preparation, such as selecting a target, watching and studying the target, preparing weapons and explosives, and finally making a decision about the time to take action and carry out the attack. Lone wolf attacks need this preparation, but less so than a major organization. Lone wolves can also be impulsive and not have an exit strategy, like the Boston Marathon bomber brothers, who improvised their escape, hijacking a car and even wandering through the streets, with one brother ending up hiding in a boat in someone's backyard.

The term itself can on the surface imply some contradictions for untrained people. The terrorist Boston bomb brothers were students, with roommates. They were not totally alone. Lone wolves may seem like loners, but usually someone knows them. Thus, an effective counterterrorism strategy calls for appeals to friends and associates—and even to the wider public—to be on the alert and to report their suspicions. I recall the important slogan for a public service announcement (PSA) of the Metropolitan Transit Authority to increase safety, reminding New York's mass transit riders, "If you see something, say something." PSAs and education programs in schools are recommended in my counterterrorism strategy.

Following the process of carrying out an attack, a lone wolf has to make contacts with people, to buy materials, and maybe even to assemble explosives and execute the attacks. Therefore, the lone wolf leaves clues and leads, which if caught by anyone involved in that process, much less by intelligence agencies or the police, could identify the terrorists before the attack actually takes place.

There are signs that help identify a terrorist before an attack. Friends and associates can be alert to strange behavior. Things to look for run the gamut from casual statements to anything that points to radicalization, including extremist statements and connection or communications with terrorist groups or extremist leaders. Internet activities are especially revealing. Any tips from family members, coworkers, or neighbors deserve to be investigated by intelligence agencies that need to follow any lead or indication that suggests terrorism. Investigations should not be dropped if there is any possibility of danger, and unless there is conclusive evidence to close a case.

For example, investigators believe Omar Mateen, the Pulse club attacker in Orlando, Florida, made surveillance trips to the club and to the Disney Springs shopping complex during "Gay Days," a citywide celebration. Disney security officials told the FBI they believe he also visited Disney World to conduct surveillance.[8] Mateen's wife said she went with her husband to Pulse and Disney Springs, where he scouted the places. She told investigators she was with her husband on at least one trip to buy ammunition.[9]

Michael Zehaf-Bibeau, who carried out an attack on Canadian soldier Nathan Cirillo and the Canadian Parliament, expressed extremist ideas and an intent to travel to Syria.[10] Zehaf-Bibeau was also angry that Canada supported the American bombing of ISIS in Syria and Iraq—such anger being an indication of his extremism. Propaganda videos and other materials admiring jihad, a "holy war" against enemies of Islam, appeared on his Facebook profile page, including a video featuring the logo of ISIS. These signs should have been noticed.

Another lone wolf terrorist, Martin Couture-Rouleau, changed a profile picture on Facebook five days before his attack to show a picture of two doors opening: one appearing to be leading to heaven and the other to hell. Months earlier, one of his posts read, "Allah has promised the hypocrite men and hypocrite women and the disbelievers the fire of hell, wherein they will abide eternally. It is sufficient for them. And Allah has cursed them, and for them is an enduring punishment." These are also signs that should have been noticed. Underneath that post was the image of a sheik, combined with an Israeli, an American flag, and an American dollar bill, one of a series of images critical of American foreign policy. According to information Radio-Canada obtained from a friend, Couture-Rouleau spent hours on the Internet and devoured jihadist literature and dreamed of dying as a martyr. The Commissioner of the Royal Canadian Mounted Police (RCMP), Bob Paulson, confirmed that Couture-Rouleau's passport had been seized and that he was one of 90 suspected extremists whom the RCMP believed intended to join militants fighting abroad.[11] This should have been caught before he acted.

These two lone wolves acted within days of each other. Commissioner Paulson said, "Zehaf-Bibeau had a very developed . . . non-national security criminality of violence and of drugs and of mental instability." Additionally, his e-mail was found in the hard drive of somebody who was charged with a terrorist-related offense.[12] A name, while certainly not the whole story in itself, can add to the mix of telltale signs. Radio-Canada reported that Couture-Rouleau's Facebook page identified him as Ahmad LeConverti, Ahmad the Converted.

These were many missed clues leading to Michael Zehaf-Bibeau's radicalization. If his embrace of extremist ideas, his social media activity, and his intent to travel to Syria were followed, the authorities could have put Zehaf-Bibeau on a watch list that may have stopped his terrorist attacks. In the case of the terrorist attacks in Paris in 2015, Turkish authorities warned their French counterparts twice in the previous 12 months that one of the attackers, Ismaël Omar Mostefaï, a 29-year-old French citizen, was known to the authorities as someone who had radical Islamist beliefs.[13] Sadly, nothing was done.

Leads regarding Abdelhamid Abaaoud, a leader of the Paris attacks, were also not followed. An image taken from a militant website showed Abaaoud. Additionally, he was linked to thwarted train and church attacks. He was also identified as an accomplice of two jihadists who were killed in a shootout at a jihadist safe house in the eastern Belgian town of Verviers in January 2015. Abaaoud, a Belgian of Moroccan origin, had spent time fighting in Syria. In a February 2015 issue of the online ISIS magazine *Dabiq*, Abaaoud, who uses also the name Abu Umar al-Baljiki (meaning, the Belgian), boasted about how he could operate in plain sight in Belgium and never get caught. He said in the interview that after the shootout in Verviers, the authorities "figured out that I had been with the brothers and that we had been planning operations together." Brazenly, he said, "My name and picture were all over the news, yet I was able to stay in their homeland, plan operations against them, and leave safely when doing so became necessary. He recounted how on one occasion he had been stopped by police, but they failed to recognize him and let him go."[14] He was right, the signs should not have been missed.

According to Wisconsin Senator Ron Johnson, Omar Mateen, the lone wolf attacker in the Pulse nightclub, used Facebook before and during the attack. In a letter to Facebook Chairman and CEO Mark Zuckerberg asking for the company's assistance in the investigation, Johnson said that Mateen used the social networking platform to "search for and post terrorism-related content." Mateen's messages declared his allegiance to ISIS and called for the United States and Russia to stop bombing the terror group. One message reportedly said, "now taste the Islamic state vengeance."[15] True enough, Mateen acted alone and can be considered a lone wolf, but his posts reveal his desire to be associated with terrorism. Had his social media contacts to terrorism sites been noted, many lives could have been saved.

TERRORISTS ARE KNOWN TO AUTHORITIES

Most of the extremists who carry out terrorist attacks in the West, including lone wolf attackers, were known to intelligence agencies and law enforcement before they committed atrocities. Some of them had connections with terrorist groups, some were suspected of extremist ideology, and some were involved in drugs and other petty crimes.

Abdulhakim Mujahid Muhammad shot and killed an army soldier at a Little Rock recruiting station in Arkansas on June 1, 2009. But he was charged with murder, not terrorism. The *Los Angeles Times* reports that after converting to Islam in Tennessee at age 20, he moved to Yemen, was arrested there, and then came back to the United States to attack the recruiting station. According to police, Muhammad stated he was "mad at the U.S. military because of what they had done to Muslims in the past," and he wanted to "kill as many people in the Army as he could."[16] This is a clear sign of danger. According to the perpetrator's father, the FBI did not charge Muhammad with terrorism because doing so would have shed a spotlight on their own incompetence. Apparently, Muhammad was investigated by the FBI Joint Terrorism Task Force when he returned from Yemen and his visit to Columbus, Ohio, was noted, where authorities were monitoring some Somali Americans traveling from there to Somalia to wage "*jihad*."[17] But nothing was done.

My principle of applying the NYC transit PSA slogan to terrorism applies to the case of a gunman with an arsenal who tried to kill people on a train from Amsterdam to Paris. Fortunately, he was subdued by a U.S. airman who noticed the man holding an assault rifle that "looked like it was jammed and it wasn't working."[18] Importantly, this gunman was known to intelligence agents in at least three countries, but according to his lawyer, he had been traveling internationally by rail for the previous six months. The German Interior Ministry spokesman Johannes Dimroth told the Associated Press News agency, "Germany tracked him in May flying from Berlin to Istanbul—a popular gateway to Syria for militants."[19] But the governments did nothing.

Several terrorists involved in the attacks in Paris and Brussels had ties with terrorism that were known to the authorities before the attacks. Some attackers known to French intelligence had dossiers identifying them as security risks. Abdelhamid Abaaoud, suspected mastermind of the Paris attacks mentioned previously, had been linked to several earlier plots.[20] Authorities also had the image taken from a militant website that showed Abaaoud. Worse yet, in missing the warning signs of a terrorist in the making, he had been linked to thwarted train and church attacks and had already been identified as an accomplice of two jihadists who were killed in a shootout at a jihadist safe house in eastern Belgium.[21] How this can slip through the cracks to have no action taken is unacceptable.

Some cases prove it is hard to spot the signs. Larossi Abballa, who stabbed an off-duty police officer and left him bleeding to death on his own doorstep in France, and forced his way inside the home and stabbed and killed the officer's female partner, had come to the attention of antiterrorist police years earlier. Unfortunately, at the time, "apart from traveling with the wrong crowd and some jogging for fitness, there was not much to complain about him in the strict terms of criminal prosecution."[22] Abballa received only a three-year sentence with a six-month suspended sentence and was allowed to go free after his conviction because he had spent two years and two months in jail awaiting trial.[23] After that, he was only under surveillance for two years and two months. Abballa's case reveals the importance of taking strong steps in the strategy of counterterrorism. These steps should include not just detection and preventive action, but also longer imprisonment and longer surveillance for potential terrorist actions after they leave prison.

In another incident, on April 7, 2017, a 39-year-old lone wolf terrorist killed 4 people and injured 15 in Stockholm, Sweden. Rakhmat Akilov, from Uzbekistan, had been known to intelligence services; he had applied for residency in Sweden in 2014, but his application was rejected in December 2016. He was given four weeks to leave the country, and in February 2017, his case was handed to police to deport him. Police said that Akilov had shown "sympathies to extreme groups such as ISIS."[24] Akilov was arrested on "reasonable suspicion of terrorist homicide,"[25] but security services had not viewed him as a militant threat. A Facebook page appearing to belong to him showed he was following a group called "Friends of Libya and Syria," dedicated to exposing "terrorism of the imperialistic financial capitals" of the United States, Britain, and Arab "dictatorships."[26] Despite all this, he still managed to carry out an attack. Clearly, security forces and police need to be more vigilant.

INTELLIGENCE SHOULD ACT SWIFTLY

Admittedly, it is hard to detect terrorists. Lone wolves may be sloppier than organizations, because they are untrained. In contrast, terrorists in organizations are trained to blend in, as Al Qaeda's terrorists did who carried out the 9/11 attacks. But even the latter can arouse suspicion, as in the case of Zacarias Moussaoui, a French citizen, who was arrested by the FBI when he took flight training courses in Eagan, Minnesota.

Lone wolves can come from abroad, or they may be homegrown. This is what happened in the case of the subway attackers in London, when homegrown suicide bombers attacked the London transportation system on July 7, 2005.

Like lone wolves, terrorists acting with organizations blend in. As Karen Greenberg, Director of the Center on National Security at Fordham Law School said:

I think we are moving towards what we call the "British" model, something that the United States has taken great pride in differentiating itself from over the past seven or eight years. The British radicalization model typically involved someone from South Asia or Pakistan who went to the U.K. for an education, built a life there, and then for some reason—personal, political or both—made their way to terrorist training camps, usually in Pakistan. Then they returned to the U.K. to carry out terrorist acts. The Times Square bomber seems to have taken that very path. He came to the U.S. 11 years ago, went to college, earned an MBA, worked as a financial analyst and owned a house in Connecticut. In 2009, he became a naturalized citizen. Then, just a short time after that, according to court papers, Shahzad traveled to Pakistan, where he got explosives training with a militant group. He may have met with leaders in the Pakistani Taliban before returning to the U.S.[27]

People who knew terrorist Fisal Shahzad in Connecticut and in Pakistan said that in the previous year he had changed in that he became more reserved and more religious, in the face of what a family friend described as "financial troubles." A year earlier, one Pakistani friend said that he even asked his father, Bahar ul-Haq, a retired high-ranking air force pilot in Pakistan, for permission to fight in Afghanistan.[28]

Whether Shahzad decided to attack on his own or not, his Times Square plot should have ended any complacency about homegrown terrorism in the United States. The United Kingdom had made the same mistake before the subway attacks there. They thought it couldn't happen in the United Kingdom, claiming that, "British society is very different," adding, "This is a problem that only exists on the European continent and won't affect us."[29] They were wrong. And other attacks have since been carried out in London.

In Shahzad's case, as for many lone wolves, the bomb's components were common—everyday products that would not raise undue suspicion when purchased especially if they were bought separately. The fact that Shahzad could collect all of the materials, construct an IED (even a poorly designed one), and maneuver it to the intended target without being detected exhibits considerable progress along the attack cycle.[30] Lone wolves may not construct explosive devices expertly, but sometimes neither do terrorists from organizations. In either case the damage can be devastating. If Shahzad had constructed his bomb properly and if the material had detonated, the explosion and the fire, which would have followed, could have caused a large number of casualties because of the high density of people in Times Square—especially on a weekend evening.

Lone wolves usually stay in their country, making it easier to notice their behavior when it is erratic. While ISIS sent terrorists on missions to foreign soil, even to blend in and gain citizenship (e.g., to cross porous European borders easily), they started to ask followers and sympathizers in the West to stay in their countries instead of immigrating to Syria. ISIS is focusing more on radicalizing people in the West through the Internet and to inspire lone wolves to do their dirty work. This inspires a part of my strategy that advises authorities to be on the lookout not just for travelers, but for those on home soil.

Policies to counterterrorism are usually developed as a result of events, developments, and actions either at home or on the international stage. In fact, American officials and intelligence agencies felt that terrorist attacks in the United States were less likely after the Paris attacks because of the difficulties facing terrorists in getting to the United States across the borders. One of the weak points in the Western policies to counterterrorism is that they are reactive when responding to lone wolf threats, when instead they need to be proactive. Although lone wolf terrorist attacks started many years ago, the focus on them shifted only after Mateen's attack on the Florida gay nightclub on June 12, 2016. The U.S. intelligence agencies could have focused on lone wolves much earlier, when ISIS shifted its strategy and many lone wolf attacks started occurring in Europe.

After the attacks in Paris in November 2015 and Brussels in March 2016, U.S. intelligence agencies should have warned the people of similar attacks at home, terrorist attacks like the attacks of California in December 2015, in Florida in June 2016, and in New Jersey and New York in November 2016. Fortunately, U.S. intelligence agencies managed to thwart lone wolf terrorist attacks inside the United States. However, in certain lone wolf cases, intelligence could have acted earlier if some clues and signs of radicalization, especially sympathy for terrorist groups or communications with terrorist leaders, had been investigated.

MISTAKES IN DEALING WITH LONE WOLVES

As I point out, mistakes have been made in dealing with lone wolf terrorists. One major mistake is a lack of coordination and information exchange between different intelligence agencies. This was a major reason that prevented intelligence agencies from uncovering many terrorist threats, including the 9/11 attack. According to FBI agent Ali Souafan, the situation might have had a different conclusion if the CIA provided the FBI with information they requested regarding terrorists' connection to the Yemen attack in 2000 against the USS *Cole*.

One example of devastating mistakes made with respect to lone wolves is the terrorist attack committed by Tamerlan Tsarnaev and his brother at the finish line on Boston Marathon on April 15, 2013, where three people were killed and over 260 were wounded, some severely. The two brothers were known to the FBI. The FBI, acting on a request from Russia, had interviewed Tamerlan Tsarnaev in January 2011, yet unfortunately did not share that activity with the Boston Police Department (BPD).[31]

Coordination between local and international agencies and between similar levels of agencies is essential to my counterterrorism strategy. The Boston Police Department had no knowledge of Tsarnaev's potential links to terrorism uncovered by the FBI. Had the BPD been aware of the 2011 interview, pieces of the puzzle that went unconnected before the Boston Marathon might have been pieced together, elevating the attention on Tsarnaev, and perhaps preventing the attack.[32]

Matt Viser, Deputy Washington Bureau Chief for the *Boston Globe* newspaper, wrote regarding a congressional report about the terrorist attack:

The Federal Security Service, or FSB, the Russian intelligence agency, warned that Tamerlan was known to have associated with radical Islamists. The FBI opened an investigation and interviewed Tsarnaev in person. Based off of its investigation, Tsarnaev's name was entered into a database called The Enforcement Communications System of Department of Homeland Security that would trigger alerts if he left or reentered the United States. In June 2011, the FBI closed its investigation and concluded the assessment found no links to terrorism. A congressional report provides one of the most detailed chronologies available of the distressing failures to connect all the dots in the months before the Boston Marathon bombings. The report highlights the ways intelligence agencies missed an opportunity to detain Tsarnaev less than a year before he planned the attack, when he returned from a trip to Dagestan in July 2012. The report examines Tamerlan Tsarnaev's history and "It largely focuses on questions surrounding his travel, and the sharing of information between federal and state agencies." The House committee produced a timeline of Tamerlan Tsarnaev's trips to Russia, and some of the early warning signs that may have been overlooked. In August 2012, an extremist video was posted to a YouTube account opened in Tsarnaev's name. Because the account was an open-source piece of intelligence, a cyber security team could have found the videos and engaged in a more detailed review of Tsarnaev's Internet activities. This video served as yet another piece of evidence that could have established a reasonable suspicion of criminal case.[33]

Another example of mistakes made in dealing with lone wolves is the case of Mateen who attacked the Florida nightclub. Mateen, an American-born son of parents from Afghanistan, was known to the FBI, who investigated him after he made several remarks claiming connections to terrorism.[34] Mateen was killed in a shootout with police after taking a number of hostages. During the attack, he called 911 and pledged allegiance to ISIS.

FBI Director at the time, James Comey, said that agents opened a preliminary investigation when Mateen was working as a contract security guard at the St. Lucie criminal courthouse. The FBI questioned Mateen again, but that time about possible connections to Moner Mohammad Abusalha, who had blown himself up for Al-Nusra Front in Syria—a group affiliated with Al Qaeda.[35] Coworkers reported that Mateen made some statements that were "inflammatory and contradictory" about terrorism, including claiming family connections to Al Qaeda and then saying he was a member of a West Bank terrorist group. But Mateen was deemed to no longer be a potential threat, and so the FBI closed its 10-month investigation.[36]

No one likes a snitch, but if friends or family care about the welfare of someone who shows suspicious behavior they should report it. This is evident in another case. The father of Ahmad Khan Rahimi—who launched pressure cooker bombs attacks in New Jersey and New York City that resulted in 31 people being injured—called his son a terrorist during a domestic quarrel in which Ahmad was allegedly wielding a knife in a confrontation with a brother. Local police were called and, as part of the investigation, the statement was passed to the FBI as part of the bureau's "guardian" program, which pursues tips from the public about possible terror activity. The official said the FBI reviewed Rahimi's prior activity and interviewed the father twice.[37] However, according to an official, the father later told agents that he made the terrorist claim out of anger, even though he did express concerns about Rahimi's choice of friends. Mistakenly in retrospect, the FBI and local police took no further action about Rahimi.

STOP SELLING ARMS TO PEOPLE ON TERROR LISTS

It is a surprising fact that although some lawmakers, officials, and citizens consider counterterrorism a priority and pledge to do everything they can to prevent lone wolf terror attacks, egregious events still occur. For example, people who are on the government terror watch list can still buy weapons despite the fact that they are flagged because of radical ideology, sympathy with terrorist groups, or suspicion of connection to terrorism. These weapons include handguns, shotguns, and semiautomatic weapons, which are lethal and could cause massive amounts of death and damage. Some lawmakers tried to convince their colleagues to adopt a new law to forbid individuals on government terror watch lists from buying weapons, but there was rejection of the law in the Senate.

President Obama said, "Enough talking about being tough on terrorism. Actually be tough on terrorism, and stop making it as easy as possible for terrorists to buy assault weapons."[38] Permissive U.S. gun laws allow someone like Mateen, who allegedly abused his spouse and was repeatedly investigated by the FBI, to legally purchase a semiautomatic weapon because at that time he had not yet openly supported a terrorist group.[39] Mateen, who bought an AR-15-style semiautomatic rifle and Glock 9 mm pistol from a Port St. Lucie gun dealer a week before his attack, had been on the FBI watch list but was taken off after he was no longer considered a possible threat.[40]

Democrat Congressman Patrick Murphy from Florida, a member of the House Intelligence Committee, said, "The fact that the terrorist loophole is still open is asinine," noting that suspected terrorists on the no-fly list are still be able to purchase weapons. He also said cyberwarfare needs to be a part of the solution. "I hope and I pray that something finally will happen."[41] He added, "It's now time that Congress act. I'll be the first to tell you that these lone wolf attacks are the strategy and the angle of many terrorist groups." He suggested a better way to track lone wolves and share information with federal agencies to better help the intelligence community: "We have to be honest and admit that this has to do with gun violence in this country."[42]

Senate Republicans rejected a bill that aimed to stop suspected terrorists from legally buying guns in 2015. The vote came a day after at least 14 people were killed during the San Bernardino massacre in California I have referred to in this book. Forty-five senators voted for the bill and 54 voted against it.

In my view, it is a tragic mistake to allow people on a terrorist watch list to buy weapons, just because there is a possibility that a name appears on a watch list by mistake. There are other ways to solve this problem. Those whose names are on the list by mistake should be able to get their name removed from the list through an accessible and transparent process of administrative review. I would rather have forbidden someone whose name is in the no-fly list by mistake from buying weapons, than to allow suspect terrorists to buy weapons and potentially do harm to innocent people.

The issues of terrorism should be a priority for governments and all agencies charged with the protection of the country and its people. Congressional bipartisan committees should be able to come to an agreement on how to solve the problem. Every day that a solution is delayed, results in exposing the lives of innocent people to attacks by lone wolf operatives who can easily purchase bomb making materials and weapons from local stores.

Besides action about lone wolves, action must be taken about foreign fighters, according to my comprehensive counterterrorism strategy, as outlined in the next chapter.

CHAPTER 12

Strategy to Stop Foreign Fighters

Stopping foreign fighters is a crucial measure in my 12-step plan to stop terrorist attacks. Foreign fighters, who travel to Syria and Iraq to join ISIS or Al-Nusra Front, the Al Qaeda franchise, need to be tracked. When they return to the countries that they came from after their visit or training, they pose a threat. Tracking them is vital for security in peace-seeking countries.

Foreign fighters can form sleeper cells and carry out attacks when they are ready, or when terrorist groups give them instructions to act. The attacks in Paris and Brussels in November 2015 and March 2016 respectively demonstrate how dangerous returning ISIS fighters can be and demonstrate the devastating results of their actions. They also provide important proof that terrorists can easily cross the porous borders in European Union countries. During the summer of 2015 and 2016, I traveled to Germany to visit my brother. From there, we went to several European countries by car without being stopped or checked at any cross-border checkpoints. In certain cases, we were crossing borders from one country to another without even realizing we were in a different country until we saw a sign on the highway that welcomed us into that country.

ISIS vowed to destroy Europe and the United States and to murder massive numbers of their civilians, so it is safe to say that ISIS is at war with the West. As such, in my strategy, ISIS's fighters should not be allowed to return home but should in fact be treated as enemy combatants.[1]

Among returning foreign fighters from previous generations, perhaps one in nine would eventually take up terrorism when they returned home. But the current fighters returning from time with ISIS are a new and untested breed. Journalists Jessica Stern and J.M. Berger said, "If they and their families someday attempt to return to their home countries, they will be unimaginably different from their predecessors."[2] Military success against ISIS on the ground in Iraq and Syria is the best way to stop the foreign fighter pipeline. But monitoring their travel is crucial. The United

States must implement policies that will prevent terrorist attacks by returning foreign fighters in their home countries.[3]

A report from the House of Representatives Homeland Security Committee Task Force on foreign fighters released in late September 2014 laid out numerous recommendations for countering terrorist travel. The report suggests that the U.S. government must share information on terrorist travel with international partners, to bolster law enforcement in dealing with the growing threat and to enhance community awareness about the problem of youth radicalization.[4]

THE UNITED NATIONS EFFORTS TO STOP FOREIGN FIGHTERS

The Obama administration organized a summit about terrorism for world leaders on the margins of the United Nations General Assembly session in September 2014, presided over by Obama, opened by UN Secretary-General Ban Ki-moon, and addressed by scores of national leaders. Obama has said, "We will take action against threats to our security, and our allies, while building an architecture of counterterrorism cooperation." The Security Council must address the growing foreign-fighter threat, but, as Obama acknowledged, adherence to the rule of law and human rights must be part of any counterterrorism strategy. Anything less would end up fueling more violent extremism.[5]

The issue of travel was addressed. Traveling to Syria or Iraq to join an extremist group is not a crime in many countries. The UN Security Council adopted a resolution that called on all states to cooperate urgently on preventing the international flow of terrorist fighters to and from conflict zones.[6] The resolution reflected concern over the establishment of international terrorist networks. The Council underscored the "particular and urgent need" to prevent the travel and support for foreign terrorist fighters associated with the Islamic State in Iraq and the Levant (ISIS), Al-Nusra Front (ANL), and other affiliates or splinter groups of Al Qaeda,[7] but the resolution also has significant weaknesses. Although enacted under Chapter VII of the United Nations Charter, which means it is legally binding, the resolution has no real enforcement measures and relies on the countries to follow through.[8]

Obama welcomed the international, high-level interest and consensus on the issue. He added that international cooperation had already increased, with foreign fighters arrested, plots disrupted, and lives saved, but more capacity was needed to tackle the problem and to prevent fighters from reaching Syria and slipping back over its borders. Reformed former fighters should speak out against groups like ISIS that say they betrayed Islam.[9]

The resolution also compelled governments to require airlines to share passenger lists and for nations to share information about terrorism suspects. The resolution should have led to increased pressure on American allies to take tougher action against ISIS. Turkey, for instance, needs to tighten controls on its border, which has been a major channel for foreign fighters, money, and arms flowing to ISIS.[10]

The problem in my view is that while the UN Resolution specifically mentions ISIS and Al Qaeda, it also refers to other unnamed foreign terrorist fighters, leaving the term open to different interpretations by different nations. This gives countries leeway to shirk on their international security responsibilities. This problem is not new; an attempt by the United Nations to reach a comprehensive agreement on international terrorism as noted above has been deadlocked for years over what constitutes a terrorist organization.[11]

In my comprehensive strategy, the world should be united in paying close attention to those who cross borders and become foreign fighters. This cooperation would extend to the fight against ISIS and its evil actions against humanity during this difficult time when we are facing the extensive challenge of global terrorism.

WESTERN EFFORTS TO STOP FOREIGN FIGHTERS

Certain countries need to step up and take the lead in stopping foreign fighters. These should include countries that have experienced terrorism carried out by such fighters before. Although attacks seem to occur in different countries over time, certain countries are more vulnerable.

Others countries, due to international affairs, can emerge as ones that should be leaders. For example, Thomas Joscelyn, a senior fellow at the Foundation for Defense of Democracies, in his testimony to the Foreign Affairs Subcommittee on Europe, Eurasia, and Emerging Threats, said that throughout much of the war in Syria, Turkey has had an open-door policy for jihadist and non-jihadist fighters alike. Turkey's policy of distinguishing between ISIS and other extremists, including Jabhat al-Nusrah, an official branch of Al Qaeda, has been a failure.[12]

The *New York Times* reported that "under pressure from its allies in the West, Turkey made it harder for would-be jihadists to slip across the border and join the ranks of ISIS at its base in northern Syria. It has however been unable or unwilling to halt the flow completely because ISIS continues to replenish forces depleted in battle and the majority of them have traveled through Turkey."[13] Turkey was also the focus of testimony before Congress in Washington, by James R. Clapper Jr., then-Director of National Intelligence. When asked if he was optimistic that Turkey would do more in the fight against ISIS, Clapper frankly said, "No, I'm not . . . I think Turkey has other priorities and other interests."[14]

France is vulnerable, given its history of attacks. Under French law, a court order was required to stop a citizen from leaving the country, but in September 2014, the government was evaluating new rules that would enable the police to make that decision without judicial review. Germany is also vulnerable; passports can be revoked in certain cases and the country was considering a provision enabling it to revoke national identity cards that allow German citizens to travel to many countries, including Turkey.[15]

The Netherlands proposed amending its nationality laws to be able to revoke Dutch citizenship if a person has volunteered with a terrorist organization. This would apply only to dual citizens, according to the Dutch Foreign Ministry.[16] In 2014, France's parliament opened a debate on a bill to provide new tools to fight terrorism. The bill aimed to take passports from people suspected of becoming terrorist fighters and blocking Internet sites designed to lure French nationals to the battlefield. French authorities stressed the need to adapt national law to cope with the terrorism threat. The West fears the return of battle-hardened citizens from Syria and Iraq after their time waging jihad, especially with ISIS groups.[17] Confiscating the passports of suspected "wannabe" terrorists as part of a larger system to prevent them from leaving France is among prime measures in the bill. Broadening legal instruments to go after "individuals" is another key change. France's current anti-terror law targets "groups."[18]

The French Parliament overwhelmingly approved the sweeping new anti-terrorism bill even though the bill raised serious civil liberties concerns. Following a similar path, President Abdel-Fattah el-Sisi of Egypt ordered a bloody crackdown against extremists that killed more than 1,000 people and imprisoned 20,000, saying that the world's alarm over extremism justified his approach.[19]

Some French politicians fear the bill is too soft. Others believe the proposed law, which would allow the authorities to confiscate passports and close websites, is an attack on civil liberties. But Gilles de Kerchove, EU counterterrorism coordinator, and Jean-Charles Brisard, a French international consultant and expert on terrorism, say the bill would align French legislation with other European countries, in particular, the United Kingdom, and is vital to French domestic security. [20]

HOW TO STOP FOREIGN FIGHTERS
FROM JOINING ISIS

Thousands of foreign fighters from the United States, Canada, Australia, and Europe travel to Syria and Iraq to join terrorist groups such as ISIS, Al Qaeda, Al-Nusra Front, and other organizations. The terrorists manage to cross the borders of several countries to reach their destinations without being stopped by the authorities in these countries.

Since 2013, and especially after two bombs were exploded at the Boston marathon, I raised warnings of the dangers of foreign fighters when they return to their countries after fighting for a terrorist organizations.

However, the world did not deal seriously with this sensitive and dangerous issue until the terrorist attacks in Paris in November 2015 killed around 130 people. The attacks were carried out by terrorists who traveled to Syria to fight with ISIS and then returned to Europe. Terrorist attacks that killed around 32 people followed in Brussels in March 2016 by the same groups of ISIS terrorists.

The two bombs hidden inside backpacks that exploded on April 15, 2013, near the finish line of the Boston Marathon were planted by 26-year-old Tamerlan Tsarnaev and his brother 19-year-old Dzhokhar Tsarnaev.[21] Federal investigators reported that one of the brothers had visited Chechnya and Dagestan, predominantly Muslim republics in the north Caucasus region of Russia that have active militant separatist movements.[22]

ISIS supporters made the frontline in Syria easy to reach by taking a comfortable flight to southern Turkey and a hike across the border. According to a Saudi citizen who joined ISIS in Syria, it was an easy walk from Turkey to the small Syrian town of Atmeh. There, in a hilly landscape marked with olive groves, recruits are received by a Syrian who runs a terrorist camp and organizes them into fighting units.[23] Each team is assigned an Arabic speaker and given 10 days basic training, the point of which was not to learn how to shoot but to learn to communicate and work together. The fighters were then dispersed among the different terrorist organizations, including Ahrar al-Sham and Jabhat al-Nusra.[24]

The Syrian terrorist groups refer to the international fighters collectively as "Turkish brothers," to hide the real nationalities of the foreign fighters, and because they all came through Turkey crossing the border between Turkey and Syria. The best route to take for foreign fighters traveling to Syria is through Turkey because of its geographic proximity to the Syrian border areas. Turkey's bilateral agreements and visa-free travel arrangements with about 69 governments, including European Union states, facilitate an uneventful trip. Of course, it helps foreign fighters navigate the territory when Turkey turns a blind eye to what happens on their borders. This was especially true during the period from 2011 to 2015. At that time the Turkish strategy was to support Syrian opposition groups in their efforts to overthrow Bashar al-Assad's regime. The most serious opposition came from extremist Salafi-jihadi groups such as Al-Nusra Front.

At a hearing on February 11, 2015, the Republican chairman of the House Homeland Security committee, Michael McCaul, said he was "worried about our ability to combat this threat abroad, but also here at home." He added, "The threat of homegrown extremism, in which individuals inspired by propaganda are motivated to launch attacks, also remains a cause for concern but has not intensified." [25]

A U.S. official familiar with the data said that through the end of 2015, slightly more than 1,000 foreign fighters a month were joining ISIS. The official also noted that crossing into Syria from Turkey continued to be the most popular route. Some attention focused on terrorist networks, but there really wasn't a strong desire to attack the networks and to make sure that the framework that was supposed to be used for the defeat of ISIS was applied.[26]

HOW TO STOP FOREIGN FIGHTERS FROM RETURNING TO THE UNITED STATES

The fact that 250 ISIS fighters come from the United States has raised alarm about the threats they pose to the U.S. homeland. Armed with a U.S. passport and with radical, violent ideologies, these individuals can return to strike inside the United States. Those who have joined ISIS have been trained and have seen combat. They return to the United States with that training and connections to terrorist groups, and become a serious threat to the U.S. homeland.[27] Former FBI Director Comey said that tracking Americans who have returned from Syria is one of the FBI's top counterterrorism priorities. Comey revealed that the FBI is investigating suspected ISIS supporters in all 50 states.[28]

In November 2014, Michael McCaul, Chairman of the House Committee on Homeland Security, said:

The U.S. government has not released a strategy for combating terrorist travel since 2006, and watchdog groups have identified vulnerabilities in everything from U.S. biometric information collection to visa security. The Obama Administration has taken positive steps to reconcile some of these deficiencies, including enhancing security at overseas airports and requiring more information from foreign passengers prior to travel, but we need to do much more. Accordingly, the House Committee on Homeland Security is launching a comprehensive review of U.S. government efforts to deter, detect and disrupt terrorist travel. This investigation is also looking closely at foreign fighter travel routes and security gaps our foreign partners can help us fill. Connecting the dots to catch terrorists is not an easy task for a single nation, let alone a group of them like the EU. But if we do not work together better to improve our defenses—and quickly—we will be meeting the threat face-to-face at home, not overseas.[29]

The *New York Times* reported in April 2014 that Europeans and Americans of Syrian heritage are fighting to liberate their homeland from the Assad regime. Sunnis from Saudi Arabia and Libya have been drawn by their solidarity with co-religionists.[30] This statement shows that terrorist groups and foreign fighters, particularly ISIS and its followers, are misunderstood. As the West was helping Syrian rebels fight the Assad regime, ISIS kidnapped American and European hostages who were helping displaced Syrians. ISIS slaughtered many of the hostages and distributed gruesome videos on the Internet of those they beheaded for propaganda purposes. Foreign fighters who returned from Syria killed and injured hundreds of innocent civilians in attacks in France in November 2015 and in Belgium in March 2016. Foreign fighter terrorists inspired by ISIS also committed atrocities in Germany, Canada, and the United States during 2015 and 2016. In the United Kingdom four terrorist attacks took place in the first half of 2017.

When compared to foreign fighters in other places such as Bosnia and Afghanistan, foreign fighters attracted to ISIS are more brutal when they return home. They are also more extreme, as was evident in the attacks in Paris and Brussels, when hundreds of people were killed and injured at the hands of terrorists who returned to France and Belgium after fighting alongside ISIS in Syria. Reflecting on the damage done by returning fighters, Karen Greenberg, Director of the Center on National Security at Fordham Law School, said, "Law enforcement is concerned that once in Syria or Iraq, radical terrorists will attempt to recruit them for such missions."[31]

Some evidence suggests that U.S. foreign fighters recruited for ISIS is on the decline. U.S. officials say the rate of Americans trying to join ISIS ground to a near halt in December 2015, down to roughly two per month. Some analysts warn that this could be a sign that ISIS intends to shift its focus toward encouraging home-grown "lone wolf" attacks or Al Qaeda–style strikes as its territory shrinks in Syria and Iraq.[32]

Journalist Michael Pizzi reported for Al Jazeera that a growing body of evidence suggests that ISIS is much less likely to gain traction in a country like the United States, where the Muslim community tends to be highly diverse, and more educated and affluent than the Muslims in the suburbs of Paris, and therefore more inclined toward integration.[33] However, in contradiction, the shootings in San Bernadino and Orlando, and the bombings in New Jersey and New York, all inspired by ISIS, can be considered to show that ISIS is *more* likely to gain traction in a country like the United States than in other countries in the world. One reason relates to money.

In the United States, affluence is sought after and admired. Some people on the fringes of society see things as a zero-sum game, a mindset that provides fertile ground for indoctrination into extremist ideologies. The world should not in any way underestimate the danger of terrorist groups such as ISIS, as previous experience proves that underestimating extremist groups was always followed by tragic attacks and barbaric atrocities committed by the evil of terrorism.

The once-distant civil war in Syria "has become a matter of homeland security," said former Secretary of Homeland Security Jeh C. Johnson. With an estimated 1,500 groups fighting in Syria, the conflict is clearly far more complex than the Afghan War.[34] Foreign fighters for ISIS have begun to find their ways back to their countries of origin and as much as 30 percent may have already done so. This is based on a report from the Counter-Terrorism Committee of the United Nations Security Council.

The problem is that militarily trained extremists from a failed war are returning to peaceful towns and cities and that international databases can identify barely more than 7,000 of them.[35]

HOW TO STOP FOREIGN FIGHTERS FROM RETURNING TO EUROPE

Between 20 percent and 30 percent of foreign fighters were returning to their home countries by the end of 2015, creating major challenges for domestic security agencies. ISIS uses returning fighters to carry out an increasing number of attacks overseas, and the threat has sparked widespread debate, particularly in Western countries, many of which have criminalized traveling to Syria to fight in the country's years-long conflict.[36]

French officials have been preparing the public for what might happen if some among the almost 700 French citizens or residents who were still fighting in Syria and Iraq decide to come home. "Their return represents an additional threat for our national security," said Manuel Valls, who served as French Prime Minister from 2014–2016, and whose country has been hit by several terrorist attacks in two years.[37]

"If you look at the summer of 2016, you see what kind of attacks we've had," said Wil M. van Gemert, head of the operations department at Europol, the European Union law enforcement agency, listing incidents in France, Germany, and Belgium. He also added, "We had people who had been radically inspired, and IS [ISIS] took a position where they claimed them to be their soldiers."[38]

Overstretched European security agencies remain ill-prepared to deal with the consequences if ISIS calls on sympathizers to attack. "It's a five-letter word, and it's called intel," said François Heisbourg, a former member of a French presidential commission on defense and national security. "The only thing you can seriously do is upgrade the ability to track and keep track of those who are here and those who are coming here."[39]

In Germany, Federal Criminal Police Office Holger Münch said that those who "have already spent a long time with ISIS, have been exposed to brutal war experiences and established many contacts" represent "a special threat" to German security if they return. Concern over a reverse flow or extremists who decide to strike at home rather than go abroad is hardly limited to the West.[40] Although as I mentioned earlier, when I was in Germany in May 2016 to visit my brother who is Council General in Frankfort, there were hardly any border security checks when we traveled to other European countries by car; however, I did notice that in Frankfurt the police were on high alert. Also, reportedly, a large number of police cars and vans arrived in a short amount of time when an alarm happened.

Some Western officials, such as Britain's counterterrorism chief Helen Ball, distinguished between "romantic freedom fighters" and "those who get themselves trained to use weapons or build bombs and engage in fighting." Her concern was that the young volunteers, radicalized and combat-trained, will wreak havoc on their return.[41]

THE DECLINE OF FOREIGN FIGHTERS JOINING ISIS

As I mentioned, the numbers of foreign fighters traveling to Syria to join ISIS, Al-Nusra Front, and Ahrar Al-Sham to fight against Bashar al-Assad's regime have decreased drastically. French Interior Minister Bernard Cazeneuve announced that there was "a fourfold decrease" in the number of French citizens who have traveled to ISIS's domain in the first six months of 2016. And in Germany, the flow of foreign fighters to Syria decreased from an average of dozens a month to a small handful.[42]

There were many reasons for the sharp decline. I highlight some of these. Air strikes by the United States and its allies and the military defeat of these terrorist groups on the ground, especially in Iraq, led to scrutiny by the West on people traveling to Syria. The arrest of some sympathizers who were on their way to Syria is also one of the reasons of the decline. A significant deterrent is the disappointment experienced by the majority of fighters who travel to Syria and discover that the harsh reality of fighting with terrorist groups is vastly different from the rosy picture that these groups portray in their recruitment propaganda. Recruits were misled to believe they would live in heaven on earth.

ISIS leaders no longer ask foreign fighters to travel to Syria because they faced new difficulties including arrest and indictment. Instead, ISIS started to ask sympathizers to remain in their countries and to launch terrorist attacks in the areas where they live. In May 2016, the now-deceased ISIS spokesman Abu Muhammad al-Adnani said, "If the tyrants have closed in your faces the door of hijrah [migration], then open in their face the door of jihad and make their act a source of pain for them. The smallest action you do in the heart of their land is dearer to us than the largest action by us, and more effective and more damaging to them." He urged his followers to strike civilian rather than military targets.[43]

The terrorist attacks carried out by Mateen in the Florida gay nightclub, bomb attacks of Ahmed Khan Rahimi in New Jersey and New York, the knife rampage at a Minnesota mall, and the attack at Ohio State University—all in 2016—have impacted the public, fearing that no place is safe, whether it be on a campus, or in a mall or nightclub. While this is not a happy realization, it makes people alert and aware.

In August 2016, a United Nations report warned that:

Somewhere between 10 and 30 percent of the foreign fighters that have gone to serve as troops for the ISIS in Iraq and Syria have already made it back home, having left the war-torn Middle Eastern countries as the self-proclaimed caliphate (June 2014) finds itself fighting both a conventional and urban guerrilla war with Syrian government troops backed by Russian airpower, Iraqi defense forces supported by American special forces and airpower, Peshmerga troops from the autonomous Iraqi Kurdistan, and various militias and rebel groups. Be that as it may, quite a few of those foreign fighters who once fought for the extremist ISIS are now back in their respective home countries.[44]

Stopping lone wolves and foreign fighters is essential, but the root causes—including that of ideology—must be extinguished. That is part of my counterterrorism strategy described in the next chapter.

CHAPTER 13

Strategy for the War of Ideology

Fundamentalists and extremists join terrorist groups for many reasons. Some may be looking for a sense of identity, adventure, money, or fame. The subversive Salafi-jihadi ideology can also be an important tool for terrorist organizations to recruit vulnerable youth. Extremist ideology is the essential motive behind terrorist attacks.

ISIS has used more suicide bombers than any other terrorist group, and suicidal people cannot be motivated by money or other materialistic benefits. Therefore, it is imperative to plan and execute a war of ideology as part of any new comprehensive strategy to counterterrorism. This is the counterterrorism element of my strategy that I address in this chapter.

The war of ideology should explain the misleading ideology, wrongful practices, and the dangers of considering other people, such as Christian, Jews, Sabians, Magians, and even Muslims as disbelievers and infidels. The War on Terror needs to revisit some terms in the fight against what terrorists describe as "holy war" or "jihad."

ISIS started as a terrorist organization in Iraq, with its leader Abo Bakr al-Baghdad being from Iraq. Most of its commanders are army officers and Ba'ath Party leaders from remnants of the Saddam's regime. However, ISIS's ideology and belief system did not originate in Iraq; it is, and always has been, deeply rooted in a strategic plan initiated by Osama bin Laden, a Saudi who adopted the extremist Wahhabi-Salafi-jihadi ideology.[1]

The major fronts to fight terrorism must focus on many underlying factors. These include the root conditions and issues that gave rise to terrorist groups in the first place and on conditions that motivate individuals to join them, the ability of such groups to conduct terrorist attacks, the intentions of groups regarding whether to launch terrorist attacks, and the defenses against such attacks.[2]

In November 2016, NPR reported that a commission chaired by former British Prime Minister Tony Blair and former U.S. Secretary of Defense Leon Panetta called for a U.S.-led strategy focusing on stopping radicalization before it happens and partnering with tech companies to fight extremism online. Blair wisely said, "We will defeat ISIS in the end. But defeating ISIS isn't going to defeat the problem. So you've got to go down and deal with the roots of it."[3]

Fordham University Professor of Psychology Harold Takooshian asked a class, "How much do we know today about the psychology of terrorism—its causes and effects?" In answering the question, he quoted social psychology professor Stanley Milgram, who conducted famous historic research about obedience even to orders to torture others by administering electric shocks to participants. This research proved that "The fact that we label some odious behavior as evil is no substitute for understanding the mechanisms that underline the evil behavior." This conclusion certainly seems to apply to the unthinkable evil of terrorism, in which large networks of individuals and even institutions among us decided to invest so much effort and creativity into the intentional destruction of strangers, including infants and families, and sometimes do so in the name of their God.[4]

WAR ON TERRORISM IS NOT AGAINST ISLAM

Terrorist groups accused the West, especially the United States, of being against Islam and Muslims. They use certain situations such as U.S. occupation of some Muslim countries to support that claim. When Saddam invaded Kuwait and U.S. forces landed in Saudi Arabia, Osama bin Laden considered it a colonial occupation of Muslim holy places in Mecca and Medina. Bin Laden exploited the situation to recruit youth and attack the U.S. forces in Somalia, Saudi Arabia, Yemen, and other parts of the world.

When the United States declared occupation in Iraq after the fall of Saddam's regime in 2003 in spite of my advice to set up an Iraq government, terrorists such as Abu Musaab al-Zarqawi, then-leader of Al Qaeda in Iraq (AQI) and his successors, used the situation to mobilize fighters against American troops. ISIS leader Abo Bakr al-Baghdadi followed in the steps of Al-Zarqawi and used the presence of American forces in Iraq as a tool to recruit Iraqi rebels and foreign fighters to fight Americans, the Iraqi government, and Iraqi people, especially Shiites in Iraq.

Lawrence Wright, journalist and author of *The Looming Tower*, wrote in January 1998 that Ayman al-Zawahiri, Al Qaeda leader, "began writing a draft of a formal declaration that would unite all terrorist groups that had gathered in Afghanistan under a single banner. Al-Zawahiri protested on three counts against the Americans: American troops stayed in Saudi Arabia, America's occupation of Iraq, and the American goal of sustaining Israel by devastating the Arab states, whose weakness and disunion are Israel's only guarantee of survival."[5]

Al-Zawahiri said a million civilians were killed in Iraq during the occupation. In fact, it is difficult to know exactly how many civilians were

killed during the occupation, and how many were killed by the terrorist attacks of Al Qaeda, the insurgency, ISIS, and other terrorist groups.
These groups consisted mainly of military officers from Saddam's army
and Ba'ath Party leaders. They used suicide bombers and detonated
car and truck bombs in crowded civilian areas all over Iraq. In most of
these attacks, dozens of Iraqis were killed and many others were injured.
Al-Zawahiri's declaration proves how the U.S. occupation of Iraq, which
I opposed, has been exploited by terrorist groups to recruit people and
to launch a campaign against U.S. and Iraqi governments after 2003.

Some politicians, experts, and writers in the West fell into the trap set
by terrorist groups when they tried to present their evil terrorist actions
as a war between the West and Islam. Some wrote books and said, "Islam
is the problem," and claimed that Islam encourages violence and the
Quran justifies the killing of innocent people. Some politicians like President Trump said the United States should ban the entry of Muslims
from certain countries. However, other politicians appealed for deeper
insight, with the view that the war against terrorism should not be a war
against Islam.

After 9/11, President Bush emphasized in his statements and inside the
administration that the United States was in no way at war with the religion of Islam. "The extremist ideology we were fighting was that of an
international network—in the nature of a political movement—that selec-
tively used Islamic ideas and vocabulary to put itself at war, not only with
all non-Muslims, but with virtually all Muslims, too," he explained.[6]

This is an important point to focus on, regarding my strategy about ideology in counterterrorism efforts. When most Western readers think of
Muslim terrorists, they think of 9/11 or plots to bomb subways or bridges
in the West. In the West, it may be hard to realize that the main targets of
terrorists are Muslims. Al Qaeda, ISIS, and other terrorist groups are virtually at war with the whole Muslim world in their attempt to create a caliphate based on an extremely strict interpretation of Islamic law.

In his memoirs, entitled "The Envoy, From Kabul to the White House,
My Journey through a Turbulent World," Ambassador Zalmay Khalilzad, who served as U.S. Ambassador to the UN under George Bush,
and as Ambassador to Iraq from 2005 to March 2007, praised President
Bush for insisting the United States was not at war with Islam. I roundly
agree. It is not surprising that we both strongly hold this view. We're
good friends. I worked with Khalilzad since the time he was appointed
as President Bush's "Special Envoy for Free Iraqis" in 2002. I received
his credentials when he came to Iraq as a U.S. Ambassador, while I was
Deputy Foreign Minister of Iraq, and when he served as U.S. Ambassador to the UN.

Khalilzad wrote about a meeting with Bush shortly after 9/11 when
he described the agony of Muslims about the decline of caliphate from a
time when it led the world in education and science. "It was a civilization

on the march," Khalilzad said. "Now, come on, Zal," Bush interrupted teasingly. White House Chief of Staff Andrew Card intervened, "I think Zal is referring to the Ottoman Empire." Khalilzad writes, "I gently noted that . . . the apex of Islamic civilization . . . had come earlier, under Arab leadership."[7]

Former Secretary of Defense Donald Rumsfeld explored the idea that the War on Terrorism was, in part, a civil war within the world of Islam. Al Qaeda is an extremist organization whose views oppose those of most Muslims. Terrorist actions threaten the interests of the Muslim world and are aimed at part in preventing Muslim people from engaging with the rest of the world.[8]

President Obama said Al Qaeda and ISIS and similar groups are desperate for legitimacy. They try to portray themselves as religious leaders and holy warriors in defense of Islam. "We must never accept the premise that they put forth because it is a lie. Nor should we grant these terrorists the religious legitimacy that they seek," he said. They are not religious leaders. They are terrorists.[9]

A critical point that cannot be overstated is that Islam is founded on a doctrine of peace and living according to God's word and law. Based upon the teachings of the Prophet Mohammed, Islam emphasizes respect for human life and human rights.[10] This must be taught in schools and to the public on a large scale, to prevent discrimination.

One of the important battles with terrorism is the battle of ideas. Terrorist groups try to brainwash people, especially youth, with their ideology about holy war (jihad) against the West. A new counterterrorism strategy must include a war of ideology that focuses on atrocities committed by terrorists against Muslims, especially civilians and vulnerable citizens such as elderly people, women, and children.

MISTAKES IN THE WAR OF IDEOLOGY

Many mistakes have been made in dealing with the sensitive and important issue of ideology that have had a negative impact on the international "War on Terror." In order to make the picture clear, I will explain some of the mistakes, starting with the war against Al Qaeda and the Taliban's regime in Afghanistan shortly after the devastating 9/11 terrorist attacks in 2001.

Under Secretary of Defense for Policy Douglas Feith, who served from 2001 to 2005, said the challenging problem was how the U.S. government should organize for the battle of ideas. "The ideological element of the struggle was essential, but no office in the U.S. government was well suited to handle it, and no official was appointed to take the lead . . . and the Bush Administration never put together a comprehensive strategy to counter ideological support for Islamist extremism."[11]

Even 16 years after the 9/11 terrorist attacks, in 2017, there was still no office in the U.S. government well suited to handle a war of ideology, no competent expert was appointed to take the lead, and the Obama or Trump Administration never put together a comprehensive strategy to counter ideological support for terrorism. I cannot underscore enough how important it is to assure Muslims that the war against terrorists is not a war against Islam. Using the wrong terminology to describe terrorists and their acts, such as describing them as Islamists or jihadists and their terrorist acts as jihad—which means a holy war in Islam—raises fear in the majority of Muslims.

President Bush wrote, "Before 9/11, most of the Americans had never heard of Al Qaeda. I had received my first briefing on the terrorist network as a presidential candidate. . . . Al Qaeda was a fundamental Islamic terror network hosted and supported by the Taliban government in Afghanistan. . . . The groups held extreme views and considered it their duty to kill anyone who stood in their way."[12]

At a meeting in 2001, Rumsfeld told Douglas Feith to review the leaflets that General Tommy Franks, then-Commander of the U.S. Central Command, planned to drop over Afghanistan by the thousands. When Feith and his staff started reviewing those materials, they discovered a few problems. One leaflet used graphics that could be seen as unfriendly to Muslims in general, not only just the Taliban. Another would make sense only to people who recognized the World Trade Center towers, and many Afghans might not understand that. And a third leaflet featured a drawing of an Afghan family happily eating from packages of food from the United States, but the father's turban was black—a distinctive Taliban symbol recognizable by anyone in Afghanistan.[13]

This shows the importance of properly understanding the culture of any country where terrorism is an issue. Cultural misunderstandings could prove costly and embarrassing for the United States or any other foreign country. It is an unacceptable mistake that some of the leaflets to be dropped by U.S. military planes on Afghanistan during the war against Taliban's regime contained messages directly opposite to those the United States wished to deliver to the people in Afghanistan.

In fact, many American leaders, especially military commanders and intelligence agents, think only of military and intelligence solutions to counterterrorist groups. After 9/11, Secretary of Defense Rumsfeld, his deputy Paul Wolfowitz, General Richard Myers who became Chairman of the Joint Chiefs in 2001, General Peter Pace who became Vice Chairman of the Joint Chiefs of Staff, and Under Secretary of Defense for Policy Douglas Feith often discussed the crucial importance of information and influence on operations, subjects also raised in interagency meetings.

Rumsfeld was critical of any "discussion that overemphasized the military dimension and understated the significance of . . . enemies' beliefs, ambitions, and ideological frame of mind. Ideas were an important element in recruiting young people into their ranks."[14]

In Iraq, mistakes were made by the United States forces. For example, when the Americans entered Baghdad and wanted to pull down the statue of Saddam in Fardous Square, they covered the dictator's head with an American flag, which upset Iraqis. When they were advised to replace it with the Iraqi flag, the Iraqis were cheerful, and proceeded to express their displeasure of the dictator by striking the statue with their shoes, sandals, and slippers—a culture sign of disrespect and dismissal.

Some American soldiers disrespected Saddam's Iraqi flag even though it contained a sacred text for Muslims, Allahu Akbar, meaning "God is Great." In addition, American soldiers began to search Iraqi women, touching their bodies to find out if they were carrying arms, a behavior Iraqis deemed unacceptable.

Journalists imbedded with soldiers filmed videos where American forces raided houses at night searching for suspects. The wives wearing nighties, and shivering children, were shown in the videos, another unacceptable sight. In another unacceptable act that I observed, U.S. troops gathered arms and ammunitions and detonated them in residential neighborhoods, which caused damage to the homes of some Iraqi people. American tanks and armored vehicles caused damage to houses and cars of Iraqi citizens. All of this is culturally inappropriate and causes division when troops need to be accepted and embraced by the locals in a spirit of respect and trust.

REACH OUT TO MUSLIMS IN THE WORLD

A new strategy to counterterrorism should reach out to Muslims all over the world. Terrorists try their best to use all pretexts to ignite a war against the West in order to get the support of Muslim nations. They use a distorted interpretation of the Quran and Prophet Mohammed's sayings to justify killing Muslims and non-Muslims. Reaching out to law abiding Muslims is imperative to help isolate the extremists, fundamentalists, and terrorists. The United States should launch a campaign for Muslim religious scholars to explain the falsehood of extreme misinterpretation of Islam, the Quran, and Prophet sayings. The dialogue of the "greatest strategic importance is not the one between America and the Muslim world, but one within the Muslim world. The key question is not what U.S. officials should say, but what American could do to encourage Muslims to speak openly against the extremists' views and to make extremist ideology less attractive."[15]

Osama bin Laden told his followers and other Muslims a simple story about the world that is easy to understand, even for those of his followers who did not had a chance to sit with him. He told Muslims that, "there is a global conspiracy by the West and its puppet allies in the Muslim world to destroy true Islam, a conspiracy that is led by the United States." Keep in mind that history repeats itself; despite bin Laden no longer being alive, his message can prevail. Those who want an idea to make them feel relevant stick to bin Laden's story because it is easy to understand, and the one-sided story makes sense.[16]

The U.S. government needs, first of all, a better understanding of the ideological battlefield. The United States also need a strategy that would help find clerics, journalists, educators, politicians, and influential persons throughout the Muslim world who are opposed to terrorist violence and find ways to amplify these moderate voices. The United States should help them to be funded and to improve their ability to communicate their messages, through print, broadcast, and the Internet.[17]

An important example is that Muslims practice fasting during the lunar month Ramadan like Christians fasting during Lent. The White House invited Muslim leaders for iftar to break their fast every year. In 2017, for the first time in nearly two decades, the holy month Ramadan has come and gone without the White House recognizing it with an iftar or Eid celebration, as had taken place each year under the Clinton, Bush, and Obama administrations.[18] These positions could be used by terrorist organization as a proof that the U.S. administration is against Islam and Muslims.

REACH OUT TO MUSLIMS IN THE WEST

Reaching out to Muslims in the West is also important in a new strategy to counterterrorism. Terrorist organizations always try to recruit Muslims in the West, and ISIS attracted thousands foreign fighters from Europe and the United States including women and youth. Terrorist groups also try to inspire Muslims in the West to attack military bases, police officers, and civilians. If Muslims in the West share information, they can help authorities stop terrorists before they attack innocent people.

In every European country, there is a minority of immigrants who have come from the Muslim world. If terrorists reach disaffected youth in these countries and organize them into terrorist operations, they can really wreak havoc, as we saw in France, Belgium, Germany, the United Kingdom, and the United States during 2015–2017.[19] Therefore, positive forces must reach out to these factors of society.

A critical step in addressing terrorism is to distinguish between Islam and Muslims. As a religion, Islam, like other religions such as Judaism and Christianity, calls for love, peace, and harmony among all humanity regardless of their ethnic, religious, and sectarian background. Muslim communities on the other hand have some extremists who terrorize people under religious slogans, but they are small in number among the majority of moderate Muslims.

When some politicians, experts, or journalists accuse Islam of being the reason for radicalism, which leads to terrorism, they serve terrorist groups who claim that the West, in general, and the United States, in particular, are against Islam and Muslims. Also, Western governments, especially the U.S. administration, need to foster better relations with Muslim communities in their countries—nonviolent Muslims who could help point a finger at radical Muslims and potential terrorists. If Western governments neglect to involve the Muslim majority, their communities will feel alienated. An important component of any counterterrorism strategy must focus on Muslims in the West who could help fill the big gap in the large number of linguists needed to adequately respond to Arabic Internet messaging.

Before 9/11, John O'Neill at the FBI National Security Division wanted to prove that bin Laden was behind terrorist attacks. He brought Ali Soufan from another squad, as he was the only FBI agent in New York who actually spoke Arabic, and one of eight in the entire country. Ali had studied bin Laden's fatwas and interviews, so when a claim of responsibility was sent to press, Soufan immediately recognized bin Laden as the author.[20] Harnessing this type of knowledge, and expertise, is essential in a counterterrorism strategy.

Investigations after the 9/11 attacks found that the FBI needed more Arabic-speaking people to translate statements issued by Al Qaeda terrorist groups and its leader Osama bin Laden. In addition, a large quantity of documents in Arabic were gathered before 9/11 about Al Qaeda but not translated because there were not enough Arab-speaking linguists.

As I mentioned earlier in this book, it is shocking that many years after the 9/11 attacks, lessons learned still have not been implemented. In a 2015 FBI report, the 9/11 Review Commission said, "the FBI urgently needs to improve its intelligence capabilities, hire more linguists and elevate the stature of its analysts to counter the rapidly evolving threats to the United States."[21]

This should have been done long ago, and needs to be done now.

FBI agents and individuals in other intelligence agencies need to understand the language of their adversaries to understand their intentions, and their plans. They need more than language skills, and they need to understand the culture, traditions, and mentality of terrorist groups—especially their leaders and planners. Since I pointed out that Al Qaeda leader Osama bin Laden and ISIS Leader Abo Bakr al-Baghdadi, both Arabs, only spoke Arabic to their followers, with all their statements in Arabic, it is essential to have had fluent Arab speakers. We need such fluent experts now on our side.

Unfortunately, many FBI agents are not familiar with the world beyond America; indeed, some had not even been given passports until the day of their departure for a mission outside the United States thousands of miles away. They knew little about the laws and customs of the countries they were working in.[22]

On June 14, 2016, after a meeting with his national security team, Obama addressed criticism that he has not used the term "radical Islam" when referring to a shooting. He called the criticism of his neglect to use the term a "political distraction" and said, "calling a threat by a different name does not make it go away." But Hillary Clinton said on June 13, 2016, that she was not afraid to use the phrase "radical Islam."[23]

Obama lashed out at Trump, who has called him soft on terrorism, and warned him that "loose talk" about Muslims has harmed the United States' campaign against militant groups. Obama challenged the demand by his critics that he characterize acts of terrorism as the work of "radical Islam"—a phrase Obama has refused to use because he believes it unfairly implicates an entire religious group for the acts of militant extremists.[24] Obama administration officials said that reaching into America's toughest neighborhoods was key to discrediting the appeal that terrorists might have, and preventing young people who want to escape marginalization and isolation from turning to extremist ideologies.[25]

STOP ATTACKS AGAINST MUSLIMS IN WEST

Attacks of terrorist groups such as Al Qaeda and ISIS in Europe and the United States resulted in a dramatic increase of hate crimes and terrorist attacks against Muslims in the West in the last few years. In reaction to this, Amnesty International USA said, "We are deeply concerned about the growing number of reports of crimes committed against Muslims and of other anti-Muslim sentiment and activity in the United States. Amnesty International deplored the stabbing of a Muslim cab driver in New York, the arson attack against a mosque construction site in Tennessee, and the vandalizing of an Islamic center in California.[26] In November 2015, an FBI report said, "Hate crimes against Muslims are on the rise."[27] The murder of three Muslim university students in Chapel Hill, North Carolina, on February 10, 2015, was seen by some as an example of a religiously motivated hate crime.[28] Many maintain the rise of Islamophobia. For example, the cold-blooded killing of a New York imam and his assistant on August 14, 2016, was said to have heightened Muslim American fears of rising violence against the 3.5 million people in the Muslim community. To many Muslims, the murders illustrated the increasingly violent face of Islamophobia in the United States.[29]

Since 9/11, activists in the United States identified Islamophobia in anti-Muslim rhetoric in news coverage by mainstream media, calls for profiling by political leaders and policymakers, acts of discrimination and violence targeting Muslim, Arab, and South Asian communities, and government actions and policies that single them out in the name of national security.[30] Reports in 2016 by the Council on American-Islamic Relations (CAIR), a Washington-based Muslim advocacy organization, recorded 18 incidents per month during a 12-month period against Muslims, including

12 murders, 34 physical assaults, 49 verbal assaults or threats against individuals and institutions, 56 acts of vandalism or destruction of property, 9 arsons, and 8 shootings and bombings.[31] And the *Huffington Post's* Islamophobia tracker, launched in January 2016, shows a steady uptick in cases of aggression against Muslims. Between January and July 2016, the tracker recorded 87 acts of aggression, a broad category that includes threats, physical assaults, and vandalism of mosques.[32]

Attacks against Muslims in Europe increased after the Paris terrorist attacks in November 2015 and Brussels terrorist attacks in March 2016. On June 19, 2017, U.K. police launched their fourth major terrorism investigation in three months after a van plowed into a crowd gathered near a mosque in one of the capital's northern neighborhoods. One man was killed and 10 others injured.[33] The mowing down of a crowd exiting Ramadan prayers at a London mosque by 47-year-old Darren Osborne of Cardiff, Wales, was considered a religious-motivated crime.[34] Attacks against Muslims could alienate Muslims in general, and make them hesitant to cooperate with authorities and reluctant to report signs of radicalism, fundamentalism, and extremism in their midst, among the Muslims communities. Also Muslims could be less enthusiastic to help police in their enquiries and investigations about suspects and potential terrorists. This cannot be allowed to happen.

STOP EXTREME RELIGIOUS DECREES

Most foreign fighters, especially from Gulf countries that were arrested in Iraq, confessed that there were two major motives that led them to join terrorist groups in Iraq. One motive is the religious decree (fatwa), which states that "jihad" or holy war is legitimate in Iraq. The second motive is Arabic TV Channels, which advocate jihad in Iraq.

The Salafi-jihadi terrorist groups allow unknowledgeable young people to issue religious decrees, without religious qualification, whereby they justify killing whoever disagrees with them, taking women as slaves and confiscating money. It is imperative that all Muslims—Sunnis, Shiites, and other sects—stand together today to face the Salafi-jihadi movement because they consider both Sunnis and Shiites as disbelievers.[35]

In a critique of non-Wahhabist Muslims, Saudi author Bin Gannam claimed that the majority of Muslims descended into polytheism. They started to worship holy and religious people, and beg them for their needs. Many believed that stones and trees can give them benefits and push bad things away. They continued to worship idols and practice polytheism, blasphemy, and immorality by worshiping people in graves, and praying for them and giving them gifts, which made them considered worse than those who worshipped idols during the Prophet's time.[36]

One the highest ranking religious scholars in Saudi Arabia, Mohammed bin Salih al-Athaimeen, a member of the Committee of High

Religious Scholars, Professor at Mohammed Bin Saud University, and preacher of Grand Mosque in Unaiza,[37] fanned flames. When asked, "Are Shiites considered as Infidels?," his answer was that Shaykh Al-Islam Ibn Taymiyyah said polytheism is based on lying, slur, and slander, so whoever is far from monotheism and the Prophet's traditions is closer to polytheism, slur, and slander, such as the Shiite rejectionists, who he said are the most lying sect among the followers of desires and the most polytheistic.[38]

Mohammed Al-Kathiri, author of *The Salafis: Between the Sunnis and Shiites*, wrote, "The Saudi Salafi extremists launched a vicious and open campaign against the Shiites. They fabricated stories and accused the Shiites of wrong beliefs and practices such as considering the Quran distorted and having a different Quran than the Sunnis, worshipping Imams (grandsons of Prophet Mohammed), and cursing the followers and companions of the Prophet."

A large number of Sunni scholars and jurists consider Shiites as moderate Muslims and have praised them for their loyalty to Prophet Mohammed and his progeny. For example, well-known Sunni scholar and writer Dr. Mustafa Al-Shakaa said, "The Jafari Shiite who follow the twelve Imams of Prophet progeny are far from fundamentalism and extremism, have wisdom and logic in their religious practices, and are the closest to the majority of Sunni Muslims." He added, "The Jafari Shiites are the majority of Shiites who live among the Sunnis in peace and harmony because the essence of the religion is the same for both and Islam calls for unity and against disunity."[39]

U.S. Ambassador Paul Bremer wrote that the Shiite tradition is to mourn Imam Hussein on the 10th day of the lunar month of Muharram, the anniversary of Ashura in which Hussein, the grandson of Prophet Mohammed, and 73 members of his family and companions were slaughtered during the rule of Umayyad Caliph Yazid Ibn Muawiya. Terrorist groups such as Al Qaeda in Iraq and ISIS have targeted Shiite civilians who were mourning the martyrdom of Imam Hussein almost every year since 2003.

On March 2, 2004, the holy day of Ashura, bombs set off by Abu Musab al-Zarqawi's Sunni organization killed 270 and wounded hundreds of people in the Karbala and Kadhimiya areas.[40] Islam forbids killings, so the murders carried out by groups cannot be rationalized. These attacks happen even to the Iraqis, perpetrated by supposedly Muslim people. Here are some examples.

On July 3, 2016, as reported in the *New York Times*, Muslims were celebrating the holy month of Ramadan in central Baghdad, when a vehicle packed with explosives crashed into a three-story complex there. Families with children had come to that complex of restaurants and stores that day to celebrate the end of the school, as well as the end of the fasting month of Ramadan. This suicide bombing, the deadliest attack in Baghdad in more

than six years, came less than a week after Iraqi security forces backed by
U.S. air strikes had liberated Falluja from ISIS. More than 140 people were
killed by the explosion. ISIS quickly boasted that it had executed the attack. ISIS claimed its suicide bomber had killed Shiite Muslims, but Sunnis
also died in the blast.

In May 2017, I was in Baghdad visiting my sick mother. My brother, a
friend of mine, and I went to have dinner in a restaurant in Al-Karrada
Al-Sharqiyya neighborhood, where I was born and lived. I left Iraq on
May 20, and 10 days later during the fasting month of Ramadhan, a car
bomb exploded outside that restaurant and killed at least 17 people and
wounded 32 more. The blast outside a popular shop in the Karrada district of the Iraqi capital was followed by another attack, outside an office where people collect their government pensions, which killed 14 and
wounded at least 37, according to police. ISIS quickly claimed responsibility for both attacks.[41]

My own history was one that fostered interreligious harmony. Born in
Karrada, I grew up in the same neighborhood where all members of my
family live. I was born into a Muslim family but my father sent me to a
private Christian school that was part of a compound with a church and
a hospital. I started to go to the church when I was four years old. I also
grew up with Christian friends in the neighborhood and at school.

My two nephews own a store 150 meters away from an explosion in
Karrada. They told me that they escaped death miraculously because
the resulting fire reached their store but retreated. They sent me a video
from a CCTV camera in the mall where they work, and I could see one of
them standing with a few other people when the explosion took place. My
nephew ducked and the dust and debris was flying everywhere.

All Islamic seminaries and religious schools for Sunnis and Shiites, such
as al-Azhar in Egypt and Al-Najaf Seminary for the Shiites, must work together to fight extreme ideology that considers other people as disbelievers. All Muslim religious scholars, jurists, intellectuals, and writers should
explain to Muslims that all extreme ideologies, especially the Salafi-jihadi
ideology, which allows killing other people, are forbidden in Islam because
the Quran and Prophet Mohammed's sayings forbid killing both innocent
Muslims and non-Muslims.

The world needs a large media campaign against extremist Salafi-jihadi
ideology to be launched on TV, newspapers, magazines, and the Internet
especially using the social networks such as Facebook, Twitter, YouTube,
LinkedIn, Google, Instagram, and all other popular social networks.

Osama bin Laden declared war against the United States by issuing
two religious decrees (fatwas) before the 9/11 attacks. The first one was
in August 1996, entitled "Declaration of war against the Americans occupying the land of the two holy places." It was published in a London
Arabic newspaper called Al Quds al Arabi.[42] The second fatwa was published on February 23, 1998, also in Al Quds al Arabi. Unlike the first fatwa,

which was issued by Osama bin Laden alone, this fatwa was signed by several leaders, including Osama bin Laden; Ayman al-Zawahiri, leader of jihad group in Egypt and Al Qaeda second-in-command; Abu-Yasir Rafa'i Ahmad Taha, leader of the Islamic Group; Sheikh Mir Hamzah, secretary of the Jumiat-ut-Ulema-e-Pakistan; and Fazlur Rahman, leader of the Jihad Movement in Bangladesh.[43]

It is imperative to know that a religious decree should be issued only by a qualified religious scholar called a jurist (mujtahid) who understands the correct interpretation of the Quran and Prophet Mohammed's sayings, and can conclude a religious decree from these two major sources. The jurist is the highest religious rank, which can be reached by a scholar after long and deep religious studies. However, it is the case in all terrorist groups, such as Al Qaeda, the Taliban, ISIS, Al-Shabab, Boko Haram, and other organizations, that the people who issue the religious decrees are not qualified, and they are not religious scholars, let alone jurists.

Al Qaeda leader Osama bin Laden was an engineer, and Ayman al-Zawahiri who replaced bin Laden after his death was a physician, but neither was a religious scholar. ISIS leader Abo Bakr al-Baghdadi is not a religious scholar either; therefore, none of the three terrorists were qualified to issue religious decrees. In spite of this, al-Baghdadi established a caliphate and appointed himself as a caliph following the Umayyad dynasty, which had established a caliphate in the seventh and eighth centuries with caliphs who committed the many atrocities I mentioned earlier.

Patrick Cockburn, author of *The Rise of the Islamic State: ISIS and the Sunni Revolution*, wrote, "In fact there are many fatwas that come out of Saudi Arabia that explicitly target Shiites and Christians. In 2009, a Saudi Imam issued a fatwa calling on Shia to be killed and Sunni Arab governments in the region failed to condemn the statement."[44]

On the Al Jazeera Arabic TV channel based in Qatar, Othman Othman on the "Al-Shariaa and Life" program asked the well-known Muslim Brotherhood scholar Sheikh Yusuf Al-Qardhawi about who is the infidel in Islam. Al-Qardhawi answered that there are two types of people—believers and infidels. In his view, you are born a believer; there is no discussion about who is being judged infidel. These infidels include Jews, Christians, and atheists who are not originally Muslim. But you can also become an infidel, as happened with the apostate (al-Murtad), even after being Muslim.

All Muslims, Sunnis and Shiites, even some Salafi religious scholars believe that the killing of Prophet Mohammed's grandson Imam Hussein along with his family and companions by Umayyad Caliph Yazid bin Muawiya (that I described earlier) was a crime, because the Quran ordered Muslims to be kind to Prophet Mohammed's family. The Prophet himself said many kind things about his grandsons Hasan and Hussein. Even so, the Saudi grand religious scholar Abdul Aziz

Al-Shaikh said on February 1, 2009, that the Yazid Caliphate was legitimate, Imam Hussein was wrong, and Yazid was right in killing the
Prophet's grandson.[45]

In 2016, ISIS issued a similar statement regarding the month of Muharram when the Shiites mourn their Imam Hussein bin Ali. They claimed
the Caliphate of Yazid is legitimate and killing Hussein was right. The
statement added that ISIS will kill Shiites during the month of Muharram
to send them to join their revered Imam.

I have emphasized in this chapter how crucial it is to understand
Islamic ideology that is true Islam, which is distinguished drastically from
the distorted ideology that is advocated by the terrorists. The ideology
adopted by the terrorists must be eradicated and replaced by true Islamic
ideology of co-existence, peace, tolerance, and harmony. In the next chapter, I outline my strategies to stop future terrorism.

CHAPTER 14

Strategy to Stop Future Terrorism

Terrorist groups will continue to be a real threat to world peace and security unless we have a comprehensive strategy to rout them out. They will not disappear, and worse, they are likely to evolve and adapt, and increase. We can assume that Al Qaeda represents the past of terrorism, ISIS represents the present, and we have to think of the future of terrorism, which could be more extreme, more brutal, and more complicated. In this chapter, I outline my counterterrorism strategy, to avert this from happening.

An effective counterterrorism strategy is urgent now. Just like the new human generation is now more familiar with modern technology, especially electronic devices, the Internet, and social media networks, future generations of terrorism will also be more familiar with accessing information, assembling homemade bombs, evading intelligence surveillance, and utilizing encrypted communications.

Future terrorists will depend more on the Internet to radicalize people, especially youth, from thousands of miles away and to inspire lone wolves to carry out terrorist attacks. After defeating ISIS and its caliphate, the future terrorists will not need a caliphate like the one ISIS established. They will need only a small area as a safe haven or a secret base from which they control operations. After the fall of the Taliban regime in Afghanistan, Osama bin Laden and Al Qaeda went into hiding and continued to organize terrorist attacks throughout the world.

ISIS focused on recruiting, educating, and training children who could evolve into future terrorists. Since the beginning of the operation to liberate Mosul on October 17, 2016, by the Iraqi security forces, children in liberated areas described how ISIS took thousands of children from mosques and put them in camps for ideological education and military training. In the future, the world will be threatened by the children of those adults who believed in the cause, or even those who were killed fighting alongside ISIS in Iraq and Syria. The latter children will be motivated by a desire to avenge their fathers' death. When I went back to Iraq from exile after the fall of Saddam's regime, I met with an Iraqi widow of a Palestinian who was killed fighting the Americans during the war of 2003. She told me her son, who was only fifteen years old, kept telling her he wanted to fight the Americans because they killed his father.

In the future, a terrorist group needs only one creative evil genius—like bin Laden was in his own way and day—who can use innovative ideas and new techniques to make undetectable bombs and formulate new plans to carry out attacks. A computer and an Internet-savvy person is all that is needed to orchestrate a propaganda campaign to radicalize people. The future is close at hand. For example, bin Laden changed the history of terrorism when he established Al Qaeda and declared a war against the United States. Khalid Shaikh Mohammed masterminded the intricate 9/11 attacks with four planes aimed at prized targets; he had also financed his nephew Ramzi Yousef who planned and executed the first attack against the World Trade Center in 1993.

Before 9/11, no one imagined that a commercial airplane could ever be taken over by terrorists; hence security screeners who detected box cutters in passengers' possession allowed them to board with them. It was those very tools that were used to take over the planes.[1] Another innovative move was to use fake journalists to assassinate Ahmed Shah Masood, with IEDs hidden in camera gear. The shoe bomb, underwear bomb, printer ink cartridge bomb, and bombs hidden in the human body were also innovative.[2]

Scott Stewart of Stratfor think tank said for safety officials it is a "cat and mouse" game between terrorists and security services. Militants develop new "weapons," security measures are raised after an incident where those are used, militants develop new tactics and "weapons," or develop new targets, and the cycle continues.

Throughout a short period in 2016–2017, many terrorist attacks were carried out in many European countries, including England, France, and Germany. It is upsetting to know how many of these have happened recently, and how violent the individual acts have been. The terrorists used easily available weapons, such as kitchen knives, trucks, and cars to kill, like those described in my chapter about lone wolves. For example, on July 14, 2016, a terrorist drove a rented, refrigerated truck weighing about 20 tons into thousands of people celebrating Bastille Day in the coastal French city of Nice, killing nearly 100 people and injuring several others. In December 2016, a Tunisian ISIS-inspired refugee drove a truck into crowded Berlin Christmas market, killing 12 people. On March 22, 2017, three people were killed, including a police officer, and at least 29 people were hospitalized in an attack in London that authorities declared as a terrorist incident. On April 7, 2017, a terrorist killed four people and injured 15 in Stockholm Sweden, by driving a stolen beer truck into a crowd of shoppers and through the side of a department store.

On June 3, 2017, three terrorists attacked pedestrians by driving a van into the crowd on the London Bridge, and then used knives to attack people at Borough Market. On June 19, 2017, a terrorist tried to attack security forces on the Champs-Elysees shopping district in Paris when he rammed his car into a police van. In the United States on November 28, 2016, a Somali-born Ohio State University student plowed his car into a group of pedestrians on campus and then got out and began stabbing people with a butcher knife before he was shot to death by a police officer. Eleven people were hurt, one critically.

Security service must not wait for militants to adopt new tactics in order to counter them. They must be proactive rather than reactive, and they should be a step ahead and figure out in advance by having human intelligence on the ground about what new terrorist tactics are being devised. The intelligence community needs to be more innovative and creative than terrorists. They must anticipate these new tactics and probable locations where the attacks might take place. In this cat and mouse scenario, terrorists should be the weaker party, "the mouse." The mouse should not win the game as happens in the Tom and Jerry cartoons.

SAUDI BOMB MAKER IBRAHIM AL-ASIRI

After killing Osama bin Laden in Pakistan on May 1, 2011, the leader of Al Qaeda in Arabian Peninsula (AQAP), Anwar al-Awlaki, became the number one terrorist until he was killed in a drone attack in Yemen on September 30, 2011. After Awlaki's death, Saudi bomb maker Ibrahim Al-Asiri became the most dangerous person with AQAP.

Ibrahim Al-Asiri was described by a U.S. official as an "evil genius." He was born into a well-off family in 1982. Ibrahim and his brother, Abdullah, disappeared in 2007 and reappeared in Yemen in 2009 with AQAP. Al-Asiri was named by the United States as one of the most wanted terrorists and was Al Qaeda's most valued bomb maker and the creator of explosives so dangerous that only a genius could have come up with those ideas.[3]

Ibrahim created a unique bomb to assassinate the head of Saudi Arabia's antiterrorism efforts, unlike any other, using 100 grams of PETN, a white, powdery explosive that was virtually undetectable. In a video posted later on jihadist websites, Al-Asiri embraced and kissed his brother goodbye, as the brother was chosen to deliver the device, hidden inside his rectum. The brother crossed the border and gained entry to the palace of the target, the Saudi head of intelligence Mohammed Bin Nayef (who had been next in line to the throne until he was deposed by the King in favor of his son) by claiming he was defecting.[4] On August 28, 2009, a spokesman for the Saudi Interior Ministry General Mansour al-Turki said that this suicide bomber was foiled because he stumbled just short of his target and fell, detonating the explosion.[5]

Although the assassination proved unsuccessful, AQAP demonstrated a shift in the operational paradigm in a manner that allowed them to achieve tactical surprise. The element of surprise worked, such that the Saudis did not see the attack coming—the operation could have succeeded had it been better executed.[6] This is the first time Al Qaeda managed to hide a bomb inside the rectum of a human body. A device used in this way could be used to bring a civilian airplane down because a terrorist could smuggle it through the screening machine at the airports.

In his next attempt, Ibrahim Al-Asiri plotted his attack with Umar Farouk Abdulmutallab, the underwear bomber, who was introduced to him by Anwar al-Awlaki. A Justice Department sentencing memo in the underwear bomber Abdulmutallab case describes that Al-Asiri had the Nigerian "practice the manner in which the bomb would be detonated; that is, by pushing the plunger of a syringe, causing two chemicals to mix, and initiating a fire which would then detonate the explosive."[7]

Abdulmutallab's act sent shockwaves throughout the world when he successfully smuggled the bomb onto a Detroit-bound airliner on Christmas day in 2009. He was able to light the bomb, but it failed to explode, causing minor burns to himself but sparing fellow passengers. John Pistole, the head of the Transportation Security Administration (TSA), said that the bomb did not detonate because Abdulmutallab had been wearing the same underwear for more than two weeks.[8]

On October 28, 2010, a parcel shipped aboard a UPS plane included a printer containing an ink cartridge with protruding wires, a circuit board, partly covered in a white powder. The parcel turned out to contain explosives. Pictures released of the suspected package were intercepted in the United Kingdom, showing a printer ink cartridge containing white powder and a mobile phone circuit board. The white substance was confirmed to be PETN.[9]

Intelligence uncovered that Al-Asiri created even more sophisticated bombs inside ink printer cartridges. They passed undetected through airport security. It took nine inspections by authorities in Dubai and Britain before they found the devices. The attempt with the ink printer cartridges, using no metal, was a further refinement to evade airport security scanners.[10]

Al-Asiri continued his efforts to develop new kinds of undetectable bombs. On May 8, 2012, the White House said a plot had been foiled when authorities in the Middle East seized another underwear bomb. The bomber involved in the plot to attack a U.S.-bound jet was working as an informant with the CIA. The revelation was another twist in a bizarre story about this attempt by Al Qaeda to strike at a high-profile American target.[11] Al Qaeda considered Al-Asiri a treasure that could not be lost, because he was such an innovative and creative (though evil) genius, who could develop new generations of bombs. Al-Asiri also was actively training the next generation of bomb makers in the event that he is killed.

FUTURE BOMBS INSIDE HUMAN BODIES

These incidents show that terrorism has reached new heights of creativity to carry out their destructive deeds. This has included new iterations of human bombs. U.S. intelligence experts admitted that Al Qaeda's master bomb maker Ibrahim Al-Asiri devised a way of concealing explosives inside the body that can avoid detection by sophisticated scanners. They also warned that terrorist groups had developed an undetectable liquid explosive that can be soaked into clothing and ignited when dry.

In 2012, Taliban terrorist groups used a bomb inside the body of a terrorist to assassinate Asadullah Khalid, head of Afghanistan's National Directorate of Security. On December 6, the terrorist with the bomb presented himself to Khalid, claiming that he was a "peace envoy" sent by the Taliban's ruling Shura Council. Since Khalid had been the target of two previous assassination attempts, he asked his security team to make sure the envoy had no explosives on him. Security took the strange visitor to a basement safe room, "where he was ordered to strip under the gaze of closed-circuit TV cameras. Satisfied that the man had no weapons or explosives, he was presented to Khalid. In that instant, the 'peace envoy' ignited his suicide bomb device. Khalid survived, but with severe abdominal injuries and wounds to his hands and arms."[12]

It was not clear where the bomb was hidden, though Afghan security experts think it was inside the bomber's rectum or scrotum. In addition to inserted bombs in the rectum or scrotum, there were reports about terrorist implanting bombs in other parts of the human body such as in the belly known as "belly bombs." It was also unclear how the device was triggered. In my view, if a terrorist group managed to hide a bomb inside a human body, then thinking of a new way to detonate it would be another easy part of the innovative terrorist technique.

The act of implanting a bomb in a terrorist's body before boarding airplanes has led to increased scrutiny for travelers to the United States who appear to have had recent surgery. The Department of Homeland Security issued a bulletin warning of renewed interest in the tactic of planting a bomb inside the human body. According to U.S. officials, a terrorist could easily slip through airport security, board a plane, and detonate the bomb using a chemical-filled syringe.[13]

Bombs can be surgically implanted in areas such as the abdominal cavity, the buttocks, or female breasts. Hiding things inside the human body is not new. Wartime U.S. intelligence agents had tiny maps and messages hidden inside their rectum. Drug mules swallow packets of cocaine that they then pass, or attempt to vomit up. Intelligence agencies have picked up terrorist operatives discussing the subject online, where one asked, "What is your opinion about surgeries through which I can implant the bomb inside the operative's body?"[14]

One might imagine that explosives detectors and X-ray scanners in modern airports would pick up bombs implanted in the body. But security scanners are designed specifically to identify explosive on the body, not inside it. Until a safe technology is invented, the detection of these human bombs will still mainly be reliant on psychological profiling, and human ability to spot would-be bombers before they act.[15]

Terrorists and intelligence agencies are playing that cat and mouse game I mentioned, as they are engaged in a technological race. So far, terrorists have managed to develop bombs inside shoes, underwear, printer ink cartridges, and the human body. Intelligence officials must develop human intelligence as well as technical intelligence to stop these bombers. They also have to develop new technology and machines capable of detecting bombs in all creatively placed cavities and places.

SAFE HAVENS OF FUTURE TERRORISM

The Iraqi government and the security forces were determined to take Mosul back from ISIS with the support of the United States and its allies. Mosul is the last big city under ISIS control, and it is their headquarters in Iraq. The problem in Syria is more complicated, so ISIS, as well as Al-Nusra Front affiliated with Al Qaeda, and other terrorist groups, may continue to have a safe haven there. Although the UN, the United States, Europe, and many countries in the Middle East are discussing a political solution for the War in Syria, there is little progress reported on achieving peace and defeating ISIS in Syria. It is imperative that the U.S. administration find a way to defeat ISIS in Syria before the latter move to a new safe haven.

President Trump's decision to attack Syria with more than 50 Tomahawk missiles on April 6, 2017, was a bold move, but also backfired, and serve to embolden ISIS and other terrorist groups in Syria and Iraq. Further, the reactions of Russia and some other countries in the region could make an international alliance to fight terrorism more complicated and more difficult.

If ISIS is defeated, fighters can leave Iraq and Syria, and scatter across many counties such as Lebanon, Libya, Yemen, Philippines, Nigeria and other countries. I will shed a light on some of potential future safe havens for ISIS. When the United States and Europe decided to intervene militarily in Libya to remove Qaddafi's regime in 2011, they committed the same mistake as they did in Afghanistan and Iraq. The lack of planning for post-Qaddafi Libya caused a power vacuum, instability, and chaos, which provided extremist groups a good opportunity to consolidate their power and feel empowered. As a result, Al Qaeda attacked the U.S. diplomatic post in Benghazi, where the terrorists killed U.S. Ambassador to Libya Christopher Stevens and three Americans on September 11, 2012.

ISIS will use a similar opportunity to create new safe havens as they did in Syria and Iraq, exploiting the power vacuum, chaos, and civil war. The leader of ISIS, Abo Bakr Al-Baghdadi, sent some of his military commanders and fighters to areas in eastern Libya, which are far from the capital Tripoli. Many Western high-ranking officials admitted that the NATO military campaign and the bombardment of Qaddafi forces was a mistake when they realized that terrorist groups in Libya became a real threat to security in Libya, the region, and the world.

On December 5, 2014, the United States announced plans to expand its anti-ISIS military campaign to Libya. Among Western concerns was Libya's political instability, which could be used by the ISIS terrorists in their favor. A top U.S. general confirmed ISIS runs terrorists training camps in eastern Libya.[16] One U.S. air strike in June 2015 targeted the Algerian militant Mokhtar Belmokhtar, while another in November 2015 killed Abu Nabil, also known as Wissam Najm Abd Zayd al Zubaydi, an Iraqi who led ISIS's arm in Libya. On February 19, 2016, a strike on a seaside town 50 miles west of Tripoli targeted Noureddine Chouchane, a Tunisian who had helped arrange the arrival of ISIS recruits into Libya.[17]

There are other future potential safe havens for ISIS, for example, in areas with no central government control, in failed states, or in sites plagued by civil war, or countries like Yemen, Nigeria, and the Philippines. Iraqi security forces learned that the leader of ISIS gave instructions to some of his aides to move to northern Lebanon, a majority Sunni area with some extreme Salafi-jihadi fighters. In Yemen, the conflict between different Yemeni factions and the war led by Saudi Arabia and supported by the United States against the Huthis (a branch of Shiites) left some areas with no central control, where terrorist groups such as Al Qaeda and ISIS are thriving. The Abu Sayyaf terrorist group in Philippines announced its allegiance to ISIS in August 2014, two months after ISIS leader Abu Bakr Al-Baghdadi announced the establishment of an Islamic State "caliphate" in areas under his control in Iraq and Syria. A global comprehensive strategy for counterterrorism should look into all potential future safe havens for terrorist groups, especially for ISIS after its defeat in Iraq and Syria.

FUTURE LONE WOLF TERRORISTS

Future terrorism in the West will depend more on foreign fighters returning to their countries from Syria and Iraq. The foreign fighters can go into hiding by themselves or among refugees, using fake passports, or through illegal smuggling to Europe, the United States, Canada, and Australia. ISIS, Al Qaeda, and other terrorist groups will also focus more and more on lone wolves, who are already in the West and have never traveled to fight in Iraq or Syria. These lone wolves could be encouraged to attack in the West, particularly in those countries that participated in air strikes against ISIS in Iraq and Syria.

After killing Ibrahim Al-Asiri, the master bomb maker with Al Qaeda in the Arabian Peninsula (AQAP), another senior AQAP leader, Khaled Batarfi, released a video, praising lone wolf style attacks against the West and calling for more of them. "We urge you to strike America in its own home and beyond."[18] White House Press Secretary for the Obama administration Josh Earnest stressed that, "The president himself has identified the risk of a lone wolf terrorist as something that is significant."[19]

It is imperative for the new U.S. administration to study cases of lone wolf attacks in Europe and in the United States as well as foiled attempts, during the four years of 2014–2017 when attacks were frequent, to understand the processes and methods of radicalization, bomb making, acquiring weapons, as well as how attacks are planned and executed. It is also important to study the mistakes and shortfalls in dealing with lone wolf actors to learn lessons and to stop future attacks by lone wolves.

TERRORISTS AND FUTURE CYBERWAR

Future terrorism will depend more on the Internet as a tool for radicalization and recruitment, especially for youth. The Internet provides quick and wide access to people all over the world, and is cheaper and easier than face-to-face recruiting. The Internet is also a secure way to cover the identity of terrorists, and provides encrypted communications.

In 2012, Birmingham teenager Junaid Hussain went on trial for hacking U.K. Prime Minister Tony Blair's address book, and taking down an anti-terror hotline. Defense lawyers described him as "shy and unassuming" and dismissed the online exploits as a childish joke. "They weren't terrorists in any way, shape or form," his attorney argued in court.[20] Less than two years later, Junaid was in Syria to join ISIS whose leaders' enthusiasm for medieval barbarity is matched by an equally eager embrace of modern technology. They know that a hacker like Junaid is as intimidating to some of their enemies transmitting from a machine from afar as the gunmen who terrorizes people up close and personal on the ground.[21]

After ISIS declared its Islamic State (caliphate) on June 29, 2014, a group of hackers who claim to be affiliated with ISIS declared a "Cyber Caliphate" and made headlines over months for a series of online incidents that received worldwide news coverage.[22] On January 12, 2015, the "Cyber Caliphate" hacked into the Twitter and YouTube accounts for the U.S. military's Central Command. The hackers claimed that they had penetrated military networks and had details of U.S. military officers. They even threatened these military officers by saying, "We will come after you, watch your back." The Pentagon said that only the social media sites themselves were compromised.[23] Once again the terrorists were a step ahead of governments and intelligence agencies. In reaction, in April 2015, the Obama administration issued an executive order that created a new targeted authority for the U.S. government to better respond to the most significant of these online threats, particularly in situations where malicious cyber actors may operate beyond the reach of existing authorities.[24]

During 2014 and 2015, ISIS is believed to have inspired the development of at least five different hacking groups that launched cyber attacks in favor of the terrorist group. On April 4, 2016, Cyber Caliphate Army (CCA), ISIS's main hacking unit, and other pro-ISIS groups like the Sons Caliphate Army (SCA) and Kalachnikov.TN (KTN) merged and formed The United Cyber Caliphate (UCC).[25] In May 2015, Britain's new spy chief Alex Younger warned that the country was now in a "technology arms race" with enemies "often unconstrained by consideration of ethics and law . . . terrorists, malicious actors in cyberspace and criminals." "The technology allows them to see what we are doing and to put our people and agents at risk."[26] Also when the section chief from the FBI Cyber Division Outreach, John Riggi, delivered the opening keynote address at the ISC2 CyberSecureGov event in Washington, D.C., in May 2015, he responded to a question on the top new and emerging global cyber threats by pointing to ISIS and the emerging cyber threats coming from the Middle East as needing more attention.[27]

Attackers often share their success, or what they have learned from failure, amplifying the world's future vulnerability to other hackers, regardless of their affiliation. One well-known hacker database, Shodan, provides tips on how to exploit everything from power plants to wind turbines, searchable by country, company, or device, providing detailed "how-to" information and greatly lowering the technical bar and knowledge for any rogue individual to hack critical infrastructures.[28]

Concern about the future of ISIS cyber terrorism is high, not because they have sophisticated hacking skills but because they are utilizing multiple ways of attracting new talent, utilizing all the freely available tools online, utilizing malware that's already available and building their own malware.[29]

U.S. vulnerability to cyber attacks is well known. Nearly 22 million individual records were stolen when hackers penetrated the government's central personnel office computers. American companies' annual losses to cyber thieves total roughly $115 billion. The U.S. government spends more than $5 billion annually on cyber defense, with responsibility divided among the Department of Defense, the Department of Homeland Security, the National Security Agency, and the FBI.[30]

The December 2015 cyber attack in the Ukraine, which affected electricity for 225,000 customers, was unique in that it is the first confirmed attack that took down a power grid. In addition, in March 2016, the United States officially charged a hacker with access to a computer control system for New York's Bowman Avenue Dam. Luckily, a gate on the dam had been disconnected for maintenance issues; otherwise, the hacker could have operated and manipulated the gate.[31] A lot of Americans do not take this seriously, but it is possible that a group like ISIS can get control and decide when they want to take out part of the power grid. Plots can take years to develop and just because you cannot imagine it happening right now does not mean it is not being worked on or it is not being plotted.[32]

Former FBI Director James Comey said, in reference to malicious software that disables or wrecks computer networks, that ISIS also recognizes that it might be easier to strike at the United States from afar using digital weapons than to infiltrate terrorists across the border. He said, "I see them already starting to explore things that are concerning, critical infrastructure, things like that. The logic of it tells me it's coming, and so of course I'm worried about it."[33]

Destructive malware is a bomb and terrorists want bombs. In October 2015, U.S. Assistant Secretary of Homeland Security for Infrastructure Protection Caitlin Durkovich said at an electric industry conference that ISIS terrorists have launched cyber attacks on the U.S. national power grid.[34] ISIS is merging their brand and increasing their numbers, skills, and even languages, which means they are increasing the channels through which they operate and distribute their claims of responsibility for successful terrorist acts. They have a much more powerful message and a more robust structure than before. They are combining their ranks to become a hacking powerhouse.[35]

On April 5, 2016, former Secretary of Defense Ashton Carter told an audience at the Center for Strategic and International Studies that U.S. Cyber Command has its "first wartime assignment" in the fight against ISIS. That cyber fight includes techniques to disrupt the group's ability to communicate, organize, and finance its operations.[36]

On the same day, the head of U.S. Cyber Command Admiral Michael Rogers told the Senate Armed Services Committee that among his biggest fears are the possibility of groups like ISIS manipulating electronic data records, impacting critical infrastructure such as the electrical grid or air traffic control systems, and using cyber tools "as a weapons system."[37]

Accessing and obtaining information from a protected computer without authorization is possible, as was done by Ardit Ferizi, also known as Th3Dir3ctorY, 20, a citizen of Kosovo, who was sentenced to 20 years in prison for providing material support to ISIS. "This case represents the first time we have seen the very real and dangerous national security cyber threat that results from the combination of terrorism and hacking," said Assistant Attorney General Carlin.[38] Ferizi hacked a U.S. retailer and collected the data from tens of thousands of customers. He then used it to compile a hit list of some 1,300 military and government personnel. The ISIS supporter announced on Twitter that he had gained access to personally identifiable information that ISIS intended to use as a hit list. After sharing the document with Junaid Hussain—an ISIS hacker—a link to the document was published on Twitter.[39]

ISIS wrote to the Americans on the hit list, "We are in your emails and computer systems, watching and recording your every move, we have your names and addresses, we are in your emails and social media accounts, we are extracting confidential data and passing on your personal information to the soldiers of the Caliphate, who soon with the permission of Allah will strike at your necks in your own lands!"[40] Assistant Attorney General Carlin warned, "This was a wake-up call not only to those of us in law enforcement, but also to those in private industry."[41]

So, the question is that how many wake-up calls are needed to awaken American intelligence agencies and to have them heed the message. There have been many wake-up calls including terrorist attacks by Al Qaeda before and after 9/11, and terrorist attacks by ISIS before and after the Paris attacks on November 2015, which has been called Europe's 9/11. Is the new U.S. administration ready to step up to the cyber challenges? It is time to get serious.

By now in this book I have reviewed major issues and strategies in my comprehensive plan to counterterrorism. In the next chapter, I present a concise view of the steps I have explored in these pages.

CHAPTER 15

Conclusion: The New 12-Step Counterterrorism Strategy to Defeat Terrorists

The chapters in this book have outlined how the world failed to stop the terrorist group Al Qaeda, which carried out many terrorist attacks around the world since 1992, including attacks in Europe and the United States. Al Qaeda was also behind the 9/11 attacks in the United States, the most devastating attacks on U.S. soil since the attack on Pearl Harbor. Over time, other terrorist groups have evolved, including the Islamic State in Iraq and the Levant/Syria (ISIL/ISIS), an organization that has increased the number and the extent of terror threats worldwide.

Osama bin Laden, the founder of Al Qaeda, was responsible for many terrorist attacks against U.S. interests. These include the attacks on U.S. troops in Yemen in 1992 and Somalia in 1993; the first attack against the World Trade Center in 1993; the attacks on the U.S. Embassies in Kenya and Tanzania in 1998; the attack on the USS *Cole* destroyer in Yemen in 2000; and the attacks that occurred in the United States in 2001 on 9/11. The United States had many golden opportunities to kill or capture bin Laden before his eventual 2011 assassination by Navy SEALS in Pakistan, but these opportunities were squandered due to political, military, and intelligence mistakes.

After the 9/11 attacks—an intricately orchestrated use of four airplanes targeting major sites in New York and Washington, D.C., in the United States—Al Qaeda continued its attempts to bring down a U.S. passenger airplane. Examples include the shoe bomber in December 2001, the underwear bomber on Christmas Day in 2009, the two printer ink cartridge bombs in October 2010, and the modified underwear bomb in May 2012, all of which are discussed in this book.

This book has shown how the world failed to stop the terrorist group ISIS, which emerged after the killing of Osama bin Laden in 2011. ISIS proved to be more extreme and more brutal than Al Qaeda and managed to control huge swathes of lands in Iraq and Syria. ISIS's leader Abu Bakr Al-Baghdadi declared an Islamic State "caliphate" and proclaimed himself to be the "caliph" or leader of the Islamic State. As this book explains, ISIS it is not a state, and it is certainly not Islamic.

But a new brand of terror emerged full blown in the United States and Europe dramatically in the years 2015–2017. Attacks were increasingly carried out by lone wolves—homegrown violent individuals and terrorist organizations, and terrorist organizations like ISIS claim credit for all of them. And simpler homemade weapons were used, rather than largescale complicated methods. In the United States, lone wolves carried out shootings on a gay night club, a college campus, and an army post and suicide bombings on pedestrian streets and at a popular marathon. Europe was not spared, with suicide bombings at an airport and metro station (in Brussels) and in a Christmas market (in Berlin), a truck driven into crowds celebrating Bastille Day in France and on the London Bridge, suicide bombing at a concert arena (in Manchester), and shootings at a magazine headquarters, football match, cafe, and concert (in Paris). Much to widespread surprise, even Muslim nations have not been spared, as terrorist attacks also hit Turkey, Lebanon, Syria, and Iraq.

These frequent attacks, which have terrorized the world, motivated me to write this book, based on my personal and professional experience, from rebelling against the terrorist regime in my native Iraq, and being imprisoned and tortured, to exile, to serving as Deputy Foreign Minister and Ambassador of Iraq at the United Nations. I have seen terror firsthand, stood up against it, and now propose the urgency of an effective counterterrorism strategy, and the 12-step plan that I propose and summarize below.

URGENCY CONSIDERING
THREATS OF WORLD WAR

A new counterterrorism strategy as I have outlined here is essential at this time considering the escalation of world tensions, specifically over the Syrian crisis. As of July 2017, a threat of Syria carrying out another chemical attack loomed on the international stage. The United States currently has troops in Syria, so its commitment to a role in the tensions is great on that level as well as its responsibility as a superpower. Tensions could escalate between the United States and Russia, which has carried out air strikes in support of President Assad since 2015. Meanwhile, the conflict in Syria rages, threatening confrontation between the United States and Russia. U.S. tension could lead to other wars with North Korea, and even China.

By the end of June 2017, coalition military forces conducted strikes consisting of over 70 engagements against ISIS terrorists as part of Operation Inherent Resolve, the operation to destroy ISIS in Iraq and Syria. In Syria, these hit a storage facility, a tank, a refinery, and storage facilities. In Iraq, military forces conducted five strikes consisting of almost

30 engagements, including near Bayji, Tel Afar, destroying an ISIS head-quarters there, and Mosul, destroying fighting positions there. The destruction of ISIS targets in Syria and Iraq limits ISIS's ability of project terror, and to conduct operations throughout the region and the world.[1]

WHY THE UNITED STATES FAILED
TO STOP AL QAEDA AND ISIS

Throughout these chapters, I have shed light on mistakes and shortfalls in dealing with terrorist groups in Afghanistan, Iraq, Libya, and Syria, as well as other countries such as Yemen, Somalia, and Nigeria. I have shown that there are many lessons to be learned from the birth and evolution of terrorist organizations, and from the Western world's approach to dealing with them. I have discussed mistakes in U.S. counterterrorism strategies during the administrations of Presidents Bill Clinton, George W. Bush, Barack Obama, and Donald Trump that have resulted in the failure to stop Al Qaeda and ISIS, despite the goal to do so. Tracing U.S. mistakes back in time, the administration of President Bill Clinton underestimated the threat of Al Qaeda, in spite of evidence that terrorists connected to Al Qaeda bombed the World Trade Center in New York in 1993. In October 2000, Al Qaeda attacked the USS *Cole* in Yemen killing 17 U.S. sailors, injuring many more, and almost sinking the destroyer. Yet, the Clinton cabinet was reluctant to respond militarily to what was quite obviously an act of war perpetrated by Al Qaeda.

Clinton's term expired three months after the bombing of the USS *Cole*. In June 2001 and five months after Bush had been sworn in, Al Qaeda released a videotape claiming responsibility for the *Cole* operation. If the Bush administration needed a reason to destroy Al Qaeda, this was the best one, because the videotape was broadcast around the world firmly showing where the responsibility lay. Instead, the response from the United States was to do absolutely nothing. This was a big mistake.

By the summer of 2001, the CIA was convinced that Al Qaeda was on the verge of a devastating attack. On August 6, 2001, President Bush received intelligence in the Presidential Daily Briefing (PDB) entitled "Bin Laden Determined to Strike in US." On September 4, 2001, at a meeting of the Principal's Committee of Bush's national-security advisers, "No one around the table seemed to have a can-do attitude. Everyone seemed to have an excuse." A week later on 9/11, the world witnessed the worst terrorist attacks in history, carried out at bin Laden's direction.[2] Nearly three thousand people were killed and twice that number were wounded. Therefore President Bush declared "War on Terror" and launched wars in Afghanistan and Iraq.

The Obama administration thought the previous President, George W. Bush, overstretched the U.S. Army and had motivated terrorists by putting a large number of ground troops in Afghanistan and Iraq. In addition, in

2011 Obama did not pressure the Iraqi government to keep residual forces, although military commanders suggested leaving some residual forces in Iraq. Such a move could have made a big difference in stopping ISIS. Later in 2013 and 2014, this terrorist group overran much of Iraq. In my opinion, just a small number of U.S. troops, along with a few jet fighters, could have prevented much of the unspeakable carnage that unfolded in Iraq over the years of 2014–2017.

Obama's election campaign promised to withdraw U.S. troops from Afghanistan and Iraq, so he worked hard to achieve that, by withdrawing troops from Iraq by the end of 2011 and from Afghanistan by the end of 2016 before the end of his second term. When ISIS took control of several important cities and towns in Iraq in 2013–2014, including Mosul, the second largest city in Iraq, President Obama was hesitant to take military action. In 2014, the Obama administration declined requests from the Iraqi government to provide air strikes against ISIS, even as the group seemed poised to overrun Baghdad. In an interview with Jon Stewart on *The Daily Show* on June 19, 2014, I said I am not suggesting a military invasion but air strikes to stop ISIS. In my opinion, lack of action was another big mistake that is evident when reviewing the outcome.

As a result, ISIS managed to control huge swathes of land in Syria and Iraq; additionally, they erased and redrew the borders drawn up in the 1916 Sykes-Picot agreement, and declared an Islamic State "caliphate." While doing this, they attracted thousands of fighters from Europe, the United States, and many other countries, and some of these recruits went on to commit atrocities and mass killings in Paris in November 2015, Brussels in March 2016, and the U.K. in 2017.

This book also explains how President Trump's policies regarding immigration and his travel ban on Muslim majority nations could embolden terrorism and help terrorist groups in their propaganda that claims the United States is against Islam and is waging a war targeting Muslims. His statements about bringing back enhanced interrogation techniques, which are considered torture and were forbidden by President Obama, have raised concern among international organizations and human rights advocates.

In light of the above and all the events outlined in these pages, this book shows the urgent need for a new comprehensive and long-term counterterrorism strategy. Unless such a strategy is adopted, the scourge of terrorism that we are now witnessing will continue.

THE NEW COUNTERTERRORISM STRATEGY

This book presents a new, 12-step counterterrorism strategy to defeat terrorists now and in the future. This strategy is based on understanding the history, roots, ideology, and mentality behind fundamentalism, extremism, and terrorism. From my perspective, terrorism is a virulent and contagious disease. If we fail to adequately treat this disease now, it will quickly spread further and engulf other countries such as Libya, Tunisia, Egypt, Turkey, and even the West, leaving fear and destruction in its wake. Time is of the essence for the world to respond. The new counterterrorism strategy is based on many tactics explored in detail in this text. The summary of these tactics is as follows.

Cut Terrorism Funding

One of the major calls to action involves cutting off the funding of terrorist organizations. Funds are the lifeline of terrorism, and ISIS has managed to get billions of dollars through, among other things, selling crude oil and oil products, selling artifacts, enslaving women, taxing people in its territories, and kidnappings for ransom.

Beyond stopping terrorists from accessing these sources of revenue, it is imperative to stop private donors and states from providing funds to groups engaging in terrorism. The international community has been too lax for too long when it comes to holding the financiers of terrorism accountable. With the United States taking the lead, individuals who support terrorism financially can be brought to justice.

Shut Down Internet Terrorism

Terrorist groups exploit the Internet and social media networks to radicalize people, recruit youth, and carry out terrorist attacks throughout the world. As one example, Al Qaeda posted an article about making pressure cooker bombs on the Internet, entitled "Make a Bomb in the Kitchen of Your Mom," which was followed to make bombs in three terrorist attacks in the United States, in 2010, 2013, and 2016.

Future terrorist groups could potentially put instructions online for making chemical weapons at home that are easy to make, such as mustard gas and sarin. Imagine a future article with a title like "Make Chemical Weapons in the backyard of Your Mom." We cannot allow terrorists to weaponize the Internet by disseminating such content. This book also has shown how the new strategy should address the problem of cyber terrorism and shut it down.

Step Up Tech

Many officials in the United States and Europe, terrorism experts, and intelligence agents believe that tech firms and experts are not doing enough to stop terrorists from exploiting the Internet and social networks. For example, terrorists exploit social networks and applications to send encrypted communications. An appropriate balance between the right to privacy and the ability to thwart terrorism online needs to be implemented.

It is imperative that the right of privacy and encryption remain both guaranteed and respected by governments and tech firms, but extremist groups must not be allowed to use coded communication to avoid intelligence surveillance and encrypted messages to coordinate attacks. Tech firms can play a leading role in stopping terrorists from using encrypted messages to plan attacks and to recruit people. They can and should develop and use effective software to locate terrorists online. They also must increase the number of staff and resources dedicated to tracking down terrorist networks using social media so that they can alert authorities about potential attacks. Tech firms do not have to do this alone; they should receive support and incentives from governments for their assistance in fighting terrorism.

Root Out Lone Wolves

Lone wolves are among the most dangerous terrorists, especially in the West, where it has become increasingly difficult for terrorist organizations to embed their own networks. Lone wolves are difficult to detect and predict; they act alone, plan their attacks secretly, and decide when and where to attack, without requiring the sorts of contacts with terrorist organizations that would make them easy to locate and track.

Lone wolves must be prevented from exploiting the ease of getting weapons in some countries in Europe and in the United States. For example, people on the no-fly list in the United States for suspicions of connections to terrorist groups can still easily buy weapons. This must be stopped.

Prevent Foreign Fighters' Attacks

Thousands of foreign fighters have joined ISIS and other terrorist groups. They have traveled from the United States, Europe, Canada, Australia, and other countries, and could return to their countries to carry out attacks. This is what happened in the November 2015 attacks in Paris and the March 2016 attacks in Brussels.

This book discusses how foreign fighters can be prevented from joining terrorist groups such as Al Qaeda in Afghanistan, ISIS in Iraq and Syria, and Al-Shabab in Somalia. Foreign fighters who traveled to these countries and fought alongside terrorist groups should also be prevented from returning home to wreak havoc.

Debunk Terrorists' Ideology

This book explains how terrorist groups utilize a distorted, subversive, and seditious ideology to brainwash youth, and to justify killing innocent people and civilians, including women and children. This ideology is the major motive behind extremism and terrorism. This distorted ideology is poisonous and has to be addressed.

Extreme ideologies should not be allowed in educational curricula, on TV, and on the Internet. A major source of recruitment of terrorists is religious schools or *madrassas*. Religious schools or madrassas must be prevented from teaching extremism. Those who finance and support extremist educational institutions need to be brought to justice and the madrassas that teach this ideology need to either be reformed or shut down.

Reach Out to Muslims

Western governments have to follow a policy of reaching out to Muslims in the West to assure them that they are not discriminated against. Education, healthcare, and jobs should be provided to deprived poor neighborhoods and Muslim communities. Muslims in Western countries can serve as a valuable source of information that can be used to root out radicals. They could provide warnings about extremist groups and individuals who might plan terrorist attacks. Western intelligence agencies should depend on such human intelligence from within the Muslim communities, as well as on tech intelligence, given that both are important.

Muslims must be assured that the "War on Terror" is not a war against Islam and Muslims. It is necessary to understand the language of terrorist groups. Terrorist groups such as Al Qaeda, ISIS, and Al-Nusra Front use Arabic as their main language of communication. Employing an adequate numbers of linguists who are capable of decoding the communications between fundamentalists, extremists and terrorists, is an important component in my proposed counterterrorism strategy.

It is vital that Muslims are involved in policy-study centers and think tanks that study the ideologies, strategies, and tactics of terrorist groups. These types of organizations play a pivotal role in devising strategies and setting policies, and thus they need to employ people from the countries where terrorist groups are most active, such as Iraq, Syria, Pakistan, and Afghanistan.

It is also important to study the differences and problems between terrorist groups and to use this information to undermine these groups. Curricula in schools, colleges, and universities should include special courses about radicalism, extremism, and terrorism, and the various groups that promote these tactics. The atrocities terrorists perpetrate on countries and societies should be highlighted; even more importantly, they should be made aware of strategies for counterterrorism such as those outlined in this book. All individuals need to know what governments as well as individuals can do to thwart terrorism. Translating and publishing articles, booklets, and books written by extremists who changed their minds and turned against radicalism and extremism is an important measure in counterterrorism strategy. These narratives can go a long way to educate the public and to bring doubt to the minds of those who may sympathize with terrorist groups.

Thwart Future Terrorist Attacks

Future generations of terrorists will depend more on sleeper cells, terrorist clusters, and lone wolves to carry out attacks. They will use modern technology for encrypted communication, and will recruit terrorists through the Internet and social networks. Terrorists who have managed to carry out attacks have been able to do so by staying a step ahead of intelligence agencies and security forces. To thwart future terrorist plans and attacks, intelligence, law enforcement, and security forces should be focused on being a step ahead instead of constantly playing a game of catch-up. They should be able to predict what terrorists think and what new ideas and plans terrorist might come up with so that they can lay out preventative measures ahead of time.

In addition, intelligence should be able to infiltrate terrorist groups and have firsthand information about future plans, moves, and tactics. The United States should depend more on human intelligence instead of relying on overly broad technical intelligence, which is often only useful in figuring out what terrorists were up to after they have already struck. Defectors from terrorist groups should be given attention and media coverage to uncover the real world of terrorism and to highlight their distorted ideology, evil practices, and atrocities. Preventing terrorists from using prisons and detention centers to radicalize other inmates and recruit them for terrorist organizations is also crucial.

Deprive Terrorists of Safe Havens

The world failed to stop Al Qaeda and ISIS, because they had safe havens in Afghanistan, Iraq, and Syria. A new counterterrorism strategy cannot allow any terrorist groups to have access to any potential safe haven in the future for any reason and under any circumstances.

New safe havens and potential places to grow and spread fundamentalism, extremism, and terrorism have to be examined closely, such as those in Libya, Yemen, Nigeria, Philippines, and Somalia. The new counterterrorism strategy should prevent terrorist groups from taking advantage of chaos. So-called failed states, as well as countries in turmoil and civil war, must be given particular attention by the international community so that they do not become breeding grounds for terrorism.

Stop Support for Extreme Opposition Groups

Support for extreme opposition elements in Afghanistan, Iraq, Libya, and Syria with money, weapons, and arms contributed to the rise of terrorist groups in these countries. The world needs to stop providing extreme opposition groups with any kind of assistance that enables them to carry out atrocities.

U.S. allies have to stop helping terrorist groups in any way and under any circumstances. Countries like Pakistan that have supported the Taliban and Al Qaeda should choose either to align with terrorism or with the free world. Turkey, a NATO member, cannot be allowed to turn a blind eye to thousands of foreign fighters crossing its borders to join ISIS and other jihadist groups such as Al-Nusra Front—an Al Qaeda franchise. After all, Turkey itself has been the target of terrorist attacks.

Form an International Counterterrorism Alliance

The United States could lead a serious, strong, and competent international alliance, with European superpowers as well as with Canada, Australia, and even Arab nations. It is also imperative that the United States have an alliance with some countries in the Middle East if it wants to be effective in fighting fundamentalism, extremism, and terrorism.

A successful alliance should include only countries that are sincere and serious in fighting extremism and combatting terrorism. Some U.S. allies had a double standard policy of supporting extreme groups in Iraq, Libya, and Syria on one hand and claiming to fight terrorism on the other hand. For example, an alliance with Iraq is essential for the international war on terrorism. Iraq could be a base in the Middle East to fight the spread of terrorism. A regional alliance with countries that are sincere in their fight against terrorism is imperative.

Take into Account Psychological Factors

All the above issues involve psychological components. These have been pointed out by my friend, United Nations NGO leader and terrorism expert Dr. Judy Kuriansky. For example, consistent with the analyses of the personality and cultural factors described in the cases in this book, terrorism arises and thrives when factions are obsessed with dynamics like power, insecurity, fears, and anger. As explicated well in *Weapons of Mass Psychological Destruction* by psychologists Larry C. James and Terry L. Oroszi, terrorists manipulate public reactions to incite maximum fear beyond the annihilation of specific targets; thus, it is crucial for the public to control emotional reactions to reduce the impact of evil intentions. Therefore, my counterterrorism strategy requires taking these psychological dynamics into account, both on the micro level—with regard to individuals—and also on the macro level, with regard to societies, countries, and international relations.

Enact a Global and Comprehensive New Strategy

Al Qaeda under Osama bin Laden's leadership and ISIS under Abo Bakr Al-Baghdadi's leadership created global terrorism networks and launched an international holy war "jihad" against the West, and especially the United States. To combat this, the United States should draw up a new global and comprehensive counterterrorism strategy that takes into consideration all areas around the world where fundamentalism, extremism, and terrorism are flourishing. If the United States and allies want to be effective in taking on these global terrorist networks, the strategy should address the roots of the problem, and not just the symptoms.

Cooperation and coordination among the world's intelligence agencies is vital. Intelligence agencies in the United States, Europe, and other countries must be willing to share information with each other regarding the identities, movements, and activities of foreign fighters. Regional powers can also play an important role in providing intelligence about foreign fighters.

Hope for the Future

In summary, effectively combating terrorism will not be simple or uncomplicated, but it is possible. Terrorism is a global phenomenon that requires a global solution. The members of the international community need to set aside their differences and work together in order to deal with this issue properly. This can be possible with effective leadership from the United States given its position as a world superpower. The Trump administration must carefully study the mistakes that have been made by previous administrations so that, instead of repeating them, it can use the lessons learned to develop and implement a coherent strategy for the future. All sectors of society can play a role in defeating terrorism. This is my hope for the future.

Notes

INTRODUCTION

1. "Security Council Resolution 688," *UN.Org*, April 5, 1991 (accessed January 15, 2017), https://documents-dds-ny.un.org/doc/RESOLUTION/GEN/NR0/596/24/IMG/NR059624.pdf?OpenElement

2. See Hamid Al-Bayati, *Destruction of Southern Marshes, in Iraq since the Gulf War*, edited by Fran Hazelton (London: Zed Books, 1994).

3. Amar U.S. Rebuilding Lives, *Amar Foundation* (accessed December 5, 2016), http://www.amarfoundation.org/en-us/

4. Jan Eliasson (Sweden), UN Deputy Secretary-General, *UN. Org*, July 1, 2012 (accessed on December 5, 2016), https://www.un.org/millenniumgoals/advocates/members/jan-eliasson.shtml

5. "US Ups Iraqi Opposition Support," *BBC*, January 22, 1999 (accessed October 30, 2016), http://news.bbc.co.uk/2/hi/events/crisis_in_the_gulf/latest_news/260264.stm

6. Hamid Al-Bayati, *Terrorism Game* (London: Al-Rafid, 2001).

7. Hamid Al-Bayati, *Terrorism in Iraq* (Baghdad: Iraqi Center for Strategic Studies, 2005).

8. "Security Council Resolution 949 Adopted by the Security Council at Its 3438th Meeting," *UN.Org*, October 15, 1994 (accessed January 15, 2017), https://documents-dds-ny.un.org/doc/UNDOC/GEN/N94/401/71/PDF/N9440171.pdf?OpenElement

9. Hamid al-Bayati, *From Dictatorship to Democracy: An Insider's Account of the Iraqi Opposition to Saddam* (Philadelphia: University of Pennsylvania Press, 2011).

10. Rt. Hon. Ann Clwyd, MP, *Parliament UK* (accessed December 5, 2016), http://www.parliament.uk/biographies/commons/Ann-Clwyd/553

11. Peter W. Galbraith, *The End of Iraq: How American Incompetence Created a War without End* (New York: Simon and Schuster, 2007).

12. Sharon Otterman, "IRAQ: Debaathification," *Council on Foreign Relations*, April 7, 2005 (accessed January 16, 2017), http://www.cfr.org/iraq/iraq-deba athification/p7853

13. "UN Security Council Resolution 1483, Iraq," *Council on Foreign Relations*, May 22, 2003 (accessed January 16, 2017), http://www.cfr.org/sanctions/ un-security-council-resolution-1483-iraq/p8471

14. Fred Kaplan, "Who Disbanded the Iraqi Army? And Why Was Nobody Held Accountable?" *Slate*, September 7, 2007 (accessed January 17, 2017), http:// www.slate.com/articles/news_and_politics/war_stories/2007/09/who_dis banded_the_iraqi_army.html

15. Edmund L. Andrews, "After the War: Baghdad; Iraqi Civilians Allowed to Keep Assault Rifles," *New York Times*, June 1, 2003 (accessed January 17, 2017), http://www.nytimes.com/2003/06/01/world/after-the-war-baghdad-iraqi-civilians-allowed-to-keep-assault-rifles.html

16. Linda Robinson, *Tell Me How This Ends: General David Petraeus & the Search for a Way Out of Iraq* (New York: Simon and Schuster, 2013), 251.

17. Ananya Roy, "Who Could Be ISIS Leader Abu Bakr al-Baghdadi's Successor If He Is Confirmed Dead?" *International Business Times*, June 24, 2017 (accessed June 24, 2017), http://www.ibtimes.co.uk/who-could-be-isis-leader-abu-bakr-al-baghdadis-successor-if-he-confirmed-dead-1627635

18. Zeina Karam and Vladimir Isachenkov, "Uncertainty over Islamic State Leader's Fate after Airstrike," *AP News*, June 16, 2017 (accessed June 24, 2017), https://apnews.com/5077aa8c02784a8d81eab1b7dc02aa5b

19. Roy, "Who Could Be ISIS Leader Abu Bakr al-Baghdadi's Successor If He Is Confirmed Dead?"

CHAPTER 1

1. Lawrence Right, *The Looming Tower, Al-Qaeda and the Road to 9/11* (New York: Thompson Press 2006), 174.

2. "What a Downed Black Hawk in Somalia Taught America," *NPR*, October 5, 2013 (accessed March 7, 2017), http://www.npr.org/2013/10/05/229561805/ what-a-downed-black-hawk-in-somalia-taught-america

3. Usama bin Ladin, "American Soldiers Are Paper Tigers," *Middle East Quarterly* 5, no. 4, December 1998 (accessed March 7, 2017), http://www.meforum .org/435/usama-bin-ladin-american-soldiers-are-paper-tigers

4. "FBI Adds bin Laden, Kopp to Most Wanted List," *CNN*, June 7, 1999 (accessed December 21, 2016), http://www.cnn.com/US/9906/07/fbi.most.wanted .02/index.html?_s=PM:US

5. Jeffrey Hays, "Combating Terrorism under Clinton," *Facts and Details*, July 2012 (accessed December 21, 2016), http://factsanddetails.com/world/cat58/ sub384/item2381.html

6. Ibid.

7. "Transcript: Bin Laden Determined to Strike in US," *CNN*, April 10, 2004 (accessed February 28, 2017), http://www.cnn.com/2004/ALLPOLITICS/04/10/ august6.memo/

8. Jane Mayer, "The Search for Osama, Did the Government Let bin Laden's Trail Go Cold?" *New Yorker*, August 4, 2003 (accessed February 28, 2017), http:// www.newyorker.com/magazine/2003/08/04/the-search-for-osama

9. Samantha Power, "Our War on Terror," *New York Times*, July 29, 2007 (accessed February 28, 2017), http://www.nytimes.com/2007/07/29/books/review/Power-t.html

10. "Trump's Counterterrorism Challenge," *The Soufan Group*, January 25, 2017 (accessed February 9, 2017), http://soufangroup.com/tsg-intelbrief-trumps-counterterrorism-challenge/

11. "Dana Priest, Bush's 'War' on Terror Comes to a Sudden End," *Washington Post*, January 23, 2009 (accessed February 28, 2017), http://www.washingtonpost.com/wp-dyn/content/article/2009/01/22/AR2009012203929.html

12. "US Terror Fight to Focus on Surgical Hits," *CBS News*, June 30, 2011 (accessed February 28, 2017), http://www.cbsnews.com/news/us-terror-fight-to-focus-on-surgical-hits/

13. "Correcting for Bush's Mistakes," *Boston Globe*, July 16, 2011 (accessed February 25, 2017), http://archive.boston.com/bostonglobe/editorial_opinion/editorials/articles/2011/07/16/correcting_for_bushs_mistakes/

14. "Cindy Saine, Obama Defends Counterterrorism Record, Offers Guidance for Trump," *VOA*, December 7, 2016 (accessed February 9, 2017), http://www.voanews.com/a/obama-to-tout-counterterrorism-success-in-final-national-security-speech/3624947.html

15. Eli Stokols and Nolan D. Mccaskill, "Full Text: Donald Trump's Speech on Fighting Terrorism," *Politico Magazine*, August 15, 2016 (accessed February 9, 2017), http://www.politico.com/story/2016/08/donald-trump-terrorism-speech-227025

16. David Jackson, "Trump Calls for New Approach to Anti-Terror Fight," *USA Today*, August 15, 2016 (accessed February 9, 2017), http//www.usatoday.com/story/news/politics/elections/2016/08/15/donald-trump-islamic-state-terrorism-clinton/88752090/

17. Charles R. Kubic, "Hilary's Huge Libyan Disaster," *The National Interest*, June 15, 2016 (accessed June 28, 2017), http://nationalinterest.org/feature/hillarys-huge-libya-disaster-16600

18. Daniel White, "Read Donald Trump's Ohio Speech on Immigration and Terrorism," *Time* August 15, 2016 (accessed February 15, 2017), http://time.com/4453110/donald-trump-national-security-immigration-terrorism-speech/

19. Staff and Agencies, "Barack Obama Says Libya Was 'Worst Mistake' of His Presidency," *Guardian*, April 11, 2016 (accessed June 28, 2017), https://www.theguardian.com/us-news/2016/apr/12/barack-obama-says-libya-was-worst-mistake-of-his-presidency

20. Jonathan Landay and Warren Strobel, "Exclusive: Trump Counterterrorism Strategy Urges Allies to Do More," *Reuters*, May 5, 2017 (accessed June 15, 2017), http://www.reuters.com/article/us-usa-extremism-idUSKBN1812AN

21. Reuters, "Trump Counterterrorism Strategy Urges Allies to Do More," *The Counter Jihad Report*, May 5, 2017 (accessed June 15, 2017), https://counterjihadreport.com/2017/05/05/reuters-trump-counterterrorism-strategy-urges-allies-to-do-more/

22. "Trump Counterterrorism Strategy Urges Allies to Do More," CNBC, May 6, 2017 (accessed June 15, 2017), http://www.cnbc.com/2017/05/06/trump-counterterrorism-strategy-allies.html

23. Ian Bremer, "Trumps and the World, What Could Actually Go Wrong, the Definitive Guide to the Global Risks of a Donald Trump Presidency," *Politico*

Magazine, June 3, 2016 (accessed March 7, 2017), http://www.politico.com/magazine/story/2016/06/2016-donald-trump-international-foreign-policy-global-risk-security-guide-213936

24. David Shariatmadari, "How War on Islam Became Central to the Trump Doctrine," *Guardian*, February 9, 2017 (accessed February 9, 2017), https://www.theguardian.com/us-news/2017/jan/30/war-on-islam-central-trump-doctrine-terrorism-immigration

25. Ibid.

26. Greg Miller and Missy Ryan, "Officials Worry That U.S Counterterrorism Defenses Will Be Weakened by Trump Actions," *Washington Post*, January 29, 2017 (accessed February 9, 2017), https://www.washingtonpost.com/world/national-security/officials-worry-that-us-counterterrorism-defenses-will-be-weakened-by-trump-actions/2017/01/29/1f045074-e644-11e6-b82f-687d6e6a3e7c_story.html?utm_term=.2ce4c87ded8f

27. Ibid.

28. Landay and Strobel, "Exclusive: Trump Counterterrorism Strategy Urges Allies to Do More."

29. John Hannah, "Will Trump Stay or Go in Iraq?" *Foreign Policy*, December 9, 2016 (accessed June 20, 2017), http://foreignpolicy.com/2016/12/09/will-trump-stay-or-go-in-iraq/

30. Ibid.

31. Lukman Faily, "Donald Trump Should Not Treat Iraq as an Afterthought," Newsweek, May 28, 2017 (accessed June 20, 2017), http://www.newsweek.com/trump-treating-iraq-afterthought-we-need-each-other-616146

32. Mark Vargas, "Why Trump Must Make a Surprise Visit to Iraq on His First Foreign Trip," *Washington Examiner*, May 19, 2017 (accessed June 20, 2017), http://www.washingtonexaminer.com/why-trump-must-make-a-surprise-visit-to-iraq-on-his-first-foreign-trip/article/2623658

33. "The Five Most Bizarre Decisions in Gulf-Qatar Crisis," *Al Jazeera*, June 12, 2017 (accessed June 15, 2017), http://www.aljazeera.com/indepth/features/2017/06/bizarre-decisions-gulf-qatar-crisis-170611075123926.html

34. Zainab Fattah, Dana Khraiche, and Zaid Sabah, "Qatar Shrugs Off Pressure with No End in Sight to Gulf Crisis," June 12, 2017 (accessed June 15, 2017), https://www.bloomberg.com/politics/articles/2017-06-12/qatar-shrugs-off-pressure-with-no-end-in-sight-to-gulf-crisis

35. Katie Hunt and Victoria Brown, "Gulf Rift: Qatar Not Ready to Surrender," *CNN*, June 10, 2017 (accessed June 15, 2017), http://www.cnn.com/2017/06/09/middleeast/qatar-diplomatic-crisis/index.html

36. Nicole Gaouette, Dan Merica, and Ryan Browne, "Trump: Qatar Must Stop Funding Terrorism," *CNN*, June 10, 2017 (accessed June 15, 2017), http://www.cnn.com/2017/06/09/politics/trump-qatar-saudi-gulf-crisis/index.html

37. Zahraa Alkhalisi, "Qatar Airways CEO: U.S. 'Fueling' the Fire of Gulf Crisis," *CNN*, June 12, 2017 (accessed June 13, 2017), http://money.cnn.com/2017/06/12/news/qatar-airways-ceo-fuel-fire-gulf-crisis/index.html

38. Reiss Smith, "Qatar News Live: Warships Arrive in Doha amid Row with Saudi Arabia—Gulf Crisis Latest," *Express*, June 17, 2017 (accessed June 19, 2017), http://www.express.co.uk/news/world/817527/qatar-news-crisis-latest-news-saudi-arabia-update-gulf-doha

39. Ryan Browne, "Amid Diplomatic Crisis Pentagon Agrees $12 Billion Jet Deal with Qatar," *CNN*, June 14, 2017 (accessed June 16, 2017), http://www.cnn.com/2017/06/14/politics/qatar-f35-trump-pentagon/index.html

40. Stephen Kalin and William Maclean, "Saudi King Empowers Young Reformer Son in Succession Shake-Up," *Reuters*, June 22, 2017 (accessed June 24, 2017), http://in.reuters.com/article/saudi-succession-son-idINKBN19C0AX

41. Edmund DeMarche, "Saudi Arabia Rewrites Succession Plan Months after Trump Meeting," *Fox News*, June 21, 2017 (accessed June 20, 2017), http://www.foxnews.com/politics/2017/06/21/saudi-arabia-rewrites-succession-plan-months-after-trump-meeting.html

42. Ibid.

43. Abdullah Al-Shihri and Aya Batrawy, "Saudi King's Moves Change Line of Succession to the Throne," *Boston Globe*, June 21, 2017 (accessed June 24, 2017), https://www.bostonglobe.com/news/world/2017/06/20/saudi-arabia-king-upends-royal-succession/8IGjzw7OGfEglwrCHgRvMP/story.html

44. Nicole Chavez, Tamara Qiblawi, and James Griffiths, "Saudi Arabia's King Replaces Nephew with Son as Heir to Throne," *CNN*, June 21, 2017 (accessed June 24, 2017), http://www.cnn.com/2017/06/21/middleeast/saudi-arabia-crown-prince/index.html

45. Bruce Riedel, "The Long-Term Cost of Saudi Succession Shake-Up," *al-Monitor*, June 21, 2017 (accessed June 24, 2017), http://www.al-monitor.com/pulse/originals/2017/06/saudi-arabia-crown-prince-king-muhammad-bin-salman-cost.html

46. Ibid.

47. Ben Hubbard, "Saudi King Rewrites Succession, Replacing Heir with Son, 31," *New York Times*, June 21, 2017, https://www.nytimes.com/2017/06/21/world/middleeast/saudi-arabia-crown-prince-mohammed-bin-salman.html?_r=0

48. Mohamad Bazzi, "Saudi Arabia's Aggressive New Heir to the Throne," *The Atlantic*, June 21, 2017 (accessed June 23, 2017), https://www.theatlantic.com/international/archive/2017/06/saudi-arabia-iran-salman-trump-kushner/531153/

49. Ibid.

50. Hubbard, "Saudi King Rewrites Succession, Replacing Heir with Son, 31."

51. Thomas Erdbrink and Mujib Mashal, "At Least 12 Killed in Pair of Terrorist Attacks in Iran," *New York Times*, June 7, 2017 (accessed June 24, 2017), https://www.nytimes.com/2017/06/07/world/middleeast/iran-parliament-attack-khomeini-mausoleum.html

52. "Iran's Guards Says Saudi Arabia behind Deadly Attacks in Tehran," *Daily Star*, June 7, 2017 (accessed June 24, 2017), http://www.dailystar.com.lb/News/Middle-East/2017/Jun-07/408822-irans-revolutionary-guards-say-saudi-arabia-was-behind-deadly-attacks-in-tehran-statement.ashx

53. Fareed Zakaria, "How Saudi Arabia Played Donald Trump," *Washington Post*, May 25, 2017 (accessed June 3, 2017), https://www.washingtonpost.com/opinions/global-opinions/saudi-arabia-just-played-donald-trump/2017/05/25/d0932702-4184-11e7-8c25-44d09ff5a4a8_story.html?utm_term=.78e1e86f52ee

54. Steven Erlanger, "As Trump Era Arrives, a Sense of Uncertainty Grips the World," *New York Times*, January 16, 2017 (accessed March 7, 2017), https://www

.nytimes.com/2017/01/16/world/europe/trump-eu-nato-merkel-brexit-russia-germany-china.html

55. "U.S.–North Korea Tensions: Japan Discussing Evacuation Plan for Citizens in South Korea," *ABC News*, April 14, 2017 (accessed April 15, 2017), http://www.abc.net.au/news/2017-04-14/us-north-korea-japan-discusses-how-to-evacuate-its-citizens/8445202

56. David Choi, "Tensions between the U.S. and North Korea Are Ramping Up amid Nuclear Threats," *Business Insider,* April 13, 2017 (accessed April 15, 2017), http://www.businessinsider.com/north-korea-threat-to-us-nuclear-trump-2017-4

57. "North Korea Threat: Mattis Says War with Isolated Nation Would Be 'Catastrophic,'" *Fox News*, May 29, 2017 (accessed June 2, 2017), http://www.foxnews.com/politics/2017/05/29/north-korea-threat-mattis-said-war-with-isolated-nation-would-be-catastrophic.html

58. Stephen Collinson, "Trump and China on Collision Course," *CNN*, December 5, 2016 (accessed March 5, 2017), http://www.cnn.com/2016/12/05/politics/donald-trump-china-taiwan-clash/

59. John Pilger, "Is War between China and America Inevitable? Investigates as Donald Trump Provokes Beijing," *Mirror*, December 7, 2017 (accessed March 5, 2017), http://www.mirror.co.uk/news/world-news/war-between-china-america-9398234

60. Anne Gearan, Philip Rucker, and Simon Denyer, "Trump's Taiwan Phone Call Was Long Planned, Say People Who Were Involved," *Washington Post*, December 4, 2016 (accessed March 5, 2017), https://www.washingtonpost.com/politics/trumps-taiwan-phone-call-was-weeks-in-the-planning-say-people-who-were-involved/2016/12/04/f8be4b0c-ba4e-11e6-94ac-3d324840106c_story.html?utm_term=.a37139af15cd

61. Jared Malsin, "A U.S. Warplane Shot Down a Syrian Jet. Here's Why That's a Big Deal," *Time*, June 19, 2017 (accessed June 25, 2017), http://time.com/4823314/syria-fighter-jet-shot-down-american/

62. Thomas Gibbons-Neff, "In Third Shoot-Down in a Month, U.S. Jet Destroys Another Iranian Drone over Syria," *Washington Post*, June 20, 2017 (accessed June 25, 2017), https://www.washingtonpost.com/news/checkpoint/wp/2017/06/20/in-third-shoot-down-in-a-month-u-s-jet-destroys-another-iranian-drone-over-syria/?utm_term=.3ecbeef24038

63. Nabih Bulos and W. J. Hennigan, "U.S. Warplane Shoots down Syrian Jet Near Raqqah," *Los Angeles Times*, June 19, 2017 (accessed June 25, 2017), http://www.latimes.com/world/middleeast/la-fg-syria-us-jet-20170619-story.html

64. Gibbons-Neff, "In Third Shoot-Down in a Month, U.S. Jet Destroys Another Iranian Drone over Syria."

65. Luis Martinez, "US Fighter Jet Shoots down Pro-Syrian-Regime Drone," *ABC News*, June 20, 2017 (accessed June 25, 2017), http://abcnews.go.com/International/syrian-drone-shot-us-fighter-jet/story?id=48154826

66. Malsin, "A U.S. Warplane Shot Down a Syrian Jet."

67. U.S. Plane Shoots Down Syrian Aircraft That Attacked U.S.-Backed Fighters," *Guardian*, June 18, 2017 (accessed June 25, 2017), https://www.theguardian.com/us-news/2017/jun/18/us-plane-shoots-down-syrian-aircraft

68. Ryan Browne, "New Details on U.S. Shoot Down of Syrian Jet," *CNN*, June 21, 2017 (accessed June 25, 2017), http://www.cnn.com/2017/06/21/politics/us-syria-russia-dogfight/index.html

69. Michael R. Gordon and Thomas Erdbrink, "U.S. Fighter Jet Shoots Down Syrian Warplane," *New York Times*, June 18, 2017 (accessed June 25, 2017), https://

www.nytimes.com/2017/06/18/world/middleeast/iran-syria-missile-launch-islamic-state.html?_r=0

70. Rebecca Kheel, "Senate Panel Demands Trump's Legal Rationale for Shooting Syrian Jet," *The Hill*, June 22, 2017 (accessed June 25, 2017), http://thehill.com/policy/defense/339041-foreign-relations-requests-legal-justification-for-syrian-jet-shoot-down

71. Ibid.

72. James Vaughan, "British General Says a Nuclear War with Russia in 2017 Is 'Entirely Plausible,' " *Infowars*, May 19, 2017 (accessed June 25, 2017), https://www.infowars.com/british-general-says-a-nuclear-war-with-russia-in-2017-is-entirely-plausible/

73. Madison Park and Steve Brusk, "White House: Syria Could Be Preparing Another Chemical Weapons Attack," CNN, June 26, 2017 (accessed June 28, 2017), http://www.cnn.com/2017/06/26/politics/syria-chemical-weapons-white-house-warning/index.html

74. Abby Ohillip and Dan Lamothe, "White House Says Syria's Assad Preparing Another Chemical Attack, Warns of 'Heavy' Penalty," *Washington Post*, June 27, 2017 (accessed June 28, 2017), https://www.washingtonpost.com/news/post-politics/wp/2017/06/26/white-house-says-syrias-assad-preparing-another-chemical-attack-warns-of-heavy-penalty/?utm_term=.5d57a4b3ff1a

75. Seymour M. Hersh, "Trump's Red Line," *Welt*, June 25, 2017 (accessed June 28, 2017), https://www.welt.de/politik/ausland/article165905578/Trump-s-Red-Line.html

76. Stokols and Mccaskill, "Full Text: Donald Trump's Speech on Fighting Terrorism."

77. David Greene, "How Trump Anti-Terrorism Policies May Differ from Obama," *NPR*, December 28, 2016 (accessed February 15, 2017), http://www.npr.org/2016/12/28/507208524/what-the-next-administrations-anti-terrorism-policies-may-look-like

78. Stokols and Mccaskill, "Full Text: Donald Trump's Speech on Fighting Terrorism."

79. Julia Edwards Ainsley, Dustin Volz and Kristina Cooke, "Exclusive: Trump to Focus Counter-Extremism Program Solely on Islam—Sources," *Reuters*, February 2, 2017 (accessed February 25, 2017), http://www.reuters.com/article/us-usa-trump-extremists-program-exclusiv-idUSKBN15G5VO

80. Bruce Weinstein, "Why President Obama Was Right Not to Say 'Radical Islamic Terrorism'," *Fortune*, June 13, 2016 (accessed February 9, 2017), http://fortune.com/2016/06/13/obama-trump-clinton-radical-islamic-terrorism/

81. "Fact Sheet: The White House Summit on Countering Violent Extremism," The White House, President Barack Obama, February 18, 2015 (accessed March 7, 2017), https://obamawhitehouse.archives.gov/the-press-office/2015/02/18/fact-sheet-white-house-summit-countering-violent-extremism

82. "Countering Violent Extremism," *Department of State* (accessed March 7, 2017), https://www.state.gov/j/cve/

83. Max Greenwood, "Trump Plans to Reshape Counter-Extremism Program to Focus on Islam: Report," *The Hill*, February 2, 2017 (accessed February 27, 2017), http://thehill.com/policy/national-security/317465-trump-plans-to-reshape-counter-extremism-program-to-focus-on-islam

84. Ainsley et al., "Exclusive: Trump to Focus Counter-Extremism Program Solely on Islam—Sources."

85. "3 Counterterrorism Mistakes in 1 Week," *Arc*, February 4, 2017 (accessed February 25, 2017), https://thearcmag.com/3-counterterrorism-mistakes-in-1-week-89e7a398ec82#.mmwkn3jb8

86. "Trump Administration Reportedly Set to Refocus Counterterrorism Efforts," *Fox News*, February 2, 2017 (accessed February 27, 2017), http://www.foxnews.com/politics/2017/02/02/trump-administration-reportedly-set-to-refocus-counterterrorism-efforts.html

87. Jackson, "Trump Calls for New Approach to Anti-Terror Fight."

88. Daniella Diaz, "Obama: Why I Won't Say 'Islamic Terrorism,'" *CNN*, September 29, 2016 (accessed February 9, 2017), http://www.cnn.com/2016/09/28/politics/obama-radical-islamic-terrorism-cnn-town-hall/

89. Saine, "Obama Defends Counterterrorism Record, Offers Guidance for Trump."

90. Diaz, "Obama: Why I Won't Say 'Islamic Terrorism.'"

91. Miller and Ryan, "Officials Worry That U.S Counterterrorism Defenses Will Be Weakened by Trump Actions."

92. Ibid.

93. "CIA Tactics: What Is 'Enhanced Interrogation'?" *BBC*, December 10, 2014 (accessed February 27, 2017), http://www.bbc.com/news/world-us-canada-117 23189

94. Ibid.

95. Siddhartha Mahanta, "Fighting Terrorism in the Age of Trump," *The Atlantic*, November 12, 2016 (accessed February 9, 2017), https://www.theatlantic.com/international/archive/2016/11/trump-torture-soufan-fbi-al-qaeda-isis-islam/507380/

96. Stokols and Mccaskill, "Full Text: Donald Trump's Speech on Fighting Terrorism."

97. Feliz Solomon, "The Secret Target of Yemen Raid Escaped and Is Now 'Taunting Trump,' Report Says," *Time*, February 6, 2017 (accessed February 9, 2017), http://time.com/4662150/yemen-raid-qaeda-al-rimi-trump-audio-fool-white-house/

98. Ibid.

99. AP, "Leader of Al Qaeda in Yemen Mocks Trump after Raid," *Fox News*, February 5, 2017 (accessed March 1, 2017), http://www.foxnews.com/world/2017/02/05/leader-al-qaeda-in-yemen-mocks-trump-after-raid.html

100. Maxwell Tani, "'This Was a Mission That Was Started before I Got Here': Trump Suggests Obama Is to Blame for the Raid That Lost a Navy SEAL," *Business Insider*, February 28, 2017 (accessed March 1, 2017), http://www.businessinsider.com/trump-blames-obama-yemen-raid-navy-seal-2017-2

101. Eric Schmitt, "U.S. Commando Killed in Yemen in Trump's First Counterterrorism Operation," *New York Times*, January 29, 2017 (accessed February 28, 2017), https://www.nytimes.com/2017/01/29/world/middleeast/american-com mando-killed-in-yemen-in-trumps-first-counterterror-operation.html?_r=0

102. "3 Counterterrorism Mistakes in 1 Week."

103. Alex Lockie, "Father of Navy SEAL killed in Yemen Raid to Trump Administration: 'Don't Hide Behind My Son's Death'," *Business Insider*, February 26, 2017 (accessed February 28, 2017), http://www.businessinsider.com/navy-seal-yemen-trump-raid-father-2017-2

104. White, "Read Donald Trump's Ohio Speech .on Immigration and Terrorism."

105. Jackson, "Trump Calls for New Approach to Anti-Terror Fight."

106. David E. Sanger, "Donald Trump Likely to End Aid for Rebels Fighting Syrian Government," *New York Times*, November 11, 2016 (accessed March 1, 2017), https://www.nytimes.com/2016/11/12/world/middleeast/donald-trump-syria.html?_r=0

107. Ibid.

108. Michael R. Gordon and Eric Schmitt, "Trump to Arm Syrian Kurds, Even as Turkey Strongly Objects," *New York Times*, May 29, 2017 (accessed June 28, 2017), https://www.nytimes.com/2017/05/09/us/politics/trump-kurds-syria-army.html

109. Tom Perry, Suleiman Al-Khalidi, and John Walcott, "Exclusive: CIA-Backed Aid for Syrian Rebels Frozen after Islamist Attack—Sources," *Reuters*, February 21, 2017 (accessed March 1, 2017), http://www.reuters.com/article/us-mideast-crisis-syria-rebels-idUSKBN1601BD

110. White, "Read Donald Trump's Ohio Speech on Immigration and Terrorism."

111. David E. Sanger and Maggie Haberman, "Donald Trump's Terrorism Plan Mixes Cold War Concepts and Limits on Immigrants," *The New York Times*, August 15, 2016 (accessed February 9, 2017), https://www.nytimes.com/2016/08/16/us/politics/donald-trump-terrorism.html?_r=0

112. Stokols and Mccaskill, "Full Text: Donald Trump's Speech on Fighting Terrorism."

113. Franz-Stefan Gady, "Trump and Offensive Cyber Warfare," *The Diplomat*, January 16, 2017 (accessed March 5, 2017), http://thediplomat.com/2017/01/trump-and-offensive-cyber-warfare/

114. Ibid.

115. Adrienne Lafrance, "Trump's Incoherent Ideas about 'the Cyber' Wait, What?" *The Atlantic*, September 27, 2016 (Accessed March 5, 2017), https://Www.Theatlantic.Com/Technology/Archive/2016/09/Trumps-Incoherent-Ideas-About-The-Cyber/501839/

CHAPTER 2

1. "President George Bush Announcing War against Iraq," *The History Place* (accessed January 16, 2017), http://www.historyplace.com/speeches/bush-war.htm

2. George W. Bush, *Decisions Points* (New York: Crowns Publishers, 2010), 186.

3. Condoleezza Rice, *No Higher Honor: A Memoirs of My Years in Washington* (New York: Crowns Publishers, 2011), 85.

4. "Afghanistan: A History of Occupation," *Telegraph*, November 26, 2010 (accessed January 16, 2017), http://www.telegraph.co.uk/news/worldnews/asia/afghanistan/8162559/Afghanistan-a-history-of-occupation.html

5. Bush, *Decision Points*, 186.

6. Ibid.

7. Ibid., 191.

8. Peter L. Bergen, *Manhunt: The Ten-Year Search for Bin Laden: From 9/11 to Abbottabad* (New York: Crown Print, 2012), 18.

9. Donald Rumsfield, *Known and Unknown: A Memoir* (New York: Penguin, 2011), 16.

10. Rumsfield, *Known and Unknown*, 316.

11. "War in the Gulf: Bush Statement; Excerpts from 2 Statements by Bush on Iraq's Proposal for Ending Conflict," *New York Times*, February 16, 1991 (accessed October 30, 2016), http://www.nytimes.com/1991/02/16/world/war-gulf-bush-statement-excerpts-2-statements-bush-iraq-s-proposal-for-ending.html

12. Bush, *Decisions Points*, 396–397.

13. Patrick Cockburn, *The Rise of Islamic State: ISIS and the New Sunni Revolution* (London: Verso, 2015), 5.

14. "Pakistan Says Investigation into Bin al-Shibh Arrest Complete," *USA Today*, September 16, 2012 (accessed October 24, 2016), http://usatoday30.usato day.com/news/world/2002-09-16-bin-al-shibh_x.htm

15. Chris McGreal, "Khalid Sheikh Mohammed: Former Military Prosecutor Denounces Trial," *The Guardian*, May 4, 2012 (accessed October 24, 2016), https://www.theguardian.com/world/2012/may/04/khalid-sheikh-mohammed-military-prosecutor

16. Brian Dakss, "Another Al Qaeda Big Arrested," *CBS New*, March 15, 2003 (accessed October 24, 2016), http://www.cbsnews.com/news/another-al-qaeda-big-arrested/

17. "Pakistan Arrests Al Qaeda's No. 3 Leader," *Fox News*, May 5, 2005 (accessed October 24, 2016), http://www.foxnews.com/story/2005/05/05/paki stan-arrests-al-qaeda-no-3-leader.html

18. "Pakistan Arrests 'Senior Al-Qaeda Operative'," *BBC*, May 17, 2011 (accessed October 24, 2016), http://www.bbc.co.uk/news/mobile/world-south-asia-13429316

19. "Top Al Qaeda Leader Arrested in Pakistan," *CNN*, September 5, 2011 (accessed October 24, 2016), http://www.cnn.com/2011/WORLD/asiapcf/09/05/pakistan.al.qaeda.arrest/index.html

20. Bergen, *The Longest War*, 59.

21. Bush, *Decisions Points*, 207.

22. Bergen, *Manhunt*, 54.

23. Bergen, *The Longest War*, 248.

24. Tony Blair, *A Journey: My Political Life, Alfred* (New York: A. Knopf, 2010), 362.

25. Bergen, *The Longest War*, 309.

26. Terry McDermott and Josh Meyer, *The Hunt for KSM: Inside the Pursuit and Takedown of the Real 9/11 Mastermind, Khalid Sheikh Mohammed* (New York: Little, Brown and Company, 2012), 46.

27. Bush, *Decisions Points*, 135.

28. Rice, *No Higher Honor, A Memoirs of my years in Washington*, xvii.

29. Jonathan Stevenson, *Counter-Terrorism: Containment and Beyond* (Oxford: Oxford University Press, 2004), 7.

30. McDermott and Meyer, *The Hunt for KSM*, 4.

31. Bush, *Decisions Points*, 187.

CHAPTER 3

1. Marc A. Thissen, "Defense Intelligence Agency Warned Obama about ISIS in 2012," *American Enterprise Institute* 2015 (accessed October 24, 2016), https://www.aei.org/publication/defense-intelligence-agency-warned-obama-about-isis-in-2012/

2. Reuters, "Trump Counterterrorism Strategy Urges Allies to Do More," *The Counter Jihad Report*, May 5, 2017 (accessed June 15, 2017), https://counterjihadreport.com/2017/05/05/reuters-trump-counterterrorism-strategy-urges-allies-to-do-more/

3. Steven Erlanger, "After London Attack, Prime Minister Says, 'Enough Is Enough'," *New York Times*, June 4, 2017 (accessed June 14, 2017), https://www.nytimes.com/2017/06/04/world/europe/uk-london-attacks.html?_r=0

4. Mary Louise Kelly, "Report Offers New Counterterrorism Strategy for Trump Administration," NPR, November 15, 2016 (accessed June 15, 2017), http://www.npr.org/2016/11/15/502211137/report-offers-new-counterrorism-strategy-for-trump-administration

5. "Key Controversies and Missteps of Postwar Period," *PBS*, October 17, 2006 (accessed October 24, 2016), http://www.pbs.org/wgbh/pages/frontline/yeariniraq/analysis/fuel.html

6. Bush, *Decision Points*.

7. Thomas E. Ricks, *Fiasco: The American Military Adventure in Iraq* (New York: Penguin, 2007), 430.

8. Andrew Sharp, *The Rise of ISIS: The West's New Crusade* (Redmond, WA: Fusion Publications, 2014), 23.

9. Peter L. Bergen, "Did Barack Obama and Hillary Clinton Create ISIS?" *CNN*, January 4, 2016 (accessed March 12, 2016), http://www.cnn.com/2016/01/04/opinions/bergen-trump-obama-clinton-creation-of-isis/index.html

10. Dexter Filkins, "The Fight of Their Lives, the White House Wants the Kurds to Help Save Iraq from ISIS. The Kurds May Be More Interested in Breaking Away," *New Yorker*, September 29, 2014 Issue (accessed October 24, 2016), http://www.newyorker.com/magazine/2014/09/29/fight-lives

11. Malcolm Nance, *Defeating ISIS: Who They Are, How They Fight, What They Believe* (New York: Skyhorse Publishing, 2016), 339.

12. Kevin Rawlison, "How ISIS Spread Its Deadly Ideology—A Timeline, Since Taking the Iraqi City of Mosul, the Terror Group Have Killed Dozens of Hostages and Often Used the Footage of the Murders as Grisly Propaganda," *Guardian*, January 3, 2016 (accessed October 24, 2016), https://www.theguardian.com/world/2016/jan/03/how-isis-spread-its-deadly-ideology-a-timeline

13. Rawlison, "How ISIS Spread Its Deadly Ideology."

14. Heather Saul, "ISIS Publishes Penal Code Listing Amputation, Crucifixion and Stoning as Punishments—And Vows to Vigilantly Enforce It," *The Independent*, January 22, 2015 (accessed October 24, 2016), http://www.independent.co.uk/news/world/middle-east/isis-publishes-penal-code-listing-amputation-crucifixion-and-stoning-as-punishments-and-vows-to-9994878.html

15. Helene Cooper, "Obama Requests Money to Train 'Appropriately Vetted' Syrian Rebels," *New York Times*, June 26, 2014 (accessed October 29, 2016), http://www.nytimes.com/2014/06/27/world/middleeast/obama-seeks-500-million-to-train-and-equip-syrian-opposition.html?_r=0

16. Tara McKelvey, "Arming Syrian Rebels: Where the US Went Wrong," *BBC News*, October 10, 2015 (accessed October 29, 2016), http://www.bbc.com/news/magazine-33997408

17. Damian Pletta and Kristina Pterson, "Obama Says U.S. Intelligence Underestimated Islamic State Threat," *Wall Street Journal*, September 28, 2014 (accessed October 29, 2016), http://www.wsj.com/articles/obama-says-u-s-intelligence-underestimated-developments-in-syria-1411918072

18. McKelvey, "Arming Syrian Rebels: Where the US Went Wrong."

19. David E. Sanger, "Rebel Arms Flow Is Said to Benefit Jihadists in Syria," *New York Times*, October 14, 2012 (accessed October 29, 2016), http://www.ny times.com/2012/10/15/world/middleeast/jihadists-receiving-most-arms-sent-to-syrian-rebels.html

20. Ernesto Londoño and Greg Miller, "CIA Begins Weapons Delivery to Syrian Rebels," *Washington Post*, September 11, 2013 (accessed October 29, 2016), https:// www.washingtonpost.com/world/national-security/cia-begins-weapons-deliv ery-to-syrian-rebels/2013/09/11/9fcf2ed8-1b0c-11e3-a628-7e6dde8f889d_story .html

21. Barbara Starr, "Official Says CIA-Funded Weapons Have Begun to Reach Syrian Rebels; Rebels Deny Receipt," *CNN*, September 12, 2013 (accessed October 29, 2016), http://www.cnn.com/2013/09/12/politics/syria-arming-rebels/index.html

22. Ibid.

23. Syrian Rebels, "Key Part of Obama's War Strategy, Gets Crucial Support from House GOP," *Fox News*, September 15, 2014 (accessed October 29, 2016), http://www.foxnews.com/us/2014/09/15/arming-syrian-rebels-key-part-obama-war-strategy-gets-crucial-

24. Adam Entous, "Covert CIA Mission to Arm Syrian Rebels Goes Awry," *Wall Street Journal*, January 26, 2015 (accessed October 29, 2016), http://www.wsj .com/articles/covert-cia-mission-to-arm-syrian-rebels-goes-awry-1422329582

25. Martin Chulov, "Amid the Ruins of Syria, Is Bashar al-Assad Now Finally Facing the End?" *Guardian*, May 23, 2015 (accessed October 29, 2016), http:// www.theguardian.com/world/2015/may/24/syria-iran-isis-battle-arab-world

26. David Blair and Richard Spencer, "How Qatar Is Funding the Rise of Islamist Extremists," *Telegraph*, September 20, 2014 (accessed October 29, 2016), http://www.telegraph.co.uk/news/worldnews/middleeast/qatar/11110931/How-Qatar-is-funding-the-rise-of-Islamist-extremists.html

27. Video Library Clips and Descriptions Are Created by My C-SPAN Users, and Are Not the Editorial Selections of C-Span. September 16, 2014 (accessed October 29, 2016), Secretary Hagel and General Dempsey on ISIS Threat, http://www.c-span .org/video/?c4509231/general-dempsey-acknowledges-us-arab-allies-funding-isis

28. Blair and Spencer, "How Qatar Is Funding the Rise of Islamist Extremists."

29. Entous, "Covert CIA Mission to Arm Syrian Rebels Goes Awry."

30. "Barzani to US: Don't sell F-16 to Iraqi PM," *Hurriyet Daily News*, April 24, 2012 (accessed April 11, 2017), http://www.hurriyetdailynews.com/barzani-to-us-dont-sell-f-16-to-iraqi-pm.aspx?pageID=238&nid=19128

31. "Iraq Receives F-16 Fighter Jets from the US," *Middle East Monitor*, July 14, 2015 (accessed October 24, 2016).

32. Joshua Gillin, "Obama Refused to Sign Plan in Place to Leave 10,000 Troops in Iraq, Bush Says," *Politifact*, May 18, 2015 (accessed October 29, 2016), http://www .politifact.com/truth-o-meter/statements/2015/may/18/jeb-bush/obama-refused-sign-plan-place-leave-10000-troops-i/

33. Katie Sanders, "Obama Wanted to Keep 10,000 Troops in Iraq, ABC's Raddatz claims," *Politifact*, August 24, 2014, http://www.politifact.com/punditfact/statements/2014/aug/24/martha-raddatz/obama-wanted-keep-10000-troops-iraq-abcs-raddatz-c/

34. James Franklin Jeffery, "Behind the U.S. Withdrawal from Iraq, Negotiations Were Repeatedly Disrupted by Obama White House Staffers' Inaccurate Public Statements," *Wall Street Journal*, last updated Nov. 2, 2014 (accessed October 29, 2016), http://www.wsj.com/articles/james-franklin-jeffrey-behind-the-u-s-withdrawal-from-iraq-1414972705

35. Eli Lake, "Why the White House Ignored All Those Warnings about ISIS," *Daily Beast*, July 6, 2014 (accessed October 29, 2016), http://www.thedailybeast.com/articles/2014/07/06/why-the-white-house-ignored-all-those-warnings-about-isis.html

36. Andrea Mitchell, "Leon Panetta: U.S. Mistakes Helped Create 'Vacuum' That Spawned ISIS," *NBC News*, October 7, 2014 (accessed October 15, 2016), http://www.nbcnews.com/storyline/isis-terror/leon-panetta-u-s-mistakes-helped-create-vacuum-spawned-isis-n220586

37. Rowan Scarborough, "U.S. Troop Withdrawal Let Islamic State Enter Iraq, Military Leaders Say," *Washington Times*, July 26, 2015 (accessed October 29, 2016), http://www.washingtontimes.com/news/2015/jul/26/us-troop-withdrawal-let-islamic-state-enter-iraq-m/?page=all

38. David Blair, "Qatar and Saudi Arabia 'Have Ignited Time Bomb by Funding Global Spread of Radical Islam'," *Telegraph*, October 4, 2014 (accessed October 15, 2016), http://www.telegraph.co.uk/news/worldnews/middleeast/iraq/11140860/Qatar-and-Saudi-Arabia-have-ignited-time-bomb-by-funding-global-spread-of-radical-Islam.html

39. Kevin Liptak, "How Could Obama Have 'Underestimated' ISIS?," *CNN*, September 30, 2014, http://www.cnn.com/2014/09/29/politics/obama-under estimates-isis/

40. Michale B. Kelley, "Obama Now Owns a War He Helped Create," *Business Insider*, September 11, 2014, http://www.businessinsider.com/issues-with-obamas-war-on-isis-2014-9#ixzz3FeEdugHZ

41. Thissen, "Defense Intelligence Agency Warned Obama about ISIS in 2012."

42. Liptak, "How Could Obama Have 'Underestimated' ISIS?"

43. Ibid.

44. Lake, "Why the White House Ignored All Those Warnings about ISIS."

45. "Why Obama Can't Say His Spies Underestimated ISIS."

46. Michael T. Flynn, "Director, Defense Intelligence Agency, Statement before Senate Armed Services Committee," February 11, 2014, http://www.armed-services.senate.gov/imo/media/doc/Flynn_02-11-14.pdf

47. Lake, "Why Obama Can't Say His Spies Underestimated ISIS."

48. Ibid.

CHAPTER 4

1. Abdul Bari Atwan, *ISIL, Roots, Savagery, and Future* (Beirut: Dar Al-Saqi, 2015), 46–47.

2. Hisham al-Hashimi, *ISIL Organization from Inside* (London: Dar Al-Hikma, 2016), 7.

3. Juan C. Zarate, *Treasury's War: The Unleashing of a New Era of Financial Warfare* (New York: Public Affairs, 2013), 2.

4. Tom Keatinge, "Finances of Jihad: How Extremist Groups Raise Money," *BBC*, December 12, 2014 (accessed November 4, 2016), http://www.bbc.com/news/world-middle-east-30393832

5. Juan Miguel del Cid Gómez, "A Financial Profile of the Terrorism of Al-Qaeda and Its Affiliates," *Terrorism Analysts*, 4, no 4 (2010) (accessed November 4, 2016), http://www.businessinsider.com/how-isis-and-al-qaeda-make-their-money-2015-12/#6-

6. Mohammed Al-Oamr, *The Legend of ISIS, The Caliphates Terrorism and the Corridors of Fund* (in Arabic) (Dubai: Madarek Publisher, 2014), 103.

7. Gómez, "A Financial Profile of the Terrorism of Al-Qaeda and Its Affiliates."

8. Ibid.

9. Rachel Ehrenfeld, "Drug Trafficking, Kidnapping Fund Al Qaeda," *CNN*, May 4, 2011 (accessed November 4, 2016), http://www.cnn.com/2011/OPINION/05/03/ehrenfeld.al.qaeda.funding/

10. Tom Keatinge, "Finances of Jihad."

11. Rachel Ehrenfeld, *Funding Evil: How Terrorism Is financed—And How to Stop It* (Chicago: Bonus Books, 2003), 24.

12. Loretta Napoleoni, *Terrorism and the Economy, How the War on Terror Is Bankrupting the World* (New York: Seven Stories Press, 2010), 13.

13. Testimony of Dennis M. Lormel, Chief, Financial Crimes Section, Federal Bureau of Investigation FBI, Before the House Committee on Financial Services, Subcommittee on Oversight and Investigations, Washington, DC, February 12, 2002 (accessed November 4, 2016), https://archives.fbi.gov/archives/news/testimony/financing-patterns-associated-with-al-qaeda-and-global-terrorist-networks

14. Oscar Williams-Grut, "Here's Where Terrorist Groups Like ISIS and Al Qaeda Get Their Money," *Business Insider*, December 7, 2015 (accessed November 4, 2016), http://www.businessinsider.com/how-isis-and-al-qaeda-make-their-money-2015-12/#6-

15. Ehrenfeld, *Funding Evil: How Terrorism Is Financed—and How to Stop It*, 24.

16. Gómez, "A Financial Profile of the Terrorism of Al-Qaeda and Its Affiliates."

17. Nance, *Defeating ISIS*, 653.

18. Tulin Daloglu, "Biden's Apology Hides the Truth, Joe Biden's Technically Apologies to Recep Tayyip Erdogan, but Didn't Deny the Merits of What He Said," *US News*, October 4, 2014 (accessed September 7, 2016), http://www.usnews.com/news/articles/2014/10/07/bidens-apology-hides-the-truth

19. Nance, *Defeating ISIS: Who They Are, How They Fight, What They Believe.*

20. Cockburn, *The Rise of the Islamic State ISIS and the New Sunni Revolution*, 35–36.

21. Charles River, *The Islamic State of Iraq and Syria: The History of ISIS/ISIL* (n.p. Charles River Editors, n.d.), Ch 5: "ISIL's Current Composition and Structure."

22. Armin Rosen, "ISIS Now Controls a Shocking Percentage of Iraq and Syria," *Business Insider*, June 11, 2014 (accessed November 5, 2016), http://www.businessinsider.com/isis-controls-shocking-percentage-of-iraq-and-syria-2014-6

23. "ISIL 'Controls Half' of Syria's Land Area," *Al-Jazeera TV*, June 1, 2015 (accessed November 5, 2016), http://www.aljazeera.com/news/2015/06/isil-controls-syria-land-area-150601131558568.html

24. Mohammed Alwash, *ISIL/ISIS and Its Sisters, from Al-Qaeda to Islamic State* (in Arabic) (Beirut: Riad el-Rayyes Books, 2015), 164.

25. Michael Weiss and Hassan Hassan, *ISIS: Inside the Army of Terror* (New York: Regan Arts, 2015), 44.

26. Nance, *Defeating ISIS: Who They Are, How They Fight, What They Believe,* 904–905.

27. Atwan, *ISIL, Roots, Savagery, and Future,* 46–47.

28. Luay Al-Khatteeb, "Will U.S. Strikes Hurt ISIS' Oil Riches?" *CNN,* 25 September, 2014 (accessed November 5, 2016), http://www.cnn.com/2014/09/22/business/isis-oil-luay-al-khatteeb/

29. Ibid.

30. Jerem Bender, "ISIS Is Turning Food and Water into a Weapon in Iraq." *Business Insider,* August 15, 2014 (accessed November 5, 2016), http://www.businessinsider.com/isis-has-two-major-weapons-in-iraq-2014-8

31. Hamdi Alkhshali and Laura Smith-Spark, "Iraq: ISIS Fighters Close Ramadi Dam Gates," *CNN,* June 4, 2015 (accessed November 5, 2016), http://www.cnn.com/2015/06/04/middleeast/iraq-isis-ramadi/

32. Tom Keatinge, "Rampant Ransoms," *Foreign Affairs,* January 26, 2015 (accessed November 5, 2016), https://www.foreignaffairs.com/articles/middle-east/2015-01-26/rampant-ransoms

33. Rukmini Callimachi, "Paying Ransoms, Europe Bankrolls Qaeda Terror," *New York Times,* July 29, 2014 (accessed November 5, 2016), http://www.nytimes.com/2014/07/30/world/africa/ransoming-citizens-europe-becomes-al-qaedas-patron.html

34. Kashmira Gander, "ISIS Hostage Threat: Which Countries Pay Ransoms to Release Their Citizens?" *The Independent,* September 3, 2014 (accessed November 5, 2016), http://www.independent.co.uk/news/world/politics/isis-hostage-threat-which-countries-pay-ransoms-to-release-their-citizens-9710129.html

35. Ashley Fantz, "How ISIS Makes (and Takes) Money," *CNN,* February 19, 2015 (accessed October 29, 2016), http://www.cnn.com/2015/02/19/world/how-isis-makes-money/index.html

36. Mohammed Al-Oamr, *The Legend of ISIS,* 104–105.

37. Sarah Almukhtar, "ISIS Finances Are Strong," *New York Times,* May 18, 2015 (accessed November 5, 2016), http://www.nytimes.com/interactive/2015/05/19/world/middleeast/isis-finances.html

38. Joseph Thorndike, "How ISIS Is Using Taxes to Build a Terrorist State," *Forbes,* August 18, 2014 (accessed November 5, 2016), http://www.forbes.com/sites/taxanalysts/2014/08/18/how-isis-is-using-taxes-to-build-a-terrorist-state/

39. Atwan, *ISIL, Roots, Savagery, and Future,* 46–47.

40. Loveday Morris, "Islamic State Isn't Just Destroying Ancient Artifacts—It's Selling Them." *Washington Post,* June 8, 2015 (accessed November 5, 2016), https://www.washingtonpost.com/world/middle_east/islamic-state-isnt-just-destroying-ancient-artifacts—its-selling-them/2015/06/08/ca5ea964-08a2-11e5-951e-8e15090d64ae_story.html

41. Atwan, *ISIL, Roots, Savagery, and Future,* 46–47.

42. Alissa Rubin, "Among the Wounded in Syria's War: Ancient History," *New York Times,* March 7, 2014, https://www.nytimes.com/2014/03/08/world/middleeast/among-the-wounded-in-syrias-war-ancient-history.html?_r=0

CHAPTER 5

1. Eben Kaplan, "Terrorist and the Internet, Council on Foreign Relations," Council on Foreign Relations, January 8, 2009 (accessed September 11, 2016), http://www.cfr.org/terrorism-and-technology/terrorists-internet/p10005

2. Timothy L. Thomas, "Information-Age 'De-Terror-ence'," *Military Review*, September-October 2001 (accessed September 11, 2016), http://fmso.leavenworth .army.mil/documents/de-terror/de-terror.htm

3. Kaplan, "Terrorist and the Internet, Council on Foreign Relations."

4. Matthew G. Devost, Brian K. Houghton, and Neal A. Pollard, "Information Terrorism: Can You Trust Your Toaster? The Terrorism Research Center," April 1996, p. 10 (accessed September 11, 2016), https://www.devost.net/papers/suntzu.pdf

5. Weiss and Hassan, *ISIS: Inside the Army of Terror*, 28.

6. Kaplan, "Terrorists and the Internet, Council on Foreign Relations."

7. Laura Ryan, "ISIS Is Better Than Al-Qaeda at Using the Internet," October 10, 2014 (accessed September 11, 2016), http://www.defenseone.com/tech nology/2014/10/isis-better-al-qaeda-using-internet/96308/

8. Jane Wakefield, "GCHQ, Terrorists, and the Internet: What Are the Issues?" *BBC*, November 4, 2014 (accessed September 11, 2016), http //www.bbc.com/news/technology-29897196

9. Grass, "USMC, Understanding and Combating Terrorism."

10. Cockburn, *The Rise of the Islamic State ISIS and the New Sunni Revolution*, 38.

11. Weiss and Hassan, *ISIS: Inside the Army of Terror*, 107.

12. Sharp, *The Rise of ISIS The West's New Crusade*, 92.

13. Jessica Stern and J. M. Berger, *ISIS: The State of Terror* (London: William Collins, 2015), 69.

14. Sharp, *The Rise of ISIS the West's New Crusade*, 94.

15. Stern and Berger, *ISIS—The State of Terror*, 114.

16. John Matthews, "Chattanooga Shootings: America, Let's Use Social Media to Stop Terrorist Attacks," *Fox News*, July 17, 2015 (accessed September 11, 2016), http://www.foxnews.com/opinion/2015/07/17/chattanooga-shootings-amer ica-lets-use-social-media-to-stop-terrorist-attacks.html

17. Service, Indo-Asian News, "No Silver Bullet to Stop Terrorist Use of Internet: Microsoft," *NDTV.com*, 2016 (accessed December 5, 2016), http://www.ndtv .com/world-news/no-silver-bullet-to-stop-terrorist-use-of-internet-microsoft-1405383

18. Alastair Jamieson, "Stockholm Truck Attack Suspect Rakhmat Akilov Admits Terrorism: Lawyer," NBC News, April 11, 2017 (accessed April 13, 2017), http://www.nbcnews.com/news/world/stockholm-truck-attack-suspect-rakhmat-akilov-admits-terrorism-lawyer-n745016

19. Steve Robson, "Stockholm Terror Attack: First Picture of Girl, 11, Killed as She Walked Home from School," *Mirror*, April 12, 2017 (accessed April 13, 2017), http://www.mirror.co.uk/news/world-news/stockholm-terror-attack-first-pic ture-10208553. Ebba Åkerlund had been reported missing by her family and it was later confirmed she was among those tragically murdered.

20. "Somali Migrants in Minnesota Are a Terror Threat to the Mall of America," *Frontpage Mag*, 2015 (accessed December 5, 2016), http://www.frontpagemag .com/point/251812/somali-migrants-minnesota-are-terror-threat-mall-daniel-greenfield

21. Nanct Crotti and Larry McShane, "Why Radical Jihadists Are Cropping Up in Minnesota, Leaving to Join Terrorist Groups," *New York Daily News*, August 30, 2014 (accessed September 11, 2016), http://www.nydailynews.com/news/national/jihadi-fiends-grow-minnesota-article-1.1922724

22. Jessica Stern, "We Need to Worry about Somali Terrorists in the U.S.," *Time*, September 26, 2013 (accessed September 11, 2016), http://ideas.time.com/2013/09/26/we-need-to-worry-about-somali-terrorists-in-the-u-s/

23. Leo Hohmann, "U.S. Government 'Breeding Terrorists'—In Minnesota," *WND*, September 2, 2014 (accessed September 11, 2016), http://www.wnd.com/2014/09/u-s-government-breeding-terrorists-in-minnesota/#!

24. Stern, "We Need to Worry about Somali Terrorists in the U.S."

25. Kaplan, "Terrorist and the Internet."

26. Goldman, "ISIS Recruits Fighters through Powerful Online Campaign."

27. Paul Tassi, "ISIS Uses 'GTA 5' in New Teen Recruitment Video," *Forbes*, September 20, 2014 (accessed September 11, 2016), http://www.forbes.com/sites/insertcoin/2014/09/20/isis-uses-gta-5-in-new-teen-recruitment-video/#67d35 59a3d29

28. Tassi, "ISIS Uses 'GTA 5' in New Teen Recruitment Video."

29. Ibid.

30. Pamela Engel, "ISIS Has Mastered a Crucial Recruiting Tactic No Terrorist Group Has Ever Conquered," *Business Insider*, May 9, 2015 (accessed September 11, 2016), http://www.businessinsider.com/isis-is-revolutionizing-international-terrorism-2015-5

31. Goldman, "ISIS Recruits Fighters through Powerful Online Campaign."

32. Thomas, "Information-Age 'De-Terror-ence'."

33. McDermott and Meyer, *The Hunt for KSM*, 142–143.

34. Kaplan, "Terrorist and the Internet, Council on Foreign Relations."

35. Thomas, "Information-Age 'De-Terror-ence'."

36. "Al Qaeda, Terrorists Changing Communication Methods after NSA Leaks, US Officials Say," *Fox News*, June 26, 2013 (accessed September 11, 2016), http://www.foxnews.com/us/2013/06/26/al-qaida-other-militants-said-to-be-changing-procedures-to-avoid-surveillance.html

37. Kathy Gilsinan, "ISIS and the 'Internet Radicalization' Trope," *The Atlantic*, December 8, 2015 (accessed September 11, 2016), http://www.theatlantic.com/international/archive/2015/12/isis-internet-radicalization/419148/

38. Peter Baker and Eric Schmitt, "California Attack Has U.S. Rethinking Strategy on Homegrown Terror," *New York Times*, December 5, 2015 (accessed September 11, 2016), http://www.nytimes.com/2015/12/06/us/politics/california-attack-has-us-rethinking-strategy-on-homegrown-terror.html?emc=edit_th_20151 206&nl=todaysheadlines&nlid=68648138&_r=0

39. Kristen V. Brown, "How Did ISIS Radicalize the Orlando Shooter?" *Fusion*, June 13, 2016 (accessed September 11, 2016), http://fusion.net/story/313671/orlando-nightclub-shooting-omar-mateen-isis-internet-radicalization/

40. Spencer S. Hsu, "Hasan's Ties to Radical Imam Raise Questions of 'Self-Radicalization'," *Washington Post*, Wednesday, November 18, 2009 (accessed September 11, 2016), http://www.washingtonpost.com/wp-dyn/content/artile/2009/11/17/AR2009111703830.html

41. David Johnston and Scott Shane, "U.S. Knew of Suspect's Tie to Radical Cleric," *New York Times*, November 9, 2009 (accessed September 11, 2016), http://www.nytimes.com/2009/11/10/us/10inquire.html?_r=0

42. Ann O'Neill, "Tsarnaev Trial: Timeline of the Bombings, Manhunt and Aftermath," *CNN*, May 15, 2015 (accessed September 11, 2016), http://www.cnn.com/2015/03/04/us/tsarnaev-trial-timeline/

43. James Gordon Meek, "FBI Feared Boston Bombers 'Received Training' and Aid from Terror Group, Docs Say," *CNN*, May 22, 2014 (accessed September 11, 2016), http://abcnews.go.com/Blotter/fbi-feared-boston-bombers-received-training-aid-terror/story?id=23819429

44. Brown, "How Did ISIS Radicalize the Orlando Shooter?"

45. Marisa Schultz, "Obama: Orlando Shooter Self-Radicalized over the Internet," *New York Post*, June 13, 2016 (accessed September 11, 2016), http://nypost.com/2016/06/13/obama-orlando-shooter-self-radicalized-over-the-internet/

46. "Ahmad Khan Rahimi Indicted in Manhattan Federal Court on Terrorism Charges," *Department of Justice*, November 16, 2016 (accessed December 11, 2016), https://www.justice.gov/usao-sdny/pr/ahmad-khan-rahimi-indicted-manhattan-federal-court-terrorism-charges

47. Renae Merle, Matt Zapotosky, Amy B. Wang, and Mark Berman, "Suspect in New York, N.J. Bombings Taken into Custody," *Washington Post*, September 19, 2015 (accessed September 11, 2016), https://www.washingtonpost.com/news/post-nation/wp/2016/09/18/three-mysterious-incidents-in-new-york-new-jersey-and-minnesota-raise-fears-of-terrorism/?utm_term=.6ea6ffdf4e40

48. Mubaraz Ahmed, "How the New York Bombing Suspect Was Radicalized Online by a Man Who Had Been Dead for Five Years," *The Independent*, September 22, 2016 (accessed November 27, 2016), http://www.independent.co.uk/voices/new-york-new-jersey-bomb-suspect-ahmad-khan-rahami-islamist-terrorism-radicalised-online-dead-man-a7323406.html

49. Mitch Smith, Richard Pérez-Peña, and Adam Goldman, "Suspect Is Killed in Attack at Ohio State University That Injured 11," *New York Times*, November 28, 2016 (accessed November 30, 2016), http://www.nytimes.com/2016/11/28/us/active-shooter-ohio-state-university.html

CHAPTER 6

1. George Michael, "What's to Stop a 'Lone Wolf' Terrorist?" *Chronicle*, September 5, 2012 (accessed September 15, 2016), http://chronicle.com/blogs/conversation/2012/09/05/whats-to-stop-a-lone-wolf-terrorist/

2. Bakker and Graaf, "Preventing Lone Wolf Terrorism: Some CT Approaches Addressed."

3. Fred Burton and Scott Stewart, "The 'Lone Wolf' Disconnect," *Security Weekly*, January 30, 2008 (accessed September 15, 2016), http://www.stratfor.com/weekly/lone_wolf_disconnect

4. Charles Krauthammer, "How to Stop a Lone Terrorist," *Washington Post*, December 22, 2014 (accessed September 15, 2016), http://www.detroitnews.com/story/opinion/columnists/charles-krauthammer/2014/12/22/stop-lone-terrorist/20660719/

5. Charles Krauthammer, "How to Stop a Lone Terrorist."

6. Isaac Chotinerm, "A Lone-Wolf Terrorist Is Never Quite Alone," *Slate*, June 2016, http://www.slate.com/articles/news_and_politics/interrogation/2016/06/why_isis_loves_lone_wolf_terrorists.html

7. Greg Gutfeld, "Stop Calling Them 'Lone Wolves'," *Fox News*, October 27, 2014 (accessed September 15, 2016), http://www.foxnews.com/on-air/the-five/article/2014/10/27/gutfeld-stop-calling-them-lone-wolves

8. Bakker and Graff, "Preventing Lone Wolf Terrorism."

9. Bergen, *The Longest War*, 202–203.

10. Bakker and Graff, "Preventing Lone Wolf Terrorism."

11. Michael, "What's to Stop a 'Lone Wolf' Terrorist?"

12. Stern and Berger, *ISIS—The State of Terror*, 95.

13. Chotinerm, "A Lone-Wolf Terrorist Is Never Quite Alone."

14. Jay Weaver and David Ovalle, "Terror Enemy No. 1: Lone Wolves Like Orlando Killer Omar Mateen," *Miami Herald*, June 14, 2016 (accessed September 15, 2016), http://www.miamiherald.com/news/local/community/miami-dade/article 83819372.html

15. Weaver and Ovalle, "Terror Enemy No. 1: Lone Wolves Like Orlando Killer Omar Mateen."

16. Ben Shapiro, "7 Other Lone Wolf Islamic Attacks Inside the U.S.," *Breitbart*, September 28, 2014 (accessed September 15, 2016), http://www.breitbart.com/ national-security/2014/09/28/7-other-lone-wolf-islamic-attacks/

17. Fausset et al., "Gunman Kills 4 Marines at Military Site in Chattanooga."

18. Weaver and Ovalle, "Terror Enemy No. 1: Lone Wolves Like Orlando Killer Omar Mateen."

19. Bakker and Graff, "Lone Wolves: How to Stop This Phenomenon?"

20. Daniel Byman, "Omar Mateen, Lone-Wolf Terrorist," *Slate*, June 2016 (accessed September 15, 2016), http://www.slate.com/articles/news_and_politics/ foreigners/2016/06/lone_wolf_terrorists_like_omar_mateen_present_a_differ ent_kind_of_threat.html

21. Weaver and Ovalle, "Terror Enemy No. 1: Lone Wolves Like Orlando Killer Omar Mateen."

22. Jeffery D. Simon, *Lone Wolf Terrorism, Understanding the Growing Threat* (New York: Prometheus Books, 2013), 20.

23. Byman, "Omar Mateen, Lone-Wolf Terrorist."

24. Chotinerm, "A Lone-Wolf Terrorist Is Never Quite Alone."

25. Tim Lister, "How Do We Stop 'Lone Wolf' Attacks?" *CNN*, October 27, 2014 (accessed September 15, 2016), http://www.cnn.com/2014/10/27/world/ lone-wolves/index.html

26. Ibid.

27. Byman, "Omar Mateen, Lone-Wolf Terrorist."

28. Ibid.

29. Chotinerm, "A Lone-Wolf Terrorist Is Never Quite Alone."

30. Weaver and Ovalle, "Terror Enemy No. 1: Lone Wolves Like Orlando Killer Omar Mateen."

31. Lister, "How Do We Stop 'Lone Wolf' Attacks?"

32. Chotinerm, "A Lone-Wolf Terrorist Is Never Quite Alone."

33. Rubin and Blaise, "Killing Twice for ISIS and Saying So Live on Facebook."

34. Michael, "What's to Stop a 'Lone Wolf' Terrorist?"

35. Chotinerm, "A Lone-Wolf Terrorist Is Never Quite Alone."

36. Krauthammer, "How to Stop a Lone Terrorist."

37. Christine Williams, "Stop Minimizing the Reality of Lone Wolf Jihadists," *Jihad Watch*, June 19, 2016 (accessed September 15, 2016), https://Www.Jihad watch.Org/2016/06/Stop-Minimizing-The-Reality-Of-Lone-Wolf-jihadists

38. Krauthammer, "How to Stop a Lone Terrorist."

CHAPTER 7

1. Kukil Bora, "Terrorist Groups Like ISIS, Al Qaeda Attract More Than 25,000 Foreign Fighters: UN Report," *International Business Times*, April 2, 2015 (accessed November 13, 2016), Http://Www.Ibtimes.Com/Terrorist-Groups-Isis-Al-Qaeda-Attract-More-25000-Foreign-Fighters-Un-Report-1867392

2. Lisa Curtis, Luke Coffey, David Inserra, Daniel Kochis, Walter Lohman, Joshua Meservey, James Phillips, and Robin Simcox, "Combatting the ISIS Foreign Fighter Pipeline: A Global Approach," *Heritage*, January 6, 2016 (accessed October 1, 2016), http://www.heritage.org/research/reports/2016/01/combatting-the-isis-foreign-fighter-pipeline-a-global-approach

3. Masood Farivar, "The Foreign Fighters and Me," *New York Times*, April 1, 2014 (accessed October 1, 2016), http://www.nytimes.com/2014/04/02/opinion/the-foreign-fighters-and-me.html?_r=0

4. Matthew Levitt, "Foreign Fighters and Their Economic Impact: A Case Study of Syria and Al-Qaeda in Iraq (AQI)," *Terrorism Research Institute*, 2009 (accessed November 13, 2016), http://www.terrorismanalysts.com/pt/index.php/pot/article/view/74/html

5. Jessica Stern and J.M. Berger, "ISIS and the Foreign-Fighter Phenomenon," *The Atlantic*, March 8, 2015 (accessed October 1, 2016), http://www.theatlantic.com/international/archive/2015/03/isis-and-the-foreign-fighter-problem/387166/

6. Ibid.

7. River, *The Islamic State of Iraq and Syria.*

8. Aaron Y. Zelin, "Who Are the Foreign Fighters in Syria?" Carnegie Middle East Center, December 5, 2013 (accessed October 1, 2016), http://www.washingtoninstitute.org/policy-analysis/view/who-are-the-foreign-fighters-in-syria

9. Mohanad Hashim, "Iraq and Syria: Who Are the Foreign Fighters?" *BBC Monitoring*, September 3, 2014 (accessed October 1, 2016), http://www.bbc.com/news/world- middle-east-29043331

10. Chris Francescani and Robert Windom, "Foreign Fighters Pouring into Syria Faster Than Ever, Say Officials," *NBC News*, October 29, 2014 (accessed October 1, 2016), http://www.nbcnews.com/storyline/isis-terror/foreign-fighters-pouring-syria-faster-ever-say-officials-n236546

11. Ibid.

12. Zelin, "Who Are the Foreign Fighters in Syria?"

13. Hashim, "Iraq and Syria: Who Are the Foreign Fighters?"

14. "French Lawmakers Tackle Tough New Anti-Terror Bill," *Daily Mail*, September 15, 2014 (accessed October 1, 2016), http://www.dailymail.co.uk/wires/ap/article-2756409/French-lawmakers-tackle-tough-new-anti-terror-bill.html

15. "A New Focus on Foreign Fighters," *New York Times*, September 24, 2014 (accessed October 1, 2016), http://www.nytimes.com/2014/09/25/opinion/a-new-focus-on-foreign-fighters.html

16. Francescani and Windom, "Foreign Fighters Pouring into Syria Faster Than Ever, Say Officials."

17. "20,000 Foreign Fighters Head to Syria: US," *Agence France Presse*, February 10, 2015 (accessed October 1, 2016), https://www.yahoo.com/news/20-000-foreign-fighters-head-syria-000443048.html?ref=gs

18. Tim Arango and Eric Schmitt, "A Path to ISIS, through a Porous Turkish Border," *New York Times*, March 9, 2015 (accessed November 13, 2016),

http://www.nytimes.com/2015/03/10/world/europe/despite-crackdown-path-to-join-isis-often-winds-through-porous-turkish-border.html

19. "Number of Foreign Fighters in Iraq and Syria Doubles in a Year, Report Finds," *Guardian*, December 8, 2015 (accessed October 1, 2016), https://www.the guardian.com/world/2015/dec/08/isis-foreign-fighters-iraq-syria-doubles-report

20. Curtis et al., "Combatting the ISIS Foreign Fighter Pipeline."

21. "Flow of Foreign ISIS Recruits Much Slower Now, U.S. Says," *CBS NEWS*, April 26, 2016 (accessed October 1, 2016), http://www.cbsnews.com/news/less-foreign-isis-recruits/

22. Griff Witte, Sudarsan Raghavan, and James McAuley, "Flow of Foreign Fighters Plummets as Islamic State Loses Its Edge," *Washington Post*, September 10, 2016 (accessed October 1, 2016), https://www.washingtonpost.com/world/europe/flow-of-foreign-fighters-plummets-as-isis-loses-its-edge/2016/09/09/ed3e0dda-751b-11e6-9781-49e591781754_story.html

23. Zelin, "Who Are the Foreign Fighters in Syria?"

24. Stern and Berger, "ISIS and the Foreign-Fighter Phenomenon."

25. Ibid.

26. Michael Pizzi, "Foreign Fighters in Syria, Iraq Have Doubled Since Anti-ISIL Intervention," *Aljazeera*, December 7, 2015 (accessed October 1, 2016), http://america.aljazeera.com/articles/2015/12/7/foreign-fighters-in-syria-iraq-have-doubled-since-anti-isil-intervention.html

27. Stern and Berger, "ISIS and the Foreign-Fighter Phenomenon."

28. Pizzi, "Foreign Fighters in Syria, Iraq Have Doubled Since Anti-ISIL Intervention."

29. Curtis et al., "Combatting the ISIS Foreign Fighter Pipeline."

30. Francescani and Windom, "Foreign Fighters Pouring into Syria Faster Than Ever, Say Officials."

31. Santora and Goldman, "Ahmad Khan Rahami Was Inspired by Bin Laden, Charges Say."

32. Stern and Berger, "ISIS and the Foreign-Fighter Phenomenon."

33. Pizzi, "Foreign Fighters in Syria, Iraq Have Doubled Since Anti-ISIL Intervention."

34. Mark Gollom and Tracey Lindeman, "Who Is Martin Couture-Rouleau?" *CBS*, October 22, 2014 (accessed November 12, 2016), http://www.cbc.ca/news/canada/who-is-martin-couture-rouleau-1.2807285

35. William McCants and Christopher Meserole, "The French Connection, Explaining Sunni Militancy around the World," *Foreign Affairs*, March 24, 2016 (accessed October 1, 2016), https://www.foreignaffairs.com/articles/2016-03-24/french-connection

36. Francescani and Windom, "Foreign Fighters Pouring into Syria Faster Than Ever, Say Officials."

37. Jeff Seldin, "Flow of Foreign Fighters to Iraq, Syria Unrelenting," *Voice of America News*, January 8, 2016 (accessed October 1, 2016), http://www.voanews.com/a/flow-of-foreign-fighters-to-syria-iraq-unrelenting/3135549.html

38. Stern and Berger, *ISIS—The State of Terror*, 80.

39. Curtis et al., "Combatting the ISIS Foreign Fighter Pipeline."

40. Stern and Berger, *ISIS—The State of Terror*, 80.

41. Ghaith Abdul-Ahad, "Syria: the Foreign Fighters Joining the War against Bashar Al-Assad," *Guardian*, September 23 2012 (accessed October 1, 2016), https://www.theguardian.com/world/2012/sep/23/syria-foreign-fighters-joining-war

42. Ibid.

CHAPTER 8

1. Yosri Fouda, "The Story of Planners of the 9/11 Attacks (Arabic)," *Yel*, September 25, 2002 (accessed October 18, 2016), http://www.ye1.org/vb/show thread.php?p=110457

2. Ibid.

3. "What Is the Position of Islam towards the Followers of the Book at This Time: Are They Believers or Infidels?" *Islam Web*, April 19, 2000 (accessed August 5, 2016), http://fatwa.islamweb.net/fatwa/index.php?page=showfatwa&Option=FatwaId&Id=29

4. "Surely those who believe and those who are Jews and the Sabians and the Christians whoever believes in Allah and the last day and does good—they shall have no fear nor shall they grieve." (Quran 2: 69)

5. "Say: We believe in Allah, and the revelation given to us, and to Abraham, Isma'il, Isaac, Jacob, and the Tribes, and that given to Moses and Jesus, and that given to (all) prophets from their Lord: We make no difference between one and another of them: And we submit to Allah." (Quran 2:136)

6. "It was We [God] who revealed the law [to Moses]: therein was guidance and light. By its standard have been judged the Jews, by the prophets who submit-ted to Allah's will, by the rabbis and believers in God: for to them was entrusted the protection of Allah's book, and they were witnesses thereto: therefore, fear not men, but fear me, and sell not my signs for a miserable price. If any do fail to judge by (the light of) what Allah hath revealed, they are (no better than) Unbelievers . . . And in their footsteps we sent Jesus the son of Mary, confirming the Torah that had come before him: We sent him the Gospel: therein was guidance and light, and confirmation of Torah that had come before him: a guidance and an admonition to those who fear Allah." (Quran 5: 44, 46)

7. Yahya R. Kamalipour and Nancy Snow (eds.), *War, Media, and Propaganda* (New York: Rowan & Littlefield, 2004), 108.

8. Ali S. Awadh Asseri, *Combating Terrorism: Saudi Arabia's Role in the War on Terror*, (New York: Oxford University Press, 2009), 36.

9. Kamalipour and Snow, *War, Media, and Propaganda*, 108.

10. "The Twelve Imams," *Al-Islam*, (n.d) (accessed August 5, 2016), https://www.al-islam.org/shiite-encyclopedia-ahlul-bayt-dilp-team/twelve-imams-part-1

11. "What Are the Major Similarities and Differences in the Different Sects of Islam?" *Detroit Interfaith Council* (n.d), (accessed August 5, 2016), https://detroit interfaithcouncil.com/2013/06/10/what-are-the-major-similarities-and-differ ences-in-the-different-sects-of-islam/

12. "Umayyad Caliphate," *The Oxford Dictionary of Islam* (n.d.), (accessed Sep-tember 4, 2016), http://www.oxfordislamicstudies.com/article/opr/t125/e2421

13. Henri Laoust, *"Ibn Taymiyyah, Muslim Theologian,"* Encyclopedia Britannica (n.d.), (accessed September 4, 2016), https://Www.Britannica.Com/Biography/Ibn-Taymiyyah

14. "Political Assassinations in Egypt and Assassination of Judge Ahmed Beg Al-Khazidar," *Muslim Brotherhood Official Encyclopedia* (n.d.), (accessed August 5, 2016),

http://www.ikhwanwiki.com/index.php?title=%D8%AD%D8%A7%D8%AF%D8%AB_%D8%A7%D8%BA%D8%AA%D9%8A%D8%A7%D9%84_%D8%A7%D9%84%D8%AE%D8%A7%D8%B2%D9%86%D8%AF%D8%A7%D8%B1_%D9%81%D9%89_%D8%A7%D9%84%D9%85%D9%8A%D8%B2%D8%A7%D9%86

15. Kamal Hassan Wahbi, *Terrorism Ideology, The Savage Wolves, A psychodynamic Analysis of Terrorist Personality* (Beirut: Dar Al-Mawasim, 2014), 183.

16. Ibid.

17. Hisham al-Hashimi, *ISIL World, The Islamic State in Iraq and the Levant* (London: Dar al-Hikma, London, 2015), 175.

18. Hasan Farhan al-Maliki, *The Roots of ISIL/ISIS, A Reading in the Heritage of Wahhabism and Saudi Scholars* (in Arabic) (Beirut: Dar Al-Mahajja, 2014), 38.

19. Ibid.

20. Patrick Cockburn, "Iraq Crisis: How Saudi Arabia Helped ISIS Take over the North of the Country," *The Independent*, July 12, 2014 (accessed September 30, 2016), http://www.independent.co.uk/voices/comment/iraq-crisis-how-saudi-arabia-helped-isis-take-over-the-north-of-the-country-9602312.html

21. Ibid.

22. Al-Hashimi, *ISIL World*, 38.

23. Cockburn, *The Rise of the Islamic State: ISIS and the Sunni Revolution*, 6.

24. Foaud Ibrahim, *ISIL: From Najdi to Baghdadi* (in Arabic) (Beirut: Awal Center, 2015), 106.

25. Ibid.

26. Alwash, *ISIL/ISIS and Its Sisters, from Al-Qaeda to Islamic State* (in Arabic), 23.

27. Zarate, *Treasury's War*, 2.

28. Ibrahim, *ISIL: From Najdi to Baghdadi* (in Arabic), 106.

29. Ibid.

30. Alastair Crooke, "You Can't Understand ISIS If You Don't Know the History of Wahhabism in Saudi Arabia," *Huffington Post*, September 5, 2014 (accessed September 30, 2016), http://www.huffingtonpost.com/alastair-crooke/isis-wahhabism-saudi-arabia_b_5717157.html

31. Ibrahim, *ISIL: From Najdi to Baghdadi* (in Arabic), 9.

32. Ibid.

33. Scott Shane, "Saudis and Extremism: Both the Arsonists and the Firefighters," *New York Times*, August 25, 2016 (accessed August 27, 2016), http://www.nytimes.com/2016/08/26/world/middleeast/saudi-arabia-islam.html?_r=0

34. Jeffrey Goldberg, "Obama Doctrine," *The Atlantic*, August 30, 2013 (accessed October 14, 2016), http://www.theatlantic.com/magazine/archive/2016/04/the-obama-doctrine/471525/

35. Hasan Farhan al-Maliki, *The Roots of ISIL/ISIS, A Reading in the Heritage of Wahhabism and Saudi Scholars* (in Arabic) (Beirut: Dar Al-Mahajja, 2014), 52.

36. Ibid.

37. Rachel Ehrenfeld, "Turning Off the Tap of Terrorist Funding," *Middle East Forum*, September 19, 2003 (accessed October 29, 2016), http://www.meforum.org/572/turning-off-the-tap-of-terrorist-funding

CHAPTER 9

1. "Why Is Washington Turning Blind Eye to ISIS's Gulf Funding Sources?" *Sputnic News*, November 19, 2015 (accessed October 29, 2016), https://sputniknews.com/politics/201511191030406241-washington-gulf-saudi-funding-ISIS/

2. Juan Miguel del Cid Gómez, "A Financial Profile of the Terrorism of Al-Qaeda and Its Affiliates," *Terrorism Analysts*, 4, No 4 (2010) (accessed November 4, 2016), http://www.terrorismanalysts.com/pt/index.php/pot/article/view/113/htm

3. Testimony of Dennis M. Lormel, Chief, Financial Crimes Section, FBI, before the House Committee on Financial Services, Subcommittee on Oversight and Investigations, *FBI.Gov*. February 12, 2002 (accessed November 4, 2016), https://www2.fbi.gov/congress/congress02/lormel021202.htm

4. UN Security Council Resolution 1267, October 15, 1999 (accessed October 29, 2016), http://www.state.gov/j/ct/rls/other/un/5110.htm

5. Douglas Farahm, "How to Stop Terrorism Financing," *Islam Daily*, October 12, 2005 (accessed October 29, 2016), http://islamdaily.org/en/charities/3567.how-to-stop-terrorism-financing.htm

6. Nidhal Hamada, *Secrets and Mysterious of ISIS, from Osama Bian Laden's Turban to Saddam Hussein Hat* (in Arabic) (Beirut: Bissan Publishers, Beirut 2015), 161–165.

7. David E. Sanger and Julie Hirschfeld Davis, "Struggling to Starve ISIS of Oil Revenue, U.S. Seeks Assistance from Turkey," *New York Times*, September 13, 2014 (accessed October 29, 2016), https://www.nytimes.com/2014/09/14/world/middleeast/struggling-to-starve-isis-of-oil-revenue-us-seeks-assistance-from-turkey.html?_r=0

8. Sam Jones, Piotr Zalewski, and Erika Solomon, "ISIS Sells Smuggled Oil to Turkey and Iraqi Kurds Says US Treasury," *Financial Times*, October 23, 2014 (accessed November 4, 2016), https://www.ft.com/content/6c269c4e-5ace-11e4-b449-00144feab7de

9. Ibid.

10. Remarks of Under Secretary for Terrorism and Financial Intelligence David S. Cohen at The Carnegie Endowment for International Peace, "Attacking ISI's Financial Foundation," U.S. Department of Treasury, October 23, 2014 (accessed June 10, 2017), https://www.treasury.gov/press-center/press-releases/Pages/jl2672.aspx

11. Erika Solomon and Guy Chazan, "ISIS Inc: How Oil Fuels the Jihadi Terrorists," *Financial Times*, October 14, 2015 (accessed November 4, 2016), https://www.ft.com/content/b8234932-719b-11e5-ad6d-f4ed76f0900a

12. Guler Vilmaz, "Opposition MP Says ISIS Is Selling Oil in Turkey," *Al-Monitor*, June 13, 2014 (accessed October 29, 2016), http://www.al-monitor.com/pulse/tr/business/2014/06/turkey-syria-isis-selling-smuggled-oil.html

13. "Most Smuggled ISIS Oil Goes to Turkey, Sold at Low Prices—Norwegian Report," *RT*, December 20, 2015 (accessed October 29, 2016) https://www.rt.com/news/326567-is-export-oil-turkey/

14. Ibid.

15. Alexi Druzhinin, "Putin: ISIS Financed from 40 Countries, Including G20 Members," *RT*, November 16, 2015 (accessed October 29, 2016), https://www.rt.com/news/322305-isis-financed-40-countries/

16. Tyler Durden, "How Turkey Exports ISIS Oil to the World: The Scientific Evidence," *Zero Hedge*, November 28, 2015 (accessed October 29, 2016), http://www.zerohedge.com/news/2015-11-27/how-turkey-exports-isis-oil-world-scientific-evidenceTwitterFacebookReddit

17. Ibid.

18. "Obama Allows US Hostage Families to Pay Ransoms," *BBC*, June 24, 2015 (accessed October 29, 2016), http://www.bbc.com/news/world-us-canada-33260645

19. Anita Kumar, "US to Allow Families of Hostages to Pay Ransom, but Government Will Not Do It," *RT*, June 24, 2015 (accessed October 29, 2016), https://www.rt.com/usa/269473-obama-hostages-ransom-pay/

20. Testimony of John S. Pistole, Deputy Assistant Director, Counterterrorism Division, *FBI*, Before the Senate Committee on Governmental Affairs, July 31, 2003 (accessed October 29, 2016), https://archives.fbi.gov/archives/news/testimony/terrorism-financing-origination-organization-and-prevention

21. "If We Want to Stop Terrorism, We Should Stop Supporting Terrorists," *Washington's Blog*, November 18, 2015 (accessed October 29, 2016), http://www.washingtonsblog.com/2015/11/if-we-want-to-stop-terrorism-we-should-stop-supporting-terrorists.html

22. Farahm, "How to Stop Terrorism Financing."

23. Sanger and Hirschfeld, "Struggling to Starve ISIS of Oil Revenue."

24. Ashley Fantz, "How ISIS Makes (and Takes) Money," *CNN*, February 19, 2015 (accessed October 29, 2016), http://www.cnn.com/2015/02/19/world/how-isis-makes-money/index.html

25. Ibid.

26. Staff Writer, "ISIS Selling Iraq's Artifacts in Black Market: UNESCO," *Al Arabiya News*, September 30, 2014 (accessed October 29, 2016), http://english.alarabiya.net/en/News/middle-east/2014/09/30/ISIS-selling-Iraq-s-artifacts-in-black-market.html

27. Fantz, "How ISIS Makes (and Takes) Money."

28. Will Freeman, "How ISIS Is Making a Fortune on the Black Market for Ancient Artifacts," Jul 10, 2014 (accessed October 29, 2016), https://thinkprogress.org/how-isis-is-making-a-fortune-on-the-black-market-for-ancient-artifacts-4d9168805ef7#.7srlla35k

29. Jack Crone, "2,000-Year-Old Artefacts Looted by ISIS from Ancient Sites in Iraq and Syria Are Being Sold on Ebay," *Daily Mail*, March 14, 2015 (accessed October 29, 2016), http://www.dailymail.co.uk/news/article-2994538/2-000-year-old-artefacts-looted-ISIS-ancient-sites-Iraq-Syria-sold-EBAY.html

30. Christopher Jones, "In Battle against ISIS, Saving Lives or Ancient Artifacts," *Hyper Allergic*, April 17, 2015 (accessed October 29, 2016), http://hyperallergic.com/200005/in-battle-against-isis-saving-lives-or-ancient-artifacts/

31. Ibid.

32. Ibid.

33. Cecilia Martin, "4,400 Year-Old Artifact Returned to Iraqi Government, IIP US Embassy," July 27, 2006 (accessed October 29, 2016), http://iipdigital.usembassy.gov/st/english/article/2006/07/20060727173413mlenuhret0.1980097.html#axzz4HRrOB6OK

34. Sophie Shevardnadze, "Children Born to ISIS Sex Slaves Are Taken to Be Trained into Murderers—Yazidi Aid Worker," *RT*, December 4, 2015 (accessed October 29, 2016), https://www.rt.com/shows/sophieco/324712-children-ISIS-sex-slaves/

35. Nick Squires, "Yazidi Girl Tells of Horrific Ordeal as ISIS Sex Slave," *Telegraph*, September 7, 2014 (accessed October 29, 2016), http://www.telegraph.co.uk/news/worldnews/middleeast/iraq/11080165/Yazidi-girl-tells-of-horrific-ordeal-as-ISIS-sex-slave.html

36. "Ban Ki-moon 'Dismayed' by Plight of Yazidi Refugees on Iraq's Mount Sinjar," *Telegraph*, August 12, 2014 (accessed October 29, 2016), http://www.tele graph.co.uk/news/worldnews/middleeast/iraq/11029997/Ban-Ki-moon-dis mayed-by-plight-of-Yazidi-refugees-on-Iraqs-Mount-Sinjar.html

37. Remarks of Under Secretary for Terrorism and Financial Intelligence David S. Cohen at The Carnegie Endowment for International Peace, "Attacking ISIS's Financial Foundation" October 23, 2014 (accessed December 2, 2016), https://www.treasury.gov/press-center/press-releases/Pages/jl2672.aspx

38. Ibid.

39. Ibid.

CHAPTER 10

1. Gabriel Weimann, "How Terrorism Uses the Internet," *US Institute of Peace*, March 13, 2004 (accessed December 2, 2016), http://www.usip.org/publications/wwwterrornet-how-modern-terrorism-uses-the-internet

2. Mattathias Schwartz, "The Whole Haystack," *New Yorker*, January 26, 2015 Issue (accessed December 2, 2016), http://www.newyorker.com/magazine/2015/01/26/whole-haystack

3. Mary Pascaline, "Orlando Shooting: Gunman a 'Homegrown Extremist' 'Radicalized' on the Internet, Obama Says," *International Business Times*, June 14, 2016 (accessed December 2, 2016), http://Www.Ibtimes.Com/Orlando-Shooting-Gunman-Homegrown-Extremist-Radicalized-Internet-Obama-Says-2381851

4. Baker and Schmitt, "California Attack Has U.S. Rethinking Strategy on Homegrown Terror."

5. "No Silver Bullet to Stop Terrorist Use of Internet: Microsoft," *ND TV*, May 12, 2016 (accessed December 2, 2016), http://www.ndtv.com/world-news/no-silver-bullet-to-stop-terrorist-use-of-internet-microsoft-1405383

6. Kashmir Hill, "Let's Stop Blaming 'The Internet' for Terrorism," *Huffington Post*, December 14, 2015 (accessed December 2, 2016), http://www.huffington post.com/entry/internet-terrorism_us_566ed1dee4b0fccee16f1960

7. Richard Spencer, "ISIL Tweeter 'ShamiWitness' Arrested in India," *Telegraph*, December 13, 2014 (accessed December 2, 2016), http://www.telegraph.co .uk/news/worldnews/islamic-state/11292412/Isil-tweeter-ShamiWitness-arrested-in-India.html

8. "Channel 4 Investigation Uncovers the British Women Supporting ISIS," *Channel 4*, November 22, 2015 (accessed December 2, 2016), http://www.channel4 .com/info/press/news/channel-4-investigation-uncovers-the-british-women-supporting-isis?hootPostID=96f1d4d4e339b272c5f7adf23ebe8e96

9. Associated Press, "Al Qaeda, Terrorists Changing Communication Methods after NSA Leaks, US Officials Say," *Fox News*, June 26, 2013 (accessed December 2, 2016), http://www.foxnews.com/us/2013/06/26/al-qaida-other-militants-said-to-be-changing-procedures-to-avoid-surveillance.html

10. Ibid.

11. Gabriel Weimann, "www.terror.net: How Terrorism Uses the Internet," *US Institute of Peace*, March 13, 2004 (accessed December 2, 2016), http://www.usip .org/publications/wwwterrornet-how-modern-terrorism-uses-the-internet

12. Schwartz, "The Whole Haystack."

13. Ibid.

14. Associated Press, "Al Qaeda, Terrorists Changing Communication Methods."

15. Schwartz, "The Whole Haystack."

16. Ibid.

17. al-Hashimi, *ISIL Organization from Inside*, 310.

18. Sharp, *The Rise of ISIS the West's New Crusade*, 95.

19. "No Silver Bullet to Stop Terrorist Use of Internet: Microsoft."

20. Ibid.

21. "Lost in Translation," *Middle East Quarterly*, 12, no 3 (summer 2005), 82–86, http://www.meforum.org/754/lost-in-translation

22. Ibid.

23. Donald A. DePalma, "FBI Still Lagging on Translation to Thwart Terrorists," *Common Sense Advisory*, October 27, 2009 (accessed December 2, 2016), http://www.commonsenseadvisory.com/Default.aspx?Contenttype=ArticleDet AD&tabID=63&Aid=1200&moduleId=391

24. "Counterterrorism FBI Needs to Improve Intelligence Capabilities, Hire More Linguists: Report," *Homeland Security Newswire*, March 26, 2015 (accessed December 2, 2016), http://www.homelandsecuritynewswire.com/dr20150326-fbi-needs-to-improve-intelligence-capabilities-hire-more-linguists-report

25. Adam Goldman, "FBI Adapts to Face Terrorism Threats but Still Faces Challenges, Report Finds," *Washington Post*, March 25, 2015 (accessed December 2, 2016), https://www.washingtonpost.com/world/national-security/fbi-adapts-to-face-terrorism-threats-but-still-faces-challenges-report-finds/2015/03/25/9af 5d042-d2d5-11e4-8fce-3941fc548f1c_story.html

26. Matthews, "Chattanooga Shootings: America, Let's Use Social Media to Stop Terrorist Attacks."

27. "Censoring the Internet Won't Stop Terrorism," *Web Pro News*, December 9, 2012 (accessed December 2, 2016), http://www.webpronews.com/censoring-the-internet-wont-stop-terrorism-2012-12/

28. Jon Brodkin, "Terrorists Are Using the Internet against Us, Lawmaker Says," *ARS Technica*, November 17, 2015 (accessed December 2, 2016), http://Ars technica.Com/Tech-Policy/2015/11/Congressman-To-Stop-Isis-Lets-Shut-Down-Websites-And-Social-Media/

29. Mario Trujillo, "FCC Says It Can't Shut Down ISIS Websites," *The Hill*, November 17, 2015 (accessed December 2, 2016), http://thehill.com/policy/technology/260438-fcc-says-it-cant-shutdown-online-terrorist-activity

30. "Terrorism: Ahmad Khan Rahami Pressure Cooker Bomb Blast 131 W. 23rd St NYC Just Like Failed Times Square Attempt by Faisal Shahzad," *PI Bill Warner*, Sunday, September 18, 2016, https://pibillwarner.wordpress.com/2016/09/18/terrorism-ahmad-khan-rahami-pressure-cooker-bomb-blast-131-w-23rd-st-nyc-just-like-failed-times-square-attempt-by-faisal-shahzad/

31. Thomas Durante, "Home-Made Devices in Boston Marathon Attack Were Made from Pressure Cooker Bombs—Al Qaeda's 'Most Effective Weapon'—And Featured in Terror Guide 'Make a Bomb in the Kitchen of Your Mom'," *Daily Mail*, April 16, 2013 (accessed December 2, 2016), http://www.dailymail.co.uk/news/article-2309728/Boston-Marathon-2013-explosions-Home-bombs-pressure-cook ers.html

32. "Terrorists Utilize the Internet to Spread Hate, Recruit," *The Jakarta Post*, July 13, 2013, http://www.thejakartapost.com/news/2013/07/13/terrorists-uti lize-internet-spread-hate-recruit.html

33. M.L. Nestel, Gilad Shiloach, and Amit Weiss, "ISIS Forums Share Pipe Bomb Instructions for Attacks on NYC, Las Vegas," *Vocative*, September 16, 2014 (accessed December 2, 2016), http://www.vocativ.com/world/isis-2/isis-pipe-bomb-at

34. Marc Santora, William K. Rashbaum, Al Baker, and Adam Goldman, "Manhattan Bombs Built for Carnage Provide Clues into Attack," *New York Times*, September 18, 2016 (accessed December 2, 2016), http://www.nytimes .com/2016/09/19/nyregion/new-york-explosion chelsea.html?emc=edit_na_201 60918&nlid=68648138&ref=cta

35. Renae Merle, Matt Zapotosky, Amy B Wang, and Mark Berman, "Suspect in New York, N.J. Bombings Taken into Custody," *Washington Post*, September 19, 2015 (accessed December 2, 2016), https://www.washingtonpost.com/news/post-nation/wp/2016/09/18/three-mysterious-incidents-in-new-york-new-jersey-and-minnesota-raise-fears-of-terrorism/?utm_term=.6ea6ffdf4e40

36. Santora et al., "Manhattan Bombs Built for Carnage Provide Clues into Attack."

CHAPTER 11

1. Simon, *Lone Wolf Terrorism*, 125.

2. J. Kuriansky (ed.), *Beyond Bullets and Bombs: Grassroots Peacebuilding between Israelis and Palestinians* (Westport, CT: Praeger Press, 2007).

3. M.L. Nestel, Gilad Shiloach, and Amit Weiss, "ISIS Forums Share Pipe Bomb Instructions for Attacks on NYC, Las Vegas," *Vocativ*, September 16, 2014 (accessed November 12, 2016), http://www.vocativ.com/world/isis-2/isis-pipe-bomb-at

4. David Wright, "Poll: Americans Fear 'Lone Wolf' Attacks," *CNN*, December 17, 2015 (accessed November 12, 2016), http://www.cnn.com/2015/12/17/ politics/washington-post-abc-news-security-poll/index.html

5. Scott Clement, "Americans Doubt U.S. Can Stop 'Lone Wolf' Attacks, Poll Finds," *Washington Post*, December 16, 2015 (accessed November 12, 2016), https:// www.washingtonpost.com/politics/americans-doubt-us-can-stop-lone-wolf-at tacks-poll-finds/2015/12/16/bfcaa102-a3ba-11e5-ad3f-991ce3374e23_story.html

6. "Poll: On Terrorism, Americans Favor Clinton over Trump," *Voice of America News*, June 28, 2016 (accessed November 12, 2016), http://www.voanews .com/a/us-terrorism-poll-clinton-trump/3395258.html

7. Clement, "Americans Doubt U.S. Can Stop 'Lone Wolf' Attacks, Poll Finds."

8. Pamela Brown, Evan Perez, Holly Yan, and Joe Sterling, "Sources: Grand Jury to Investigate Orlando Shooter's Widow," *CNN*, June 16, 2016 (accessed November 12, 2016), http://www.cnn.com/2016/06/15/us/orlando-shooter-omar-mateen/

9. Ibid.

10. David Gomez, "The Myth of the Big Bad Lone Wolf," *The Foreign Policy*, October 25, 2014 (accessed November 12, 2016), http://foreignpolicy.com/ 2014/10/25/the-myth-of-the-big-bad-lone-wolf/

11. Mark Gollom and Tracey Lindeman, "Who Is Martin Couture-Rouleau?" *CBS*, October 22, 2014 (accessed November 12, 2016), http://www.cbc.ca/news/ canada/who-is-martin-couture-rouleau-1.2807285

12. Saeed Ahmed and Greg Botelho, "Who Is Michael Zehaf-Bibeau, the Man Behind the Deadly Ottawa Attacks?" *CNN*, October 23, 2014 (accessed November 12, 2016), http://www.cnn.com/2014/10/22/world/canada-shooter/

13. Ceylan Yeginsu, "Turkey Warned French Twice about Attacker, Official Says," *New York Times*, November 16, 2015 (accessed November 12, 2016), http://www.nytimes.com/live/paris-attacks-live-updates/turkey-warned-french-twice-about-attacker-official-says/

14. Jamie Dettmer, "Fumbles, Mistakes Prompt Talk of Major French Intelligence Failure," *VOA News*, November 17, 2015 (accessed November 12, 2016), http://www.voanews.com/content/fumbles-mistakes-prompt-talk-of-major-french-intelligence-failure/3061990.html

15. Brown, Perez, Yan, and Sterling, "Sources: Grand Jury to Investigate Orlando Shooter's Widow."

16. Andrew C. McCarthy, "Willful Blindness: A Memoir of the Jihad," *Encounter Books*, p XIX (n.d.) (accessed November 12, 2016), https://books.google.com/books?id=qOVxG5_NK3oC&pg=PR19&dq=%22Ezeagwula%22&hl=en&ei=wdXiTPn8IcH58AbI-vXgDA&sa=X&oi=book_result&ct=result&resnum=1&ved=0CCUQ6AEwAA#v=onepage&q=%22Ezeagwula%22&f=false

17. Ibid.

18. Lori Hinnant, "France-Stopping the Wolves Story," *Associated Press*, August 29, 2015 (accessed November 12, 2016), https://www.yahoo.com/news/security-worry-stop-lone-wolf-attacks-190051028.html?ref=gs

19. Ibid.

20. Larry Buchanan and Haeyoun Park, "Uncovering the Links between the Brussels and Paris Attackers," April 9, 2016 (accessed November 12, 2016), http://www.nytimes.com/interactive/2016/03/23/world/europe/how-the-brussels-and-paris-attackers-could-be-connected.html

21. Dettmer, "Fumbles, Mistakes Prompt Talk of Major French Intelligence Failure."

22. David A. Andelman, "Lone Wolves Are a Global Dilemma," *USA Today*, June 16, 2016 (accessed November 12, 2016), http://www.usatoday.com/story/opinion/2016/06/15/lone-wolves-terrorism-orlando-france-islamic-state-trump-andelman-column/85921600/

23. Alissa J. Rubin and Lilia Blaise, "Killing Twice for ISIS and Saying So Live on Facebook," *New York Times*, June 14, 2016 (accessed November 12, 2016), http://www.nytimes.com/2016/06/15/world/europe/france-stabbing-police-magnanville-isis.html?_r=0

24. Per Nyberg and James Masters, "Sweden Terror Suspect 'Confesses' to Stockholm Attack," *CNN*, April 11, 2017 (accessed April 13, 2017), http://www.cnn.com/2017/04/11/europe/stockholm-terror-attack-rakhmat-akilov/

25. Nadia Khomami, "Stockholm Attack Suspect Rakhmat Akilov Admits Terrorist Crime," *Guardian*, April 11, 2017 (accessed April 13, 2017), https://www.theguardian.com/world/2017/apr/11/stockholm-attack-suspect-rakhmat-akilov-admits-terrorist

26. Robson, "Stockholm Terror Attack."

27. Dina Temple-Raston, "Terrorism in the U.S. Takes on a U.K. Pattern," *National Public Radio*, May 9, 2010 (accessed November 12, 2016), http://www.npr.org/templates/story/story.php?storyId=126646911May 9, 20108:00 AM ET

28. James Barron and Sabrina Tavernise, "Money Woes, Long Silences and a Zeal for Islam," *New York Times*, May 5, 2010 (accessed November 12, 2016), http://www.nytimes.com/2010/05/06/nyregion/06profile.html?_r=0

29. Temple-Raston, "Terrorism in the U.S. Takes on a U.K. Pattern."

30. Ben West and Scott Stewart, "Uncomfortable Truths and the Times Square Attack," *Security Weekly*, May 6, 2010 (accessed November 12, 2016), https://www.stratfor.com/weekly/20100505_uncomfortable_truths_times_square_a

31. Michael P. Downing and Matt A. Mayer, "Preventing the Next 'Lone Wolf' Terrorist Attack Requires Stronger Federal–State–Local Capabilities," *The Heritage Foundation*, June 18, 2013 (accessed November 12, 2016), http://www.heritage.org/research/reports/2013/06/preventing-the-next-lone-wolf-terrorist-attack-requires-stronger-federalstatelocal-capabilities

32. Ibid.

33. Ibid.

34. Byron Tau, "Hillary Clinton Declares Stopping 'Lone Wolf' Attackers Is National Priority," *Wall Street Journal*, June 15, 2016 (accessed November 12, 2016), http://blogs.wsj.com/washwire/2016/06/15/hillary-clinton-declares-stopping-lone-wolf-attackers-is-national-priority/

35. Rubin and Blaise, "Killing Twice for ISIS and Saying So Live on Facebook."

36. Ibid.

37. Kevin Johnson, Tariq Zehawi, and Andrew Wyrich, "Ahmad Rahami's Dad Accused Son of Being a Terrorist in 2014," *USA Today*, September 20, 2016 (accessed November 12, 2016), http://www.usatoday.com/story/news/nation/2016/09/20/ahmad-rahamis-dad-accused-son-being-terrorist-2014/90734892/

38. Sarah Wheaton, "Obama Argues for Gun Controls as Way to Fight Terror," *Politico*, June 14, 2016 (accessed November 12, 2016), http://www.politico.com/story/2016/06/barack-obama-gun-control-terror-224331

39. Daniel Byman, "Omar Mateen, Lone-Wolf Terrorist," *Slate*, June 2016 (accessed November 12, 2016), http://www.slate.com/articles/news_and_politics/foreigners/2016/06/lone_wolf_terrorists_like_omar_mateen_present_a_different_kind_of_threat.html

40. Weaver and Ovalle, "Terror Enemy No. 1: Lone Wolves Like Orlando Killer Omar Mateen."

41. "Lawmakers Reflect on How to Stop Lone Wolf Terror Attacks," *Sinclair Broadcast Group*, June 13, 2016 (accessed November 12, 2016), http://wjla.com/news/nation-world/lawmakers-reflect-on-how-to-stop-lone-wolf-terror-attacks

42. Ibid.

CHAPTER 12

1. Robert Spencer, "European Authorities Overwhelmed as Hundreds of Islamic State Fighters Return Home," *Jihad Watch*, March 28, 2016 (accessed November 13, 2016), https://Www.Jihadwatch.Org/2016/03/European-Authorities-Overwhelmed-As-Hundreds-Of-Islamic-State-Fighters-Return-Home

2. Stern and Berger, *ISIS—The State of Terror*, 197.

3. Curtis et al., "Combatting the ISIS Foreign Fighter Pipeline."

4. Ibid.

5. The Editorial Board, "A New Focus on Foreign Fighters," *NYT*, September 24, 2014 (accessed October 1, 2016), http://www.nytimes.com/2014/09/25/opinion/a-new-focus-on-foreign-fighters.html

6. Security Council Resolution 11580 of September 24, 2014 (accessed September 14, 2016), http://www.un.org/press/en/2014/sc11580.doc.htm

7. Ibid.

8. "A New Focus on Foreign Fighters."

9. Security Council Resolution 11580.

10. "A New Focus on Foreign Fighters."

11. Ibid.

12. Thomas Joscelyn, "Islamist Foreign Fighters Returning Home and the Threat to Europe," *Long War Journal*, September 19, 2014 (accessed November 13, 2016), http://www.longwarjournal.org/archives/2014/09/islamist_foreign_fig.php

13. Tim Arango and Eric Schmitt, "A Path to ISIS, through a Porous Turkish Border," *NYT*, March 9, 2015 (accessed November 13, 2016), http://www.nytimes.com/2015/03/10/world/europe/despite-crackdown-path-to-join-isis-often-winds-through-porous-turkish-border.html

14. Ibid.

15. Somini Sengupta, "Nations Trying to Stop Their Citizens from Going to Middle East to Fight for ISIS," *New York Times*, September 12, 2014 (accessed November 13, 2016), http://www.nytimes.com/2014/09/13/world/middleeast/isis-recruits-prompt-laws-against-foreign-fighters.html?_r=0

16. Ibid.

17. Associated Press, "French Lawmakers Tackle Tough New Anti-Terror Bill," *Daily Mail*, September 15, 2014 (accessed October 1, 2016), http://www.dailymail.co.uk/wires/ap/article-2756409/French-lawmakers-tackle-tough-new-anti-terror-bill.html

18. Ibid.

19. "A New Focus on Foreign Fighters."

20. "France's Parliament on Monday Began to Debate a New Anti-Terrorism Bill That Aims to Stop Would-Be Jihadists from Travelling to Foreign Battlefields," *France 24*, September 16, 2015 (accessed October 1, 2016), http://www.france24.com/en/20140916-france-debates-tough-new-anti-terror-bill-what-do-experts-think

21. "Boston Marathon Terror Attack Fast Facts," *CNN Library*, April 8, 2016 (accessed October 5, 2016) http://www.cnn.com/2013/06/03/us/boston-marathon-terror-attack-fast-facts/

22. Eric Schmitt, Michael S. Schmidt, and Ellen Barry, "Bombing Inquiry Turns to Motive and Russian Trip," *New York Times*, April 20, 2013 (accessed October 5, 2016), http://www.nytimes.com/2013/04/21/us/boston-marathon-bombings.html?pagewanted=all&_r=0

23. Abdul-Ahad, "Syria: The Foreign Fighters Joining the War against Bashar al-Assad."

24. Ibid.

25. "20,000 Foreign Fighters Head to Syria: US."

26. *Jeff Seldin*, "Flow of Foreign Fighters to Iraq, Syria Unrelenting," *Voice of America News*, January 8, 2016 (accessed October 1, 2016), http://www.voanews.com/a/flow-of-foreign-fighters-to-syria-iraq-unrelenting/3135549.html

27. Curtis et al., "Combatting the ISIS Foreign Fighter Pipeline."

28. Ibid.

29. Michael McCaul, "Europe Has a Jihadi Superhighway Problem," *Time*, November 11, 2014 (accessed November 13, 2016), http://time.com/3578462/european-union-security-gap-foreign-fighters-terrorists/

30. Masood Farivar, "The Foreign Fighters and Me," *NYT*, April 1, 2014 (accessed October 1, 2016), http://www.nytimes.com/2014/04/02/opinion/the-foreign-fighters-and-me.html?_r=0

31. Francescani and Windom, "Foreign Fighters Pouring into Syria Faster Than Ever, Say Officials."

32. Pizzi, "Foreign Fighters in Syria, Iraq Have Doubled Since Anti-ISIL Intervention."

33. Ibid.

34. Farivar, "The Foreign Fighters and Me."

35. Norman Byrd, "Are Isis Foreign Fighters Terrorist Time Bombs? Chilling Report Says 30 Percent Are Already Home from the Middle East," *Inquisitr*, August 24, 2016, http://www.inquisitr.com/3450236/isis-foreign-fighters-going-home-30-percent-have-already-returned-some-30000-still-fighting/http://www.inquisitr.com/3450236/isis-foreign-fighters-going-hohttp://www.inquisitr.com/3450236/isis-foreign-fighters-going-home-30-percent-have-already-returned-some-

36. "Number of Foreign Fighters in Iraq and Syria Doubles in a Year, Report Finds."

37. Griff Witte, Sudarsan Raghavan, and James McAuley, "Flow of Foreign Fighters Plummets as Islamic State Loses Its Edge," *Washington Post*, September 10, 2016 (accessed October 1, 2016), https://www.washingtonpost.com/world/europe/flow-of-foreign-fighters-plummets-as-isis-loses-its-edge/2016/09/09/ed3e0dda-751b-11e6-9781-49e591781754_story.html

38. Ibid.

39. Ibid.

40. Ibid.

41. Farivar, "The Foreign Fighters and Me."

42. Ibid.

43. Witte, Raghavan, and McAuley, "Flow of Foreign Fighters Plummets as Islamic State Loses Its Edge."

44. Byrd, "Are Isis Foreign Fighters Terrorist Time Bombs? Chilling Report Says 30 Percent Are Already Home from The Middle East."

CHAPTER 13

1. Nance, *Defeating ISIS*, 290.

2. Stevenson, *Counter-Terrorism*, 7.

3. Mary Louise Kelly, Report Offers New Counterterrorism Strategy For Trump Administration, NPR, November 15, 2016 (Accessed June 15, 2017), http://www.npr.org/2016/11/15/502211137/report-offers-new-counterrorism-strategy-for-trump-administration

4. Harold Takooshian, "Understanding Terrorism," *Journal of Social Distress and the Homeless*, 12, no. 4 (2003), 245.

5. Lawrence Wright, *The Looming Tower: Al-Qaeda and the Road to 9/11* (New York: Knopf, 2006), 260.

6. Douglas J. Feith, *War and Decision: Inside the Pentagon at the Dawn of the War on Terrorism* (New York: HarperCollins Books, 2008), 168.

7. Geoff Dyer, "The Envoy: From Kabul to the White House, by Zalmay Khalilzad," *Financial Times*, March 18, 2016 (accessed August 30, 2016), http://www.ft.eom/intl/cms/s/0/840fa0ec-ec3d" 11 e5-bb79-2303682345c8.html

8. Feith, *War and Decision*, 57.

9. Nance, *Defeating ISIS*, 339.

10. Shaykh Muhammad Hisham Kabbani, Shakh Seraj Hendricks, "Jihad: A Misunderstood Concept from Islam," *Islamic Supreme Council* (accessed August 30, 2016), http://islamicsupremecouncil.org/understanding-islam/legal-rulings/5-jihad-a-misunderstood-concept-from-islam.html

11. Feith, *War and Decision*, 139.

12. Bush, *Decisions Points*, 134.

13. Feith, *War and Decision*, 103.

14. Ibid., 167.

15. Ibid., 168.

16. Bergen, *The Longest War*, 26.

17. Feith, *War and Decision*, 169.

18. Amy B Wang, "President Trump Just Ended a Long Tradition of Celebrating Ramadan at the White House," *Washington Post*, June 17, 2017 (accessed June 28, 2017), https://www.washingtonpost.com/news/retropolis/wp/2017/06/17/thomas-jeffersons-iftar-dinner-and-the-history-of-ramadan-at-the-white-house/?utm_term=.6764926b8411

19. Sharp, *The Rise of ISIS, The West's New Crusade*, 97.

20. Wright, *The Looming Tower*, 273.

21. Michael S. Schmidt, "Report Credits F.B.I. with Progress Since 9/11, but Says More Is Needed," *New York Times*, March 25, 2015 (accessed August 30, 2016).

22. Wright, *The Looming Tower*, 274.

23. David Nakamura, "Obama Lashes Out at Trump, Says Using the Phrase 'Radical Islam' Is Not a Strategy," *Washington Post*, June 14, 2016 (accessed August 30, 2016).

24. Ibid.

25. Luis Ramirez, "White House Opens Summit on Countering Extremism," *VOA*, February 17, 2015 (accessed August 30, 2016).

26. The Editors, "Increase in Crimes against Muslims," *Amnesty USA*, September 10, 2010 (accessed June 19, 2017), http://blog.amnestyusa.org/us/increase-in-crimes-against-muslims/

27. Betsy Woodruff, "Hate Crimes against Muslims Rise in US," *Daily Beast*, November 18, 2015 (accessed June 19, 2017), http://www.thedailybeast.com/hate-crimes-against-muslims-rise-in-us

28. "Hate Crimes against Muslims in US Have Skyrocketed during 'War on Terror,'" *RT*, February 12, 2015 (accessed November 16, 2015), https://www.rt.com/usa/231839-muslim-hate-crime-religion/

29. Masood Farivar, "Attacks against US Muslims Growing in Frequency, Violence," *VOA News*, August 17, 2016 (accessed June 19, 2017), https://www.voanews.com/a/us-rising-islamophobia/3469525.html

30. Deepa Iyer, "Here We Go Again? Muslim Americans Brace for a Backlash after Paris," *The Nation*, November 16, 2015 (accessed November 16, 2015), https://www.thenation.com/article/here-we-go-again-muslim-americans-brace-for-backlash-after-paris/

31. Farivar, "Attacks against US Muslims Growing in Frequency, Violence."

32. Ibid.

33. Zainab Fattah Ladane Nasseri, "Here Are the Major Terror Attacks in Europe, From Paris to Oslo, Bloomberg," June 19, 2017 (accessed June 22, 2017), https://www.bloomberg.com/news/articles/2017-06-19/here-are-the-major-terror-attacks-in-europe-from-paris-to-oslo

34. "London Van Attack: Suspect Identified, Arrested in Terror Investigation," *Fox News,* June 19, 2017 (accessed June 19, 2017), http://www.foxnews.com/world/2017/06/19/london-van-attack-suspect-identified-arrested-in-terror-

35. Mohammed Al-Kathiri, *The Salafis: Between the Sunnis and Shiites* (Beirut: Al-Ghadeer, 2008), 9.

36. Mohammed Nima al-Simawi, *Wahhabi Project to Obliterate Islamic Artifacts and Antiquities* (in Arabic) (USA: Dar al-Kutub, 2015), 15.

37. "Stops in the Life of Shaikh Mohammed Bin Salih al-Athaimeen." *Saaid* (accessed August 30, 2016), www.saaid.net

38. Mohammed bin Salih al-Athaimeen, Do Shiites Considered as Infidels? *Islam Way* (accessed August 30, 2016), http://ar.islamway.net/fatwa/13964/%D9%87%D9%84-%D9%8A%D8%B9%D8%AA%D8%A8%D8%B1-%D8%A7%D9%84%D8%B4%D9%8A%D8%B9%D8%A9-%D9%81%D9%8A-%D8%AD%D9%83%D9%85-%D8%A7%D9%84%D9%83%D9%81%D8%A7%D8%B1

39. Mutafa Al-Shakaa, *Islam without Sects* (in Arabic) (Cairo: Al-Dar Al-Masriya, 1991), 80.

40. Paul Bremer, *My Year in Iraq* (New York: Simon and Schuster, 2006), 312.

41. Martin Chulov, "Dozens of Iraqis Killed as Isis Targets Baghdad during Ramadan," *Guardian,* May 30, 2017 (accessed June 28, 2017), https://www.theguardian.com/world/2017/may/30/baghdad-ice-cream-shop-isis-car-bomb-attack

42. "Al-Qaeda: Declarations & Acts of War," *The Heritage Foundation* (accessed August 30, 2016), http://www.heritage.org/research/projects/enemy-detention/al-qaeda-declarations

43. Ibid.

44. Cockburn, *The Rise of the Islamic State: ISIS and the Sunni Revolution*, 32.

45. "The Mufti of Saudi Arabia" Says "Yazid's Caliphate Is Legitimate and Hussein Was Wrong" *Youtube*, February 4, 2009 (accessed August 30, 2016), https://www.youtube.com/watch?v=v0Yoeg7k1s4

CHAPTER 14

1. Scott Stewart, "AQAP: Paradigm Shifts and Lessons Learned," *Stratfor*, September 2, 2009 (accessed September 23, 2016), https://www.stratfor.com/weekly/20090902_aqap_paradigm_shifts_and_lessons_learned

2. Stewart, "AQAP: Paradigm Shifts and Lessons Learned."

3. Rebecca Evans, "Devices That Can be Sewn into the Body and Are Virtually Undetectable," *Daily Mail*, July 3, 2014 (accessed September 24, 2016), http://www.dailymail.co.uk/news/article-2680052/Master-explosives-turned-brother-bomb-Evil-genius-created-devices-sewn-body-virtually-undetectable.html

4. Sudarsan Raghavan and Peter Finn, "Al-Qaeda Bombmaker Ibrahim Hassan al-Asiri Has Tried to Attack the U.S. Three Times, Officials Say," *Washington Post*, May 8, 2012 (accessed September 24, 2016), https://www.washingtonpost.com/world/middle_east/al-qaeda-bomb-maker-ibrahim-hassan-al-asiri-has-tried-to-attack-the-us-three-times-officials-say/2012/05/08/gIQA16pkBU_story.html

5. Michael Slackman, "Would-Be Killer Linked to Al Qaeda, Saudis Say," *New York Times*, August 28, 2009 (accessed September 23, 2016), http://www.nytimes.com/2009/08/29/world/middleeast/29saudi.html

6. Stewart, "AQAP: Paradigm Shifts and Lessons Learned."

7. Raghavan and Finn, "Al-Qaeda Bombmaker Ibrahim Hassan Al-Asiri Has Tried to Attack the U.S. Three Times."

8. "Underwear Bomber Plot Failed Because He 'Wore Same Pants for Two Weeks'," *Telegraph*, July 25, 2014 (accessed September 24, 2016), http://www.telegraph.co.uk/news/worldnews/al-qaeda/10989843/Underwear-bomber-plot-failed-because-he-wore-same-pants-for-two-weeks.html

9. Khaled Wassef, "Timeline of Yemen Bomb Plot," *CBS News*, October 30, 2010 (accessed September 24, 2016), http://www.cbsnews.com/news/timeline-of-yemen-bomb-plot/

10. Raghavan and Finn, "Al-Qaeda Bombmaker Ibrahim Hassan al-Asiri Has Tried to Attack the U.S. Three Times."

11. Paul Harris and Ed Pilkington, "'Underwear Bomber' Was Working for the CIA," *Guardian*, May 9, 2012 (accessed September 24, 2016), https://www.theguardian.com/world/2012/may/09/underwear-bomber-working-for-cia

12. Michael Burleigh, "Nightmare with Terrorists with Bombs Surgically Implanted INSIDE Their Bodies," *Daily Mail*, August 9, 2013 (accessed September 24, 2016), http://www.dailymail.co.uk/news/article-2387332/Nightmare-terrorists-bombs-surgically-implanted-INSIDE-bodies.html

13. Brian Ross, "Al Qaeda 'Belly Bombs' Entirely Possible, Doctor Says," *ABC News*, July 6, 2011 (accessed September 24, 2016, http://abcnews.go.com/Blotter/us-al-qaeda-designing-belly-bombs-beat-airbort/story?id=14008049

14. Burleigh, "Nightmare with Terrorists with Bombs Surgically Implanted INSIDE Their Bodies."

15. Ibid.

16. "West's Action in Libya in 2011 Was a 'Mistake'—Italy's Foreign Ministry," *RT*, December 5, 2014 (accessed September 24, 2016), https://www.rt.com/news/211883-italy-libya-conflict-mistake/

17. "Declan Walsh Ben Hubbard and Eric Schmitt," "U.S. Bombing in Libya Reveals Limits of Strategy against ISIS," *New York Times*, February 19, 2016 (accessed September 24, 2016), http://www.nytimes.com/2016/02/20/world/middleeast/us-airstrike-isis-libya.html?_r=0

18. Dugald McConnell and Brian Todd, "Al Qaeda Branch Calls for New Attacks against United States," *CNN*, August 5, 2015 (accessed September 22, 2016), http://www.cnn.com/2015/08/04/middleeast/al-qaeda-branch-yemen-united-sta

19. "Greg Gutfeld: Stop Calling Them 'Lone Wolves'," *Fox News*, October 27, 2014 (accessed September 22, 2016), http://www.foxnews.com/on-air/the-five/article/2014/10/27/gutfeld-stop-calling-them-lone-wolves

20. Emma Graham-Harrison, "Could ISIS's 'Cyber Caliphate' Unleash a Deadly Attack on Key Targets?" *Guardian*, June 14, 2016 (accessed September 27, 2016), https://www.theguardian.com/world/2015/apr/12/isis-cyber-caliphate-hacking-technology-arms-race

21. Ibid.

22. Jason Stapleton, Jason Rips Centcom over Social Media Hack, *YouTube*, January 13, 2015 (accessed September 27, 2016), https://www.youtube.com/watch?v=TuhOR8kYUV0

23. Ibid.

24. Dan Lohrmann, "Cyber Terrorism: How Dangerous Is the ISIS Cyber Caliphate Threat?" *Government Technology*, May 18, 2015 (accessed September 27,

2016), http://www.govtech.com/blogs/lohrmann-on-cybersecurity/Cyber-Ter
rorism-How-Dangerous-is-the-ISIS-Cyber-Caliphate-Threat.html

25. Pierluigi Paganini, "Analyzing Cyber Capabilities of the ISIS," *Security Affairs*, April 30, 2016 (accessed September 27, 2016), http://securityaffairs.co/wordpress/46831/terrorism/report-cyber-capability-evaluation-isis.html

26. Lohrmann, "Cyber Terrorism: How Dangerous Is the ISIS Cyber Caliphate Threat?"

27. Ibid.

28. Graham-Harrison, "Could ISIS'S 'Cyber Caliphate' Unleash a Deadly Attack on Key Targets?"

29. John P. Mello, "ISIS Cyberthreat: Puny but Gaining Power," *Tech News World*, May 5, 2016 (accessed on September 27, 2016), http://www.technews world.com/story/83468.html

30. Joseph Marks, "ISIL Aims to Launch Cyberattacks on U.S.," *Politico Magazine*, December 29, 2015 (accessed September 27, 2016), http://www.politico.com/story/2015/12/isil-terrorism-cyber-attacks-217179

31. Jeff Peters, "Talking Cyber-Terrorism and ISIS with Morgan Wright," *Surf Watch Labs*, April 13, 2016 (accessed September 27, 2016), https://blog.surfwatch labs.com/2016/04/13/talking-cyber-terrorism-and-isis-with-morgan-wright/

32. Ibid.

33. Marks, "ISIL Aims to Launch Cyberattacks on U.S."

34. Ibid.

35. Mello, "ISIS Cyberthreat: Puny but Gaining Power."

36. Marks, "ISIL Aims to Launch Cyberattacks on U.S."

37. Ibid.

38. "ISIL-Linked Kosovo Hacker Sentenced to 20 Years in Prison," *Justice Department* (accessed September 23, 2016), https://www.justice.gov/opa/pr/isil-linked-kosovo-hacker-sentenced-20-years-prison

39. Iuana Pascu, "ISIS Supporter Gets 20 Years for Cyber Terrorism," *Hot for Security* (accessed September 27, 2016), https://www.hotforsecurity.com/blog/isis-supporter-gets-20-years-for-cyber-terrorism-16738.html

40. Ibid.

41. "ISIL-Linked Kosovo Hacker Sentenced to 20 Years in Prison."

CHAPTER 15

1. "June 28: Military Airstrikes Continue against ISIS Terrorists in Syria and Iraq, U.S. Central Command," Release No: 17-245, June 28, 2017 (accessed June 28, 2017), http://www.centcom.mil/MEDIA/PRESS-RELEASES/Press-Release-View/Article/1231343/june-28-military-airstrikes-continue-against-isis-terrorists-in-syria-and-iraq/

2. Jane Mayer, "The Search for Osama, Did the Government Let bin Laden's Trail Go Cold?" *New Yorker*, August 4, 2003 (accessed February 28, 2017), http://www.newyorker.com/magazine/2003/08/04/the-search-for-osama

Selected Bibliography

Abdul-Ahad, Ghaith. "Syria: The Foreign Fighters Joining the War against Bashar al-Assad." *Guardian*. September 23, 2012. https://www.theguardian.com/world/2012/sep/23/syria-foreign-fighters-joining-war (accessed October 1, 2016).

Ahmed, Mubaraz. "How the New York Bombing Suspect Was Radicalised Online by a Man Who Had Been Dead for Five Years." *The Independent*. September 22, 2016. http://www.independent.co.uk/voices/new-york-new-jersey-bomb-suspect-ahmad-khan-rahami-islamist-terrorism-radicalised-online-dead-man-a7323406.html (accessed November 27, 2016).

Ahmed, Saeed, and Greg Botelho. "Who Is Michael Zehaf-Bibeau, the Man Behind the Deadly Ottawa Attack?" *CNN*. October 23, 2014. http://www.cnn.com/2014/10/22/world/canada-shooter/ (accessed September 28, 2016).

Al-Bayati, Hamid. *Terrorism Game*. London: Al-Rafid, 2001.

Al-Bayati, Hamid. *Terrorism in Iraq*. Baghdad: Iraqi Center for Strategic Studies, 2005.

Al-Bayati, Hamid. *From Dictatorship to Democracy: An Insider's Account of the Iraqi Opposition to Saddam*. Philadephia: University of Pennsylvania Press, 2011.

Al-Hashimi, Hisham. *ISIL World: The Islamic State in Iraq and the Levant* (in Arabic). London: Dar al-Hikma, 2015.

Al-Hashimi, Hisham. *ISIL Organization from Inside* (in Arabic). London: Dar Al-Hikma, 2016.

Al-Kathiri, Mohammed. *The Salafis: Between the Sunnis and Shiites* (in Arabic). Beirut: Al-Ghadeer, 2008.

Al-Khatteeb, Lucy. "Will U.S. Strikes Hurt ISIS' Oil Riches?" *CNN*. September 25, 2014. http://www.cnn.com/2014/09/22/business/isis-oil-luay-al-khatteeb/ (accessed November 5, 2015).

Alkhshali, Hamdi, and Laura Smith-Spark. "Alkhshali, Hamdi, and Laura Smith-spark. Iraq: ISIS Fighters Close Ramadi Dam Gates." *CNN*. June 4, 2015. http://www.cnn.com/2015/06/04/middleeast/iraq-isis-ramadi/ (accessed November 5, 2016).

Al-Maliki, Hasan Farhan. *The Roots of ISIL/ISIS: A Reading in the Heritage of Wahhabism and Saudi Scholars* (in Arabic). Beirut: Dar Al-Mahajja, 2014.

Almukhtar, Sarah. "ISIS Finances Are Strong." *New York Times*. May 18, 2015. http://www.nytimes.com/interactive/2015/05/19/world/middleeast/isis-finances.html (accessed November 1, 2016).

Al-Oamr, Mohammed. *The Legend of ISIS: The Caliphates Terrorism and the Corridors of Fund* (in Arabic). Dubai: Madarek, 2014.

Al-Shakaa, Mustafa. *Islam without Sects* (in Arabic). Cairo: Al-Dar Al-Masriya, 1991.

Al-Simawi, Mohammed Nima. *Wahhabi Project to Obliterate Islamic Artifacts and Antiquities* (in Arabic). USA: Dar al-Kutub, 2015.

Alwash, Mohammed. *ISIL/ISIS and Its Sisters, from al-Qaeda to Islamic State* (in Arabic). Beirut: Riad el-Rayyes Books, 2015.

Andelman, David A. "Lone Wolves Are a Global Dilemma." *USA Today*. June 16, 2016. http://www.usatoday.com/story/opinion/2016/06/15/lone-wolves-terrorism-orlando-france-islamic-state-trump-andelman-column/85921600/ (accessed September 8, 2016).

Arango, Tim, and Eric Schmitt. "A Path to ISIS, Through a Porous Turkish Border." *New York Times*. March 9, 2015 (accessed November 13, 2016).

Asseri, Ali S. Awadh. *Combating Terrorism: Saudi Arabia's Role in the War on Terror*. New York: Oxford University Press, 2009.

Atkinson, Khorri. "GOP Blocks Bill to Stop Terrorists from Buying Guns." *MSNBC*. December 4, 2015. http://www.msnbc.com/msnbc/gop-blocks-bill-stop-terrorists-buying-guns (accessed October 3, 2016).

Atwan, Abdul Bari. *ISIL, Roots, Savagery, and Future*. Beirut: Dar Al-Saqi, 2015.

Baker, Peter, and Eric Schmitt. "California Attack Has U.S. Rethinking Strategy on Homegrown Terror." *New York Times*. December 5, 2015. http://www.nytimes.com/2015/12/06/us/politics/california-attack-has-us-rethinking-strategy-on-homegrown-terror.html?emc=edit_th_20151206&nl=todayshe adlines&nlid=68648138&_r=0 (accessed September 8, 2016).

Bakker, Edwin, and Beatrice Graff. "Preventing Lone Wolf Terrorism: Some CT Approaches Addressed." *Terrorism Analysts*. 2011. http://www.terrorismanalysts.com/pt/index.php/pot/article/view/preventing-lone-wolf/html (accessed September 13, 2016).

Barrett, Devlin, and Damian Paletta. "Top U.S. Officials to Meet with Tech CEOs on Terror Concerns." *Wall Street Journal*. January 7, 2016. http://www.wsj.com/articles/top-u-s-officials-to-meet-with-tech-ceos-on-terror-concerns-1452195796 (accessed September 15, 2016).

Barron, James, and Sabrina Tavernise. "Money Woes, Long Silences and a Zeal for Islam." *New York Times*. May 5, 2010. http://www.nytimes.com/2010/05/06/nyregion/06profile.html?_r=0 (accessed September 6, 2016).

Bender, Jeremy. "ISIS Is Turning Food and Water into a Weapon in Iraq." *Business Insider*. August 15, 2014. http://www.businessinsider.com/isis-has-two-major-weapons-in-iraq-2014-8 (accessed November 3, 2016).

Bergen, Peter L. *Did Barack Obama and Hillary Clinton create ISIS?* January 4, 2016. http://www.cnn.com/2016/01/04/opinions/bergen-trump-obama-clinton-creation-of-isis/index.html.

Bergen, Peter L. *The Longest War: The Enduring Conflict between America and Al-Qaeda.* New York: Free Press, 2011.

Bergen, Peter L. *Manhunt: The Ten-year Search for Bin Laden: From 9/11 to Abbottabad.* New York: Crown, 2012.

Blair, David. "Qatar and Saudi Arabia 'Have Ignited Time Bomb by Funding Global Spread of Radical Islam'." *Telegraph.* October 4, 2014. http://www.telegraph.co.uk/news/worldnews/middleeast/iraq/11140860/Qatar-and-Saudi-Arabia-have-ignited-time-bomb-by-funding-global-spread-of-radical-Islam.html (accessed October 29, 2016).

Blair, David, and Richard Spencer. "How Qatar Is Funding the Rise of Islamist Extremists." *Telegraph.* September 20, 2014. http://www.telegraph.co.uk/news/worldnews/middleeast/qatar/11110931/How-Qatar-is-funding-the-rise-of-Islamist-extremists.html (accessed October 29, 2016).

Blair, Tony. *A Journey: My Political Life, Alfred.* New York: A. Knopf, 2010.

Bora, Kukil. "Terrorist Groups Like ISIS, Al Qaeda Attract More Than 25,000 Foreign Fighters: UN Report." *International Business Times.* April 2, 2015. Http://Www.Ibtimes.Com/Terrorist-Groups-Isis-Al-Qaeda-Attract-More-25000-Foreign-Fighters-Un-Report-1867392 (accessed November 13, 2016).

Bremer, Paul L. *My Year in Iraq: The Struggle to Build a Future of Hope.* New York: Simon and Schuster, 2006.

Brodkin, Jon. "Terrorists Are Using the Internet Against Us, Lawmaker Says." *ARS Technica.* November 17, 2015. Http://Arstechnica.Com/Tech-Policy/2015/11/Congressman-To-Stop-Isis-Lets-Shut-Down-Websites-And-Social-Media/ (accessed November 21, 2916).

Brown, Kristen V. "How Did ISIS Radicalize the Orlando Shooter?" *Fusion.* June 13, 2016. http://fusion.net/story/313671/orlando-nightclub-shooting-omar-mateen-isis-internet-radicalization/ (accessed September 5, 2016).

Brown, Pamela, Evan Perez, Holly Yan, and Joe Sterling. "Sources: Grand Jury to Investigate Orlando Shooter's Widow." *CNN.* June 16, 2016. http://www.cnn.com/2016/06/15/us/orlando-shooter-omar-mateen/ (accessed September 2, 2016).

Buchanan, Larry, and Haeyoun Park. "Uncovering the Links between the Brussels and Paris Attackers." *New York Times.* April 9, 2016. http://www.nytimes.com/interactive/2016/03/23/world/europe/how-the-brussels-and-paris-attackers-could-be-connected.html (accessed September 28, 2016).

Burr, Edmondo. "Google to Show Wrong Search Results to Combat Terrorism." *Your News Wire.* February, 3, 2016. http://yournewswire.com/google-to-show-wrong-search-results-to-combat-terrorism/ (accessed September 15, 2016).

Burton, Fred, and Scott Stewart. "The 'Lone Wolf' Disconnect." *Security Weekly.* January 30, 2008 (accessed September 15, 2016).

Bush, George W. *Decisions Points.* New York: Crowns Publishers, 2010.

Byman, Daniel. "Omar Mateen, Lone-Wolf Terrorist." *Slate.* June 2016 (accessed September 8, 2016).

Byrd, Norman. "Are ISIS Foreign Fighters Terrorist Time Bombs? Chilling Report Says 30 Percent Are Already Home from the Middle East." *Inquisitr.* August 24, 2016. http://www.inquisitr.com/3450236/isis-foreign-fighters-going-home-30-percent-have-already-returned-some-30000-still-fighting/http://www.inquisitr.com/3450236/isis-foreign-fighters-going-hohttp://www.inquisitr.com/3450236/isis-foreign-fighters-going-home-3 (accessed November 7, 2016).

Callimachi, Rukmini. "Paying Ransoms, Europe Bankrolls Qaeda Terror." *New York Times.* July 29, 2014. http://www.nytimes.com/2014/07/30/world/africa/ransoming-citizens-europe-becomes-al-qaedas-patron.html (accessed November 3, 2016).

Charles River. *The Islamic State of Iraq and Syria: The History of ISIS/ISIL.* Charles River Editors, USA. n.d.

Chotinerm, Isaac. "A Lone-Wolf Terrorist Is Never Quite Alone." *Slate.* June 2016. http://www.slate.com/articles/news_and_politics/interrogation/2016/06/why_isis_loves_lone_wolf_terrorists.html (accessed September 15, 2016).

Chulov, Martin. "Amid the Ruins of Syria, Is Bashar al-Assad Now Finally Facing the End?" *Guardian.* May 23, 2015. http://www.theguardian.com/world/2015/may/24/syria-iran-isis-battle-arab-world (accessed October 18, 2016).

Clement, Scott. "Americans Doubt U.S. Can Stop 'Lone Wolf' Attacks, Poll Finds." *Washington Post.* December 16, 2015. https://www.washingtonpost.com/politics/americans-doubt-us-can-stop-lone-wolf-attacks-poll-finds/2015/12/16/bfcaa102-a3ba-11e5-ad3f-991ce3374e23_story.html (accessed September 14, 2016).

Cockburn, Patrick. "Iraq Crisis: How Saudi Arabia Helped ISIS Take over the North of the Country." *The Independent.* July 12, 2014. http://www.independent.co.uk/voices/comment/iraq-crisis-how-saudi-arabia-helped-isis-take-over-the-north-of-the-country-9602312.html (accessed September 30, 2016).

Cockburn, Patrick. *The Rise of Islamic State: ISIS and the New Sunni Revolution.* London: Verso, 2015.

Coldewey, Devin. "Manhattan DA Pushes for Lawful Backdoor into Encrypted Phones." *NBC News.* November 18, 2015 (accessed September 15, 2016).

Cooper, Helene. "Obama Requests Money to Train 'Appropriately Vetted' Syrian Rebels." *NYT.* June 26, 2014. http://www.nytimes.com/2014/06/27/world/middleeast/obama-seeks-500-million-to-train-and-equip-syrian-opposition.html?_r=0 (accessed October 29, 2016).

Crone, Jack. "2,000-Year-Old Artefacts Looted by ISIS from Ancient Sites in Iraq and Syria Are Being Sold on Ebay." *Daily Mail.* March 14, 2015. http://www.dailymail.co.uk/news/article-2994538/2-000-year-old-artefacts-looted-ISIS-ancient-sites-Iraq-Syria-sold-EBAY.html (accessed October 29, 2016).

Crotti, Nanct, and Larry McShane. "Why Radical Jihadists Are Cropping Up in Minnesota, Leaving to Join Terrorist Groups." *New York Daily News.* August 30, 2014. http://www.nydailynews.com/news/national/jihadi-fiends-grow-minnesota-article-1.1922724 (accessed September 5, 2016).

Curtis, Lisa, et al. "Combatting the ISIS Foreign Fighter Pipeline: A Global Approach." *Heritage.* January 6, 2016. http://www.heritage.org/research/reports/2016/01/combatting-the-isis-foreign-fighter-pipeline-a-global-approach (accessed November 14, 2016).

Dakss, Brian. "Another Al Qaeda Big Arrested." *CBS News*. March 15, 2003. http://www.cbsnews.com/news/another-al-qaeda-big-arrested/ (accessed October 24, 2016).

Daloglu, Tulin. "Biden's Apology Hides the Truth, Joe Biden's Technically Apologies to Recep Tayyip Erdogan, but Didn't Deny the Merits of What He Said." *US News*. October 4, 2014. http://www.usnews.com/news/articles/2014/10/07/bidens-apology-hides-the-truth (accessed September 7, 2016).

DePalma, Donald A. "FBI Still Lagging on Translation to Thwart Terrorists." *Common Sense Advisory*. October 20, 2009 (accessed September 20, 2016).

Dettmer, Jamie. "Fumbles, Mistakes Prompt Talk of Major French Intelligence Failure." *VOA News*. November 17, 2015. http://www.voanews.com/content/fumbles-mistakes-prompt-talk-of-major-french-intelligence-failure/3061990.html (accessed September 3, 2016).

Devost, Matthew, Brian Houghton, and Pollard Neal. "Information Terrorism: Can You Trust Your Toaster?" *The Terrorism Research Center*. April 1996. https://www.devost.net/papers/suntzu.pdf (accessed September 11, 2016).

Downing, Michael P., and Matt A. Mayer. "Preventing the Next 'Lone Wolf' Terrorist Attack Requires Stronger Federal–State–Local Capabilities." *Heritage Foundation*. June 18, 2013 (accessed October 12, 2016).

Druzhinin, Alexi. "Putin: ISIS Financed from 40 Countries, Including G20 Members." *RT*. November 16, 2015. https://www.rt.com/news/322305-isis-financed-40-countries/ (accessed October 21, 2016).

Durante, Thomas. "Home-Made Devices in Boston Marathon Attack Were Made from Pressure Cooker Bombs—Al Qaeda's 'Most Effective Weapon'—and Featured in Terror Guide 'Make a Bomb in the Kitchen of Your Mom'." *Daily Mail*. April 16, 2013. http://www.dailymail.co.uk/news/article-2309728/Boston-Marathon-2013-explosions-Home-bombs-pressure-cookers.html (accessed November 19, 2016).

Durden, Tyler. "How Turkey Exports ISIS Oil to the World." *The Scientific Evidence*. November 28, 2015. http://www.zerohedge.com/news/2015-11-27/how-turkey-exports-isis-oil-world-scientific-evidenceTwitterFacebookReddit (accessed October 29, 2016).

Ehrenfeld, Rachel. "Drug Trafficking, Kidnapping Fund Al Qaeda." *CNN*. May 4, 2011. http://www.cnn.com/2011/OPINION/05/03/ehrenfeld.al.qaeda.funding/ (accessed November 4, 2016).

Ehrenfeld, Rachel. *Funding Evil: How Terrorism is financed—And How to Stop It*. Chicago: Bonus Books, 2003.

Engel, Pamela. "ISIS Has Mastered a Crucial Recruiting Tactic No Terrorist Group Has Ever Conquered." *Business Insider*. May 9, 2015. http://www.businessinsider.com/isis-is-revolutionizing-international-terrorism-2015-5 (accessed September 29, 2016).

Entous, Adam. "Covert CIA Mission to Arm Syrian Rebels Goes Awry." *Wall Street Journal*. January 26, 2015. http://www.wsj.com/articles/covert-cia-mission-to-arm-syrian-rebels-goes-awry-1422329582 (accessed October 21, 2016).

Fanz, Ashley. "How ISIS Makes (and Takes) Money." *CNN*. February 19, 2015. http://www.cnn.com/2015/02/19/world/how-isis-makes-money/index.html (accessed November 2, 2016).

Farahm, Douglas. "How to Stop Terrorism Financing." *Islam Daily.* October 12, 2005. http://islamdaily.org/en/charities/3567.how-to-stop-terrorism-financing .htm (accessed October 19, 2016).

Farivar, Masood. "The Foreign Fighters and Me." *New York Times.* April 1, 2014. http://www.nytimes.com/2014/04/02/opinion/the-foreign-fighters-and-me.html?_r=0 (accessed October 1, 2016).

Fausset, Richard, Alan Blinder, and Michael S. Schmidt. "Gunman Kills 4 Marines at Military Site in Chattanooga." *New York Times.* July 16, 2015. http://www .nytimes.com/2015/07/17/us/chattanooga-tennessee-shooting.html (accessed September 9, 2016).

Feith, Douglas J. *War and Decision: Inside the Pentagon at the Dawn of the War on Terrorism.* New York: HarperCollins Books, 2008.

Filkins, Dexter. "The Fight of Their Lives, the White House Wants the Kurds to Help Save Iraq from ISIS." *New Yorker.* September 29, 2014. http://www .newyorker.com/magazine/2014/09/29/fight-lives (accessed October 24, 2016).

Flynn, Michael T. "Statement before Senate Armed Services Committee." *Defence Intelligence Agency.* February 11, 2014. http://www.armed-services.senate .gov/imo/media/doc/Flynn_02-11-14.pdf (accessed October 2016).

Francesscani, Chris, and Robert Windom. "Foreign Fighters Pouring into Syria Faster Than Ever, Say Officials." *NBC News.* October 29, 2014. http://www .nbcnews.com/storyline/isis-terror/foreign-fighters-pouring-syria-faster-ever-say-officials-n236546 (accessed October 1, 2016).

Freeman, Will. "How ISIS Is Making a Fortune on the Black Market for Ancient Artifacts." *ThinkProgress.* July 10, 2014. https://thinkprogress.org/how-isis-is-making-a-fortune-on-the-black-market-for-ancient-artifacts-4d9168805 ef7#.xt9k7e4hk (accessed October 29, 2016).

Galbriath, Peter W. *The End of Iraq: How American Incompetence Created a War without End.* New York: Simon and Schuster, 2007.

Gander, Kashmira. "ISIS Hostage Threat: Which Countries Pay Ransoms to Release Their Citizens?" *Independent Digital News and Media.* September 3, 2014. http://www.independent.co.uk/news/world/politics/isis-hostage-threat-which-countries-pay-ransoms-to-release-their-citizens-9710129.html (accessed November 3, 2016).

Gillin, Joshua. "Obama Refused to Sign Plan in Place to Leave 10,000 Troops in Iraq, Bush Says." *politifact.* May 18, 2015. http://www.com/truth-o-meter/ statements/2015/may/18/jeb-bush/obama-refused-sign-plan-place-leave-10000-troops-i/ (accessed October 20, 2016).

Gilsinan, Kathy. "ISIS and the 'Internet Radicalization' Trope." *The Atlantic.* December 8, 2015. http://www.theatlantic.com/international/archive/2015/12/ isis-internet-radicalization/419148/ (accessed September 5, 2016).

Goldman, Adam. "FBI Adapts to Face Terrorism Threats but Still Faces Challenges, Report Finds." *Washington Post.* March 25, 2015. https://www.washington post.com/world/national-security/fbi-adapts-to-face-terrorism-threats-but-still-faces-challenges-report-finds/2015/03/25/9af5d042-d2d5-11e4-8fce-3941fc548f1c_story.html (accessed November 23, 2016).

Goldman, Julianna. "ISIS Recruits Fighters through Powerful Online Campaign." *CBSNews.* August 29, 2014. http://www.cbsnews.com/news/isis-uses-social-media-to-recruit-western-allies/.

Gollom, Mark, and Tracey Lindeman. "Who Is Martin Couture-Rouleau?" *CBS News*. October 22, 2014. http://www.cbc.ca/news/canada/who-is-martin-couture-rouleau-1.2807285 (accessed November 12, 2016).

Gomez, David. "The Myth of the Big Bad Lone Wolf." *The Foreign Policy*. October 25, 2014. http://foreignpolicy.com/2014/10/25/the-myth-of-the-big-bad-lone-wolf/ (accessed September 7, 2016).

Gómez, Juan Miguel del Cid. "A Financial Profile of the Terrorism of Al-Qaeda and Its Affiliates." *Terrorism Analysts*. November 4, 2010 (accessed Noevmber 4, 2016).

Grass, S. M. "Understanding and Combating Terrorism." *Global Security*. 1989. http://www.globalsecurity.org/military/library/report/1989/GSM.htm.

Greenfield, Daniel. "Somali Migrants in Minnesota Are a Terror Threat to the Mall of America." *Front Page Magazine*. February 22, 2015 (accessed September 2, 2015).

Gutfeld, Greg. "Stop Calling Them 'Lone Wolves'." *FOX News*. October 27, 2014. http://www.foxnews.com/on-air/the-five/article/2014/10/27/gutfeld-stop-calling-them-lone-wolves (accessed September 16, 2016).

Hamada, Nidhal. *Secrets and mysterious of ISIL: From Osama Bian Laden's Turban to Saddam Hussein Hat* (in Arabic). Beirut: Bissan publishers, 2015.

Hamburger, Tom, and Kevin Sieff. "Joy about Bergdahl Release Gives Way to Questions." *Washington Post*. June 1, 2014. https://www.washingtonpost.com/world/national-security/hagel-discusses-details-of-us-operation-to-exchange (accessed October 25, 2016).

Hashim, Mohanad. "Iraq and Syria: Who Are the Foreign Fighters?" *BBC Monitoring*. September 3, 2014. http://www.bbc.com/news/world-middle-east-29043331 (accessed November 5, 2016).

Hazelton, Fran (ed.). *Iraq Since the Gulf War, Prospects for Democracy*. London: Zed Books, 1994.

Higham, Scott, and Ellen Nakashima. "Why the Islamic State Leaves Tech Companies Torn between Free Speech and Security." *Washington Post*. September 15, 2016. https://www.washingtonpost.com/world/national-security/islamic-states-embrace-of-social-media-puts-tech-companies-in-a-bind/2015/07/15/0e5624c4-169c-11e5-89f3-61410da94eb1_story.html?kmap=1 (accessed September 30, 2016).

Hill, Kashmir. "Let's Stop Blaming 'the Internet' for Terrorism." *Huffington Post*. December 14, 2015. http://www.huffingtonpost.com/entry/internet-terrorism_us_566ed1dee4b0fccee16f1960 (accessed August 23, 2016).

Hinnant, Lori. "France-Stopping the Wolves Sory." *Associated Press*. August 29, 2015 (accessed September 9, 2016).

Hohmann, Leo. "U.S. Government 'Breeding Terrorists'—In Minnesota." *WND*. September 4, 2014. http://www.wnd.com/2014/09/u-s-government-breeding-terrorists-in-minnesota/#! (accessed September 28, 2016).

Hsu, Spencer S. "Hasan's Ties to Radical Imam Raise Questions of 'Self-Radicalization'." *Washington Post*. November 18, 2009. http://www.washingtonpost.com/wp-dyn/content/article/2009/11/17/AR2009111703830.html (accessed November 6, 2016).

Ibrahim, Foaud. *ISIL: From Najdi to Baghdadi* (in Arabic). Beirut: Awal Center, 2015.

Jeffery, James Franklin. "Behind the U.S. Withdrawal from Iraq, Negotiations Were Repeatedly Disrupted by Obama White House Staffers' Inaccurate Public

Statements." *Wall Street Journal.* November 2, 2014. http://www.wsj.com/articles/james-franklin-jeffrey-behind-the-u-s-withdrawal-from-iraq-1414 972705.

Johnson, Kevin, Tariq Zehawi, and Andrew Wyrich. "Ahmad Rahami's Dad Accused Son of Being a Terrorist in 2014." *USA Today.* September 20, 2016. http://www.usatoday.com/story/news/nation/2016/09/20/ahmad-rahamis-dad-accused-son-being-terrorist-2014/90734892/ (accessed September 29, 2016).

Johnston, David, and Scott Shane. "U.S. Knew of Suspect's Tie to Radical Cleric." *New York Times.* November 9, 2009. http://www.nytimes.com/2009/11/10/us/10inquire.html?_r=0 (accessed September 9, 2016).

Jones, Christopher. "In Battle against ISIS, Saving Lives or Ancient Artifacts." *Hyperallergic.* April 17, 2015. http://hyperallergic.com/200005/in-battle-against-isis-saving-lives-or-ancient-artifacts/ (accessed October 29, 2016).

Jones, Sam, Zalewski Piotr, and Erika Solomon. "ISIS Sells Smuggled Oil to Turkey and Iraqi Kurds, Says US Treasury." *Financial Times.* October 23, 2014. https://www.ft.com/content/6c269c4e-5ace-11e4-b449-00144feab7de (accessed October 29, 2016).

Joscelyn, Thomas. "Islamist Foreign Fighters Returning Home and the Threat to Europe." *Long War Journal.* September 19, 2014. http://www.longwarjournal.org/archives/2014/09/islamist_foreign_fig.php (accessed November 6, 2016).

Kamalipour, Yahya R. and Nancy Snow (eds.). *War, Media, and Propaganda.* Maryland: Rowan & Littlefield Publishers, 2004.

Kaplan, Eben. "Terrorist and the Internet, Council on Foreign Relations." *Council on Foreign Relations.* January 8, 2009 (accessed September 2016).

Keatinge, Tom. "Rampant Ransoms." *Foreign Affairs.* January 26, 2015. https://www.foreignaffairs.com/articles/middle-east/2015-01-26/rampant-ransoms (accessed November 2016).

Kelley, Michale B. "Obama Now Owns a War He Helped Create." *Business Insider.* September 11, 2014. http://www.businessinsider.com/issues-with-obamas-war-on-isis-2014-9#ixzz3FeEdugHZ (accessed October 18, 2016).

Krauthammer, Charles. "How to Stop a Lone Terrorist." *Washington Post.* December 22, 2014. http://www.detroitnews.com/story/opinion/columnists/charles-krauthammer/2014/12/22/stop-lone-terrorist/20660719/ (accessed September 15, 2016).

Kumar, Anita. "US to Allow Families of Hostages to Pay Ransom, but Government Will Not Do It." *RT.* June 24, 2015. https://www.rt.com/usa/269473-obama-hostages-ransom-pay/ (accessed October 29, 2016).

Kuriansky, J. *Beyond Bullets and Bombs: Grassroots Peacebuilding between Israelis and Palestinians.* Westport, CT: Praeger Press, 2007.

Lake, Eli. "Why the White House Ignored All Those Warnings about ISIS." *Daily Beast.* July 6, 2014. http://www.thedailybeast.com/articles/2014/07/06/why-the-white-house-ignored-all-those-warnings-about-isis.html (accessed October 2016).

"Lawmakers Reflect on How to Stop Lone Wolf Terror Attacks." *Sinclair Broadcast Group.* June 13, 2016. http://wjla.com/news/nation-world/lawmakers-reflect-on-how-to-stop-lone-wolf-terror-attacks (accessed October 20, 2016).

Leung, Wency. "NY Restaurant Serves Food on Saddam Hussein's Plates: Would You Eat Off Them?" *The Globe and Mail.* October 7, 2011. http://www.the

globeandmail.com/life/the-hot-button/ny-restaurant-serves-food-on-saddam-husseins-plates-would-you-eat-off-them/article618133/ (accessed October 29, 2016).

Levitt, Matthew. "Foreign Fighters and Their Economic Impact: A Case Study of Syria and Al-Qaeda in Iraq (AQI)." *Terrorism Research Institute.* 2009 (accessed November 13, 2016).

Levitt, Matthew, and Sam Cutler. "UN Promotes Splitting the Taliban from al-Qaeda." *Washington Institute.* June 27, 2011. http://www.washingtoninsti tute.org/policy-analysis/view/un-promotes-splitting-the-taliban-from-al-qaeda (accessed October 24, 2016).

Liptak, Kevin. "How Could Obama Have 'Underestimated' ISIS?" *CNN.* September 30, 2014. http://www.cnn.com/2014/09/29/politics/obama-underes timates-isis/ (accessed October 23, 2016).

Lister, Tim. "How Do We Stop 'Lone Wolf' Attacks?" *CNN.* October 27, 2016. http://www.cnn.com/2014/10/27/world/lone-wolves/index.html (accessed September 17, 2016).

Londono, Ernesto, and Greg Miller. "CIA Begins Weapons Delivery to Syrian Rebels." *Washington Post.* September 11, 2013. https://www.washingtonpost .com/world/national-security/cia-begins-weapons-delivery-to-syrian-rebels/2013/09/11/9fcf2ed8-1b0c-11e3-a628-7e6dde8f889d_story.html (accessed October 20, 2016).

Lormel, Dennis M. "Subcommittee on Oversight and Investigations." *The Federal Bureau.* February 12, 2002. https://archives.fbi.gov/archives/news/testi mony/financing-patterns-associated-with-al-qaeda-and-global-terrorist-networks (accessed November 5, 2016).

MacAskill, Ewen. "How French Inteliigence Agencies Failed before the Paris Attacks." *Guardian.* November 19, 2015. https://www.theguardian.com/world/2015/nov/19/how-french-intelligence-agencies-failed-before-the-paris-attacks (accessed September 7, 2016).

Martin, Cecilia. "4,400 Year-Old Artifact Returned to Iraqi Government." *IIP US Embassy.* July 27, 2006. http://iipdigital.usembassy.gov/st/english/article/2006/07/20060727173413mlenuhret0.1980097.html#axzz4HRrOB6OK (accessed October 29, 2016).

Matthews, John. "Chattanooga Shootings: America, Let's Use Social Media to Stop Terrorist Attacks." *Fox News.* July 17, 2015. http://www.foxnews.com/opin ion/2015/07/17/chattanooga-shootings-america-lets-use-social-media-to-stop-terrorist-attacks.html (accessed September 20, 2016).

McCarthy, Andrew. *Willful Blindness: A Memoir of the Jihad.* New York: Encounter Books, 2008.

McCaul, Michael. "Europe Has a Jihadi Superhighway Problem." *Time.* November 11, 2014. http://time.com/3578462/european-union-security-gap-for eign-fighters-terrorists/ (accessed October 8, 2016).

McDermott, Terry, and Josh Meyer. *The Hunt for KSM: Inside the Pursuit and Take-down of the Real 9/11 Mastermind, Khalid Sheikh Mohammed.* New York: Little, Brown and Company, 2012.

McGreal, Chris. "Khalid Sheikh Mohammed: Former Military Prosecutor Denounces Trial." *Guardian.* May 4, 2012. https://www.theguardian.com/world/2012/may/04/khalid-sheikh-mohammed-military-prosecutor (accessed October 24, 2016).

McKelvey, Tara. "Arming Syrian Rebels: Where the US Went Wrong." *BBC News.* October 10, 2015. http://www.bbc.com/news/magazine-33997408.

Meek, James Gordon. "FBI Feared Boston Bombers 'Received Training' and Aid from Terror Group, Docs Say." *ABC News.* May 22, 2014. http://abcnews .go.com/Blotter/fbi-feared-boston-bombers-received-training-aid-terror/ story?id=23819429 (accessed September 11, 2016).

Merle, Renae, Matt Zapotosky, Amy Wang, and Mark Berman. "Suspect in New York, N.J. Bombings Taken into Custody." *Washington Post.* September 19, 2015. https://www.washingtonpost.com/news/post-nation/wp/2016/09/ 18/three-mysterious-incidents-in-new-york-new-jersey-and-minnesota- raise-fears-of- (accessed November 9, 2016).

Meserole, Christopher, and William McCants. "The French Connection, Explain- ing Sunni Militancy Around the World." *Foreign Affairs.* March 24, 2016. https://www.foreignaffairs.com/articles/2016-03-24/french-connection (accessed October 1, 2016).

Michael, George. "What's to Stop a 'Lone Wolf' Terrorist?" *Chronicle.* September 5, 2012. http://chronicle.com/blogs/conversation/2012/09/05/whats-to-stop- a-lone-wolf-terrorist/ (accessed September 20, 2016).

Mitchell, Andrea, and Leon Panetta. "U.S. Mistakes Helped Create 'Vacuum' That Spawned ISIS." *NBC News.* October 7, 2014. http://www.nbcnews.com/ storyline/isis-terror/leon-panetta-u-s-mistakes-helped-create-vacuum- spawned-isis-n220586 (accessed October 15, 2016).

Morris, Loveday. "Islamic State Isn't Just Destroying Ancient Artifacts—It's Selling Them." *Washington Post.* June 8, 2015. https://www.washingtonpost.com/ world/middle_east/islamic-state-isnt-just-destroying-ancient-artifacts— its-selling-them/2015/06/08/ca5ea964-08a2-11e5-951e-8e15090d64ae_ story.html (accessed November 3, 2016).

"Most Smuggled ISIS Oil Goes to Turkey, Sold at Low Prices—Norwegian Report." *RT.* December 20, 2015. https://www.rt.com/news/326567-is-export-oil- turkey/ (accessed November 4, 2016).

Nance, Malcolm. *Defeating ISIS: Who They Are, How They Fight, What They Believe.* New York: Skyhorse Publishing, 2016.

Napoleoni, Loretta. *Terrorism and the Economy, How the War on Terror Is Bankrupting the World.* New York: Seven Stories Press, 2010.

Nestel, M.L., Gilad Shiloach, and Amit Weiss. "ISIS Forums Share Pipe Bomb Instructions for Attacks on NYC, Las Vegas." *Vocativ.* September 16, 2014. http://www.vocativ.com/world/isis-2/isis-pipe-bomb-at (accessed November 17, 2016).

Nissenbaum, Dion. "Top 10 Revelations from Robert Gates's Memoir." *Wall Street Journal.* 2014. http://blogs.wsj.com/washwire/2014/01/07/top-10-revela tions-from-robert-gatess-memoir/ (accessed November 30, 2016).

O'Neill, Ann. "Tsarnaev Trial: Timeline of the Bombings, Manhunt and After- math." *CNN.* May 15, 2015. http://www.cnn.com/2015/03/04/us/tsarnaev- trial-timeline/ (accessed September 6, 2016).

Parker, George, and Murad Ahmed. "Cameron Warns Internet Groups to Stop Spread of Terror Material." *Financial Times.* November 14, 2014. https://www.ft .com/content/f82e7206-6bb4-11e4-9337-00144feabdc0 (accessed Septem- ber 15, 2016).

Pascaline, Mary. "Orlando Shooting: Gunman a 'Homegrown Extremist' 'Radicalized' on the Internet, Obama Says." *International Business Time.* June 14, 2016. Http://Www.Ibtimes.Com/Orlando-Shooting-Gunman-Homegrown-Extremist-Radicalized-Internet-Obama-Says-2381851 (accessed October 7, 2016).

Piper, Paul. "Nets of Terror, Terrorist Activity on the Internet." *Info Today.* November 2008. http://www.infotoday.com/searcher/nov08/Piper.shtml (accessed August 3, 2016).

Pizzi, Michael. "Foreign Fighters in Syria, Iraq Have Doubled Since Anti-ISIL Intervention." *Aljazeera.* December 7, 2015. http://america.aljazeera.com/articles/2015/12/7/foreign-fighters-in-syria-iraq-have-doubled-since-anti-isil-intervention.html (accessed October 1, 2016).

Pletta, Damian, and Kristina Pterson. "Obama Says U.S. Intelligence Underestimated Islamic State Threat." *Wall Street Journal.* September 28, 2014. http://www.wsj.com/articles/obama-says-u-s-intelligence-underestimated-developments-in-syria-1411918072.

Rawlison, Kevin. "How ISIS Spread Its Deadly Ideology—A Timeline, Since Taking the Iraqi City of Mosul, the Terror Group Have Killed Dozens of Hostages and Often Used the Footage of the Murders as Grisly Propaganda." *Guardian.* January 3, 2016. https://www.theguardian.com/world/2016/jan/03/how-isis-spread-its-deadly-ideology-a-timeline.

Rice, Condoleezza. *No Higher Honor: A Memoirs of My Years in Washington.* New York: Crowns Publishers, 2011.

Ricks, Thomas E. Fiasco. *The American Military Adventure in Iraq.* New York: Penguin, 2007.

Robinson, Linda. *Tell Me How This Ends: General David Petraeus & the Search for a Way Out of Iraq.* New York: Simon and Schuster, 2013.

Roff, Peter. "Obama's Bad Deal for Bergdahl, Swapping Taliban Prisoners Is Yet Another Costly Act of Hubris by the President." *US News.* June 5, 2014. http://www.usnews.com/opinion/blogs/peter-roff/2014/06/05/obamas-bergdahl-taliban-swap-is-a-costly-mistake (accessed October 14, 2016).

Rosen, Armin. "ISIS Now Controls a Shocking Percentage of Iraq and Syria." *Business Insider.* June 11, 2014. http://www.businessinsider.com/isis-controls-shocking-percentage-of-iraq-and-syria-2014-6 (accessed November 5, 2016).

Rubin, Alissa J. "Among the Wounded in Syria's War: Ancient History." *New York Times.* March 7, 2014 (accessed November 3, 2016).

Rubin, Alissa J., and Lilia Blaise. "Killing Twice for ISIS and Saying So Live on Facebook." *New York Times.* June 14, 2016. http://www.nytimes.com/2016/06/15/world/europe/france-stabbing-police-magnanville-isis.html?_r=0 (accessed September 26, 2016).

Rumsfield, Donald. *Known and Unknown.* New York: Penguin, 2011.

Ryan, Laura. "ISIS Is Better Than Al-Qaeda at Using the Internet." *Defense One.* October 10, 2014. http://www.defenseone.com/technology/2014/10/isis-better-al-qaeda-using-internet/96308/ (accessed September 3, 2016).

Sanders, Katie. "Obama Wanted to Keep 10,000 Troops in Iraq, ABC's Raddatz Claims." *Politifact.* August 24, 2014. http://www.politifact.com/punditfact/statements/2014/aug/24/martha-raddatz/obama-wanted-keep-10000-troops-iraq-abcs-raddatz-c/ (accessed October 22, 2016).

Sanger, David E. "Rebel Arms Flow Is Said to Benefit Jihadists in Syria." *New York Times*. October 14, 2012. http://www.nytimes.com/2012/10/15/world/middleeast/jihadists-receiving-most-arms-sent-to-syrian-rebels.html (accessed October 24, 2016).

Sanger, David, and Davis Hirschfeld. "David E. Sanger And Julie Hirschfeld Davis, Struggling to Starve ISIS of Oil Revenue, U.S. Seeks Assistance from Turkey." *New York Times*. September 13, 2014. http://www.nytimes.com/2014/09/14/world/middleeast/struggling-to-starve-isis-of-oil-revenue-us-seeks-assistance-from-turkey.html (accessed October 29, 2016).

Santora, Marc, William Rashbaum, Al Baker, and Adam Goldman. "Manhattan Bombs Built for Carnage Provide Clues into Attack." *New York Times*. September 18, 2016. http://www.nytimes.com/2016/09/19/nyregion/new-york-explosion chelsea.html?emc=edit_na_20160918&nlid=68648138&ref=cta (accessed November 19, 2016).

Saul, Heather. "ISIS Publishes Penal Code Listing Amputation, Crucifixion and Stoning as Punishments—And Vows to Vigilantly Enforce It." *The Independent*. January 22, 2015. http://www.independent.co.uk/news/world/middle-east/isis-publishes-penal-code-listing-amputation-crucifixion-and-stoning-as-punishments-and-vows-to-9994878.html.

Scarborough, Rowan. "U.S. Troop Withdrawal Let Islamic State Enter Iraq, Military Leaders Say." *Washington Post*. July 26, 2015. http://www.washingtontimes.com/news/2015/jul/26/us-troop-withdrawal-let-islamic-state-enter-iraq-m/?page=all (accessed October 12, 2016).

Schmitt, Eric, Michael Schmidt, and Ellen Barry. "Bombing Inquiry Turns to Motive and Russian Trip,." *New York Times*. April 20, 2013. http://www.nytimes.com/2013/04/21/us/boston-marathon-bombings.html?pagewanted=all&_r=0 (accessed October 5, 2016).

Schroeder, Peter. "Treasury Urges Patience in Effort to Dry Up ISIS Dollars." *The Hill*. November 13, 2014. http://thehill.com/policy/finance/224036-treasury-urges-patience-in-effort-to-dry-up-isis-dollars (accessed October 4, 2016).

Schultz, Marisa. "Obama: Orlando Shooter Self-Radicalized over the Internet." *New York Post*. June 13, 2016. http://nypost.com/2016/06/13/obama-orlando-shooter-self-radicalized-over-the-internet/ (accessed September 9, 2016).

Schwartz, Mattathias. "The Whole Haystack." *New Yorker*. Januray 26, 2015. http://www.newyorker.com/magazine/2015/01/26/whole-haystack (accessed 2016).

Seldin, Jeff. "Flow of Foreign Fighters to Iraq, Syria Unrelenting." *Voice of America News*. January 8, 2016 (accessed October 1, 2016).

Sengupta, Somini. "Nations Trying to Stop Their Citizens from Going to Middle East to Fight for ISIS." *New York Times*. September 12, 2014 (accessed October 12, 2016).

Shapiro, Ben. "7 Other Lone Wolf Islamic Attacks Inside the U.S." September 28, 2014 (accessed September 28, 2016).

Sharp, Andrew. *The Rise of ISIS The West's New Crusade*. Redmond, WA: Fusion Publications, 2014.

Shevardnadze, Sophie. "Children Born to ISIL Sex Slaves Are Taken to Be Trained into Murderers—Yazidi Aid Worker." *RT*. December 4, 2015. https://

www.rt.com/shows/sophieco/324712-children-isil-sex-slaves/ (accessed October 29, 2016).

Simon, Jeffery D. *Lone Wolf Terrorism, Understanding the Growing Threat*. New York: Prometheus, 2013.

Smith, Mitch, Adam Goldman, and Richard Pérez-Peña. "Suspect Is Killed in Attack at Ohio State University That Injured 11." *New York Times*. November 28, 2016. http://www.nytimes.com/2016/11/28/us/active-shooter-ohio-state-university.html (accessed November 30, 2016).

Somin, Ilya. "The Case against the Obama Administration's Deal Exchanging Five High-Ranking Taliban Leaders for One Captured US Soldier." *Washington Post*. June 1, 2014. https://www.washingtonpost.com/news/volokh-con spiracy/wp/2014/06/01/the-case-against-the-obama-administrations-deal-exchanging-five-high-ranking-taliban-leaders-for-one-captured-us-soldier/ (accessed October 20, 2016).

Sorcher, Sara. "Exclusive: How US Government Wants Silicon Valley Tech Leaders to Fight ISIS." *CS Monitor*. January 8, 2016. http://www.csmonitor.com/World/Passcode/2016/0108/Exclusive-How-US-government-wants-Sili con-Valley-tech-leaders-to-fight-ISIS (accessed September 15, 2016).

Spencer, Richard. "ISIL Tweeter 'ShamiWitness' Arrested in India." *Telegraph*. December 13, 2014. http://www.telegraph.co.uk/news/worldnews/islamic-state/11292412/Isil-tweeter-ShamiWitness-arrested-in-India.html (accessed December 2, 2016).

Spencer, Robert. "European Authorities Overwhelmed as Hundreds of Islamic State Fighters Return Home." *Jihad Watch*. March 28, 2016 (accessed November 13, 2016).

Squires, Nick. "Yazidi Girl Tells of Horrific Ordeal as ISIL Sex Slave." *Telegraph*. September 7, 2014. http://www.telegraph.co.uk/news/worldnews/mid dleeast/iraq/11080165/Yazidi-girl-tells-of-horrific-ordeal-as-Isil-sex-slave.html (accessed October 29, 2016).

Starr, Barbara. "Official Says CIA-Funded Weapons Have Begun to Reach Syrian Rebels: Rebels Deny Receipt." *CNN*. September 12, 2013. http://www.cnn.com/2013/09/12/politics/syria-arming-rebels/index.html (accessed October 20, 2016).

Stern, Jessica. "We Need to Worry about Somali Terrorists in the U.S." *Time*. September 26, 2013. http://ideas.time.com/2013/09/26/we-need-to-worry-about-somali-terrorists-in-the-u-s/ (accessed September 28, 2016).

Stern, Jessica, and J.M. Berger. *ISIS: The State of Terro*. New York: HarperCollins Publishers, 2015.

Stern, Jessica, and J.M. Berger. "ISIS and the Foreign-Fighter Phenomenon." *The Atlantic*. March 8, 2016. http://www.theatlantic.com/international/archive/2015/03/isis-and-the-foreign-fighter-problem/387166/ (accessed October 1, 2016).

Stevenson, Jonathan. *Counter-Terrorism: Containment and Beyond*. Oxford: Oxford University Press, 2004.

Styles, Kirsty. "Should Tech Companies Join the Government's Counter-Terrorism Unit?" *NewsStateman Tech*. August 26, 2016. http://tech.newstatesman.com/feature/tech-counter-terrorism (accessed September 15, 2016).

Takooshian, Harold. "Understanding Terrorism," *Journal of Social Distress and the Homeless* 12, no. 4 (2003).

Tassi, Paul. "ISIS Uses 'GTA 5' in New Teen Recruitment Video." *Forbes.* September 20, 2014. http://www.forbes.com/sites/insertcoin/2014/09/20/isis-uses-gta-5-in-new-teen-recruitment-video/#67d3559a3d29 (accessed September 28, 2016).

Tau, Byron. "Hillary Clinton Declares Stopping 'Lone Wolf' Attackers Is National Priority." *Wall Street Journal.* June 15, 2016 (accessed October 20, 2016).

Temple-Raston, Dina. "Terrorism in the U.S. Takes on a U.K. Pattern." *National Public Radio.* May 9, 2010. http://www.npr.org/templates/story/story.php?story Id=126646911May 9, 20108:00 AM ET (accessed September 9, 2016).

Thiessen, Marc A. "Will Obama Repeat His Iraq Mistakes in Afghanistan? If You Like the Unfolding Disaster in Obama-Abandoned Iraq, You Are Going to Love Obama-Abandoned Afghanistan." *Washington Post.* June 23, 2014. http://www.washingtonpost.com/opinions/marc-thiessen-will-obama-repeat-his-iraq-mistakes-in-afghanistan/2014/06/23/fd935084-facd-11e3-b1f4-8e77c632c07b_story.html (accessed October 23, 2016).

Thissen, Marc A. "Defense Intelligence Agency Warned Obama about ISIS in 2012." *American Enterprise Institute.* November 20, 2015. https://www.aei .org/publication/defense-intelligence-agency-warned-obama-about-isis-in-2012/ (accessed October 27, 2016).

Thomas, Timothy L. "Information-Age 'De-Terror-ence'." *Military Review.* September 2001. http://fmso.leavenworth.army.mil/documents/de-terror/de-terror .htm.

Thorndik, Joseph. "How ISIS Is Using Taxes to Build a Terrorist State." *Forbes.* August 18, 2014. http://www.forbes.com/sites/taxanalysts/2014/08/18/ how-isis-is-using-taxes-to-build-a-terrorist-state/ (accessed 2016).

Trujillo, Mario. "FCC Says It Can't Shut Down ISIS Websites." *The Hill.* November 17, 2015. http://thehill.com/policy/technology/260438-fcc-says-it-cant-shut down-online-terrorist-activity (accessed November 6, 2016).

Vilmaz, Guler. "Opposition MP Says ISIS Is Selling Oil in Turkey." *Al-Monitor.* June 13, 2014. http://www.al-monitor.com/pulse/tr/business/2014/06/ turkey-syria-isis-selling-smuggled-oil.html (accessed November 5, 2016).

Viser, Matt. "The Report Highlights Ways Agencies Failed to Detain Tamerlan Tsarnaev before He Allegedly Planned the Attack." *Boston Globe.* March 26, 2014. Https://Www.Bostonglobe.Com/News/Nation/2014/03/26/Con gressional-Report-Details-Intelligence-Failures-Prior-Marathon-Bombings/ P1ej4egwdvt1k809brq5vo/Story.Html (accessed September 20, 2016).

Wagstaff, Keith. "Paris Attack Could Renew Debate over Encrypted Messaging Apps." *NBC News.* November 16, 2016. http://www.nbcnews.com/storyline/ paris-terror-attacks/paris-attack-could-renew-debate-over-encrypted-messaging-apps-n464276 (accessed September 15, 2016).

Wahbi, Kamal Hassan. *Terrorism Ideology, the Savage Wolves, a Psychodynamic Analysis of Terrorist Personality* (in Arabic). Beirut: Dar Al-Mawasim, 2014.

Wakefield, Jane. "GCHQ, Terrorists, and the Internet: What Are the Issues?" *BBC.* November 4, 2014. http://www.bbc.com/news/technology-29897196 (accessed September 15, 2016).

Weaver, Jay, and David Ovalle. "Terror Enemy No. 1: Lone Wolves Like Orlando Killer Omar Mateen." *Miami Herald.* June 14, 2016. http://www.miami herald.com/news/local/community/miami-dade/article83819372.html (accessed September 20, 2016).

Weimann, Gabriel. "How Terrorism Uses the Internet." *US Institute of Peace.* March 13, 2004. http://www.usip.org/publications/wwwterrornet-how-modern-terrorism-uses-the-internet (accessed August 2, 2016).

Weiss, Michael, and Hasan Hasan. *ISIS: Inside the Army of Terror.* New York: Regan Arts, 2015.

West, Ben, and Scott Stewart. "Uncomfortable Truths and the Times Square Attack." *Security Weekly.* May 6, 2010. https://www.stratfor.com/weekly/20100505_uncomfortable_truths_times_square_attack (accessed September 27, 2016).

Wheaton, Sarah. "Obama Argues for Gun Controls as Way to Fight Terror." *Politico.* June 14, 2016. http://www.politico.com/story/2016/06/barack-obama-gun-control-terror-224331 (accessed October 5, 2016).

Williams, Christine. "Stop Minimizing the Reality of Lone Wolf Jihadists." *Jihad Watch.* June 19, 2016. Https://Www.Jihadwatch.Org/2016/06/Stop-Minimizing-The-Reality-Of-Lone-Wolf-JIHADISTS (accessed September 26, 2016).

Williams-Grut, Oscar. "Here's Where Terrorist Groups Like ISIS and Al Qaeda Get Their Money." *Business Insider.* December 7, 2015. http://www.businessinsider.com/how-isis-and-al-qaeda-make-their-money-2015-12/#6- (accessed November 4, 2016).

Witte, Griffe, Sudarsan Raghavan, and James McAuley. "Flow of Foreign Fighters Plummets as Islamic State Loses Its Edge." *Washington Post.* September 10, 2016 (accessed October 1, 2016).

Wright, David. "Poll: Americans Fear 'Lone Wolf' Attacks." *CNN.* December 17, 2015. http://www.cnn.com/2015/12/17/politics/washington-post-abc-news-security-poll/index.html (accessed September 15, 2016).

Wright, Lawrence. *The looming Tower, Al-Qaeda and the Road to 9/11.* New York: Thompson Press, 2006.

Yadron, Danny, and Julia Carrie Wong. "Silicon Valley Appears Open to Helping US Spy Agencies after Terrorism Summit." *Guradian.* January 8, 2016 (accessed September 15, 2016).

Yeginsu, Ceylan. "Turkey Warned French Twice about Attacker, Official Says." *New York Times.* November 16, 2015. http://www.nytimes.com/live/paris-attacks-live-updates/turkey-warned-french-twice-about-attacker-official-says/ (accessed September 23, 2016).

Zarate, Juan C. *Treasury's War: The Unleashing of a New Era of Financial Warfare.* New York: Public Affairs, 2013.

Zelin, Aaron Y. "Who Are the Foreign Fighters in Syria?" *Carnegie Middle East Center.* December 5, 2013. http://www.washingtoninstitute.org/policy-analysis/view/who-are-the-foreign-fighters-in-syria (accessed October 1, 2016).

Index

About the Author

AMBASSADOR T. HAMID AL-BAYATI, PhD, is an Iraqi diplomat, academic, and author. He is currently a distinguished professor at Fordham University and a Special Adviser at the Middle East Office, International Education, Fairleigh Dickinson University in the USA. He was the Ambassador and Permanent Representative of Iraq to the United Nations (UN) from 2006 to 2013. Previous to that post, he was Iraq's Deputy Foreign Minister for Political Affairs and Bilateral Relations from 2004 to 2006.

Since his arrival in New York in 2006, Ambassador Al-Bayati made significant progress as Iraq's Permanent Representative to the UN. He was elected to top positions at the UN, including as Chair of the Third Committee (Social, Humanitarian, and Cultural Affairs) in 2006; Vice President of the General Assembly in 2007; and Chair of the Sixth Committee (Legal Affairs) in 2008. Additionally, Ambassador Al-Bayati was elected as Chair of the United Nations Disarmament Commission (UNDC) in 2011.

Following Saddam Hussein's invasion of Kuwait in 1990, the United Nations Security Council considered Iraq a threat to world's peace and security and adopted many resolutions against Iraq under chapter VII, which authorized the Security Council to use force and impose sanctions. After the fall of Hussein's regime in 2003, there were many unresolved issues regarding the relations between Iraq and Kuwait. Al-Bayati worked to solve the issues, to lift sanctions against Iraq, and to get Iraq out of chapter VII. His efforts were successful in that on December 15, 2010, the Security Council adopted a resolution to lift sanctions against Iraq and to remove Iraq from chapter VII actions.

Throughout this career, Al-Bayati was an outspoken opposition leader against the dictatorship of Saddam Hussein, whose regime murdered many of his colleagues and family members. He went into exile in the United Kingdom, but continued to serve as a major delegate in international negotiations for democracy and peace in Iraq. He is the author of several books, including *From Dictatorship to Democracy: An Insider's Account of the Iraqi Opposition to Saddam* (2011) with a foreword by Peter Galbraith. His many media appearances have included the *Daily Show* hosted by Jon Stewart. To this day, he remains active in international affairs, both in his academic roles, speaking, and in events at the UN. Concerned about peace, notably, he was instrumental in the UN resolution about the International Day of Happiness and continued to organize events at the UN about this issue and in celebration of this world-recognized day. Most notably, he is active in analyzing the world reactions to terrorism, a topic characterizing his lifelong work.